CHOOSE AND FOCUS

CHOOSE
AND
FOCUS

JAPANESE

BUSINESS

STRATEGIES

FOR THE

21ST CENTURY

ULRIKE SCHAEDE

Cornell University Press

ITHACA AND LONDON

First published 2008 by Cornell University Press

Printed in the United States of America

Library of Congress Cataloging-in-Publication Data

Schaede, Ulrike, 1962–
  Choose and focus: Japanese business strategies for the 21st century / Ulrike Schaede.
        p. cm.
  Includes bibliographical references and index.
    ISBN 978–0–8014–4706–8 (cloth : alk. paper)
    1. Japan—Commerical policy.   2. Competition—Japan.
3. Product differentiation—Japan.   4. Strategic planning—Japan.
5. High technology industries—Japan.   6. Japan—Economic policy—
21st century.   I. Title.

  HF1601.S34 2008
  338.50952—dc22   2008006379

Cloth printing   10   9   8   7   6   5   4   3   2   1

CONTENTS

"It's awful," conference participants from Japan deplored. "Just look at Japan's electronics industry—in fast-growing markets like China or India, none of them is the market leader any more."[1] Old ways of thinking die hard. But being the largest general maker of a variety of electronics appliances cannot be—and indeed no longer is—the dominant strategy of Japanese electronics firms. They can no longer aim to sell cheap televisions to emerging consumer markets, because the competitive advantage they previously enjoyed has moved elsewhere. Instead, more and more Japanese companies are becoming leaders in high-technology categories with higher margins and profitability. The idea is no longer to compete for market share in all product categories, but to sell the most differentiated products. Japanese companies including Japan Synthetic Rubber, Fujifilm, Toppan Printing, and Nitto Denko have become global leaders in the high-tech materials components for LCD displays, such as polarizers and other layers that enhance color and viewing angle, and their dominance explains the growing trade deficits of South Korea and Taiwan (home to the leading assemblers of LCD panels) vis-à-vis Japan.

The same is true for industry after industry: Toyota's Prius is not an outlier, but just the most visible Japanese foray into leadership in 21st century technologies. A 2007 joke in Japan had it that the new Boeing 787 Dreamliner was going to be "made with Japan"—because Toray, Mitsubishi Heavy and Kawasaki Heavy Industries were to develop and supply the advanced composite materials for the fuselage and wings, one of the airplane's most celebrated technological advances. Meanwhile, IHI Corporation was to jointly develop the engines with General Electric. Japan's corporate positioning is changing from being the world leader in low-cost, high-quality "household name" products to differentiation through technological leadership in well-defined and focused market segments. For most Japanese companies and industries,

---

1. "Global Repositioning of Japan in the Global Economy" conference, held at the University of Pennsylvania and Villanova, September 2006.

profits are no longer to be earned simply through volume but through margins. And because this is mainly happening at the materials and components level, and often includes companies we have not heard of, this shift has not yet attracted the wide attention it deserves.

In this book I describe the fundamental changes in Japanese business and strategy that have occurred during the past decade, and suggest how these changes will affect global competition in the next decade. I argue that the 1998–2006 period defines a strategic inflection point for Japanese business, overturning many of the principles on which the Japanese postwar economy was built. We are seeing a transformation of the competitive landscape for Japanese business strategy. In this new regime, laws and their implementation have been changed, new markets and companies have emerged, and old market rigidities have been undermined. This sea change has forced large Japanese companies to reorganize and restructure. Japanese businesses are now clearly identifying the core areas in which to compete. In the process, previously highly diversified Japanese multinationals have become leaner, more nimble, and more competitive. Their aggressive moves in spinning off non-core businesses have, in turn, created new market opportunities for start-ups and foreign investors. A vibrant market for mergers, acquisitions, and hostile takeovers has emerged. Because of Japan's weak economy in the 1990s and the new emphasis on China, these fundamental changes have gone largely unnoticed in the West. However, the cumulative results of the many changes at the legal and corporate level point to a New Japan. This book chronicles the transformation and explains how it has affected what we used to "know" about Japanese businesses and the implications for the future competitiveness of Japanese business and for the global economy.

Our existing knowledge of Japan stems largely from the economic boom times of the late 1980s. After the bubble burst in 1991, Japan fell into a decadelong recession and popular business interest turned to China. Meanwhile, Japanese business underwent a quiet yet fundamental reorientation. Between 2002 and 2007, Japan's listed companies reported five consecutive years of combined record profit growth, and Japan boasted its longest boom in recorded history, with more than 66 consecutive months of economic growth. Large Japanese firms are now reappearing as greatly reformed entities and world-class competitors. In the face of these changes, relying on what we "know" about Japanese business from the 1980s is a recipe for disaster equivalent to that made by U.S. automobile manufacturers in the 1970s. The new business climate in Japan presents opportunities for foreign companies within Japan—and threatens those who ignore the new capabilities of resurgent Japanese firms.

Acknowledgments

This book is based on knowledge and experience that I have accumulated over two decades of research about Japan. It brings together insights regarding the postwar period derived from earlier studies and new research on ongoing change and the transformation of Japanese business organization. Over time, I have received more support than I can list, from research affiliations with the Bank of Japan, Japan's Ministry of Economy, Trade and Industry, and Hitotsubashi University, as well as from many individuals in Japan's government organizations, private companies, venture capital firms, and academia. I am particularly grateful to Sozaburō Okamatsu, Tomio Tsutsumi, Ryōzō Hayashi, and Kunio Okina for supporting my research endeavors.

In putting this book together, I have benefited from a great research environment at the University of California at San Diego, in particular at my home base, the Graduate School of International Relations and Pacific Studies (IR/PS). Takeo Hoshi, Peter Gourevitch, and Barry Naughton have long been terrific intellectual sparring partners, and their feedback was important at various stages of this project. For advancing a research idea, few things are more effective than an IR/PS faculty research lunch, and I am indebted to Craig McIntosh, Stephan Haggard, Gordon Hanson, Ellis Krauss, and other seminar participants for their help in refining the argument. I have received fabulous research assistance from Robert L. Sei, Jun Hee Oh, Kuniaki Nemoto, and Masafumi Miya. I thank Brad Glosserman, Ryōzō Hayashi, Hideichi Okada, Adrian Tschoegl, and many friends, students, and interview partners in Japan for stimulating conversations.

A first draft of the manuscript benefited tremendously from thoughtful page-by-page comments by Patricia Maclachlan. In addition, Christina Ahmadjian, Jennifer Amyx, Peter Gourevitch, Sanford Jacoby, Steven Kohlhagen, James Lincoln, Hugh Patrick, and two anonymous reviewers for Cornell University Press provided helpful feedback on various parts of the book.

And finally, I thank Charles A. O'Reilly III, whose smile is priceless.

ULRIKE SCHAEDE

Cardiff-by-the-Sea

CHOOSE AND FOCUS

1

INTRODUCTION

Between 1998 and 2006, Japan's political economy underwent a dramatic change. Some observers have referred to this period as a "lost decade" of stagnation, but it is now clear that it was a turning point toward corporate renewal that has fundamentally changed the context in which Japanese corporations compete. Profound transformation of the regulatory system, the arrival of price competition, and the opening of markets to new entrants, imports, and foreign investors has made our knowledge of Japan outdated. Japan's business organization has shifted from its old emphasis on corporate growth through diversification and long-term relationships toward a focus on core businesses and concentration of resources to increase profitability through efficiency and strategic superiority. This transformation has gone largely unnoticed, yet it represents a profound shift in the global competitive landscape for the 21st century.

This wholesale change is irreversible. It is not simply based on new laws but has been driven by a confluence of forces that cannot be undone. Globalization and the breakdown of protective barriers have brought competition to Japan's domestic markets. Aggressive economic reforms, beginning with Prime Minister Ryūtarō Hashimoto in 1998 and pushed further under Junichirō Koizumi between 2001 and 2006, included deregulation and privatization under the heading "leave it to the market," a transformation of Japan's basic regulatory philosophy, and the revision of all laws pertaining to commerce to enhance transparency and facilitate corporate renewal. Postwar-period informal industrial policies have been replaced by 21st century legal accountability. The severe banking crisis of 1998, in the context of an extended recession and a nonperforming loan debacle, was a tipping point. The insight that Japan's old system had collapsed left the government and corporations with no choice but to restructure and reorganize. The cumulative effects of these changes have fundamentally altered Japan's competitive landscape and business organization.

Thus, the period from 1998 through 2006 crystallized into what Burgelman and Grove (1996) have called a strategic inflection point. This term refers to a point in time when the competitive environment changes such that the balance of forces shifts away from previous ways of doing business to new ones.[1] A strategic inflection point affects industry dynamics and brings a complete reorientation of corporate strategy, as it necessitates a change from one winning strategy to another. For example, the arrival of internet commerce brought a strategic inflection point for the retail book industry, where the winning proposition shifted from the previous store location, shelf presentation, and ambience to immediacy in shipping, selection, and price. Similarly, the introduction of music downloads has greatly affected how record labels contract artists and how musicians compose and sell music. In the past, the arrival of telephony, mechanical refrigeration, or the semiconductor all greatly changed the ways in which businesses competed. The changes that Japan has undergone since 1998 are so elemental that they have triggered a deep-seated restructuring of Japanese business organization. In the 21st century, what we used to know about *keiretsu* (business groups), main banks, Japan's system of ownership and corporate governance, the subcontractor system, and lifetime employment is no longer true.

The effects of strategic renewal began to show in late 2002. In stark contrast to the widely held view that Japan has lost its drive, in each of the five years between 2002 and 2007 Japan's listed companies posted consecutive record-high combined pretax profits.[2] The overall economy was experiencing an unprecedented 66 months of sustained economic growth. And between early 2003 and late 2006, the Nikkei 225 stock index climbed 100 percent. After a decadelong hiatus, Japanese firms were reentering global markets as new competitors, while markets in Japan have also been transformed. Japan's leaders in the electronics, precision and electric machinery, materials and steel industries are no longer stodgy, inefficient goliaths, for they have changed into lean and driven competitors with clear profit responsibilities and a focus on winning. What is more, deregulation, consolidation, and reconfiguration of competition within Japan have led to the emergence of new and hitherto not widely known competitors from Japan, such as in the pharmaceutical, chemical materials, and telecommunications industries. Japanese firms, old and new, are rising fast in the "Global 100" lists of their respective industries, and they are very different firms from the ones we used to know. They have shifted from big, ever-expanding mass producers of high-quality standardized products to much more strategic providers of new product concepts with differentiated value propositions.

1. In mathematics, an inflection point is reached when the first derivative (the slope of the trajectory) becomes zero, and the second trajectory (the rate of change) reverses its sign. See also Grove (1996).
2. *Nikkei Weekly,* June 5, 2007.

Japan's business catchphrase to describe this transition into the 21st century was "choose and focus" (*sentaku to shūchū*, also sometimes translated as "selection and concentration"). It refers to focusing on superior market positioning in a few selected categories and winning through strength and profitability in the core businesses. Thus, "choose and focus" addresses the two basic questions of strategy: (1) What businesses should we be in? and (2) How do we compete? As we will explore, to answer the first question a company must determine its core activities. Rather than being all things to all people, as Japan's highly diversified companies used to be, companies should choose what businesses to be in and excel in those markets. For example, in 2002 the former personal computer monitor leader Matsushita Electric (Panasonic) spun off its liquid crystal display (LCD) business, whereas Toshiba has decided to be a main player in a particular type of semiconductor. To answer the second question—how to compete—a company must determine how, exactly, it will outperform its competitors in that business segment. As established by Porter (1980) there are fundamentally only two ways to do so: be better or be cheaper than the competitors. To continue the two examples, Toshiba has focused its semiconductor resources on NAND (also known as flash memory). Meanwhile, TM Display Technologies, a joint venture between Toshiba and Matsushita combining the spun-off LCD capabilities of those two companies, has itself exited the mid-sized LCD market and instead specializes in very small, high-tech displays for mobile devices where sun reflection poses a great challenge to visibility. Further changes in this fast-moving industry are on the horizon.

Implementing "choose and focus," therefore, includes three separate activities of corporate renewal. First, a company must spin off noncore activities to be better able to focus its resources on the core businesses. Next, in addition to organic growth, one way to gain market dominance in the core is to merge the business with that of a competitor, or simply to acquire a competitor (if need be, through a hostile takeover). Mergers and acquisitions in the same industry are strategic if they increase economies of scale or otherwise increase the company's competitiveness (such as a geographic extension in retailing). And finally, companies must clean house and revise their internal organization, in order to align the new strategic thrust with their human resource practices (rewards and promotions) as well as the overall corporate culture. In Japan, this also included a shift toward increased transparency and responsibility of business units, based on new disclosure and accounting rules beginning in 2000.

In many ways, this move toward "choose and focus" resembles the experience of the United States in the 1980s. During the 1960s and 1970s, strategic wisdom had argued for growth through diversification—and this advice was followed by many firms in the United States, Europe, and Japan. In the 1980s, the United States moved to greater pluralism in strategy, also based on new insights in finance theory that demanded diversification not by corporations but rather in investors' portfolios. More sophisticated insights in corporate strategy stressing the virtues of focusing on clearly identified core competencies supported this shift, as did a reinterpretation of antitrust statutes that now disadvantaged conglomerates. Moreover, conglomerates were increasingly accused of resembling inefficient bureaucracies; lean and nimble became the new buzzwords.

This 1980s' shift in U.S. strategy transpired at exactly the time when Japan was globally admired for its superior mass production techniques and seemingly could do no wrong. In chapter 3, we will see that Japan's postwar business system created strong incentives for diversification. Moreover, investors—mainly other companies and banks—believed the strategic wisdom of the time that corporate diversification was desirable. Onto four decades of continuous diversification, the bubble economy of 1987–91 added aggressive corporate growth through exuberant diversification. In the 1990s, Japan's large conglomerates found themselves unable to compete in a changed global environment, and in particular against newly restructured U.S. firms. Yet, regulatory stalemate and a lack of legal infrastructure meant there were few incentives for Japanese firms to restructure aggressively until the second half of the 1990s. However, the banking crisis of 1998, in the midst of a continued recession, brought a tipping point—the old corporate system simply collapsed. Reforms initiated by Prime Minister Hashimoto in 1998, in particular through the financial "Big Bang" that brought new transparency in accounting, began to push Japanese firms toward renewal.

This is not at all to say that Japan must or should follow the United States. It simply means that we have learned much about corporate strategy since the 1980s, and have come to realize that growth through diversification is not always the best, and certainly not the only, way for large companies to succeed. At a minimum, Japan's strategic inflection has brought more options and therefore greater diversity in corporate strategy (Aoki, Jackson, and Miyajima 2007). And similar to the United States, because many large Japanese companies approached the strategic inflection point as highly diversified firms, change has manifested itself in refocusing and strategic repositioning. What we also know from the U.S. experience is that, in terms of corporate performance, for some companies things may get worse before they get better, as it can take up to a decade to disentangle, reorganize, and find a new internal alignment to implement the new strategies.

"Choose and focus" renewal has greatly affected the overall landscape of Japanese business. Companies have begun to reformulate their corporate strategies to win in the global marketplace by shedding secondary or unprofitable businesses, reevaluating their supplier and trading partnerships, and reforming their human resource policies. As a result, the way in which they compete is different from what our 1980s-based perceptions may suggest.

Some observers have scoffed at Japan's economic recovery of the early 2000s, arguing that it was driven by exports in Old Japan industries such as steel to a booming China, and that therefore it would cease as soon as demand from China subsided. Such commentary does not reflect Japan's new reality. As table 1.1 shows, steel accounted for less than 5 percent of total Japanese exports between 2003 and 2006—as compared with 16.4 percent for cars (led by hybrids that are built only in Japan), 9 percent for chemicals and chemical materials, and 6.5 percent for electronic parts (including semiconductors and LCD display components). None of these industries sells "old stuff," as these exports are driven by an underlying qualitative upgrading. The transformation of Japan's steel industry may, in fact, be the best example.

Of Japan's total steel exports in 2006, 20 percent went to South Korea, another 20 percent to China, and 10 percent to Thailand. In other words, half of Japan's steel exports were sold to the three most aggressive low-cost competitors (SBJ 2007). How could this be possible? After great industry reorganization, Japanese steelmakers have begun to consolidate into two main groups,

TABLE 1.1. *Selected Japanese Trade Statistics, 2003–2006 (in trillion yen, %)*

	2003	2004	2005	2006
Value of exports	54.5	61.2	65.6	75.2
Value of imports	44.4	49.2	56.9	67.3
Leading industries				
Cars	8.9	9.2	9.9	12.3
% of total exports	*16.3*	*15.0*	*15.1*	*16.4*
Chemicals	4.5	5.2	5.8	6.8
% of total exports	*8.3*	*8.5*	*8.8*	*9.0*
Electronic parts	4.1	4.4	4.4	4.9
% of total exports	*7.5*	*7.2*	*6.7*	*6.5*
Iron & steel products	2.1	2.5	3.0	3.5
% of total exports	*3.9*	*4.1*	*4.6*	*4.7*
Exports to China	6.6	8.0	8.8	10.8
Imports from China	8.7	10.2	12.0	13.8
Exports to South Korea	4.0	4.8	5.1	5.8
Imports from South Korea	2.1	2.4	2.7	3.2
Exports to United States	13.4	13.7	14.8	16.9
Imports from United States	6.8	6.8	7.1	7.9

Source: Statistical Handbook of Japan 2007 (SBJ 2007).

Nippon Steel (which is growing ties with Sumitomo Metal and Kobe Steel) and JFE Holdings (a merger between NKK and Kawasaki Steel) (Yamaguchi 2003). Both have specialized in high-end, semifinished steel that other Asian competitors cannot produce, due to a lack of technological capabilities or investments after the Asian financial crisis of 1997. The play on words for JFE Holdings is that it may stand for Japan FE (iron), or alternatively for "Japan Future Enterprise"—a focused, future-oriented, steel-engineering powerhouse. Industry observers have credited the company with "one of the most formidable R&D capabilities in the global steel industry" (Kwon 2004). JFE has developed a ferritic stainless steel that is corrosion resistant and environmentally advanced as it does not contain lead. This has made JFE one of the world's leading providers of automotive steel technology, for fuel tanks, exhaust systems, and catalytic converters. Japan's stock market has begun to react to such news. Between 2003 and 2007, JFE Holding's stock price increased by over 400 percent, and its 21 percent return on equity was impressive by any standard.

The claim that the recent recovery was led by Old Japan exports is misguided. Ignoring Japan's new global competitors could be a major mistake. Being blindsided by old notions of how Japan competes could prove costly when competing against Japan's renewed and reorganized firms. Further, overlooking Japan's newly opened markets could also translate into lost opportunities. U.S. investment banks and private equity and hedge funds have recognized this and moved aggressively into the Japanese markets. Almost one third of the stocks traded on the Tokyo Stock Exchange are now held by foreign accounts. The "retail revolution" has opened inroads into Japan's consumer markets. Increased transparency in business processes and price competition have replaced previously insular trade relations.

Of course, vestiges of the old system remain and changes occur faster in some industries than in others. Laggards in many industries resist the sea change that has occurred. Like most countries, Japan also maintains its share of protected industries, such as agriculture, but it has become more similar to other countries even in those sectors. In product market after product market, the government has privatized and withdrawn. The shift in thinking also is apparent in the next generation of ministry staff, from a perceived mission of proactively guiding and interfering to one of monitoring and refereeing. Changes in Japan's regulatory system that emphasize greater transparency and reliance on rules and courts—as opposed to informal regulation through administrative guidance—have greatly reduced the postwar notion that the government should protect companies (see chapter 2). As a result, the influence of protected segments on the overall economy has begun to wane. In their place, the success of the newly refocused firms has propelled further change and reform, which in turn is eroding resistance and old-school attempts to uphold market protection.

Japan's fast-paced economic growth in the postwar period (1950s–1980s) and its growing trade surplus inspired both admiration and fear among the country's trading partners. Management scholars eagerly studied Japan's business organization, because it represented a successful alternative to arm's-length market transactions, with different processes of innovation, work flows and training, and corporate design that combined bottom-up worker participation with top-down decision making. There was a widespread belief that something about Japan's system of industrial policies and informal and situational regulation, design of research consortia, production and education systems, and human resource management made Japanese firms superior.[3] In particular, Japan's knack at commercializing new technologies that had been invented elsewhere triggered a discussion of "short-termism" versus "patience" in the management of technological innovation. According to one line of thinking, U.S. management was too myopic to foresee the technology's consumer application—such as LCDs or the fax machine—whereas Japan's smarter organizational design allowed leveraging core competencies beyond the currently served markets (Prahalad and Hamel 1990). Japan's long-term technology bets and managerial growth goals were widely admired even as the United States shifted from diversification and toward focus in the 1980s. Even some of the leading contributors to new strategy insights remained favorably disposed toward Japan. For example, Michael Porter (1992) argued that the constant pressure by U.S. financial markets for immediate results was less successful than the patience of Japanese banks in their support of diversification.

In reaction to this positive picture, some economists and political scientists suggested that Japan's success was due to industrial policies and domestic market restrictions. With the growing trade imbalance in the 1980s, foreign interest shifted to the issue of market access. Many claimed that Japan's markets were protected from foreign competition, which afforded Japanese exporters an unfair advantage. A decade of trade negotiations resulted in piecemeal liberalization that allowed partial access to selected markets but still left many critics dissatisfied. These trade disputes turned vitriolic under the rubric of "structural impediments," which referred to trade practices that created an uneven playing field, such as preferential trade among business group members and special pricing mechanisms and financial arrangements that lowered the cost of borrowing for Japanese firms. However, interest in Japan suddenly

---

3. See chapter 3 for details on postwar corporate strategy and citations of the literature.

abated as the country fell into recession in the 1990s and China emerged as the next big market in Asia.

By 2007, many were surprised to learn that Japan had experienced five years of economic growth, led by the trailblazers of "choose and focus." Japan was reemerging as a different entity. As I will detail in the next chapter, since the late 1990s Japan's government has continuously revised laws on finance, accounting, disclosure, bankruptcy, and new company formation—to a point that, as of 2007, little was left of the old legal mold. Increased transparency has invited active foreign financial participation. Most of all, the regulatory philosophy itself has moved away from preemptive and protective policies and institutions that nurture industries and firms toward managerial flexibility and postremedy solutions (post-hoc deliberations in court), with agencies monitoring transactions and markets rather than actors.

The global market environment has also helped transform Japan's postwar system of stable trade and close financial relations. Extensive government policies served the economy well in the 1950–1990 period, when Japan was catching up, but in the 21st century this no longer works. Japan has lost its cost advantages and needs its own technological innovation. World trade rules have changed, and import barriers to Japan have become unsustainable in most markets. Globalizing supply chains and production has affected labor and supplier relations. Competitive companies have begun to realize that long-term business ties, established market hierarchies, and tight supplier and employee relations no longer offer an optimal business strategy. Corporate strategy is context specific, and the ongoing changes in Japan's political economy have transformed the context in which Japanese firms compete. They must retool to win.

Structure of This Book

In this book I identify the changes brought about by the strategic inflection point of 1998–2006 and show how these have affected Japanese business organization in the 21st century. The discussion is organized into four parts. Following this introduction, Chapter 2 provides details on the legal, political, and systemic changes since 1998. Laws have been written and court processes established to create a new system in which Japanese executives are at much more liberty to design corporate strategies, but they also can be held liable for their actions. These reforms are the backdrop to Japan's strategic inflection point, which was brought about by the cumulative effects of the vast changes made between 1998 and 2006.

Part II addresses the reasons for diversification in the Old Japan. Chapter 3 reviews the incentives for and constraints on corporate strategy in Japan's political economy during the postwar period (1950–1990s). During that time, diversification was a natural and, with the exception of the bubble period, rational approach. With high growth and a rapid rate of technological change, the dominant strategic intent was to stabilize markets as much as possible, so as to grow as fast as possible. Stability was structured through interfirm relations, while growth was accomplished by diversifying into new businesses. Chapter 4 reviews the literature on diversification, as well as lessons on refocusing from the U.S. experience in the 1980s, and shows how Japan has begun to change.

Part III discusses how the strategic inflection point has affected Japan's industrial architecture as we used to know it: Business groups and main banks (chapter 5), ownership and governance (chapter 6), subcontracting (chapter 7), price competition (chapter 8), and lifetime employment (chapter 9). Each of these chapters shows how the underlying logic of these pillars of Japanese business organization has been changed, so that they have begun to fulfill a new strategic function.

In the New Japan, business groups can no longer simply offer stability—they have to provide means to increase members' competitiveness. In industry after industry, the important players are no longer clearly identifiable as group members, but where they are, they enjoy benefits beyond simple insurance and stability (chapter 5). Meanwhile, financial deregulation and the restructuring of the banking sector have greatly loosened main-bank relations. This has caused a reconfiguration of corporate governance, as cross-shareholdings and bank ownership have made way for a more diversified group of shareholders and institutional investors. Their interests are represented in new legislation, and they have changed the incentives faced by managers. The arrival of private equity funds in the 1990s has greatly affected financial flows by undermining the erstwhile dominance of banks in determining access to finance. The success of these funds has spawned a new financial industry in Japan, as a growing number of venture capital firms branched out into management buyouts and turnaround deals. The arrival of hostile takeovers has completely altered what it takes to be successful, as executive managers are now clearly oriented toward efficiency and profitability (chapter 6).

Chapter 7 explains how globalization, combined with domestic changes, has affected Japan's subcontracting system. The relocation of part manufacturing to lower-cost countries, global sourcing of standard parts, and the shift to "modulization" have inverted the previous logic of subcontractor hierarchies—first-tier suppliers are now often exclusive whereas lower-tier firms have become dispensable. Chapter 8 describes how previous relational pricing mechanisms in business-to-business transactions have been replaced by market spot pricing, and the retail revolution has opened up competition at the consumer end. In combination, the breakdowns of postwar pricing patterns have brought price competition to Japanese markets. Chapter 9 describes the shift in labor relations toward performance pay and promotion for regular (lifetime) employees and new court rulings regarding dismissals that have greatly increased flexibility in human resource management. Nonregular workers are increasing, as focused firms outsource administrative services and skilled consultants. The sudden rise in the value attached to specialization has paved the way for pay by job category and opened a market for midcareer job changers. Japanese business is being reconstituted and repositioned to serve the new strategic priorities of specialization and differentiation.

Part IV introduces companies and markets that represent the New Japan. There may be no stronger evidence that Japan's postwar system has been replaced than the ongoing decentralization of financial flows. The emergence of a viable venture capital industry means that start-ups are no longer exclusively dependent on bank loans, and the availability of funding has invited more entrepreneurship (chapter 10). Chapter 11 showcases four companies that have greatly challenged or defined the markets in which they operate: Softbank and telecommunications, kakaku.com and Internet retailing, Astellas and the pharmaceuticals industry, and SBI E*Trade and online brokerages. Chapter 12 concludes by discussing what the combined changes in Japan's political economy and business organization mean for the competitiveness of Japanese firms as well as for the global economy.

The Extent of Corporate Renewal

The three main vehicles for implementing a "choose and focus" strategy are divestitures (spinning off noncore business units); consolidation (acquiring strength in the core business); and restructuring through internal reorganization. Japanese laws and regulations for corporate reorganization began to change in 1998, and were fundamentally transformed beginning in 2000 when new laws and taxation greatly facilitated spin-offs and divestitures. Complementing these changes were new bankruptcy and liquidation laws and more efficient court processes. One of the most often-heard phrases from Japanese executives in the early 2000s was "We cannot do this any more"—regardless of whether they were asked about strategy, pricing, finance, corporate governance, or human resources.[4] Chapter 6 will demonstrate that by giving greater autonomy to managers and clarifying regulations on restructuring, these legal changes invited a veritable mergers and acquisition wave, in particular after 2003, when a market for spun-off entities as well as opportunities for friendly or hostile takeovers emerged.

---

4. Interviews with Japanese business executives, venture capitalists, and government officials, 2000–2005.

1.1. *"Choose and Focus" among Nikkei 500 Companies, 2000–2006*

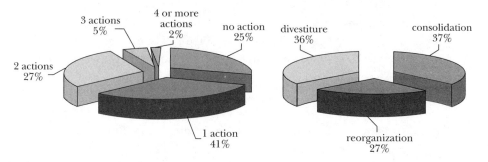

But just how extensive were these changes? One basic illustration of the incidence of reorganization and renewal can be gained from simply count- ing such activities as reported by firms themselves (see figure 1.1). The data sample consists of the *Nikkei 500* companies as of January 2007, excluding banks and investment banks, leaving a total of 472 firms.[5] The time period covered was January 2000 through December 2006, and the search was based on these companies' annual reports as well as their Japanese-language 10K form-equivalents (the *Yūka shōken hōkokusho*).

Of Japan's 472 largest companies, only 25 percent (177) did no restruc- turing, meaning that 75 percent of Japan's largest companies engaged in at least one form of reorganization during that six-year period. Breaking down these data further, we find that 41 percent (or 194 companies) adopted one measure of "choose and focus" and 34 percent adopted multiple measures. These measures were fairly evenly spread between divestitures (36%), consoli- dations (37%), and reorganizations (27%). Of the 472 firms, 33 were children of "choose and focus," created in this period through mergers. Note that it is quite possible that not all instances of restructuring were reported. There- fore, at the most conservative level, counting only instances of divestitures (refocusing, narrowly defined), we can see that 173, or 36 percent, of Japan's largest companies refocused in this period; if all activities of reorganization are counted, three quarters did.[6]

5. The banking industry is typically excluded from studies of this type because it is a focused sector due to regulation, although Japan's banking sector is also an example of con- solidation in this period.

6. In a study of divestitures and acquisitions of 770 manufacturing firms for the 1999– 2003 period, Ushijima (2007) finds that 41% of firms made at least one acquisition, 24% made at least one divestiture, and 15% did both. Because his study covers an earlier period and does not consider reorganization, the data support the findings reported here. See chapter 4 for more discussion.

One may wonder whether 75 percent (for all three measures) or 36 percent (divestitures only) is a lot of restructuring, or a little. After all, companies are constantly changing by selling or acquiring businesses. A comparative yardstick is offered by the U.S. refocusing wave of the 1980s. In a careful study of that period, Markides (1995a, 1995b) found that, by the most conservative estimate, 20 percent of Fortune 500 firms refocused during the 1980s, although he felt that the true number was closer to half. Kaplan and Weisbach (1990) estimate that 44 percent of all U.S. business units purchased in the 1960s and 1970s had been sold off by the late 1980s. Studies of refocusing face great challenges in data identification, and cross-country differences in accounting and disclosure rules make international comparisons difficult. However, the broad measures suggest that the lower boundaries for Japan (36% and 75%) are higher than those Markides found for the United States (20% and 50%), making Japan's "choose and focus" period a truly remarkable episode in global business history.

Restructuring in Japan was not driven by a handful of firms or a few select industries. The distribution of "choose and focus" intensity by industry is shown in figure 1.2, by graphing the average number of measures per firm in each industry (counting all three activities). The 472 firms in the sample were divided into 23 industries, and the overall average was 1.19 measures per firm. One might think that perhaps Old Japan industries known for a high degree of industrial policy protection (such as food processing) or industries that suffered the most from excessive diversification during the bubble (such as

1.2. *Average Number of "Choose and Focus" Actions per Firm, per Industry, 2000–2006*

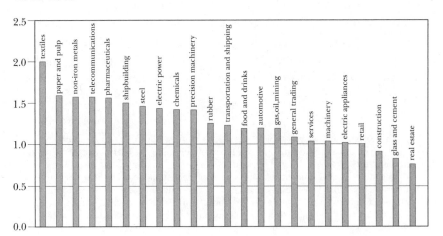

construction or shipbuilding) might be in most need of restructuring. How-ever, no such pattern emerges strongly from figure 1.2, which shows that all industries engaged in "choose and focus." To the extent that the most active refocusers share similar pressures, these might be related to deregulation and increasing global competition, such as in pharmaceuticals where protection of Japanese markets was greatly reduced in 2004 (see Astellas case study in chapter 11).

Restructuring is affecting Japan's overall industrial organization in impor-tant ways. Focus is often accomplished through spinning off noncore busi-ness units. To the extent that these are bought by competitors in that same business, the acquisition can result in increased industry concentration. In support of corporate renewal, the government revised its antitrust stance in the early 2000s. Whereas the Japan Fair Trade Commission (JFTC) previ-ously had allowed mergers if they did not result in a market share exceeding 35 percent, in the early 2000s the JFTC allowed combinations resulting in market shares of up to 50 percent and, in 2006, shifted to case-by-case review of industry concentration, including a consideration of the global competitive situation.[7]

However, this need not be a competitive concern because in many industries consolidation was counterbalanced by new market entry. In addition to new firms such as Softbank, one important group of entrants were newly formed subsidiaries resulting from spin-offs. Rather than selling business units out-right, many firms transferred the business into a new company, to keep the option to either reenter the market later or sell the company after a turnaround at a later point. Often spin-offs were structured as joint ventures between com-panies exiting the same business, that is, previous competitors. In addition to the already mentioned LCD display industry, another example comes from semiconductors. In 1999, Elpida Memory Inc. was founded when Hitachi and NEC spun off their DRAM businesses into a new joint venture (JV). In 2003, Renesas was established as a JV between Hitachi and Mitsubishi Electric when both transferred their semiconductor businesses (other than memory) to the new company.

Note that three things just happened in this process. First, the large firms are all more focused, having spun off low-margin, commoditized semicon-ductor segments. Second, the newly created firms are by definition lean and focused, and they have specialized in certain market segments. And third, these new firms cut across previous business group boundaries. For example, NEC is a formal member of the Sumitomo group and Mitsubishi Electric of the

7. See JFTC 2007; also *Nikkei*, January 10, 2006; *Nikkei*, June 16, 2006.

Mitsubishi group. Thus, in industry after industry, some of the leading firms now include companies founded after 1998 that are unencumbered by the traditional strategic pressures exerted by business groups or main banks. These new companies can structure employment and trade relations for strategic fit in the New Japan.

Why Change Takes Time: Alignment through Reorganization

During the 1990s, a new stream in the strategy literature began to call attention to the importance of execution and implementation. For organizational renewal to be successful, new strategic goals must be aligned with critical tasks, formal organization, human resource policies, and corporate culture (Tushman and O'Reilly 1996, 2002; O'Reilly and Tushman 2004). Without true alignment of "tasks, organization, people and culture," restructuring will result in little more than hot air. In Japan, the critical tasks shifted from being the biggest to being the most profitable, and accordingly, the emphasis in formal incentives had to shift to performance, in organizational design to accountability, and in corporate culture to efficiency—or, what Matsushita Electric's turnaround leader Kunio Nakamura referred to as "nothing short of a cultural revolution" (see chapter 4). By 2007, 83 percent of large firms had abandoned or greatly reduced seniority pay and promotion, and instead made efficiency an important criterion in performance appraisal. However, the need for a new alignment throughout the entire organization greatly slows down organizational renewal—which can take perhaps a decade for a company with 100,000 employees and a strong corporate culture. The first effects of new alignment of tasks, organization, people, and culture became apparent around 2002, spearheaded by Japan's early adopters of "choose and focus." For most Japanese firms, these changes will become visible in stronger performance only around 2010.

The initial realignment step was often a formal reorganization. In a 1999 survey of Japan's 100 largest firms, 47 percent announced shifts in corporate structure, and half of these planned a transition to financially autonomous business units in the so-called company system (*kanpanii seido*). This term is misleading, because this reorganization does not result in independent companies, but only in an internal shift to separate financial statements for each business unit, as if these were self-reliant entities. Most companies that have adopted this system retain centralized staff functions, such as human resources.

Thus, the "company system" is a strong version of a multidivisional organization that falls between the postwar Japanese practice of direct reporting and limited authority and the full independence given to subsidiaries of a holding company structure. This new system makes Japan's multidivisional organizations more similar to those elsewhere. Throughout the postwar period even the most diversified Japanese firms had delegated only limited decision-making authority to the heads of business units. Global subsidiaries had to check with the main office on even minor items. Decision making by consensus was the norm, not only within the head office but across divisions. Foreign business partners often found it difficult to locate the actual decision maker and were frustrated by the slow speed and apparent indecisiveness of Japanese business partners. At the turn of the century, this frustration was increasingly shared by Japanese firms themselves, and many identified a need for clearer responsibilities, increased transparency and cost efficiency, and leadership at the business-unit level. New accounting rules since 2000 have ended the covert cross-subsidization of business units that previously characterized almost all Japanese firms. Mandatory quarterly earnings reports beginning in 2005 left even the laggards among Japan's listed companies with no choice but to worry about the accuracy of their financial data.

In the early 2000s, shifting to the "company system" became the umbrella label for a reorganization of formal structure as well as processes and incentives for profitability and accountability. In many firms this shift coincided with the adoption of the so-called executive officer (*shikkō yakuin*) system, in which heads of business units do not also automatically become members of the board of directors. Boards were reduced in size and complemented by outside directors. The first company to adopt this system was Sony in 1994, followed by Mitsubishi Chemical and the electronic firms Hitachi and Toshiba. The 2007 introduction of "J-SOX" rules, a version of the U.S. Sarbanes-Oxley Act (SOX) that spells out the responsibilities and liabilities of directors, combined with the greater ease of bringing derivative lawsuits on behalf of shareholders, greatly increased pressure on board members to ensure that business units did not engage in investments or activities without clearly identifiable profit streams.

Beginning in 1998, Japanese firms also were given the option to reorganize as a holding company, when a revision of the Antimonopoly Law (AML) lifted the ban that dated back to 1947. The initial beneficiary was the banking industry, which underwent unprecedented consolidation beginning in 1998. Japan's 20 preeminent postwar banks merged into four large financial holding companies that became umbrellas for separate operations in retail, corporate, and trust banking. Manufacturing firms were slower in shifting to holding companies because previous regulations had incentives against doing so. However, new tax rules as well as new laws facilitating reorganizations invited interest in holding companies.[8] By 2006, of the 472 large firms in the *Nikkei 500* sample, 29 had switched to pure holding-company structures.

In contrast to the multidivisional organization under the "company system" the subsidiary firms of holding companies are independent. For example, shifting to a holding structure allowed Kirin to detach its beer brewing from its soft drink and pharmaceutical operations. Kirin was successful in all three of these business, even though expected synergies from core competencies (such as in fermentation and biotech) had not materialized. Instead of divesting some of these businesses, Kirin wanted them to operate separately and be focused on their markets. Thus, while Kirin Pharma Co. Ltd. is pursuing collaboration with Terumo to become one of Japan's global niche pharmaceutical firms, Kirin Brewery Co. is jockeying for position with Asahi Beer in Japan's highly competitive domestic beer market. Thus, the New Japan holding companies are very different from pre–World War II conglomerates: they do not aim to form dominating trusts spanning all important industrial sectors but are structured for clear strategic purposes.

Overall, Japan's largest firms have embarked on an all-out refocusing and specialization course. Their strategic repositioning with a new emphasis on profitability is accompanied by changes in formal organization, human resource management, and corporate culture. Although it will take perhaps a decade for these changes to manifest themselves across all large Japanese firms, the transition is clearly under way.

What the Skeptics May Say

Some readers may harbor doubts that Japan has really changed. First, they may point to smaller firms that continue traditional business practices. In this book I cover only large firms, where the strategic inflection point has manifested itself most clearly as of 2007. A study of how this trickles down throughout the entire economy is left for future research.

Skeptics may also point to large firms that continue to be laggards, seemingly unable to change their corporate culture. But one should keep in mind that no country is free of pockets of protectionism and poorly performing companies. Their existence is no proof that change is not occurring. What is relevant is the

---

8. Before the implementation of consolidated accounting standards in 2000, firms could offset losses in one division with profits in another and thereby reduce overall taxable income. Moreover, accounting rules shifted to mark-to-market evaluation of long-term shareholdings in 2001. Until then, creating a holding company would have required the transfer, and therefore mark-to-market valuation, of shares kept at book value. Because many companies held shares bought at inflated prices during the bubble period, they were loath to mark-to-market these voluntarily in the midst of the 1990s recession (Kojima 1998).

influence that such companies have on the overall economy. Japan's strategic inflection point means that the laggards' influence is waning, partially because of changes in regulatory processes and partially because they are a dying breed as Japan shifts to accountability, bolstered by a growing market for acquisitions, including of hostile takeovers.

Some business practitioners may be impatient and not see any evidence of change, as of 2007, in particular in human resource management (HRM). Promotions still seemed to be inside the company only and management continued to appear entrenched. Cross-fertilization through midcareer hires remained rare. This is not surprising, as changes in HRM practices got under way only in the early 2000s. It will be a decade before these changes are truly incorporated—or even longer, until the first generation of employees hired under performance pay will reach managerial levels. Some companies have begun to introduce market wages by job category, a first step toward transferability of talent. We will know that change has arrived in HR when we see an increase in labor mobility across companies at the midcareer level, and even more so when companies not in distress begin to hire management executives from the outside.

Scholars, too, have expressed their doubts. For example, Amyx (2004) and Vogel (2006) argue that vested interests and institutional complementarities can pose insurmountable obstacles to systemic change and reform. Others have pointed to Japan's engrained "socialist" behavior (Anchordoguy 2005) or distinctive social networks (Witt 2006) as great inhibitors to doing things differently. However, the research and data reported in these studies refer to the 1990s and up to the 2002 at most, which was before Prime Minister Koizumi implemented his unexpectedly powerful policy program of "leaving it to the market" and before the effects of restructuring began to show in corporate profits. Therefore, these studies could not have foreseen the strategic inflection point as it manifested itself in corporate renewal only after 2002. These studies were also conducted by political scientists that concern themselves with overall system change of the political economy, and they pursue the larger question of how Japan's "system of capitalism" compares to other systems.

While I leave an evaluation of the overall issue of system change to political science experts, this book will show that at the corporate level Japan has unambiguously turned to the market. The forces forming corporate strategy are no longer determined through relations with banks and business groups, but by the market. Shareholders are no longer satisfied by good relations, but demand high profitability. Low-performing companies face the new and real threat of a hostile takeover. Employees are no longer quietly suffering life-long soldiers, but they increasingly demand individual career paths, interesting work assignments, and work-life balance. Japan's answers to the new challenges will be different from those adopted by other countries, just as Japan's legal interpretations will differ from the United States even when the new laws are based on the U.S. model. It will take time for this shift to trickle through society, as Japanese employees are unlikely to turn into individually driven competitors overnight. But in terms of business processes and the approach to corporate strategy, Japan has turned away from its previous system of socializing risk and toward competition in the marketplace.

Even those who agree with the overall change argument may be skeptical of the claim that it is not reversible. For example, in chapter 5 I will show that the degree of cross-shareholdings has greatly declined since 1998, opening up the stock market to greater variety in investors and greater turnover. Yet, in 2007 news from Japan reported an uptick in corporate cross-shareholdings. How does this sit with the move toward the market? It does, because the new corporate stakes differ qualitatively from the old ones. Previously, a large portion of friendly shareholdings were based on business group membership or ongoing trade relations, as an insurance against stock price volatility. The new corporate stakes are much more strategic, for they are not predicated by business groups but based on market calculations. They often occur among competitors or technology collaborators. Where they are used as a defense against hostile takeovers, given the new takeover rules of Japan they also promise high returns on investment. Understanding this difference is critical in understanding the New Japan.

Finally, some may claim that "choose and focus" is just another fad in Japanese corporate strategy. Not only have we experienced similar reversals in other countries before, they might say, but the dominant thinking in strategy is likely to be replaced by the next big idea (e.g., Tsuchiya 2004). The validity of these doubts notwithstanding, studying Japan's "choose and focus" wave of the early 21st century is of critical importance, for this phase represents a fundamental shift in Japanese business strategy, one that will shape future strategy-making in Japan. The changes in market environment, regulation, and global competition since the late 1990s have altered Japan's business organization in such critical ways that they have altered the strategic calculations of the rational Japanese firm. This has rendered our existing knowledge and assumptions about how Japan works outdated and obsolete.

TOWARD

CHOOSE AND FOCUS

2

JAPAN'S STRATEGIC
INFLECTION POINT,
1998–2006

Between 1998 and 2006, Japan underwent changes in laws and regulation, regulatory processes and domestic and global competition so fundamental that the period defines a strategic inflection point. In business research, such an inflection demarcates a point in time when the balance of forces shifts completely away from previous structures to new ways of doing things, and therefore fundamentally alters the ways in which companies compete. For this inflection to be strategic, it has to be irreversible (Burgelman and Grove 1996; Burgelman 2002). What made change in Japan irreversible was not so much one single event but rather the cumulative effect of all these reforms and transitions.

After the burst of the bubble economy of 1987–1991, Japan fell into a decade of stagnation and recession. The year 1998 was marked by a series of watershed events, led by a near meltdown of the financial system. The banking crisis caused a credit crunch, which greatly limited the access of small firms to credit, and this in turn caused social distress that did not abate until 2002, as expressed in measures such as record-high small-firm bankruptcies and suicides. For a period of four years, Japan was confronted with an urgent necessity to do "something," and this pressure led to an improbable and previously inconceivable reconstitution of Japan's business organization. The banking crisis therefore brought a tipping point—when the combination of economic and social crisis, global competition, and the ineffectiveness of government policies suddenly revealed that the postwar system had run its course. The main difference between the reforms since 1998 and previous reforms is that multiple forces for change hit Japan concurrently, leaving no choice but to truly change the ways in which things were done.

In this chapter I begin with a review of the triggers for reform: banking crisis and social distress, the inefficiency of postwar-period economic policies, and globalization. I then analyze these changes in detail, in particular as they pertain to Japan's legal structure. These legal revisions have replaced the postwar-period tools of industrial policy and informal regulation based on government-business interaction. In the manufacturing industries, government protection of business has been greatly reduced, as has the reliance on main banks to bail out failing firms; in their stead, courts have become important in bankruptcy procedures, and their rulings are widening the options of businesses in need of restructuring. It will become clear how new laws have caused a move to the market, by establishing clear processes and easing access to the courts; how shareholder rights have been strengthened and Japanese executives are both at greater liberty to design corporate strategies and more accountable for their choices; and how these shifts have altered the competitive environment from which New Japan companies emerge.

Triggers for Reform

Social Crisis

The tipping point became widely visible in the late 1990s when unprecedented social crisis showed that postwar-period policy tools had become completely ineffective. This was obvious in indicators of social distress that all hit record highs, including unemployment, bankruptcies by small firms, homelessness, crime, divorce rates, child abuse, and suicides. A few of these indicators, indicating the rapid exacerbation of private suffering in 1998, are shown in figure 2.1. What was eye-opening about these data was how directly related they were to economic hardship. A U.S.-Japan comparison of the relation between economic data (growth, unemployment) and private distress (personal debt, bankruptcy, suicide) showed a much more direct association for Japan than for the United States (Schaede 2006). This was attributed to the fact that during the postwar period Japan had little need for a comprehensive government program of poverty relief and long-term unemployment support. During the go-go years of postwar economic growth, unemployment was not a pressing issue under the system of lifetime employment, while the working poor had usually been able to find jobs. In any event, families were expected to be the first and last resort for people in need—but in the 1990s, families often found themselves unable to help.

The suicide rate in particular worried many Japanese, not only because its scale exceeded even the immediate postwar period but because it tied to the problem of loan sharks. In 2002, police statistics reported that 41 percent of suicides were attributed to "economic" or "work-related" reasons, which was more than the 39 percent for health reasons (health problems are said to be the main cause of suicide in most developed countries) (NPA 2003). One important reason was the rapid increase of so-called high interest-rate lenders who, in the 1990s, dominated banks in the individual loan market through a superior

2.1. *Unemployment, Personal Bankruptcy, and the Suicide Rate, 1955–2004*
Sources: www.stat.go.jp/data/roudou/2.htm; www.npa.go.jp/toukei/index.htm; www.courts.go.jp.

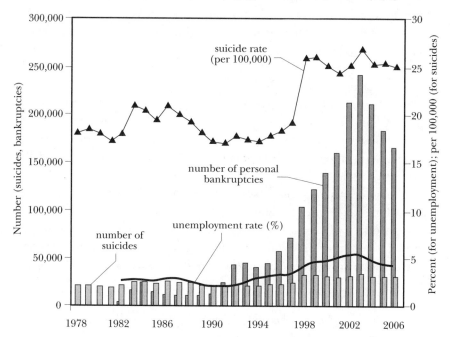

business model of offering cash loans with immediacy and respect for privacy. An underground illegal loan business grew quickly, charging interest rates of up to 1,000 percent to people unable to pay the high-interest lenders. Because Japanese life insurance companies still paid in the case of death through suicide, it became one way out for the highly indebted (jobless, previously self-employed, working poor), often committed by parents who wanted to protect their children from falling into the grasp of loan sharks (Schaede 2006).

In addition to extensive newspaper coverage, the general public was all too aware of this sad state of affairs, for one frequent method of committing suicide was throwing oneself in front of a Tokyo commuter train during the evening rush hour. The rapid increase of homeless people seeking shelter in train stations and public parks also made it painfully visible that something was seriously amiss. For Japan, one of the most affluent countries in the world and one that prides itself on social stability and security, these were shocking events. What began with the banking crisis in 1998 came to a boiling point at the turn of the century, when bankruptcies by small firms hit record highs. Anticyclical economic policies had obviously become ineffective, and in any event Japan's burgeoning budget deficit required different measures of reform. In 2001 Japan's Liberal Democratic Party elected as its leader Junichirō Koizumi, a proreform maverick. Koizumi promised, and powerfully delivered, a comprehensive program of privatization and deregulation. His policy mantra of "leave it to the market" guided policy reforms from 2001 to 2006.

Globalization

Studies of globalization have explained the sea change in competition, supply-change management, and trade that began in the 1980s. For the purposes of this book, we will note that globalization occurs at four levels: in manufacturing as separate from finance, and outside an economy (usually referred to as "in-out") as separate from inside an economy ("out-in"). As more and more Japanese manufacturing firms located some of their production facilities in other countries during the 1980s, the new trend came to be referred to as *kūdōka* (hollowing out), and globalization was discussed in terms of how "in-out" in manufacturing affected domestic industries. In contrast, domestic markets remained relatively shielded, both in manufacturing and finance.

In the 1990s, however, globalization hit Japan's domestic markets with full force, both in product markets and in finance. By 2004, the import penetration ratio in manufactured goods, which had hovered below 7 percent of total sales until the early 1990s, had doubled to 13 percent (CAO 2004, figure 3-2-1). Although perhaps still comparatively low, this doubling up was critical because imports brought price competition to intermediate and end product markets. At the same time, global parts procurement, especially in mature industries such as household appliances, continued to increase. In finance, the 1998 revision of the Foreign Exchange Law removed most of the remaining barriers to investments in Japanese companies. Foreign equity funds had developed an appetite for assets sold by banks cleaning up their bad loans, because it was apparent that the aggressive direct write-offs of loans translated into fire sales of golf courses, resort hotels, and other projects from the bubble period. Buying these up cheaply and turning them around promised to be a good investment.

Deregulation brought further financial market opening. The percentage of foreign ownership in companies listed in the first section of the Tokyo Stock Exchange more than quintupled, from 5 percent in 1991 to 28 percent in 2007. More than 50 large TSE-listed companies had foreign ownership exceeding 50 percent. In 2005, Sony appointed a non-Japanese president, and Nissan's turnaround was a story of French-Japanese cooperation. Global competition had arrived in Japan.

Banking Crisis

In late 1997 the aftermath of the bubble economy turned into crisis. A series of scandals, which had begun at banks and investment banks, had extended to the bureaucracy in 1995. In 1997 another round of widespread accounting fraud by investment banks was revealed.[1] These revelations exposed the true extent of the nonperforming loan crisis and the financial system's abysmal state of affairs. Bank failures, which had begun in 1995 with the collapse of the *jūsen* mortgage lenders and a string of smaller banks, had caused the Ministry of Finance (MOF) to intervene to avoid a bank run. In November 1997, however, these failures combined to create an explosion, when for the first time in the postwar period a large city bank failed. Hokkaido Takushoku Bank suspended operations, and was eventually merged with Hokkaido Bank. In the same month, the country's third largest investment bank, Yamaichi Securities, could no longer disguise its huge bubble-period losses. To add insult to injury, the main bank of Yamaichi's business group, Fuji Bank, reneged on the well-established practice of bailing out an integral business group member. Alas, Fuji Bank apologetically explained, it was itself overburdened with nonperforming loans and therefore unable to rescue Yamaichi Securities. And, while the Asian financial crisis of 1997 did not hit Japan directly, it caused great losses for Japanese banks that were involved in Asian trade finance and investment.

The MOF's fair-weather reporting had been exposed as fiction. In rapid succession, more trouble came to the fore. In September 1998, the collapse of Japan Leasing, a subsidiary of the Long-Term Credit Bank, with debt of ¥2.2 trillion (almost $17 billion), was the biggest failure of a Japanese firm to date. A month later, the government nationalized two of the three specialized banks that had been main contributors to the postwar system, the Long-Term Credit Bank of Japan and Nippon Credit Bank (later sold to foreign funds and restructured into Shinsei and Aozora). The year 1998 also saw the introduction of two emergency laws to support the banking industry, as well as the establishment of the Resolution and Collection Corporation (RCC, Seiri kaishū kikō) to assist banks with the liquidation of bad loans through

---

1. Scandals began in 1991, when it was revealed that brokerage houses had promised compensation for stock losses to their best clients, and had paid for it by churning (trading frequently) the accounts of unsuspecting small investors. This was followed by revelations of fraud by individual bankers and a few murders allegedly committed by so-called *sōkaiya*, corporate racketeers. In 1995, a set of bribery scandals undermined the credibility of the Bank of Japan and Ministry of Finance. In 1997, the *tokkin* scandal revealed that the large investment banks had laundered investment losses in specific investment accounts (including pension reserves by large firms) in real and fake subsidiaries; see Katz (2003) and Amyx (2004).

cash purchases and strict collection from original debtors (Hoshi and Kashyap 2001; Takeuchi 2003).[2]

In fact, the banking crisis was so severe that between March 1998 and March 1999 the government had to infuse ¥9.3 trillion (about $90 billion) into the largest banks.[3] This infusion invited fierce discussion in the media, and to appease taxpayers it came with "business improvement orders" as to what was required of recipient banks in terms of recovery. A revision of the antitrust restriction on holding companies allowed the large banks to merge and reposition strategically by combining fee income activities with their standard loan business. Japan's banking industry underwent major consolidation, as the leading banks merged into four financial holdings. Small banks, likewise, were reorganized in a process that continued beyond 2006.

Long planned by Prime Minister Ryūtarō Hashimoto, who spearheaded financial reform, 1998 also was the year of the financial "Big Bang." This reform package brought a revision of almost all laws relating to the financial industry as well as accounting and disclosure, with the goal of introducing transparency and making Japan's financial markets "free, fair, and global." No longer could banks and corporations hide their nonperforming loans in undisclosed subsidiaries, and cross-subsidization within highly diversified companies had to be declared through the introduction of consolidated balance sheet accounting. Investors could no longer easily be misguided, as a company's core and affiliated businesses and their separate performances were now regularly reported, finally allowing a full interpretation and comparison of the financial health of Japanese companies.

Though not strictly part of the Big Bang, a concurrent reform was the 1998 replacement of the previous Foreign Exchange and Foreign Trade Control Law by a new Foreign Exchange Law that liberalized cross-border financial transactions. This marked the end of government controls and restrictions on foreign participation in Japanese firms as well as foreign investments by Japanese citizens.

The revocation of this important law was indicative of an overall change in Japan's regulatory system. The postwar system had placed great emphasis on

2. The 1998 Emergency Measures Law to Resurrect Financial Functions (Kinyū kinō saisei hō) and the Emergency Measures Law for the Speedy Improvement of Financial Functions (Kinyū kinō kenzen-ka-hō) were designed to be in place until 2001, and the Deposit Insurance Corporation was chartered with recapitalizing banks. The first law included a temporary nationalization scheme that was applied to the two long-term credit banks. See Amyx (2006) for a political analysis of the banking crisis.

3. A first capital infusion was offered in March 1998 (¥1.8 trillion), and a second in March 1999 (¥7.5 trillion); both were required so that the large city banks could maintain their capital adequacy ratios of 8%, as described by the Bank for International Settlements [BIS] for international banking.

entry regulation, whereby the regulator (i.e., the ministry in charge, which was also tasked with protecting and nurturing an industry) decided which companies were allowed to engage in what business activities. Process regulation—the monitoring of firms once they were "in"—had been left to informal agreements that were implemented through frequent contacts between companies and ministries (Schaede 2003). An important tool of informal regulation was administrative guidance, which allowed for situational regulation and rested on a carrot-and-stick approach. Those who cooperated were rewarded whereas mavericks were punished. In addition to entry licenses and permits in the ministries' discretion, the Ministry of Economics, Trade and Industry (METI) had greatly relied on trade controls to evoke business cooperation in informal quid pro quo regulation. With the 1998 Foreign Exchange Control Law, METI relinquished its most important policy tool of the postwar period.

In the financial sector, the Ministry of Finance began deregulation in the 1980s by tinkering with entry rules. This meant allowing partial entry by certain banks into certain business areas, and by deregulating certain interest rates while keeping others fixed. This invited regulatory arbitrage, as banks and companies exploited the resulting price distortions in financial and real estate markets. Informal regulation became a major contributor to the bubble economy of 1987–91, during which MOF lost control over banking regulation and transgressions, however blatant, remained unsanctioned.

In the 1990s, scandals involving ministry officials led to the first revisions of administrative guidance that placed stricter limits on personal connections between firms and ministries. In 1998, the Ministry of Finance was stripped of most of its supervisory role in the financial sector. In its stead, the newly created Financial Services Agency (FSA) began operation in 1998, and soon became a prime example of how regulatory processes had begun to change. For the first time, the 1999 Inspection Manual introduced a detailed and binding rulebook on bank inspections. In defining what constituted a nonperforming loan, it wiped out decades of banks' self-reporting. The banking crisis afforded the FSA heightened authority, as banks were facing failure and the government's capital infusion had triggered public scrutiny.[4]

In 2002, Prime Minister Koizumi issued an aggressive program for structural change, with financial system reform and the clean-up of nonperforming

4. The FSA published on the Internet not only the results of its inspections but also the difference between its and the banks' own claims. Initially, the largest banks underestimated their bad loans by 36%, with five banks underreporting their nonperforming loans by more than 50%. In the third round (ending 2002), average underreporting had declined to 5.5% (www.fsa.go.jp/news/newse/e20040916-1.html). For an in-depth account of regulatory changes, see Amyx (2004); for a sixth-year review of FSA operations, see Hoshi and Ito (2004).

loans by 2004 at its core. This was indeed accomplished, as the ratio of non-performing loans at major banks declined from 8.4 percent in 2002 to 2.9 percent in 2005. Even though problems remained at the smaller banks, by 2006 the loan portfolios of Japan's major banks had improved and were profitable again.

The Need for New Economic Policies: Zombies and Government Debt

When Prime Minister Hashimoto's 1998 Big Bang was first announced, few anticipated the enormous impact it would have. Too often in the past, Japan's government had paid lip service to deregulation yet efforts had rarely been valiant enough to overcome vested interests. The reforms beginning in 1998 were different partially because of their nature (by stipulating transparency), and partially because of their timing, occurring just when Japan's economy was hopelessly stuck in a rut.

The macroeconomic dilemma of the 1990s has been reported elsewhere (e.g., Katz 1998, 2003) and can briefly be summarized here. A decadelong recession had depleted government resources and rendered postwar-period policy tools ineffective. Fast-rising unemployment was perhaps the greatest challenge, because the existing social contract had delegated a large portion of employment insurance and pensions to companies' lifetime employment system. The sudden jump in unemployment in the 1990s posed enormous challenges. In the absence of well-endowed public assistance, the government's solution was to avert unemployment by subsidizing large firms in danger of failure. Thus were born the "zombie" firms of the 1990s, that is, firms unable to earn a profit but artificially kept alive so that they could continue providing employment (Hoshi 2004; Caballero, Hoshi, and Kashyap 2005). The creation of zombies turned the problems caused by the bubble economy into calamities.

One of the industries most affected by the real estate bubble and bust had been the construction industry, which employed more than 10 percent of Japan's workforce. The government's first attempts to sustain employment were public work projects, which in previous years had often been used to jump-start the economy. The government launched new construction of highways, dams, bridges, tunnels, wave breakers, and even leisure hotels for civil servants in the most remote areas, solely to boost the construction industry.[5] Besides deplorable consequences for nature and scenery, the public work projects of the

5. See Kerr (2001) for a vivid though perhaps overstated account of what these programs did to Japan's landscape; see Lincoln (2001) and Calder (1988) for the underlying economic processes.

late 1980s and 1990s ballooned government debt. The second-worst industry on the government's zombie chart was retailing, which accounted for at least another 10 percent of the workforce due to the multiple layers of distribution and suppliers. Daiei and the Sogo Department Store were two prime examples of companies considered too big to fail in the mid-1990s. The government pushed banks to roll over loans to these failing chains, thereby only adding to the banking crisis.

Artificial life support for failing firms may have contributed to social stability, especially during the credit crunch that began in 1998 when small firms (such as Daiei's suppliers) reported increasing difficulties in receiving bank loans.[6] However, the macroeconomic consequence of zombies was unambiguously negative, as these firms occupied financial and human capital in nonproductive areas that could not be put to use in more profitable and promising activities (Caballero, Hoshi, and Kashyap 2005). The credit crunch, perceived or real, underscored this crowding-out phenomenon.

Extensive public works, bailing out large banks, and reduced tax revenues due to recession all contributed to a fiscal crisis. Tax revenues financed less than half of the government's budget in the early 2000s, and by 2003 general gross government debt had reached 170 percent of GDP (compared with 65 percent for the United States, 68 percent for Germany, and 119 percent for Italy, the long-time leader in this league). Because the Japanese government holds some portion of this debt through a variety of special accounts, net debt (gross debt minus the government's financial assets) may allow for a more meaningful comparison. Here, Japan's 85 percent compared with Italy's 90 percent, which was much higher than the OECD average (the United States stood at around 44% and Germany at 58%) (MOF 2005). The fact that almost all of Japan's public debt was held by domestic investors reduced pressure on the exchange rate, but rising debt caused great political concern nonetheless, especially in light of the looming end of the government's zero-interest-rate policy (a measure to infuse liquidity into the depressed economy from 2000 to 2006), which was to raise the government's costs of debt financing.

For economic reform, government debt meant that Japan could no longer afford to apply Band-Aids to the economic recession with public spending. Something more fundamental had to happen. Japan needed true reform.

6. The credit crunch was partially due to a 1998 rule that banks operating domestically maintain a capital adequacy ratio of 4%. This ratio measures a bank's capital base in relation to total assets and aims to ensure sound banking by prohibiting excessive leverage. It raises the cost for each loan, and in 1998 Japanese banks were unable to increase capital to sustain lending. Moreover, because a large portion of capital was in the form of equity holdings in other companies, falling stock prices negatively affected the banks' ratios, necessitating government rescue purchases of equity held by banks (Schaede 2005).

Government Reforms: Leave It to the Market

Another push forward came in 2001 through government reorganization, planned by Prime Minister Hashimoto in the late 1990s in a move labeled a "regime shift" in a highly prescient analysis by Pempel (1998). In addition to a streamlining of ministries in 2001 to reduce the size of government and clarify responsibilities, a main feature of this reform was the concentration of decision-making power in the Prime Minister's Office. Under a strong prime minister—such as Koizumi between 2001 and 2006—this reorganization curtailed ministerial influence over industry as well as over the policy-making process, as the prime minister can now pull reform deliberation away from the ministries and into his own discussion group, the Council on Economic and Fiscal Policy (CEFP). In the postwar period, ministry-based deliberation councils (*shingikai*) had played an important role in Japan's policy-making process, because in many cases they reinforced the power of the various ministries over their industries. A council's final report was often written by bureaucrats and frequently turned into law. Under the new system, the prime minister, who is also a member of the CEFP, can choose to pull a policy deliberation away from the ministry to open it for broader discussion, thereby greatly curtailing vested interests in any one policy area. Thus, the 2001 administrative reform did much more than simply reshuffle, reduce in number, and rename the various ministries. It also introduced mechanisms that, if used with authority, would weaken the role of the bureaucracy and lower the ministries' resistance to change.

Moves to reshape the Liberal Democratic Party and force out several of the old guard enabled Prime Minister Koizumi to curb resistance within the LDP against more market-oriented reforms. But perhaps his biggest achievements were in aggressively pushing privatization and, in a great reversal of previous government-business relations, in denouncing the government's role in supporting private business. Koizumi's line "leave to the private sector what the private sector can do" (*minkan ni dekiru koto wa minkan ni yaraseru*) became the core message of the 2002 Revival Program, and his relentless insistence convinced business that they could no longer sit and wait for the government to bail them out.[7]

Thus, in extending Hashimoto's reforms of the late 1990s, Koizumi ended the previous government approach of socializing business risk. Throughout the postwar period, companies often hedged against failure by discussing new projects with their ministry, and once approved, could count on that ministry

7. See, for example, http://www.kantei.go.jp/foreign/koizumispeech/2002/02/04sisei_e.html.

to support the decision even if it went afoul. This exchange of information was private and closely held, greatly empowering the ministries. Koizumi's new stance and the new "sunshine" regulation, however, brought an end to this informal decision making, transferring the discussion of business decisions to the companies and their shareholders, and leaving ministries with open and transparent regulatory decision-making powers.[8]

The New Demand for Law

The 1998 establishment of the Financial Services Agency, separate from the Ministry of Finance, was a harbinger of the reorientation of Japan's regulatory system. It was followed by a series of new laws that shifted the regulatory focus away from the actor (an industry or company) and toward transactions and markets. The postwar-period informal regulatory processes, based on the fact that a ministry in charge of nurturing an industry was also tasked with its regulation, was undermined by a shift to legal processes and a turn to the courts.

This transition built on a fundamental reorientation in Japan's legal philosophy. Japanese corporate law, as it existed through the 1990s, dated back to 19th century civil law logic of "pre-regulation." This meant that the law detailed most corporate activities ex ante, and in the event that a dispute was brought to court, judges were asked to merely interpret the code (without being bound by precedent)—as opposed to shaping the law through case precedents, as common law systems allow. In the area of corporate governance, for example, this meant that the law imposed highly detailed restrictions on management. Although this greatly limited managerial discretion, it also reduced the threat that managers would be held liable for their decision making by shareholders. However, these limitations on management had become such an obstacle that in 2001 the Ministry of Justice issued a statement that Japanese corporate law was to be reoriented toward a "postremedy" approach, under which everything is possible unless it is specifically prohibited. Any problems will be addressed upon their occurrence.[9]

As Milhaupt and Pistor (2008) argue powerfully, the differences between common and civil law applications are not nearly as stark as typically characterized. In reality, codes are not that specific even in civil law countries (such as Japan or Germany), and the courts' interpretations importantly shape corporate

---

8. Interview, METI officials, spring 2007. As one official put it, "It is no longer fun to be a METI official."

9. See Ministry of Justice, "Japanese Corporate Law: Drastic Changes in 2000–2001 and the Future," www.moj.go.jp/ENGLISH/information/jcld-01.html.

rules. Moreover, judges would be unwise to ignore prior rulings, because this increases the chance that their rulings are overturned in higher courts. A much more critical difference between ex ante and postremedy legal systems lies in the incentives they offer to invest in innovation, and in the access they provide at the lawmaking and law enforcement stages. Stock options are a fitting example of differences between the two systems. In the U.S., companies had the idea to hand out options as incentives, and rules and regulations were developed only over time, in a series of court cases. The companies innovated, the courts shaped post hoc. In contrast, because stock options were not described in the laws of Japan or Germany, companies there first had to lobby to have stock options written into the law. Even though they may have developed functional equivalents such as perquisites, the financial innovation depended on an initial move by the lawmakers, not the companies.

The Ministry of Justice's statement of a switch to ex post adjudication, therefore, is a message of increased access to lawmaking (by rewriting corporate laws to offer more managerial liberties) and to the courts (by streamlining court processes, reducing fees, and helping courts specialize in certain areas such as bankruptcy). Both have resulted in a new demand for law in Japan (Milhaupt and Pistor 2008; West 2001; Milhaupt and West 2004). What this means is a shift away from the centralized lawmaking driven by the legislature as well as a shift away from the postwar emphasis on informal regulation among insiders and toward a larger circle of participants in the legal process. For example, derivative lawsuits (brought by investors on behalf of the company) have doubled from 84 in 1993 to an annual level of over 160 in the early 2000s. This was accomplished by both a pull and a push affect. The push came from the government, in its revision of corporate law to introduce more accountability and easier access to the courts for shareholders. The pull was the market, as evidenced in the Livedoor case of 2005, Japan's first publicly played out domestic hostile-takeover battle.

In February 2005, the startup information technology (IT) company Livedoor, representing New Japan and given a face by a young, brash entrepreneur, submitted an unsolicited bid for an established, suited-up, Old Japan broadcasting company. The company attempted to fend off the hostile bid by offering warrants with special rights, based on a 2002 Commercial Code revision that allowed such warrants, at a fair price, designed to the detriment of the hostile bidder. Livedoor sued the broadcasting company on the grounds that the price was grossly unfair. The court sided with Livedoor, and the subsequent fierce battle held many Japanese enthralled for months. The main fallout from this case was that Japan had entered new territory of lawmaking. A new precedent was set, and it greatly influenced the subsequent shaping of hostile takeover legislation.[10]

Legal Change: Toward Reorganization and Restructuring

As the government pushed for economic reform in the late 1990s, it became apparent that the greatest obstacle to corporate renewal was a dearth of laws and rules structuring the processes of corporate reorganization. In 1997 Japan began to revise the Commercial Code almost every year for a decade. Related laws such as those regarding finance, accounting, taxation, labor, and bankruptcy were introduced, amended, and expanded at a rapid rate. Reflecting the new legal philosophy, these revisions increased managerial flexibility and choice but also brought new regulations, including ones on transparency, accountability (through improved corporate governance rules), corporate finance, and reorganization. This shift also aligned Japan with international practices, such as in disclosure, accounting, and bankruptcy practices. In 2006, a new Corporation Law (Kaisha-hō) superseded all laws regarding company creation, restructuring, and corporate governance. As a result, somebody who knew Japan well in the 1980s but has not looked at it since then might not recognize the new legal environment. A timeline of the most important legal changes for corporations in that decade in provided in table 2.1.

Transparency: The New "Sunshine" Laws

The financial Big Bang of 1998 contained a schedule of actions to bring Japanese corporate disclosure and accounting rules into line with international standards. During the postwar period, informal workouts by banks had often been facilitated by very lenient disclosure requirements, both for the struggling company and the banks. Bank failures after the burst of the bubble, however, had revealed dubious accounting practices, such as hiding problem loans in small subsidiaries. In 2000, Japan introduced consolidated accounting—meaning that a company has to report on its own activities as well as those of its subsidiaries. Finally, investors could learn about the full extent of a company's operations and its overall profitability, adjusted for all subsidiary operations.

In addition to having to declare it all, beginning in 2000 companies had to report mark-to-market valuations of their assets, as opposed to book (or purchase price) values; beginning in 2001 this rule also applied to cross-shareholdings.

---

10. Milhaupt and Pistor (2008) show how the Livedoor case underscores the important shift in expectations about the role of law in Japan. They find that Japan has changed much more drastically in the legal realm than other civil law countries that are also undergoing great changes, such as Germany.

TABLE 2.1. *The Most Important Legal Changes toward the New Japan*

Year	Commercial Law	Other Laws / Programs	Accounting/Tax	Labor
1997	Simplification of merger processes	Lifting ban on holding companies (AML revision); Foreign Exchange Law; Financial System Reform Law (Big Bang)		
1998	Stock repurchases allowed	Two laws to rescue financial institutions		
1999	Equity-swap system; Equity transfer system	Industrial Revitalization Law	Adoption of tax effect accounting and cash flow statements	Revision of Equal Opportunity Employment Law
2000	New spin-off system; simplification of transfer of business (spin-outs) and M&As	Civil Rehabilitation Law (bankruptcy procedures)	Consolidated accounting; Mark-to-market valuation of financial assets (except cross-shareholdings)	End of employee veto right in spin-offs and transfers
2001	Abolition of par value stocks, introduction of treasury stocks (repurchasing of own shares)	Emergency economic measures; "Guideline for Multiparty Work-outs" for bank rescues	New accounting of retirement benefits; mark-to-market for cross-shareholdings; statutory auditor system expanded; corporate reorganization tax rules	Law for Facilitating the Resolution of Individual Labor Disputes

Year				
2002	Various types of stocks allowed; new stock option system; new corporate governance rules	Program for Financial Revival; Bank Stock Ownership Limit Law	Consolidated tax return system	Revision of Labor Standards Law
2003	Treasury stock purchase system (for use in M&A)	Revision of Corporate Reorganization Law, Liquidation Law; New Business Promotion Law (¥1 firms)	New accounting rules for impaired assets; quarterly earnings reports for listed firms (TSE rule)	Working Dispatching Law
2005	Corporation Law	Revision of Antimonopoly Law; Takeover Guideline		
2006	Financial Instruments and Exchange Law	LLP Law; Statutory quarterly earnings reports for listed firms; new reporting system for large shareholdings		Revision of Law Stabilizing Employment of Older Persons

Note: For laws, dates refer to the time that the change/revision passed the Diet; implementation usually occured the following year.

The effect was twofold. Companies with assets acquired in the early postwar period could report a windfall gain by switching to present values (if they had not already done so voluntarily). However, the majority of companies had bought shares, real estate, and other assets during the bubble period of the 1980s, and the value of these had fallen precipitously since 1991.

Sunshine, it is said, is the best disinfectant. Having to lay open to the public its financial woes pushed many large companies toward reform, even ones that were not in immediate distress. The new accounting rules made corporate information much more meaningful, and the government launched an Internet website with free access to corporate annual statements.[11] Corporate websites, too, began to become more informative, and many now contain annual statements, together with the glitzy annual report.

In 2003, the Tokyo Stock Exchange followed suit and required listed companies to post quarterly earnings reports. This caused initial resistance, in particular in industries governed by relational pricing that was often not settled within one quarter, as discussed in detail in chapter 8. Still, the rules on quarterly earnings reports were tightened annually, and in 2007 they were incorporated into the new Financial Instruments and Exchange Law.

Bankruptcy and Liquidation

If market capitalism means freedom of entry and exit, between 2000 and 2003 Japan made a huge leap toward that system. A first step in cleaning up the nonperforming loan crisis was to facilitate bankruptcy-based restructuring or simply exiting a business through liquidation. In the postwar period, banks had addressed looming business failures by working out informal debt restructuring that left the loans on the books, to be covered by loss reserves taken from bank profits. The goal was to save the company and recoup the loans in the long run. However, in the 1990s banks could no longer afford a "refinance-and-wait" approach, as bank profits were insufficient to cover loss reserves. This necessitated a switch to direct bad-loan disposals, in which the bank suffers a one-time extraordinary loss by writing off the loan and initiates bankruptcy procedures and restructuring by selling off nonprofitable business units. One way for the banks to hold on to something of value was to structure debt forgiveness whereby bad loans were swapped into equity shares that might gain value with a successful turnaround. These shares were sold, typically at only a few cents for each dollar of bad debt, to outside investors, such as U.S. equity funds.

---

11. This report, the *Yūka shōken hōkokusho*, is the functional equivalent to 10(k) statements in the United States. The website is https://info.edinet.go.jp.

However, banks and companies needed new procedures to switch to direct bad-loan disposals. Given the postwar-period reliance on informal workouts, existing bankruptcy laws were inadequate to handle swift reorganization. The 2000 Civil Rehabilitation Law (Minji saisei-hō) replaced the clumsy Composition Law (Wagi-hō) of 1927 to design new bankruptcy procedures for corporations and individuals. In 2003, the Corporate Reorganization Law (Kaisha kōsei-hō) of 1951 was revised to allow Chapter 11-type turnarounds adjudicated in courts. Moreover, the 2001 Guideline for Out-of-Court Workouts addressed bank-led workouts by stipulating how debt forgiveness should be organized in cases with multiple lenders but uncertain claims.[12] In 2004, the old Liquidation Law (Hasan-hō) was revised to simplify legal procedures for a shutdown and fair distribution of assets. Thus, the three main venues of dealing with failing companies—shutdown, reorganization, and informal workout—were clarified and streamlined to increase transparence and speed in bankruptcy and liquidation.

Court reforms made the legal shift to speed and transparency real. It is now possible to file a reorganization petition with a court in Tokyo or Osaka even if these two cities are not the location of the business or of a lender. These two district courts established special reorganization departments to handle bankruptcy cases promptly and efficiently. Data by Teikoku Databank show that bankruptcy procedures skyrocketed with the adoption of these measures. In the period between April 2000 and March 2005, 86,972 bankruptcies were reported with liabilities of ¥73 trillion, the vast majority of them under the Corporate Reorganization Law.[13]

Naturally, not all companies were excited about the idea of shedding or liquidating parts of the business empires they had so carefully built. One such example was Daiei, whose founder and president resisted reorganization to the point where the retail maverick became a zombie, artificially kept alive by banks. Others, such as Kanebo, could not reorganize because their non-performing loans affected all business units such that restructuring threatened the entire organization. In still other cases, the main bank was simply unable to orchestrate a workout due to legal uncertainty over the share of the burden to be shouldered by each lender. During the postwar period, it had not

---

12. See Higashino (2004a). Takeuchi (2003) argues that while Japanese banks had accumulated significant case law and hands-on experience in informal, multibank workouts, these were typically done behind closed doors. In contrast, companies accumulated hardly any knowledge, and until the introduction of contemporary bankruptcy legislation were dependent on the banks' expertise and whims. This may have dampened a company's enthusiasm for reorganization, and the Guideline was meant to rectify this situation.

13. See, e.g., Takagi (2003); Higashino (2004c); www.tdb.co.jp.

been common to write contracts stating a bank's specific liability in a jointly financed project, as this was left for negotiation with the main bank in the case of a bailout. In the extreme case of Kanebo more than 100 banks had, at one point or another, financed projects.

To help banks rid themselves of such nightmare clients, in April 2003 the government created the Industrial Revitalization Corporation of Japan (IRCJ). It received a fund of ¥10 trillion to use for the restructuring of firms with reasonable prospects but great resistance to reorganization. The IRCJ was to purchase a failing company's loans and assets, structure a new business plan and reorganization schedule, and sell its holdings to investors willing to execute the turnaround. In other words, the government created an organization to perform the function of a private equity fund specializing in corporate reorganization. The IRCJ had a limited life of four years, and its staff, consisting mostly of lawyers and consultants, were to enter the private sector after completion of their assignment. According to one official, the IRCJ performed three important functions. It helped shape the legal processes in cases in which banks could not agree how to divvy up losses in joint projects. It also jump-started a restructuring phase by showing that it could be done in Japan. And finally, it forced resisting companies, including Daiei, to reform. Overall the IRCJ took on over 40 projects, and when it was liquidated in March 2007 it carried forward a profit of about ¥40 billion (about $330 million).[14]

Reorganization and Restructuring

A first major push toward reorganization in the years 1998 through 2000 was to allow companies to buy back their own stock, and to facilitate the process and financing of mergers and acquisitions (M&A) by allowing mergers through stock swaps and streamlining rules on spin-offs. Allowing stock repurchases addressed an ugly legacy of the bubble period, when companies had increased new equity finance from ¥872 billion in 1986 to ¥8.8 trillion in 1989 (TSE 2006, 74; Hashimoto 2002). When the bubble burst in 1991, companies found themselves with huge amounts of equity and inefficiently used assets. In the 1990s, MOF even tried to enforce a freeze on new stock issues to prevent further depression of the stock market.

To correct the equity overhang, regulations on stock repurchases were revised, and in 1999 new stock swap and stock transfer systems allowed companies to sell off parts of the organization or merge with another firm through a stock swap. Together with a new stock-unit system (ending the clumsy stock

---

14. Interview with a board member of the Industrial Revitalization Corporation of Japan, Tokyo, 2003; *Japan Times*, December 30, 2006.

trading unit and face value regulations that posed great obstacles for capital increases and start-up funding), a 2001 revision also lifted a ban on what companies could do with the stock they repurchased, including a ban on acquiring other companies. In addition to lifting remaining limitations on the newly created stock options, the introduction of new stock categories and new rules on transactions offered unprecedented flexibility in refinancing, compensation, corporate restructuring, and takeover defense.

As we saw in chapter 1, "choose and focus" entails the shedding of noncore businesses, the purchase of other companies to strengthen the core business, and revising the formal organization. The new laws facilitated these processes by simplifying split-ups and spin-offs, acquisitions, and buyouts. The introduction of a divestiture system in 2000, together with the lifting of the ban on holding companies in 1997, created opportunities for companies to reorganize. Subsequent reforms offered a completely new set of deals in terms of asset transfers, leveraged or management buyouts, and takeovers (Hashimoto 2002; Higashino 2004a, 2004b). New rules on internal oversight made members of the board of directors liable for mismanagement and increased pressures to attach clear responsibilities to business units. Companies can now think strategically about their business portfolio—which business units to keep, which to spin off, and which to close down. Even laggards were pushed in this direction with the 2000 shift to consolidated accounting, when companies could no longer cross-subsidize or hide losses in certain business segments.

As part of its Revival Program, the government also began to revise rules on labor. Before 2000, a spin-off or transfer of operations into another organization required the consent of both creditors and labor. A company trying to reorganize by spinning off noncore businesses often faced resistance by employees who did not want to work for a smaller company because of lower wages there. Keeping the employees would have undermined the purpose of streamlining operations. Further flexibility in labor relations came with the 2003 revision of the Labor Standards Law, which increased labor turnover and mobility. For the first time the law addressed the dismissal of regular ("lifetime") employees, and the new legal interpretation opened the path to easier layoffs, especially for firms in distress.

New legislation also facilitated hostile takeovers. These had long been hindered by cross-shareholdings and a lack of rules on disclosure of large shareholdings and minority owners. In light of the rapid increase in takeovers in the early 2000s, the Ministry of Justice and METI released a Takeover Guideline in 2005 whose objectives were to ensure growth in corporate value, adopt global standards, offer equal treatment to all bidders, and expand corporate options by allowing "reasonable defense measures." With this the Guideline validated a poison pill (a mechanism that makes a hostile bid prohibitively expensive) in the form of new warrant issues that dilute the raider's stake. In 2006 the Takeover Guideline became binding by becoming part of the Corporation Law, which also clarified the rights of owners in defense situations.[15]

One concern at the time was that Japanese firms would use the new Takeover Guideline to formulate a plethora of defense mechanisms. However, whereas a June 2006 poll revealed that 27 percent of listed companies were considering the introduction of such measures, another survey in October 2007 showed that only 400 firms, or 10 percent of listed firms, had in fact adopted poison pills (*Nikkei*, June 19, 2006, October 15, 2007). As of 2007, the actual processes and defense mechanisms had yet to be established, but it was noteworthy that these mechanisms were discussed with unprecedented interest by shareholders. Perhaps most important, the possibility of hostile takeovers in and of itself pushes management toward "choose and focus." The objective with a hostile takeover is typically to purchase an underperforming company, replace its management, and revise the business model to improve performance. The best defense against such a takeover is for management to undertake these reforms itself. Therefore, the mere threat of a hostile takeover, regardless of whether it was ever launched, greatly increased managerial discipline.

The New Corporation Law

The numerous Commercial Code revisions culminated in the Corporation Law (Kaisha-hō) that became effective May 2006, replacing the archaic and in places nearly unintelligible code crafted in prewar Japanese. This law had been tested, so to speak, with the 1999 Industrial Revitalization Law that allowed METI to designate certain companies to reorganize according to new guidelines regarding spin-offs, internal reorganization, and financial restructuring. The 2006 Corporation Law accepted most of those features, and also unified many of the provisions that had been repeatedly revised in the Commercial Code.

Perhaps the most fundamental shift with the Corporation Law lies in the determination of corporate risk and responsibility. Reflecting the overall shift to postremedy thinking, the law expanded managerial freedom and introduced new, market-based means for investor protection. To begin with, the law removed minimum capital requirements for companies. Based on the idea that

---

15. Milhaupt (2005) offers a detailed analysis of how the Guideline represents an adaptation of Delaware takeover rules to the Japanese setting. See MOJ and METI (2005) for the "Guidelines for Corporate Value Protection" (Takeover Guidelines), and the Corporate Value Study Group (CVSG 2006) for the 2006 report on takeover activities and policies. See chapter 6 for details on hostile takeovers.

paid-in capital—a financial endowment at the time of establishment—would increase the chances of survival and thus protect investors, previously a company had to secure capital of ¥10 million (roughly $930,000) to be established as a stock corporation. However, this had obviously become insufficient for investor protection, yet had presented itself as a great obstacle to start-up companies. In 2003 so-called ¥1 companies, with one penny of capital, were allowed for start-ups, and this system was incorporated into the 2006 law. Moreover, the responsibility for dividend payments was moved from shareholders to the board of directors, increasing the financial flexibility of management.

To counterbalance this new flexibility, the law is also very clear about managerial responsibility and liability. Shareholder rights were greatly increased, and their standing (i.e., eligibility) to sue expanded. In other words, the law has removed previous ex ante protection and increased ex post dispute rights. By doing so in clear language, it has increased investors' access to the lawmaking process.

The Corporation Law also cleaned up the previous jungle of corporate design. It identifies four types of corporate form: the stock corporation (KK, *kabushiki kaisha*); the limited liability company (GK, *gōdō kaisha*); the unlimited partnership; and the limited partnership (LLP, introduced by separate legislation in 2005 to accommodate venture capital firms and other professional groups).[16]

In terms of corporate governance, publicly traded stock corporations can now choose from a variety of organizational designs, including whether to introduce a committee system for board monitoring (Miyazaki 2006; Takehara and Hinei 2006). To facilitate company creation and small-firm management, the Corporation Law gives smaller, closely held KK, such as start-up firms, the option of having only one director, and the statutory auditor may be replaced by an "accounting participant," that is, a corporate officer who is qualified as an accountant. Overall, the law brought more clarity and transparency to the legal environment for Japanese firms.

The Financial Instruments and Exchange Law: J-SOX

Effective October 2007, the Financial Instruments and Exchange Law (FIEL, Kinyū shōhin torihiki-hō) greatly revised regulations on corporate disclosure,

---

16. The former *yagen gaisha* (YK, limited liability company) was abolished, in a case of reform catching up with reality. Yet, this revision had real implications for foreign financial firms operating special purpose companies (SPC) for securitization transactions, because the YK had less demanding corporate governance rules, and could be treated as disregarded entities for U.S. income tax purposes. The new GK shares some of these flexible features, but is also covered by bankruptcy rules (see www.iflr.com, "Japan: SPCs under Common Law," December 2005; and PricewaterhouseCoopers, *Japan Tax Update* 14, October 2005).

internal auditing and compliance, in addition to governing financial transactions, investment funds, stock exchanges, and disclosure associated with takeover bids. This law's most significant implication for the overall regulatory system was the shift of regulation from industry-based to instrument-based, in that the new rules apply to the transaction regardless of the actor—be that a bank, a fund, or an individual. This further directed regulatory action away from individual companies and toward markets.

The FIEL combined regulations previously contained in the Securities and Exchange Law, Investment Trusts Law, Mortgage-backed Securities Law, and Financial Futures Law. It structured a new regulatory framework for the financial industry, covering a variety of instruments as well as sales, asset management and investment advice. It also further improved on corporate reorganization through mergers, stock swaps, and corporate splits by categorizing such deals as offerings of "securities" and regulating the financial transactions involved (Kodachi 2006).

But perhaps the biggest contribution of the FIEL to the strategic inflection point in Japanese corporate management is in further pushing transparency and managerial accountability. First, it makes quarterly earnings reports statutory for all listed companies. Moreover, it contains a section referred to as J-SOX—the Japanese version of the U.S. Sarbanes-Oxley Act (SOX) that prescribes internal controls and independent audits (albeit without some of the more onerous portions of the U.S. law). The J-SOX mandates certification of all statements made in the annual and quarterly reports of listed companies by qualified auditors, and makes members of the board of directors liable for lack in monitoring or oversight. No longer can a board member claim to have been unaware of a managerial decision (FSA 2006; Konishi and Shimizu 2006; Hori 2006).

Following on the heels of FIEL, the government began discussions on a new Financial Services and Market Law, to use the same new horizontal approach for the regulation of banking and insurance products. The relevance of FIEL is therefore twofold: it facilitates corporate reorganization by introducing market-based processes and rules on the exchange of securities, and it paves the way for cross-sectoral financial laws. The adoption of transparent, postremedy, transaction-based rules continues.

Antitrust Enforcement

Another area in need of reform toward "leaving it to the market" was antitrust. During the postwar period, the official as well as tacit sanctioning of cooperation among competing firms was an important feature of industrial policy. In a 2003 public speech, the secretary general of Japan's Fair Trade Commission,

Akinori Uesugi, referred to the 1955–70 period as the "Dark Ages of the Antimonopoly Act" (Uesugi 2005a). Even after a reform of the Antimonopoly Law (AML) in 1977 that introduced fines and prohibited outright price-fixing, enforcement of the law remained spotty, with some industries remaining unsanctioned even though prices were high and market shares remarkably stable. In the 1990s, Japan's Fair Trade Commission (JFTC) began to investigate repeat offenders more strictly, but during the recession many industries continued to self-regulate their markets, whether through restricting access to competitors, stipulating rules that could only be met by incumbents, division of customers, or outright price-fixing and bid rigging (Schaede 2000a).

In his inauguration speech in 2001, Prime Minister Koizumi declared that a transition to 21st century competition policy was required to referee Japan's newly reformed and newly privatized and deregulated industries. This was perhaps the first time that a Japanese prime minister commented on antitrust in his first public appearance (Suwazono 2005). Koizumi's interest was directly related to his program of privatizing the many public corporations in infrastructure provision. These were often staffed with ex-bureaucrats and had long been suspected to be involved in bid rigging (*dangō*) for public work projects, in some cases by proactively structuring a rigged bid (Schaede 2006a, 141; Takeshima 2006).

Thus empowered, during the five years between 2001 and 2005 the JFTC launched 154 cartel investigations, or an average of 31 cases per year, and more than two thirds of these were directed at bid-rigging violations. This compared to 124 cases, or an annual average of 25, for the previous five years (1996–2000) (JFTC 2005). Although the absolute numbers may look comparatively small, the move toward more aggressive antitrust enforcement is remarkable. Schaede (2000a) showed that in the postwar period, antitrust enforcement was countercyclical, that is, it increased during recessions. In contrast, in the 2001–05 period enforcement numbers increased during an economic upswing, indicating a true trend reversal.

As the JFTC took a more active stance in prosecution, its teeth were greatly sharpened in 2005 when the AML received its most substantial revision since 1977. Perhaps most important, a leniency system was introduced, granting total immunity to the first whistle-blower of a cartel and reducing immunity to the two following applicants. Leniency has long been considered one of the strongest weapons in U.S. antitrust enforcement, as it introduces suspicion and thereby destabilizes cartels. It seems to be as effective in Japan. In the course of 2006, the JFTC received an average of five leniency applications per month, and reported whistle-blowing to be a powerful investigative tool (Takeshima 2006). In addition, the JFTC was empowered in regards to criminal investigations and procedures. Whereas previously only the Ministry of Justice could launch criminal cases, the JFTC now can move beyond administrative processes and subpoena materials in search for evidence. Moreover, penalties were greatly increased. For large manufacturing firms, surcharges (fines) were raised from 6 percent to 10 percent of sales generated by the illegal activity, with special penalties for repeat offenders, and the range of violations subject to penalties was also expanded. This means that penalties now have a much greater deterrence effect. Finally, investigative procedures were streamlined to speed up cases, but defendants are also allowed to provide statements at the initial investigation stage.

This last measure was important because it tied into an overall shift in the JFTC's standing within Japan's political economy and how it investigates cases. In the 2001 government reorganization, the JFTC had been moved into what is now the Ministry of Internal Affairs and Communication, but in 2003 it was pulled into the Cabinet Office, to report directly to the prime minister. The JFTC's staff has grown to over 600, and staff expertise has been broadened to include economists, accountants, and professional lawyers (traditionally, government lawyers were not members of the Japanese bar). This reorientation of staff points to a qualitative shift in antitrust prosecution. Previously, JFTC investigations had been largely administrative: Was there tangible evidence of price fixing, or did the cartel structure sanctions to punish its own members for cartel breaking? If not, the JFTC may have issued a warning but not pursued the case. Likewise, in merger cases the JFTC used to employ a simplistic rule that the new entity could not have a market share exceeding 35 percent, unless there were strong industrial policy reasons to allow it. In the New Japan, the JFTC will instead evaluate a range of economic variables, such as the impact of a cartel on market prices, the interplay of competitive constraints with other laws (such as regarding intellectual property), and, for mergers, the global competitive situation of the industry concerned.

This qualitative change required not only a change in investigation procedures by allowing defendants to make their case early on, but it also necessitated specialization of JFTC staff. The JFTC founded a research institute to support economists in their studies of antitrust economics, which had remained an underdeveloped discipline at Japanese universities given Japan's postwar-period antitrust stance. Likewise, private law firms began to ramp up their expertise in cartel law, and the demand for law greatly increased also in the area of competition policy (Uesugi 2005b). The 2005 revision of the antitrust statute therefore marks more than just the introduction of stricter rules; it signals a qualitative shift to evaluating market economics in antitrust decision making.

Evaluation: Irreversible Change?

The strategic inflection point was triggered by a confluence of factors—things had gotten so bad in so many areas that Japan reached a tipping point. The reforms during that period were so multifaceted and deep-seated that they have completely changed the business environment in which Japanese firms compete. In 2007, some still doubted whether these changes would stick. Was this truly a strategic inflection, or was it simply an aberration caused by an overreaction to the banking crisis that was to be corrected through a partial or complete reversal to old practices? Would old rigidities resurface, and would Koizumi's successors allow vested interests to regain the upper hand?

Some of the changes described in this chapter could be reversed through changes in politics—for example in antitrust, where we know from the United States that enforcement tends to differ with changes in the ruling party. Moreover, the Cabinet Office's deliberation council, the CEFP, will only be as strong and proreform as the prime minister allows it to be, and could fall into oblivion if not charged with critical topics. Government policies in these areas will offer a good yardstick of system change in the years to come.

As for the laws themselves, they are reversible in two ways: they can be rewritten, or they can be altered in their interpretation and implementation. Rewriting business laws becomes complicated to the extent that they constitute a system of interrelated regulations, and it is precisely the plethora of legal changes in Japan, all based on new legal philosophy, that crystallized into the strategic inflection point at the turn of the century. It is impossible that all of the new reforms could be undone.

Legal doctrine, in contrast, is always subject to change, and the new demand for law and broadened access to the lawmaking process through lawsuits will only accelerate this process in Japan. In measuring shifts to clearer accountability, one tell-tale sign will be the prosecution of white collar crime. In 2007, former Livedoor founder Takafumi Horie received a 30-month prison sentence for irregular accounting, and fund manager Yoshiaki Murakami received a two-year sentence and a record personal fine of ¥1.2 billion (about $10 million) for insider trading connected to the Livedoor takeover bid. As one observer argued, "Murakami is not alone. Many people commit insider trading, but Murakami's visibility made him an obvious target. The courts wanted to send a clear signal to markets."[17] If we observe white collar crimes to be prosecuted in this way, covering Old Japan just as much

---

17. Mitsuru Yoshikawa, managing director at Daiwa Institute of Research, cited in *International Business Times,* July 19, 2007, http://uk.ibtimes.com/articles/20070719/yoshiaki-murakami-fund-manager-jailed-japan.htm.

as New Japan, we will know that the strategic inflection point has reached management's ethics.

Even if the government were to reverse its reform stance, however, in terms of corporate strategy the cumulative effect of the legal changes at the turn of the century was to completely revise the environment in which Japanese firms compete, by pushing the entire system toward market processes. Perhaps most important were the "sunshine laws" that brought transparency and full disclosure of corporate finances. The incentives and constraints faced by Japanese managers in structuring their business and competing to win have completely changed. Under old laws and practices, restructuring for clearer profit responsibilities and strategic positioning was difficult, and there were few incentives as long as cross-subsidizing did not have to be reported. Now that the cloak has been lifted, the pressures on companies to reorganize have increased.

The shift toward market-oriented, transparent decision making geared toward profitability and strategic dominance is, of course, a gradual process, with old habits dying more slowly than the laws can be rewritten. However, the process has clearly begun at the top, as executives and board members have become liable through the introduction of J-SOX, and derivative shareholder suits have become a true threat. In April 2007, an accounting scandal at the third-largest brokerage, Nikko Cordial Corporation, led to a takeover by Citigroup. Nikko was fined $4.3 million by the Tokyo Stock Exchange (the largest such fine to date) for inflating earnings in 2005 and 2006. In an unprecedented move, Nikko in turn sued three of its senior executives for fraud, for a combined ¥3.1 billion (more than $30 million).[18]

Top executives are now much concerned about the integrity of their decision-making processes and the viability of their investment decisions. According to one external board member of a large materials company, as of 2007 his board continued to receive investment applications from business-unit managers still operating in the old mind-set of copycat investment to mimic competitors. However, the board has begun to categorically reject proposals that do not promise strong returns on investment or do not fit with the company's overall strategic plan. He added: "Perhaps in some companies board members do not yet comprehend that they can end up in jail. But they will learn fast."[19]

18. "Nikko to Sue Former Executives for Accounting Fraud," *Japan Times,* February 28, 2007.
19. Interview, March 2007.

THE
OLD
JAPAN

3

POSTWAR

CORPORATE

STRATEGY

Perhaps surprisingly, there are only a few studies that look at the overall drivers of corporate strategy in postwar Japan (e.g., Yoshino 1968; Clark 1979; Abegglen 1984; Abegglen and Stalk 1985; Kagono et al. 1985). Most of the business research of the postwar period have zeroed in on one aspect of the system, such as supplier structures, research and development (R&D) organization, or corporate groups. Porter, Takeuchi, and Sakakibara (2000) consider corporate strategy in the 1990s, and dismiss postwar-period managers as having been insufficiently decisive and overly concerned with competitor imitation and market share growth through diversification. Rather than asking why companies engaged in these strategies, the authors merely conclude that Japanese managers must learn how to compete better. James Abegglen (2004), who coined the term "lifetime employment" in his early pathbreaking studies, took a fresh look at changing corporate strategy in the early 2000s through an analysis of five well-established Japanese firms he had observed over the previous five decades. The author accuses Japanese firms, in particular in the electronics industry, of "massive strategic failure" (*hisan na senryaku shippai*) in overdiversification, but he, too, does not analyze why these "failures" occurred.

In this book, in contrast, I assume that large companies in the postwar period were quite insightful about their situation, understood well the economic system and industry dynamics they operated in, and optimized their corporate strategies given the incentives and constraints of the old regime. We will see that market share growth and diversification were rational responses to postwar incentives. This holds true even when applying the more sophisticated insights of corporate strategy developed since the 1980s. The situational context for Japanese firms, that is, the industrial policy priority of export growth, is treated as exogenous here, although clearly corporations themselves helped shape this context. And just as Japanese firms lobbied the government to uphold protection then, they are now influencing the newly emerging political-economic system (Vogel 2006). Rather than discussing this interplay between government and business in shaping the system, however, in this chapter I explore the strategy context of postwar-period Japan.

The first step in an analysis of corporate strategy is the identification of the drivers of competition in a given market. Going back to Porter (1980), this can be done with the help of a market forces analysis. Porter suggested five critical forces: the threat of new entry, the threat of product substitution, the power of suppliers, the power of buyers, and the extent of rivalry. As summarized by Ghemawat (2006), there is nothing magic about the number five, and including other forces may improve the analysis. An example of an additional important force are so-called complementors, companies that create joint success by advancing each other's strategic position even though they operate in different industries.

The goal with this exercise of analyzing market forces is to identify the constraints and possibilities in a given market, as well as the means to exploit opportunities while protecting against potential threats. For example, if markets are wide open and capital requirements low, incumbent firms have to realize that profits will be squeezed by new entrants. Where entry is difficult, new competition may still emerge in the form of substitute products—that is, functional equivalents that could replace the current product or industry (such as floppy disks being replaced by USB flash drives). If either suppliers or buyers are powerful (perhaps because they have more bargaining power, are specialized, or can easily switch to other firms), they can squeeze profit margins and therefore have to be managed in some shape or form. To offer but one example, airlines face the problem that buyers can easily switch to another carrier; to tie travelers in, airlines offer frequent flyer programs. Likewise, if suppliers possess crucial technological knowledge, they need to be locked in lest they raise prices or wander off to work with a competitor. Thus, the market forces analysis aims to identify the "squeeze points," the complexities and the external contextual elements of a marketplace, in order to help design strategic levers for success: what not to worry about, where to lock in critical aspects of competition, and where to focus strategic attention.

A market forces analysis is typically conducted for an industry. However, the following takes a different approach and conducts this analysis for Japan's overall domestic market during the postwar period. Given the incentives and constraints within Japan's political economy, with its growth-promoting industrial policies, if you had been the decision maker in a large Japanese firm in the rapidly growing economy of the 1950s through 1980s, what would your competitive strategy have been?

The main points of this analysis are summarized in figure 3.1. During the postwar period, the strategic focus was the horizontal axis in figure 3.1 (stable

3.1. *A Market Forces Analysis for the Postwar Period (1950s–1980s)*

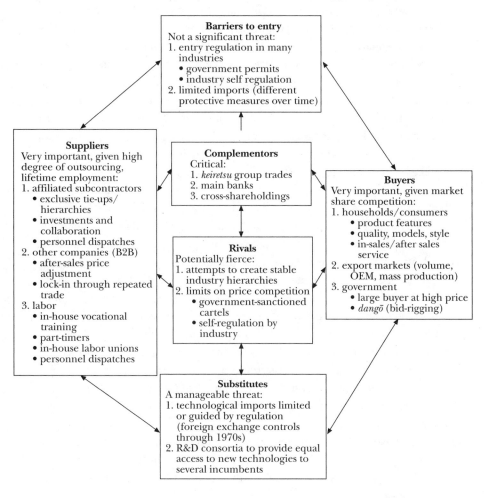

Barriers to entry
Not a significant threat:
1. entry regulation in many industries
   • government permits
   • industry self regulation
2. limited imports (different protective measures over time)

Suppliers
Very important, given high degree of outsourcing, lifetime employment:
1. affiliated subcontractors
   • exclusive tie-ups/ hierarchies
   • investments and collaboration
   • personnel dispatches
2. other companies (B2B)
   • after-sales price adjustment
   • lock-in through repeated trade
3. labor
   • in-house vocational training
   • part-timers
   • in-house labor unions
   • personnel dispatches

Complementors
Critical:
1. *keiretsu* group trades
2. main banks
3. cross-shareholdings

Rivals
Potentially fierce:
1. attempts to create stable industry hierarchies
2. limits on price competition
   • government-sanctioned cartels
   • self-regulation by industry

Buyers
Very important, given market share competition:
1. households/consumers
   • product features
   • quality, models, style
   • in-sales/after sales service
2. export markets (volume, OEM, mass production)
3. government
   • large buyer at high price
   • *dangō* (bid-rigging)

Substitutes
A manageable threat:
1. technological imports limited or guided by regulation (foreign exchange controls through 1970s)
2. R&D consortia to provide equal access to new technologies to several incumbents

relations with rivals, suppliers and customers), whereas in the 21st century this focus has shifted to the vertical axis (competition through existing or new rivals, and through innovation).

The context for corporate strategy in postwar Japan was determined by the economic growth priorities of the time. Japan's postwar political economy has been well studied and can be summarized briefly here. In what Johnson (1982) has labeled a developmental state approach, Japan's government embarked on a set of industrial policies to maximize economic growth by nurturing specific growth sectors (initially steel, chemicals, heavy machinery, energy, and shipbuilding) and by ensuring low costs of borrowing. Low interest rates invited high private investment in plant and equipment, which caused cyclical surplus production, especially in high fixed-cost industries such as steel or cement. To regulate this "excess competition," in some industries the government administered or tacitly sanctioned industry meetings during which production quotas and market share ratios were determined (Yamamura 1967, 1982). Antitrust rules were often overwritten by the growth agenda (Hadley 1970). Strict trade controls restricted imports of competing products and managed access to foreign technologies and raw materials (Ito and Kiyono 1988). Although the effectiveness of these policies has been questioned, no one denies that these policies were attempted, and therefore constituted the platform for strategic decision-making by Japanese firms in their domestic market.[1]

The biggest effect of industrial policies on corporate strategy was that it oriented companies toward competing on sales revenues: the more sales the better, almost regardless of profitability. Industry rankings were based on sales revenues, and being a top-tier company entailed prestige and free marketing. In industries identified as growth champions, such as chemicals and shipbuilding, market share was crucial because it was the main criterion in the government's formula for approving capacity expansion (Yoshino and Lifson 1986). In the trade industries the government allotted quotas based on existing market share—be it for access to imported raw materials, or export quotas such as under the voluntary export restraints in the automobile and electronics industries in the 1980s. More sales also translated into higher government allotments such as subsidies. Sales size was also important for recruiting, which occurred in a draft pick, with the order going from large to small. As we will see, banks had their own reasons for putting emphasis on their borrowers' revenues over profits. The search for ever-growing sales introduced competition into the otherwise fairly rigidly regulated economy, and the easiest way to increase sales was to diversify into new product segments and markets.

Japan's postwar economic growth was rapid but by no means linear. High swings in year-on-year GDP growth rates, as the economy undertook its technological catch-up with the West, are shown in figure 3.2. In the 1950s and 1960s, annual GDP growth averaged 10 percent, but was halved to 5 percent after the 1973 oil crisis. Especially under fixed exchange rates until 1973, the boom years caused overheating, which had to be corrected by tight monetary

1. See, among many more, Calder (1998, 1993); Johnson (1982); Yamamura (1967, 1982); Hadley (1970); Komiya, Okuno, and Suzumura (1988); Murakami (1982); Patrick and Rosovsky (1976); Patrick (1986); Pempel (1998); Samuels (1987); Schaede (2000b); Yamamura and Yasuba (1987). Doubts on the effectiveness of these polices have been voiced by, e.g., Weinstein (1995); Beason and Weinstein (1996); Callon (1995). Porter, Takeuchi, and Sakakibara (2000) and Katz (1998, 2003) claim that Japan's world-class exporting industries were successful on their own, whereas industrial policies slowed down a much larger group of inefficient domestically oriented industries.

3.2. *Annual GDP Growth Rate, 1956–2006*
Source: Constructed from government data at www.stat.go.jp.

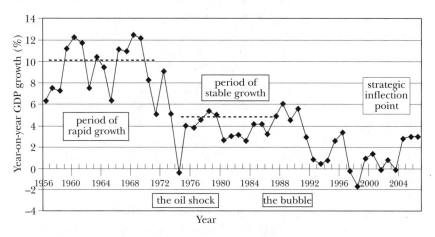

policy to reduce raw material imports. Combined with a rapid rate of technological change, this created a highly unstable environment. Yet, Japan reported fewer than 70 large-scale bankruptcies between 1960 and 1993. This was in part due to informal workouts led by the main banks, but more importantly it was the result of corporate strategies, backed by government policies, geared to ensuring stability and survival in managing the six market forces.

The Threat of New Entry

Throughout the 1950s, Japan's government pursued infant-industry protection, as foreign competition was excluded through trade and capital controls. The Foreign Exchange and Foreign Trade Control Law allowed the Ministry of International Trade and Industry (MITI, which was renamed METI in 2001) to regulate all cross-border transactions. MITI also used this law to guide Japanese firms' spending of foreign reserves, in particular for the purchase of foreign technology. Imports were further limited by special industry laws where the growth of indigenous industry was considered important. Foreign direct investment into Japan was regulated through the Foreign Capital Law, which prohibited majority-owned foreign enterprises in Japan (e.g., Ozaki 1972; Mason 1992).[2]

2. These laws were the *Gaikoku kawase oyobi gaikoku bōeki kanri hō (Gaitame hō)*, as well as the *Gaishi ni kan suru hōritsu (Gaishihō)*. Postwar trade policies were finalized in 1998, when the Foreign Exchange and Foreign Trade Control Law was replaced by the Foreign Exchange Law.

Direct controls of imports and foreign direct investment had to be revised in 1964, when Japan acquired Article 8 status at the IMF and joined the OECD and the GATT. Still, Ito and Kiyono (1988) show that protectionist policies were phased out only slowly, or were substituted for by other means to restrict imports, such as nontariff barriers. Throughout the postwar period, the import penetration ratio remained below 5 percent in most industries (except in raw materials, where Japan is almost 100 percent dependent on imports).

Even after direct import controls were abolished and nontariff trade barriers phased out in the late 1980s, many Japanese markets remained protected. This was accomplished through both official regulation and industry agreements. Japan's postwar system of regulation was predicated on entry permits in many industries, while adjusting process regulation to situational needs by keeping it informal. Both advantaged insiders over new entrants. In industries that were not considered critical for industry policy purposes, narrow product market segmentation facilitated self-regulation by the incumbent firms in terms of who to trade with. Boycotts (or what the law called "refusal to deal") were not punished in any deterring way, and many trade associations established rules that they would trade only with other members of the association, but then restricted membership (Schaede 2000a).

Market restrictions also limited entry by new domestic firms. Although the immediate postwar years had seen a wave of new firm creation, beginning in the 1960s this slowed down greatly and did not resume until the 1990s. So rigid had entry rules and market hierarchies become that founding a new business and growing it to success had become nearly impossible. It is difficult to think of more than ten successful large firms founded between 1965 and 1990, and Japanese market hierarchies were remarkably stable. Only in the 1990s did METI realize the detrimental effects of the lack of start-up innovation and begin to draft laws to facilitate new firm creation. Until then, the overlap of interests in market closure and protection by regulators and companies posed formidable barriers. Incumbent firms had little to worry about the threat of new entry.

The Threat of Substitutes

Substitutes are functional equivalents to existing products—often based on technological innovation—that can make a company's products obsolete or secondary, thereby presenting a replacement threat. Understanding the potential disruption through innovation yet also aiming at technological catch-up, Japan's government carefully managed potential substitutes by offering incumbent firms equal access to technology imports and innovation. The two main tools used to guide this process were strict controls on technology imports (implemented through foreign exchange controls) and government organization of corporate R&D in so-called research consortia. The latter have been well studied and some authors have questioned their effectiveness in producing breakthrough innovation.[3] Yet, again, it is undisputed that these policies existed and that they constituted the setting in which companies had to ponder the replacement threat.

In an in-depth case study of the transistor radio industry, Lynn (1998) shows how the "innovation superstructure" (government policies, trade associations, and professional societies) was critical in allowing not only the initiator (Sony) to push the technology forward but also in helping the established electron-tube firms to successfully adopt the new technology and account for 79 percent of Japanese semiconductor production within four years after Sony started selling portable transistor radios in 1955.[4] This is remarkable in that strategy literature on disruptive technologies shows that incumbents often fail to foresee or react nimbly to new technologies. This is because discontinuous changes are often "competence destroying" (Tushman and Anderson 1986) by negating the value of existing practices, skills, and knowledge within the firm. Faced with discontinuous change, leading firms often succumb to the liability of incumbency and inertia, as success over time has made them too big and too ossified to engage in architectural innovation (Henderson and Clark 1990; Tushman and O'Reilly 1996; Christensen 1997). As a result, disruptive technologies often cause market upheaval, leading to Schumpeter's creative destruction by replacing sluggish and ill-equipped firms with nimble innovative ones.

In the mind-set of Japan's developmental state this chain of events had to be avoided, lest it cause disruption of the industry hierarchies so carefully designed for targeted growth promotion. The government therefore structured R&D consortia, based on the concept that the initial research would be jointly done but each company would then use the results in its own marketing of commercial applications.[5] In addition to gaining access to the latest innovations,

---

3. For studies on R&D consortia, including positive and negative evaluations, see, e.g., Anchordoguy (1989, 2005); Callon (1995); Goto and Wakasugi (1988); Noble (1989); and Okimoto (1989).

4. The Sony transistor case is often cited as an example of MITI holding up innovation by denying the purchase of a license. Lynn (1998) refutes this account. Not only did Sony receive MITI permission within six months, but in the meantime had already started its own research. What is more, Japan already had resident knowledge in transistors. As early as in 1948 a set of researchers at Japan's Electrotechnical Laboratory (ETL, later merged into NTT's research arm) had begun research on transistors, and in the 1950s many of the ETL researchers joined private companies such as Sony, Sharp, and Fujitsu (including Leo Ezaki who subsequently won the Nobel Prize for his development of the tunnel diode at Sony).

5. MITI was by no means the only player in this game, though it was the largest and best studied by virtue of being in charge of manufacturing. Other ministries in charge of transportation, construction, posts and telecommunications, and health employed similar policies of technological information dissemination.

companies were often interested in participating because the consortia presented an opportunity for cross-fertilization among researchers, which was limited due to lifetime employment. MITI had two main goals with these consortia: to be efficient by avoiding duplicative efforts and to prevent a firm from building a monopoly built on innovation. A main facet of industrial policy was to support more than one company in each industry, so as to limit the power of any one company over the regulator. Therefore, whatever the success of consortia in pushing innovation further, their main effect for the Japanese economy was to diffuse information about early-stage technologies among the leading firms, and indirectly thereby to uphold industry hierarchies with three or four well-defined champions.

However, this approach to technology policy also had a major downside, as it negated first-mover advantage in innovation. One example of how worried the government was about the destabilizing effects of innovation by a single firm was in the financial sector. During financial deregulation in the 1980s, when allowing the introduction of a new financial product, the Ministry of Finance would either delay the launch while disseminating product information across the industry, or officially announce the new product but delay actual introduction so that other banks could quickly copy it. Over time, innovation will be discouraged if the innovator cannot recoup the costs of innovation through temporary monopoly rents. This was indeed identified as a problem in the 1990s, and it has triggered a reorientation in technology policy.

More important for the current analysis, as Goto and Wakasugi (1988) have argued, even though research consortia may in some cases have fostered product-market competition, they effectively limited access to new technologies to the largest firms—namely, those granted foreign exchange with which to purchase knowledge from abroad, as well as those invited to the R&D consortia. Access was determined by size, as measured in sales and employment. Thus, the system made the threat of unforeseen substitutes negligible, but also reinforced the orientation to diversification, which increased chances of technology access in several product categories.

Complementors: Business Groups and Main Banks

With the threat of displacement greatly reduced, Japanese firms turned their strategic attention to stabilizing the existing market. A first step to reduce the destabilizing effects of competition was to establish complementing relationships with other firms. In the narrow sense of the term, complementors are two companies from different industries that each offers one aspect of a total product solution, such as compact disc (CD) players and music CDs. To the extent they can tie up through specific technology and therefore dominate the market, such as Microsoft and Intel during the "Wintel" era, both gain more together than alone (Brandenburger and Nalebuff 1997). Here, the concept is used in a broader sense to refer to business allies that ensure long-term survival through long-term tie-ups and trade relations.

The most important such complementary relation was established by the six so-called horizontal business groups (keiretsu): Mitsubishi, Mitsui, Sumitomo, Fuyō, Sanwa, and Dai-Ichi Kangyō.[6] In addition to these horizontal groups, there were numerous other business groups, some centered on a retailer, others more vertical in a structure in which one large company invested in numerous smaller firms. During the postwar period, it would have been difficult to find a company that was not a member of one business grouping or another.

The main reason why a company would join one of the horizontal business groups was that these groups offered stability in the form of protection from hostile takeovers due to cross-shareholdings, and a certain, stable minimum sales volume due to preferential trade. Nakatani (1984), Hoshi and Kashyap (2001), and Lincoln and Gerlach (2004) found group member firms to have earned lower profits. Importantly, they also enjoyed lower variance in profits over time.

Cross-shareholdings were the glue in this arrangement. With all members owning small shares in each other, but no rule on mandatory submission of minority shares to a bidder acquiring a majority stake, any outside takeover attempt could be thwarted. From an individual company's perspective, the foregone return on investment incurred by owning shares in firms with stable but low profitability was the insurance premium to be paid for capital market protection (Nakatani 1984). When the government's measures to create barriers to foreign entry proved effective in the 1960s, the fear of hostile takeovers was replaced by trade insurance. Preferential trade within the groups assured a constant minimum sales volume. This helped smooth sales over the business cycle (as group companies would buy even during downturns) and provided insurance in times of crisis (as group purchases would increase to support a struggling member).

When a company encountered trouble, the group offered one additional aspect of safety through the main bank: bankruptcy insurance. A core company of the six horizontal groups, this bank had two main functions—to help highly leveraged firms to get more loans (including from other banks) and to rescue a company should it fall into distress (e.g., Sheard 1989, 1994; Aoki

---

6. Extensive research on business groups in Japan has yielded insights about the functioning of these groups. See, e.g., Gerlach (1992); Lincoln and Gerlach (2004); and Lawrence (1993). Details will be discussed in Chapter 5.

and Patrick 1994; Hoshi and Kashyap 2001). The main bank was a strategic complementor in that without a designated bank companies would have been unable to uphold very high debt-equity ratios exceeding 400 (see chapter 5). With such high leverage, for companies to keep their main bank happy, they had to maintain sales revenues. This made minimum guaranteed sales a strategic variable. In addition to joining a business group, a company would strive to maintain sales through maintaining market share, which in the go-go years of rapid growth meant keeping up with the investment of other competitors. If competitors invested heavily, and one company did not, it would by necessity lose market share (Abegglen and Stalk 1985). As observed by Porter, Takeuchi, and Sakakibara (2000), this resulted in competitive convergence as all companies seemingly moved in lockstep toward growth.

High leverage also meant risk. The general thinking at the time (including in the United States) was that this risk could be reduced through diversification, that is, through operating in several businesses with uncorrelated income streams. Moreover, from the banks' perspective regulated interest rates meant that they earned a fixed spread on every loan, and banks competed for volume: the more loans, the higher their interest income.[7] Therefore, banks were quite happy to grant more loans as companies branched out into new businesses, which was considered a reduction in risk. At the same time, stable shareholders (which included banks) were not as much concerned about profitability. Banks were satisfied as long as interest payments were made when due, and large shareholders holding their stakes for stability and insurance were also pleased with diversification.

Rivals

Rivalry in postwar Japan was the fiercest force, but fortunately for Japan's largest firms the postwar political economy allowed them to adopt measures to harness some of the forces of competition. They established stable, long-term trade relations with firms outside their groups by offering special discounts, services, and implicit promises to help out during times of trouble. If possible, they also tried to reach industry agreements not to compete, either geographically or by customer segment or through price setting. Where these were effective, competition revolved around superior product features, higher quality, better in-sales and after-sales service, and easier access to distribution outlets.

---

7. See Teranishi (2003) for an analysis of bank behavior in the postwar period. Aoki (1988, 1990) and Weinstein and Yafeh (1995) show why banks liked their clients to borrow beyond levels warranted by share value maximization, and they argue that the higher rates charged to main clients were agency fees for its *keiretsu* management services.

Price competition is viewed as a threat by any business, so that left to their own devices most companies will attempt to cooperate on prices.[8] In Japan's postwar period, the government openly invited price setting in many basic materials industries (Tilton 1996). In the 1950s and 1960s, so-called production curtailment was invited by MITI in industries where "excessive competition" appeared to have destabilizing effects. Small firm cooperatives, as well as export associations in charge of pushing sales abroad, were exempted from the antitrust statutes (Weinstein 1995; Schaede 2000a). In other industries, agreements were either tacitly allowed or sanctioned by penalties so lenient as to create few deterrents. The "public interest" stated in Japan's Antimonopoly Law was interpreted as meaning the business interest, through which consumer interests would be served in the consumers' roles as employees. In some cases prices were agreed on in the trade associations, while in others competitors would simply mimic price moves by the industry leader. These agreements were often long term because there was no new entry that could have challenged the incumbents. Whether they were always effective is less clear, but we know that industry hierarchies were stable throughout the postwar period. We also know that, compared to other countries, consumers paid dearly for many products and services. Where companies could, they attempted to create a stable business environment through limiting price competition.

Keeping prices at a high level also had another strategic purpose, as it allowed exporting industries to engage in a so-called sanctuary strategy (Schaede 2004). In this approach firms adopted a particular type of multimarket competition in that they cooperated to keep prices high at home, and used the resulting surplus profit to compete more fiercely in overseas markets, first against overseas firms but eventually also against each other. One example was the electronic appliances cartel uncovered in 1992 (JFTC 1993), at a time when Japanese companies engaged in price wars in U.S. electronics stores.

Overall, then, rivalry was a major threat and received careful strategic attention. To create stability, government and industry joined forces in their attempts to curb price competition, thus shifting competition toward locking in trading partners to ensure sales, and attracting buyers through nonprice competition. The resulting stable industry hierarchies allowed firms to be highly leveraged and to diversify into many product markets, even where they were also-rans and made little profit.

---

8. Adam Smith alerted us to this in his observation that "people of the same trade seldom meet together, even for merriment and diversion, but the conversation ends in a conspiracy against the public, or in some contrivance to raise prices" (Smith 1937 [1776], vol. 1, bk. 1, chap. 10). If this were not globally true even to date, we would not need antitrust authorities charged with preventing or prosecuting this behavior.

Suppliers

The fifth force, suppliers, consists of producers of materials, parts, and services, as well as employees (suppliers of labor). Both of these were of extraordinary importance, especially in the 1950s and early 1960s when wartime destruction and limited capital necessitated that firms outsource heavily and labor was scarce.

Subcontractors

Part suppliers were a critical force in the postwar period, because some of Japan's manufacturing firms relied extensively on parts outsourcing, typically from a hierarchy of tightly aligned companies called subcontractors. These are a well-studied facet of Japan's postwar business organization, partly because the automobile industry is the most-studied industry of that period and subcontracting is highly relevant there.[9]

As Smitka (1991) and Nishiguchi (1994) show, Japan's subcontracting system grew out of necessity in the 1950s before it turned into a virtue in the 1970s. In the immediate postwar years, in many assembling industries such as automobiles and electronics, production facilities had been destroyed and companies faced a scarcity of funds, especially if they were not among the government's handpicked champions. In the early 1950s, a smaller workforce reduced the threat from fierce labor strikes, until a change in legislation restricted the rights of unions. Wages at smaller firms were generally lower than at larger firms. Thus, for different reasons at different times, outsourcing was preferable.

Some buyers found themselves outsourcing critical parts. As transaction costs economics (Williamson 1975, 1985) suggests, using the "market" instead of within-firm "hierarchy" to outsource critical components creates dependencies that have to be managed with great care, lest the supplier runs away with the technology or squeezes the buyer on price. One solution to this holdup threat is to create long-term ties through repeated trades, technology sharing, and ownership stakes. Many Japanese manufacturers built stable groups of first-tier suppliers that in turn relied on second-tier firms and so on, so that a large number of small firms were part of the buyer's business group, a vertical keiretsu. At the height of this system, in 1981, more than 65 percent of small manufacturing firms (and almost 90% in the automobile sector) identified themselves as subcontractors to one larger firm.

---

9. See, for example, Ahmadjian and Lincoln (2001); Dyer (2000); McMillan (1990); Lincoln, Gerlach, and Ahmadjian (1996); Lincoln, Ahmadjian, and Mason (1998); Nishiguchi (1994); Smitka (1991); and others cited in chapter 7. For differences in the system in the electronics industry, see Hoetker (2004).

High dependency meant that managing supplier relations was a critical task. Some authors have described these as trust based (e.g., Smitka 1991), based on societal tendencies to value stability. Alternatively, ownership stakes by the large buyers, combined with good relationship management, created an economic rationale for both sides to value the tie-up. In either case, large Japanese firms expended enormous effort into structuring their supplier relations, in recognition that this was a strategically important force.

The significant reliance on subcontractors still contributed to diversification of the assembler. Because the structure for outsourcing was so well established, companies could enter new product segments fairly easily and still increase their workforce incrementally. Moreover, in some cases the assembler's ownership stakes were so substantial that on a consolidated basis subcontracting added to diversification, even though this was not reported under the disclosure rules of the time. For example, when Matsushita Electric began its complete reorganization and turnaround in the early 2000s, it had over 600 wholly or partially owned subsidiaries.

Labor

The second major supplier group is labor, and one of the best-known elements of Japanese business is lifetime employment. As will be explored in chapter 9, from a strictly legal perspective of who had claims to long-term retention, this system covered up to 80 percent of the workforce. Some observers put this number lower, because lifetime employment was not legally prescribed but rather developed through a sequence of court decisions. For current purposes, it suffices to say that a substantial portion of the labor force expected to be employed in the long run, and layoffs became increasingly difficult through the postwar period (e.g., Rebick 2005; Araki 2002).

For managers, lifetime employment poses great challenges by turning labor into a fixed cost. Therefore, the break-even point for Japanese firms in the postwar period was comparatively high. This meant that even a small drop in sales had a big negative effect on the company's bottom line. Combined with the high dependence on bank loans, lifetime employment explains why Japanese firms were so concerned about constantly increasing sales and market share growth.

Given these challenges, why did lifetime employment become a pillar of postwar Japanese business organization? To begin with, the government pushed this system as a critical component of Japan's social contract. To pursue the postwar goal of fast economic growth, the government chose to support large firms. In return, these were expected to grow and employ, alleviating the government burden of unemployment insurance. Only in the 1970s did the government launch a full-fledged effort to build up social welfare. During much of the postwar period, however, corporate welfarism was a reasonable trade-off for companies that paid lower effective taxes and received government support but in turn provided labor welfare. Moreover, employees were interested in this system as well, as cultural risk averseness, expressed in a preference for stability and security, made lifetime employment desirable for many.

Companies also had strategic interests in lifetime employment. First, labor scarcity in the early 1960s made them keen to lock in their core workforce. Moreover, Japan's predominant system of in-house vocational training made locking in employees beneficial as it prevented competitors from stealing them. For these reasons, companies proactively pushed lifetime employment by vesting pension benefits only late in the employee's career, and by introducing a system of seniority wages that made job changes financially disadvantageous for the employee.[10] In a setting of high innovation dynamics in which incumbents were expected to lead progress, lifetime employment also lowered employee resistance to change. This is so for two reasons: if an employee knows he (rarely she) will not be laid off, he is more willing to be retrained and accept new job assignments. Moreover, if employees feel safe about their positions and promotions, they are more willing to assume the risk of working in a business with uncertain success.

Lifetime employment also created pressures for diversification. In a system of seniority wages and promotion, the easiest way companies could reward exceptional performance was by assigning superior positions. These opened up more easily as a company entered new businesses. At the same time, exiting an existing business was difficult because layoffs were so severely constrained. Even as companies branched out into new business sectors, they had to maintain old businesses, not only to sustain sales but also to sustain jobs.

Buyers

Because this analysis covers Japanese industry as a whole, there are many different buyers, which are divided here into three broad categories: consumers, export markets, and the government (in particular in construction, infrastructure, and public works).

Given wide-ranging attempts to curb price competition among manufacturers, competition in consumer end products, too, occurred mostly through nonprice competition. The main tool to maintain prices at the retail level was

---

10. Ichinose (2001) estimates that a job change at age 45 meant losses of about ¥100 million (or almost $1 million) in pensions and earnings; cf. Chapter 9.

to control the distribution system without disruption by maverick discounters. The mavericks eventually prevailed and triggered a "retail revolution" (*ryūtsū kakumei*) in the 1990s, but until then many large consumer-goods companies managed to keep a tight lid on their distributors through what were called Japan's "customary trade practices" (*shōkankō*): retail price maintenance, rebates, return of unsold goods, and exclusive distribution networks. By printing a price on the product and enticing or coercing exclusive distributors to charge this exact price, the manufacturer could control retail prices. Retail stores were tempted to go along through progressive rebates (the more you sell the lower your purchase price and the larger your spread). The returns of unsold goods policy limited the retailer's risk of being stuck with unmovable items, and also enabled the manufacturer to ensure there would be no uncontrolled fire sales of last season's products (Kawagoe 1997; Schaede 2000a).[11]

The antitrust authorities helped in this endeavor, for although some of these practices limited competition, they were rarely stopped before the 1990s. What is more, the government may have helped start this system, because during the turmoil immediately after World War II and through the 1950s, three categories of products were specifically exempted from rules on retail price maintenance: copyrighted materials (books, records), pharmaceuticals and cosmetics, and daily-use consumer goods ranging from toothpaste, soap, and men's shirts to pens and caramel candy. Through the 1980s, consumer goods costing less than ¥1,000 were exempted from retail price maintenance rules (Kawagoe 1997).

The challenge, then, was to sell as many products as possible while charging the same price as competitors, and Japan's postwar consumer goods markets became a showcase for how to excel in nonprice competition. Marketers managed to establish the notion that high prices equaled high quality, and that Japanese consumers preferred paying high prices because they were hawks for quality. They were rewarded at the point of purchase with superior sales service, beautiful wrapping, and "free" shipping. We cannot be sure whether Japanese consumers truly enjoyed high prices or had good reason to equate them with quality. However, the breakup of distribution barriers and the way in which Japan's consumers have embraced discount stores and cheap import products since the 1990s suggests that this was more of a marketing myth than a shopping truth. Regardless, high prices meant that

---

11. These customary trade practices were one of the core discussion points in the U.S.-Japan Structural Impediments Initiative launched in 1989, as they were considered a great obstacle to foreign competitors, because they tied many distributors exclusively to one domestic manufacturer.

Japanese companies had to compete through "bells and whistles" by making their products more advanced, more hip, or more convenient (such as better TVs, pink vacuum cleaners, or fridges with the freezer at the bottom). Another path to increase sales was to entice consumers to replace products rapidly. This was accomplished through aggressive introduction of hit products through incremental improvements, as well as the commercialization of new technologies, such as the Walkman, the VCR, or the fax machine. The strategic focus of nonprice competition explains the Japanese competitive advantage, through the 1980s, in consumer product development and product improvement.

In addition to "cool" products, extensive after-sales service offered important product information and ensured regional availability (Flath 1989). Conveniently, it also supported replacement rates. Cars, for instance, were typically sold by door-to-door salesmen, and upon purchase these salesmen would return at regular intervals to remind the owner that it was time for a tune-up and drive him or her to the shop. In due course the owner would also be reminded that it was time to buy a new car.

The final element in nonprice competition was exclusive retail chains, such as in electronics and cosmetics. For example, at its height Matsushita Electric had over 25,000 National Stores and Panasonic Stores all over the country (followed by roughly 8,000 for Sony). These neighborhood stores would sell everything from lightbulbs, batteries, and extension cords to refrigerators and TV sets—and all only from one maker. Stores increased sales by pulling clients in through ubiquity, but they also helped enforce retail price maintenance (Fukunaga and Chinone 1994). Extending into the retail business also increased diversification: the manufacturer was now engaged in the retail sector (which sometimes included real estate), and had to build a sufficient array of products to stock an entire store.

Export markets served initially as a means to increase sales volume to justify high investments in production capacities. Therefore, in the 1960s and 1970s Japanese firms engaged in significant original equipment manufacturer production, whereby they produced products sold under foreign companies' brand names. Over time, and with increasing quality gains, establishing their own brand names became important if sales were to grow. It was at that time that the sanctuary strategy (using home profits from high prices to cross-subsidize cutthroat competition in foreign markets) first materialized. But price competition was not all. As Lynn (1998) points out, Japanese manufacturers such as Toyota, Honda, and Sony were perhaps most successful due to their knack at nonprice competition and at introducing high quality products with features specifically aimed at foreign consumers. As sales volume continued to grow,

Japanese manufacturers then also honed their high-quality mass production skills, which that often remained unrivaled.[12]

In the postwar period the Japanese government was a large buyer through its many so-called public corporations tasked with building infrastructure, from urban housing complexes and sewage systems to highways, tunnels, bridges, and railways. The processes in which the public corporations procured services from private firms have been well studied under *dangō* (bid rigging).[13] Perhaps its most important aspect in terms of business strategy was the government policy of predetermining a specific group of companies that were allowed to participate in a certain bid, again favoring larger companies over smaller ones. This maintained the industry hierarchy, ensured the growth and long-term survival of construction firms, and created yet another barrier to market entry. Since mid-1995, Japan's antitrust authority has come down increasingly harder on bid-rigging violations. In the early 21st century privatization and the reorganization of public corporations have greatly altered government procurement processes.

Evaluation: Diversification as a Rational Strategic Response

The strategic wisdom of the 1960s and 1970s argued for growth through diversification. But even in hindsight it would be wrong to accuse Japanese firms of strategic failure. Given the incentives and constraints of Japan's postwar political economy, diversification was a rational corporate strategy. The great international success of Japan's export industries reinforced their strategic choices. Corporate shareholders and banks pushed for diversification as one way to reduce the risk of corporate failure. The government rewarded sales growth by tying access to innovation, talent, foreign reserves, and trade quotas to market share. Lifetime employment necessitated branching out to reward talent with management positions, but also made exit from a nonprofitable business difficult.

The postwar political economy allowed companies to use a variety of mechanisms to create stability in a fast-growing, fast-changing market. To sustain high leverage, companies identified one main bank that would tolerate the exposure. More than profitability, the main bank was interested in stable growth through regular increases in sales revenue, which under fast economic growth could be accomplished by competing in a growing number of products.

12. Studies in operations management have shown this in great detail; e.g., Liker (2004). Since this goes beyond strategy, it is not further analyzed here. The competitive context within Japan that focused on nonprice competition, and thus on quality and product features, contributed to this success story.

13. E.g., Krauss and Coles (1990); McMillan (1991); Woodall (1996); and Schaede (2000a).

Business groups provided stability by guaranteeing minimum quarterly sales through preferential trades. Government policies largely shielded companies from the threats of new entry and new substitutes through trade controls and the management of innovation in R&D consortia that assured incumbents access to new innovation. Even as Japan worked hard to catch up technologically with the West, therefore, this catch-up occurred without overthrowing market hierarchies or threatening the livelihood of flagship firms.

In this context, diversification was perfectly rational, as the combination of export promotion policies with low cost of borrowing and the overall sales growth dictum meant that bigger was better. High diversification was also in line with the advanced strategic thinking at the time. The global portfolio strategies of General Electric, Philips, and Siemens in the 1960s and 1970s were all based on diversification.

This means that during the postwar years firms directed their strategic attention to the horizontal axis of figure 3.1 (suppliers, competitors and complementors, and buyers). Special effort was exerted to manage suppliers and to agree with rivals on price, while securing complementors and pleasing buyers such that they willingly paid high prices.

However, the strategic inflection point has completely altered the competitive dynamics of the Japanese market such that stability—the virtue of the postwar period—has now become a liability. As we will see, corporate dependence on bank loans has greatly declined, and profitability has become an important determinant of a firm's cost of capital. Tie-ups that ensure sales over profits are no longer an advantage. As trade and cross-border financial controls have been removed, foreign competitors challenge Japanese firms in their home markets. To compete in these more dynamic markets, firms are looking for specialized knowledge and have begun to adjust the seniority pay system in order to be better able to attract talent, including midcareer employees. Technological catch-up has long been accomplished and markets for research ideas and innovation have opened up. Research consortia in the 21st century are much reduced in number and size and mostly concerned with pushing the knowledge frontier in basic research. Given new market dynamics, benefits from long-term tie-ups with suppliers are less clear, which has led many firms to restructure their subcontractor networks. As profits become the driving variable and competition turns global, price agreements are increasingly difficult to forge. The retail revolution has undermined the manufacturers' insistence on retail prices. And as rules and regulations, whether on disclosure, financing, bankruptcies, foreign exchange flows, or firm creation, have all been rewritten, the Japanese business context has been transformed.

Therefore, Japan's strategic inflection point has shifted corporate attention away from the horizontal axis of figure 3.1 and moved it toward the vertical axis. The new strategic challenge for firms is to position themselves so as to be able to fight the threat of new entry and compete not only against existing competitors but also against potential future substitutes (global technological advances), while reevaluating complementors as to exactly how they will help increase profitability. Diversification has become a liability and "choose and focus" a winning strategy.

4

DIVERSIFICATION

VERSUS

FOCUS

Our understanding of Japan's shift toward "choose and focus" is informed by existing research in strategy, in particular as it relates to the experience of diversification and refocusing in the United States of the 1970s and 1980s. A review of the established insights of strategy research about the United States will set the stage for the discussion of Japan.

The Two Basic Questions of Strategy

At the most basic level, strategy is about making choices of how to compete along two dimensions: (1) What businesses should the company be in? and (2) How will the company compete? The latter refers to strategic positioning within a product market and is determined at the business-unit level. How can the company position itself such that it outcompetes others by offering a unique price-value combination? Porter (1980) established this trade-off by stipulating that a company either has to offer a cheaper product than others or one that is sufficiently differentiated that customers are willing to pay a higher price.[1]

One can visualize this trade-off as a competitive frontier (figure 4.1), where each position on the outer curve represents a winning price-value proposition. A company positioned below this competitive frontier (at "x" in figure 4.1) is "stuck in the middle": to be successful in the long run, it must either move up by competing at a lower price, given its degree of differentiation, or it must move to the right, to offer a more differentiated product at its current price. Barring market distortions or government protection, in the long run only companies operating along the competitive frontier will survive. In postwar Japan, cross-subsidization within multidivisional firms allowed some businesses to operate as also-rans in their industries, below the competitive frontier, for many years.

---

1. E.g., Porter (1980, 1985) and Ghemawat (1991, 2006). The source for cost leadership is a company's ability to operate more efficiently than the competition, whereas the source for differentiation is the ability to produce something sufficiently special that it can command a premium price that exceeds the extra cost of differentiating.

4.1. *The Competitive Frontier of Cost vs. Differentiation*

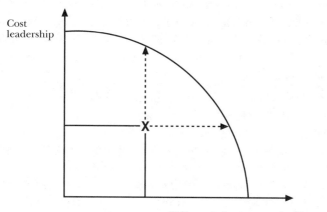

The New Japan "choose and focus" approach, in contrast, refers to refocusing resources in select businesses that compete along the frontier.

What allows a company to establish a competitive position in an industry (i.e., to create and sustain a competitive advantage over others, over time) is its particular set of assets and capabilities, referred to as core competencies (Prahalad and Hamel 1990; Barney 1991). These are valuable assets that are not imitable or fungible (meaning they cannot be copied or bought). These assets may include a brand name or reputation, but they also may entail unique technologies or production processes that may be based on tacit knowledge or organizational learning.

Theories of Core Competence Extension

The "choose" element of "choose and focus" refers to the strategic decision a company has to make in what, and how many, different product markets or industries to compete. Teece (1982) observes that if markets were completely efficient, there should be no multiproduct firm, as each firm would simply maximize profits by doing the one thing it does best and selling off any excess assets it possesses. However, either transaction costs or the quality of the core asset may be such that selling excess assets is not possible or would result in no gain. In these situations, the firm is best off employing its excess productive factors by branching out into a related business that also benefits from their utility.

However, evidence from the United States in the 1960s and 1970s shows that diversification does not necessarily increase performance; in fact, the more diversified a firm, especially into unrelated fields, the worse its performance (e.g., Rumelt 1974). Extending Teece's notion of diversification as an extension of productive factors, Montgomery and Wernerfelt (1988) explain the decline in average performance of business units that have diversified by the fact that a given productive factor will lose some of its efficiency if employed for different purposes, and the farther the company diversifies away from the core, the higher these efficiency losses. In other words, it is difficult for one company with its distinctive set of core competencies to extend capabilities to operate at the competitive frontier in multiple businesses.

This insight has led others to propose a curvilinear relation between diversification and performance: the initial extension of excess assets into related production that is still close to the core (i.e., related diversification) increases overall performance, because the efficiency losses in using the asset suboptimally are less than the company's overall gains from added scale and scope (such as production, marketing, or distribution). Learning, technological diffusion, and asset amortization may also contribute to increased profits. However, as the asset is extended too far (i.e., into unrelated businesses), efficiency losses outweigh these gains and the average performance of business units declines (e.g., Markides and Williamson 1994, 1996). This curvilinear relationship is shown in figure 4.2.

The United States went through a merger and conglomeration wave in the 1960s that were later labeled a "30-year detour away from efficiency" (Shleifer and Vishny 1991, 54). This interesting experience has given rise to a substantial body of empirical research, from the disciplines of organizational behavior, transaction costs economics, agency theory, finance, and strategic management. Although this research remains ambiguous in its findings, in a meta-analysis that quantitatively synthesized 82 studies on the relation between diversification

4.2. *The Curvilinear Relation between Diversification and Performance*

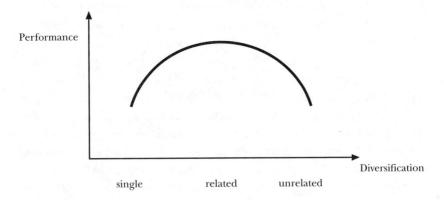

and performance, Palich, Cardinal, and Miller (2000) find strong support for the inverted U-shape of the curvilinear model: the initial (related) diversification has a positive effect on performance, whereas high (unrelated) diversification depresses the overall performance of the company. That is to say, some related diversification is superior to no diversification, yet unrelated diversification decreases overall performance.

Figure 4.2 suggests the existence of an optimal point beyond which diversification is excessive. The puzzle, then, is why companies would diversify beyond the optimal point into unrelated fields. The reason is that each company possesses a different set of core competencies, so that this point is different for each firm, and it is difficult ex ante to properly differentiate related from unrelated diversification. Prahalad and Hamel (1990) established the difference between core products and their underlying core competencies. It is the latter that must be leveraged to "escape the myopia of the currently served markets," even if such competency-based business extension may appear to be unrelated in product-market terms (Hamel and Prahalad 1994). From this emerged the concept of dynamic capabilities, which are core competencies that can be adapted over time to allow the company to compete successfully even in the face of incremental or disruptive change in its competitive environment (Teece, Pisano, and Shuen 1997; Harreld, O'Reilly, and Tushman 2007). If based on superior information regarding the nature of a firm's core competencies and dynamic capabilities, seemingly unrelated diversification can be successful, which in turn explains the remaining ambiguity in strategy research on diversification.

However, we should remind ourselves that before the above insights into core competencies and dynamic capabilities were developed, strategy research had stipulated that continuously branching out into new markets was the only way for companies to survive (Steiner 1964; Carroll 1984). Product life cycles, it was argued, necessitated that firms move on once the maturity stage was reached and demand began to subside. Moreover, the specialist strategy was considered too risky. Early strategy scholars such as Penrose (1959) had praised a certain degree of diversification because it reduced the risk of corporate failure, even in the event of failure in one market segment. Diversified firms created portfolio effects that increased the firm's chances of survival by combining businesses with less than perfectly correlated financial flows. These portfolio effects constituted a type of "co-insurance" that also increased the company's debt capacity, and perhaps lowered its cost of capital (e.g., Seth 1990; Berger and Ofek 1995).

Given this line of thinking, the United States experienced a wave of diversification in the 1960s, mostly through friendly acquisitions through stock swaps (i.e., without major involvement of deal brokers and financiers). Most of these business extensions were into unrelated businesses, with the goal to form conglomerates. Perhaps the main reason for the latter was politics, as U.S. interpretation of antitrust statutes in the 1960s and 1970s disallowed within-industry mergers. In looking at Fortune 500 companies at the time, Rumelt (1974) found that the fraction of single-business firms dropped from 22.8 percent in 1959 to 14.8 percent in 1969, while companies that engaged in unrelated diversification more than doubled from 7.3 percent to 14.8 percent. In addition to endeavored synergies and risk reduction, some authors claim that companies diversified so heavily because they could: sitting on a pile of cash and enjoying high stock market valuations, managers "bought growth" rather than paying out dividends (Shleifer and Vishny 1991, 52).

The Disadvantages of Diversification

The 1980s saw a huge change in the composition of U.S. firms' assets and corporate strategy. The decade represented a major reversal from conglomeration and toward specialization, through sell-offs or liquidations of unrelated businesses and consolidation in a few core markets. Acquisitions were mostly within the industry, with the goal of consolidating an industry position, whereas divestitures turned strategic when companies differentiated between core and noncore business and began to shed the latter to build "pure, muscular" companies (Markides 1995a, 104). One particularly aggressive deal form were so-called bust-up takeovers, sometimes structured as leveraged buyouts (LBOs), in which raiders purchased underperforming conglomerates and, within a short period of time, sold the pieces off to other bidders, often to firms in the same industries seeking to increase their market power.

Ravenscraft and Scherer (1987) estimate that one third of all business units purchased in the 1960s and 1970s had been sold off by the mid-1980s. By 1990, 44 percent of the purchases of the conglomeration period had been undone (Kaplan and Weisbach 1992). More than 28 percent (or 143 firms) of the Fortune 500 companies as of 1980 had been acquired by 1989 (Shleifer and Vishny 1991). As already reported in chapter 1, in a study on refocusing that paid special attention to restructuring through divestitures, Markides (1995a, 1995b) finds that at least 20 percent but probably closer to half of all Fortune 500 firms refocused in the 1980s. In almost all cases, these divestitures, sell-offs, and liquidations had been precipitated by managerial challenges of coordination and control. Berger and Ofek (1999) show that poor performance preceded divestitures in this period. Five main explanations have been proffered as to why the "excessive diversification" of the 1960s was detrimental and had to be reversed. Each of these is also helpful in our understanding of Japan's experience with a similar reversal two decades later.

The first set of explanations pertains to changes in the competitive environment that turned high diversification from a winning strategy into a losing proposition. Increased uncertainty and volatility through globalization raised the costs of control and coordination in highly diversified firms. Moreover, the Reagan administration's loosened antitrust stance allowed intraindustry mergers and consolidation, just as the overall poor performance of U.S. industry in the 1980s created pressure to do "something." Although some of the 1980s mergers were voluntary, there was also a rapid rise in involuntary reorganizations through hostile takeovers. Simply the fear of a hostile takeover often invited voluntary restructuring as a preemptive move. For example, Markides (1995a) shows through a survey of 150 large U.S. firms in the late 1980s that although only about 13 percent of divestitures were directly forced by a hostile takeover bid, more than 70 percent of divestitures were triggered by managers' perceptions that their firms were possible takeover targets. As we will see in more detail later, all of these factors applied equally to Japan in the early 2000s.

Second, the development of the efficient market hypothesis in finance affected the ways in which investors thought about risk. Rather than companies diversifying into a portfolio of businesses, the dominant way of thinking shifted to risk diversification on the part of the investors. Jensen and Meckling (1976) and Fama and Jensen (1983), among others, argued that the modern corporation was an efficient separation of labor, where management specializes in running the firm while owners specialize in risk bearing. Thus, it should not be the firms that diversify their portfolios, but rather their owners. Throughout the 1980s, rapid advances in financial markets such as increased disclosure, growing sophistication in the dissemination of financial information, and the liquidity and immediacy of the market through technological advances in stock trading all began to erode the erstwhile advantage of the internal capital market of the multidivisional firm in allocating resources (Bhide 1990). The new investors, aided by securities analysts, preferred specialized firms because simplicity greatly facilitated comparison across companies, whereas conglomerates were like apples and oranges. Porter (1987) advised that investors could diversify their own portfolios as long as companies operated in comparable businesses. Thus, investors began to discount highly diversified firms in favor of specialized ones in their efforts to reduce risk by diversifying their ownership stakes.

Unlike the 1960s, the 1980s mergers and acquisitions were mostly paid for in cash, and they involved increasingly intricate financial deals brokered by newly specialized investment banks. Institutional investors in search of alternative investments became important players (Bhagat, Shleifer, and Vishny

1990). Perhaps most representative of this era was the emergence of a new type of financial agent, corporate raiders and leveraged buyout funds, such as KKR (Kohlberg, Kravis Roberts & Co.). Made memorable through the 1987 movie character Gordon Gekko in *Wall Street,* these brokers were constantly on the lookout for bust-up deals, justifying executives' fear of hostile takeovers. These new investors can be viewed as intermediaries that facilitate the transfer of assets from one group of owners to another. Kaplan (1992) showed that of the 183 large leveraged buyouts completed in the United States between 1979 and 1986, by 1990 47 percent had been sold, either to other companies or by going public. In the 1990s, these intermediaries reemerged, including in Japan, under the label of private equity and hedge funds.

In addition to changes in finance, the strategic reversal in the United States was also pushed by the recognition that excessive diversification posed great challenges to organizational design and management. This line of thinking came under the heading of "failure of internal capital markets." Williamson (1975, 1985) suggested that the multidivisional organization is an efficient device where each division is a profit center but leadership allocates resources across business units based on superior information of the extendibility of firm resources. However, at some point in the process of diversification, increased breadth comes at the expense of depth (specialization). Meanwhile, internal resource allocations are increasingly subjected to opportunism, bureaucracy, corporate politics, and similar obstacles of human nature that undermine the initial efficiency consequences of the multiproduct firm. Business units that ought to be shut down are not, due to vested interests, and new businesses in unrelated areas are opened to reward successful managers. Other costs include the challenges of managerial control as the firm gets too big, coordination costs, and the distortion of information as it passes through the layers of hierarchy. Shleifer and Vishny (1990) even went so far as to describe some of the U.S. conglomerates of the early 1980s as resembling ministries in planned economies. In a return to Adam Smith and Frederick Taylor, the argument for specialization to raise productivity was revisited.

Also in the 1960s, a corporate governance argument had emerged in favor of diversified firms. Experienced managers were thought to be rare, and large conglomerates increased their role in the overall economy. However, in the 1980s we began to realize that the previously acclaimed professional manager of a conglomerate was neither as rare nor as capable as previously thought (Shleifer and Vishny 1990). Instead, diversification was explained by the hubris that results when managers are overly optimistic about their abilities (Roll 1986). If this combines with weak governance mechanisms (e.g., a board of directors dominated by insiders; captured shareholders) managers often have free reign in their plans to engage in unrelated diversification (e.g., Hoskisson and Turk 1990).

Agency theory added to these insights in explaining how incentives increase the likelihood of managerial failure. Some managers may be tempted to maximize their own utility rather than that of their shareholders. For one, managers may be interested in growth through diversification to hedge against employment risk, which is tied to the firm. Whereas shareholders can diversify risk, managers work for only one firm, and the firm's viability determines managerial lifetime income. The risk of firm failure can be reduced by diversifying into unrelated businesses (Amihud and Lev 1981). Next, there is also significant evidence that firm size and executive compensation are correlated, piquing executive interest in increasing firm size (e.g., O'Reilly and Main 2006). It was also suggested that the incentive to "buy growth" might be particularly strong for companies with free cash flow, which allowed investments in projects that the market finds dubious ex ante, but that managers believe will prove profitable ex post (Myers and Majluf 1984). Free cash flow is generated when firms have already fulfilled all projects with positive net present value within the current industry, which is often the case in mature industries (Jensen 1986). When managers have discretion because they face weak monitoring mechanisms and aspire to grow because they have little debt outstanding, it is in their interest to undertake aggressive diversification rather than return excess cash flow to owners. When such managers become desperate, their shopping spree may be to the detriment of investors.

Insights from finance and agency theory combine into the final contributor to explaining excessive diversification: fads and fashion (e.g., Morck, Shleifer, and Vishny 1990). The 1960s merger wave in the United States was strongly supported, if not driven, by a stock market highly enthusiastic about aggressive diversification (e.g., Matsusaka 1990). If the stock market rewards diversification, corporate executives would find it difficult indeed to go against it. Moreover, according to agency theory, if a manager were to stand up against a possibly misled group of investors, this would constitute a pursuit of personal interests over those of the shareholders. In other words, even if the market were to "get it completely wrong" (Shleifer and Vishny 1991), as it may have in the 1960s, the executive is still obligated to follow the wishes of the owners and do whatever it takes to increase the stock price—even if this meant excessive diversification. As we will see below, a similar story can be told about the bubble period in Japan, when the stock market gave the highest rewards to the most delirious diversifiers.

As new strategy insights regarding core competencies and the critical role of building "next horizon" dynamic capabilities around a well-defined core gain traction in Japan, the United States may be embarking on yet another reversal at the time of this writing. For example, during the 1980s and 1990s, financial markets pushed the global pharmaceutical industry to exit businesses other than the core of human drug development, even if those were related (e.g., other chemicals). This facilitated the task of comparing the performance of drug companies, and thus made the jobs of securities analysts and institutional investors easier. However, when the largest drug companies began to face a threat of empty pipelines for new drugs by 2010, these same investors and analysts suddenly accused them of not being sufficiently diversified to ensure against this industry risk. Overall, it seems that the extreme versions of both, diversification and focus, lead to suboptimal corporate strategy, although the market at times prefers these extremes.

The Effects of Refocusing

Advances in theory notwithstanding, empirical research has yet to determine the performance effects of refocusing. One reason for the continuing ambiguity in the diversification-performance literature is that the design of empirical research is fraught with data identification problems, and differs across disciplines and goals of study. Just as Rumelt (1974) and Ravenscraft and Scherer (1987) established that there was little gain in profitability or other measures of performance from conglomeration, Shleifer and Vishny (1991) find little ex post evidence that refocusing leads to improved profitability measures. In contrast, Markides (1995a, 1995b) finds strong evidence that refocusing, in any shape or form, during the 1980s in the United States was associated with improvements in profitability by the refocusing firms.

In contrast to the performance studies, stock market valuation results are clearer. Markides (1992, 1995a) shows through an event study of the United States that refocusing was often associated ex ante with an increase in the company's stock price, as well as ex post with increased performance.[2] Moreover, Kaplan and Weisbach (1992) argue that this may not simply be due to fad and fashion but to true value creation through the acquisition-divestiture reversal of the 1980s: divestitures can be based on a turnaround effort and learning, such that stock market enthusiasm at both ends of the deal (the point of purchase and of divestiture) is completely warranted. They show for the 1980s that prices obtained in divestitures in more than half of all cases were attractive enough to make the investment worthwhile, regardless of whether the diversification was related or unrelated.

---

2. Similar findings of increase in shareholder value with specialization in the 1980s were presented by Berger and Ofek (1995, 1999) and Comment and Jarrell (1995).

Furthermore, it is evident that specialization and refocusing lead to industry consolidation. For example, Bhagat, Shleifer, and Vishny (1990) show that the majority of the 62 hostile takeovers launched between 1984 and 1986 in the United States increased consolidation. In 72 percent of cases where assets were divested, these were subsequently purchased by firms in that asset's business. Similarly, Kaplan (1992) observed that at least one third of assets purchased in leveraged buyouts in the first half of the 1980s were sold off to competitors in related industries. Although some attributed this consolidation to changing antitrust policies in the United States, others have pointed to economic explanations for the consolidation (e.g., Summers in comments to Bhagat, Shleifer, and Vishney 1990). In Japan, too, the strategic inflection point has provided economic incentives for consolidation, and mergers and acquisitions have resulted in new market leaders in many product categories.

We are thus left with insights from the United States that inform our understanding of Japan. Both significant costs and benefits can be associated with diversification, and these differ by company. Managers may pursue personal interests in strategic decision making or be subject to hubris, but they may also be misled by the stock market. The challenge in answering the corporate strategy question of "What business should we be in?" is to identify the point where the company is moving too far away from its core competencies to be able to gainfully leverage its factors of production. Moreover, refocusing is likely to lead both to more product market competition because previous conglomerates are dissolved and to consolidation as competing firms buy up assets divested in their industries.

Japan's Experience: From Diversification to "Choose and Focus"

Chapter 3 showed how Japan's postwar political economy made diversification a rational strategy. Access to industrial policy allocations based on industry ranking translated into a pursuit of sales growth. Main banks were supportive of "buying growth," which also made lifetime employment possible. Thus, aggressive growth was expected by stakeholders, supported by shareholders (other firms and banks), and further pushed by government policy.

Empirical studies of Japan's postwar industrial organization confirm this trend toward increasing diversification among large Japanese firms. Looking at 124 firms for the period 1963–74, Goto (1981) found that, on average, 48 percent of the sales of these firms were in nonprimary commodities, and, as this trend increased, diversification also became less related. These results were echoed in Yoshihara et al. (1981) who found a continuing trend toward diversification and also identified the growth of bureaucracy in large organizations that were typically organized in a rather centralized way, even though they were structured on paper as multidivisional companies. Tsuru (2004) showed increasing inefficiencies in these bloated organizations. Fukui and Ushijima (2006) extended Goto's study into the period from 1973 to 1998, and confirmed a further increase in diversification. Industries that stood out as particularly diversified include textiles, machinery, and chemicals. Moreover, companies that were business group members with a clearly defined main bank were more diversified than other firms, supporting the notion that main banks were proactively pushing for diversification. One main data problem confronted by all these studies is lack of information on subsidiaries, given Japan's lenient disclosure rules until 2000. This is particularly unfortunate for the 1980s when diversification through subsidiaries became a standard practice.

Onto four decades of continuous diversification, the bubble economy from 1987–1991 added exuberant diversification—whether by steel companies into hotel chains, electronics makers into Hollywood, manufacturing firms into golf courses, or railways into department stores. Japanese managers had ample cash while stock market evaluations hit new records almost daily. One Japanese firm after another engaged in unrelated diversification that ultimately challenged organizational capabilities and internal capital market controls.

Hubris played greatly into the real estate and stock price escalation during this period. "Japan as No. 1" became the catchphrase, and executives succumbed to the temptation to extend into new business terrains. This behavior was further reinforced by an exaggerated evaluation of Japanese practices by scholars and business analysts. Even as the United States went through its reversal from conglomeration to refocusing in the 1980s, many Japanese firms were celebrated as case studies for meaningful diversification. Recall that Prahalad and Hamel's (1990) seminal core competence article hailed NEC, in particular, for its leveraging of competencies into unrelated fields. It is now clear that some of NEC's branching out was misguided, and the company has reversed its course.

Thus, while the United States underwent its strategic reversal in the 1980s, Japan was entranced in its bubble economy. In the 1990s Japan's leading firms began to realize that they could no longer compete as highly diversified, high-cost goliaths in the increasingly globalized economy. For most companies, however, recession and a lack of political initiative to push restructuring allowed "muddle through" tactics. It was only in the late 1990s, and in particular with the banking crisis of 1998, that the severity of the crisis brought true change and the reversal toward "choose and focus" set in.

A first harbinger of the strategic inflection point was a reevaluation of "performance" itself, away from sales and market share, and toward profitability. In a 1999 government survey, chief executives of the 2,370 largest firms were asked what their ultimate management goal had been until 1999, and what it was for the future. Looking backward, 47.2 percent of the executives listed "sales" as their main objective, followed by "ordinary profits" (27%) and "operating profits" (10%); only 1.4 percent said they had considered return on equity important in the past. In contrast, looking into the future, a combined 65.7 percent said that "profits" were their main objective while only 12 percent continued to endeavor to maximize sales.[3] To accomplish this shift toward profitability, companies needed to unbundle and refocus, that is, undiversify and concentrate on their core business. In the 1999 Annual Survey of Corporate Behavior, 26.4 percent of the largest firms responded that they were "excessively diversified."[4]

This response caused the government to commission an early study on the shift in corporate strategy toward refocusing. From 2002 survey data, Miyajima and Inagaki (2003) present first insights into the relationship between focusing and the performance of Japanese firms at the turn of the century. Although necessarily preliminary in its findings, the study showed that unrelated diversification was associated with reduced performance, and that Japan's business structure began to change in the mid-1990s when the trend toward diversification was reversed and more and more companies, especially in manufacturing, embarked on strategic reversal. Fukui and Ushijima (2006) support this finding of a negative association between diversification and performance. Similar to the data findings on the extent of "choose and focus" presented in chapter 1, Ushijima (2007) and Kikutani, Itoh, and Hayashida (2007) find that refocusing companies did so with a vengeance: in most cases, they adopted restructuring measures of spin-offs and acquisitions simultaneously.

In late 2003, Nikkei Needs conducted a first study of the relative performance of wholly owned subsidiaries, made possible by new mandatory consolidated accounting after 2000. In looking at the Nikkei 500 firms excluding finance (447 firms), Katō (2003a, 2003b) finds 1,380 separate businesses; that is, on average each of Japan's largest companies operated in three other businesses at the time. He identifies the "core business" as the one contributing more than 50 percent of sales, and analyzes the contribution of this core business to total return on sales, return on assets, and sales growth. Based on these data, Katō (2003b) finds Japan's preeminent "choose and focus" leaders as of 2003

3. See MHLW, *Jinji/rōdō kanri kenkyūkai, koyō kankō senmonkai, Chūkan hōkokusho*, at www2.mhlw.go.jp/topics/topics/ kigyoc/index.htm.

4. This annual survey is sent to all listed companies, excluding financial firms. The response rate in the 1999 survey was 63.4% (1,361 firms). See www5.cao.go.jp/99/f/19990420ank/menu.html.

to be Takeda Pharmaceutical (also hailed as Japan's best company for three years in a row), the office equipment manufacturer Canon, Tanabe Pharmaceuticals, Tokyo Gas, Takuma (a maker of recycling equipment), and Nihon Telecom Holdings. In the case of Takeda, the core business of medical drugs had constituted 70 percent of its sales in 1999 (with other chemicals making up for the rest), but this share had reached 90 percent of sales in 2003. Return on assets had grown in each of the previous four quarters. Canon, likewise, had increased the contribution of office equipment to total sales from 60 percent in 1999 to 70 percent in 2003 (while upholding a strong "second core" in cameras with 15% of sales). From these studies, Katō concludes that Japan's strongest companies were unambiguously adjusting their strategic positioning, and the highest performers in the early 2000s were the early movers on this trend. At the same time, even among Japan's largest firms there was room for more refocusing.

Two Examples: How Matsushita and Takeda Have Changed

Panasonic and the Electronics Industry

Japan's global electronics companies were among the most aggressive diversifiers throughout the postwar period, so much so that the term *sōgō denki* (generic electronics and electrical machinery firms) was coined to describe their branching out into ever new product segments and components markets. Since the late 1990s, however, the leading companies of this industry, such as NEC, Hitachi, and Toshiba, have all taken aggressive measures to refocus—in what the press now labels "*denki saihen*" (the reorganization of the electrical machinery industry). Perhaps the best example of turnaround in this industry is provided by Matsushita Electric Industries (MEI), which has undergone what one author has called "the largest corporate restructuring in history" (McInerney 2007).

At its height in the late 1980s, MEI was the largest electronics company in the world, selling the brands Panasonic, National, JVC, and Quasar. It had grown from humble beginnings into global leadership by excelling in the mass production of high-quality household electronics and their components, ranging from washers, dryers, and TVs to batteries, lightbulbs, and semiconductors. The "Matsushita Way" placed great emphasis on loyalty, and during the recession of the 1970s the company's founder, Konosuke Matsushita, had been instrumental in affirming Japan's system of lifetime employment through his insistence on not laying off regular employees (Nikkei 1991). MEI was also celebrated for its "one product–one division" structure based on the logic of self-sufficiency of each product division in terms of product development, manufacturing, and sales. What was sometimes overlooked was that these divisions still had to build consensus and allow cross-subsidization, and, what is more, that over time a lack of integration gave rise to duplication. In 1985, MEI rose to global fame with the VHS videotape recorder, developed by its subsidiary JVC in a triumphant technology-standard showdown against archrival Sony's Betamax. By 1991, MEI was the world's largest electronics maker, with sales exceeding ¥4.5 trillion ($36 billion).[5]

MEI also greatly affected Japan's retail system, for its network of retail stores for the Panasonic and National brands accounted for more than 60 percent of its domestic sales. At its height, over 25,000 such small neighborhood stores performed two critical functions. They allowed easy test marketing of new product ideas as well as retail price maintenance. Ubiquity meant convenience, and there was usually no competition in the immediate vicinity, so that Matsushita controlled retail prices, which helped boost profits and allowed the company to compete more forcefully in global markets.

During the bubble period of 1987 through 1991, Matsushita found itself flush with cash and engaged in increasingly unrelated diversification (e.g., the purchase of the movie studio and film library of MCA in 1991, real estate, and a financial subsidiary). At the same time, duplication through the one product–one division structure led to uncoordinated expansion of manufacturing abroad. By the early 1990s, MEI operated innumerable neighboring plants in China, all producing similar or even the same products, often of the low value-added type such as extension cords. The structure designed to spur rapid product introduction by hungry division managers had turned the company into warring camps fighting over basic products. Innovation was stifled, and during the 1990s MEI failed to produce new hit products and completely missed the video games segment. It even had to give up its market leadership in its flagship product, the TV. At the same time, competitors from Korea, and increasingly from China, began to compete heavily in MEI's core segment of basic household appliances.

By 2007, MEI was a completely reorganized, restructured, and streamlined organization aimed at superior value creation in the digital age. In 2001, MEI launched, in its own words, a "cultural revolution" under CEO Kunio Nakamura. A first step was to abolish the one product–one division structure, with the goal of deemphasizing parochial business-unit interests. Performance was now evaluated based on global results, forcing a tighter integration of global operations. The company revised its employment practices and significantly

---

5. On the old Matsushita, see Goshal and Bartlett (1988); for a celebration of Mr. Matsushita's management philosophy, see Kotter (1997).

reduced its workforce. The retail system was overhauled, with only 5,000 stores remaining for the purpose of test marketing. Thorough cost-reduction measures included reducing business-unit control over investment decisions, streamlining the subcontractor system, and cutting global production facilities by half (Yoshino and Endo 2005).

In 2003, Panasonic was made MEI's only global brand (with National continuing only in Japan; JVC was sold off in 2007). The company repositioned, away from its previous goal of being the world's largest electronics maker, to becoming a technology leader through excellence in "ideas for life" products. These are differentiated, cutting-edge products that offer high-tech solutions to everyday life needs. The core areas were identified as digital networking, home appliances, and advanced components. To gain leadership in these areas, MEI targeted R&D investments in core products. Beginning in 2004, MEI re-emerged as the world leader in plasma TVs, as a major force in mobile phone technology, and as the producer of a hit line of "tough" notebooks.

To increase profitability, MEI consolidated its previous vast network of subsidiaries, selling off those that no longer presented a fit and acquiring others that were strategically important, such as Matsushita Electric Works. In a complete reversal of its original management philosophy, the company pulled core business units closer together to create strategic cohesion.

Although pushing such radical changes through a large, strong organizational culture as that of MEI was a task to continue into the 2010s, Nakamura had promised and accomplished a "V-Shaped" recovery. After bleeding money in 2002 and 2003, MEI showed a remarkable recovery, with steep annual growth between 2003 and 2007. For the fiscal year ending in March 2007, MEI's net profits surged by 41 percent (*Nikkei,* April 28, 2007). The company has repositioned itself as a global competitor in differentiated electronic components and products, thus avoiding head-on competition with Asian mass producers. Effective October 2008, the company changed its official name to Panasonic Corporation.

Takeda Pharmaceutical Company

Takeda is Japan's largest pharmaceutical company, and in 2005 ranked 15th globally in sales. As will be discussed in more detail in chapter 11 with the case study of Astellas, Japan's health care system underwent sweeping deregulation and reform in the early 2000s. At the same time, global industry shifts toward consolidation placed great pressure on companies to gain economies of scale in R&D and marketing and to bolster their pipelines, as the year 2010 will see a number of global blockbuster drugs come off patent. To compete in this environment as a global company, in 2000 Takeda embarked on a "choose and focus" mission. As of 2007, Takeda had transformed itself from a highly diversified conglomerate operating in ethical (i.e., prescription) and over-the-counter drugs, bulk vitamins, agrochemicals, urethane chemicals, and animal health as well as in the food business, into a focused company boasting 44 percent of its sales in global markets and earning 82 percent of its revenues from ethical drugs, including four global blockbuster medications.

Takeda's history dates back to 1781, when Chōbei Takeda started a retail business in traditional Japanese and Chinese medicines in Osaka. In the 1870s, his great-grandson, Chōbei Takeda IV, built a direct import business for Western medicines, and in 1907 Takeda gained exclusive rights to sell Bayer products in Japan. Takeda's first R&D division was built in 1915. In the postwar period, the company's main business was vitamins, but it also developed sedatives and an analgesic and entered the antibiotics segment. A series of joint ventures in Japan and abroad helped the business grow, and in 1985 Takeda Pharmaceuticals Products was founded in the United States as a joint venture with Abbott Labs. In 1991, Takeda launched Prevacid, an anti–peptic ulcer agent. All the while, domestic business flourished due to continuing protective market restrictions and high prices to be garnered for vitamins in a market comparatively prone to self-medicate. Over time, the company had also entered a variety of related businesses that boosted sales.

In international comparison, however, all this still left Takeda a small player. With a research budget of ¥68 billion (about $550 million) in 1996 and a priority established by the logic of Japan's national health care system on incremental product improvement, Takeda could not compete globally. Domestic deregulation was soon to take away previous pockets of profits, and the retail revolution and import competition in the mid-1990s had already undermined margins in the vitamin segment. Takeda embarked on its first "Management Plan 2001–2005" with a mission to "choose," that is, to exit noncore businesses, to be followed by a plan for 2006–10 that aimed at consolidating resources in the core business of ethical drugs to position Takeda as a "world-class pharmaceutical company with Japanese origin."

Reorganization involved shedding six businesses: the animal health business (2000), all international operations associated with bulk vitamins (sold to Bayer in 2001), the urethane chemical business (2002, into a newly formed joint venture with Mitsui Chemicals), the food business (2002, JV with Kirin), agribusiness (2003, JV with Sumitomo Chemical), and "life-environment businesses" (2005, sold to Osaka Gas). Thus, Takeda has not completely exited these markets, but it has transferred these businesses into independent, new companies. The transfer of businesses allowed Takeda to consolidate its core business, by taking full ownership of its various global subsidiaries and joint ventures in ethical drug discovery and manufacturing. In 2005, the company merged with Syrrx Inc., a U.S. biotech company, into Takeda San Diego.

Next, resources were focused on research. R&D expenditures as a percentage of sales increased from 8.5 percent in 1996 to 14 percent in 2006, when the annual R&D budget had tripled to ¥170 billion (roughly $1.35 billion) to exceed the estimated minimum efficiency scale for global pharmaceutical companies of $1.2 billion (*Diamond Weekly* 2007b). The net result was a continuous annual increase in sales, topping $10 billion in 2006. Between 2004 and 2007, Takeda's stock price doubled. The company has identified four core drug categories in which to compete: lifestyle-related diseases, oncology and urology, the central nervous system, and gastroenterology. As of 2007, the company's four global blockbuster drugs were Blopress (hypertension), Actos (diabetes), Lupron (prostate cancer), and Prevacid (ulcers). In 2007, the new Rozerem was the fastest growing insomnia drug in the United States.

Evaluation: Increasing Performance through Unbundling

Until the 1980s, the perceived strategy favored diversification as the predominant business approach to growth. However, after four decades of continuing diversification, and a bubble interlude of excessive diversification, large Japanese firms began to realize that they could no longer compete against lower cost, high-quality producers from Asia. The banking crisis added to the pressure to restructure and focus on higher margin businesses. The strategic inflection point was a tipping point where old ways of doing business simply no longer worked.

In 2007, it was too early to evaluate the performance effects of "choose and focus" for Japan, although anecdotal evidence from the most aggressive refocusing firms—in the electronics, steel, pharmaceuticals, and chemical industries—all point to strong positive effects on profits, return on equity, and stock prices. Early successful refocusers, such as Panasonic, report changes akin to a cultural revolution. The strategic inflection point and the wave of "choose and focus" have completely altered corporate strategic thinking and how Japan's leading companies compete.

III

JAPAN'S CHANGING INDUSTRIAL ARCHITECTURE

5

CORPORATE RELATIONS:
KEIRETSU, CROSS-SHAREHOLDINGS,
AND THE MAIN BANK

Japan's corporate groups, cross-shareholdings, and main bank arrangements represent core elements of Japan's postwar industrial architecture. Admired by some for their "patient capital" implications and criticized by others as market distorting, Japan's intermarket groups and financial structure have been widely studied. From this research, we have learned three main things. In their financing, Japanese firms relied primarily on bank loans, which put one main bank in a focal position in the financial arrangements and corporate governance of a firm. The largest firms issued shares, a large portion of which were held as long-term cross-shareholdings between banks and firms, as well as among firms. These cross-shareholdings underpinned large industrial groups called keiretsu as well as long-term trade relations.

As we saw in chapter 3, the main purpose with these tie-ups was insurance. This was important to the highly leveraged and therefore potentially unstable large firms. Preferential trade among group firms guaranteed constant minimum sales revenues. In return for granting a bank the right to intervene in management at times of crisis, companies assured access to credit. There was no outright market for corporate control, and corporate governance—the monitoring of management—for large firms was left mostly in the hands of the main bank and the business group.

Evaluation of these three elements has changed over time. Initially they were cited to explain Japan's success. Patient capital allowed companies to pursue long-term corporate growth without having to please shareholders in the short term (e.g., Porter 1992). Studies on main banks argued that a corporate governance system based on superior information by banks can be seen as functionally equivalent to a takeover market, and thus was at least as good a solution as, if not in some respects superior to, the M&A-crazy U.S. market (Aoki and Patrick 1994; Hoshi 1994; Sheard 1989, 1994; Kester 1991). Corporate groups, it was shown, contributed to in-group knowledge sharing and the success of Japanese firms in global markets (e.g., Gerlach 1992; Lincoln and Gerlach 2004).

More critical evaluations pointed to preferential trade as a means to close Japanese markets to new entry. In the early 1990s, the keiretsu became one core issue of the Structural Impediments Initiative, a round of U.S.-Japan trade negotiations that lasted through the 1990s (e.g., Prestowitz 1988; Lincoln 1999). Mutual cross-shareholdings obstructed foreign direct investment in Japan. Some finance economists were skeptical about the signaling power of Japanese stock prices, given that so many of the outstanding shares were in stable ownership, which resulted in a thin (i.e., illiquid) market and therefore easy price distortions. Others challenged the notion that patient capital produces better results than constant stock market monitoring, especially given issues with transparency and disclosure in Japan (e.g., McDonald 1989; French and Poterba 1991; Fedenia, Tschoegl, and Triantis 1994).

Whatever one's evaluation, Japan's strategic inflection has undermined the previous value of insurance provided by these arrangements. More dynamic and open markets require a higher degree of specialization and competitiveness as firms need to react to changing markets fast, turning stability into a liability. As large firms orient their external financing away from banks, they need to increase profitability in order to lower their costs of external funding, just as main banks need to identify new business models. Cross-shareholdings, too, have been greatly repositioned, as they are much more strategic and no longer predicated on business group membership.

Horizontal Business Groups

In the competitive setting of the postwar period, Japanese firms were successful if they could increase their size while shielding themselves from market upheaval, and one way to accomplish this was through corporate tie-ups. These tie-ups came in three flavors: large, intermarket groups ("horizontal keiretsu"); vertical lineups of subcontractors and other suppliers; and vertical tie-ups with exclusive wholesalers and retailers in distribution. All three have undergone great transformations. As will be shown in chapters 7 and 8, supplier relations have become more diversified and the retail revolution has undermined exclusive wholesaler arrangements. The focus here is on the "Big 6" horizontal groups.

Excellent research on business groups paired with superb data unavailable for most other countries has afforded us great insights into the workings of keiretsu during the postwar period. From data based on Toyo Keizai's annual *Kigyō Keiretsu Sōran*, we could measure cross-held ownership stakes, personnel dispatches, and within-group loans. Regular surveys by the Japan Fair Trade Commission from 1977 through 2001 have added qualitative information over time. Sociologists (Gerlach 1992; Lincoln and Gerlach 2004; Lincoln, Gerlach, and Ahmadjian 1996; Lincoln, Gerlach, and Takahashi 1992) have used these data for network analyses, while economists have studied the implications for corporate finance and industrial organization (e.g., Caves and Uekusa 1976; Hoshi and Kashyap 2001; Hoshi 1994; Lawrence 1993).

From this research we recall that there are two types of horizontal groups—three direct descendants of prewar *zaibatsu* (Mitsubishi, Mitsui, and Sumitomo) and three groups anchored by banks (Fuyō, Sanwa, and Dai-Ichi Kangyō [DIK]).[1] Each of these groups had several core firms (such as the main bank, a trading company, and perhaps a heavy machinery company), but no company was dominant in terms of ownership stake; rather, each group member owned, on average, 1–2 percent of the shares of other group members. Each group had between 25 and 45 core members, so that during the postwar period more than 200 of Japan's largest firms were members of one of the Big 6 (JFTC 2001, 19). The groups followed a rule called "one-setism," meaning that there was only one competitor per industry to prevent intragroup competition (leading Caves and Uekusa [1976] to label them intermarket groups). With increasing diversification, this rule was loosened over time; for example, Mitsubishi Heavy and Mitsubishi Electric eventually began to compete in several product segments such as air conditioning. Note that "one-setism" means that a business group was not a cartel, because it did not dominate any one industry. Rather, one effect of these arrangements was repeated oligopolies, in that the top three or four largest firms in most product markets would be from one of these groups (Hadley 1970).

During the 1950s, companies sought protection from foreign hostile takeovers. When the government proved it could effectively implement foreign exchange controls, the emphasis shifted to reducing variance in sales revenues and stock prices (Lincoln and Gerlach 2004). For shareholders, one price that had to be paid for this stability was the cost of carrying a stock portfolio that, while promising future capital gains, earned no returns just when companies were strapped for cash. To alleviate this cost, a custom emerged whereby most companies paid semiannual dividends at the predetermined amount of 10 percent of the par value of a stock, regardless of corporate performance. This turned dividend payments into something akin to interest payments, albeit at a very low rate. Since the majority of stocks had a par value of ¥50, most

---

1. The group anchored by the Industrial Bank of Japan (IBJ) has not been considered in this context, although it has been referred to as the "super-elite, most influential group" ("*chō-eriito, jitsuryoku Number 1*," Ōsono 1991). Following the merger into Mizuho Financial Group, this group has amalgamated with the DIK and Fuyō groups. Members of the IBJ group included Japan's flagship companies, such as Japan Airlines, Nissan Motors, Central Glass, Japan Steel, Dai-Shōwa Paper, Aoki Construction, Kuraray, and Japan Railways West. See Calder (1993) on the role of IBJ as a signal setter for industrial policy.

companies had to pay dividends of ¥5 per share. Hodder and Tschoegl (1985) calculate that during the 1960–83 period, firms listed in the first section of the Tokyo Stock Exchange paid an average of between 5.92 and 6.88 yen per share; during that same period, the stock price index increased sevenfold, so that average dividend yields declined to roughly 1 percent of the share price during that period. It would have been easy to identify more profitable venues of investment.

Studies have shown that group firms had lower average profitability than nongroup firms, but also lower variance in profitability over time (Nakatani 1984; Hoshi and Kashyap 2001). This can be partially explained by self-selection, as conservative companies were more likely to join groups. Over time, group firms also may have increasingly been Old Japan industries that declined in Japan's changing industrial structure after the 1970s (Suzuki 2005). Another contributor to lower profits was the preferential trade agreements among group firms, at prices negotiated to smooth revenues across member firms. One ticket for group membership was for firms to buy a certain portion of their inputs from other group firms, in particular in times of crisis. Although this was most relevant in intermediate products and equipment such as steel or machine tools, it was visible even to the naked eye—at a Mitsubishi plant, only drinks from Kirin would be served. When Mazda fell into crisis in the 1970s, in addition to providing financial support and absorbing some surplus labor, Sumitomo group firms encouraged their employees to purchase a new Mazda car. As analyzed further in chapter 8, these preferential trades often overrode cost considerations. The important benefit was that sustaining sales was crucial during the go-go years of rapid growth.

Data and surveys suggest that much of this has changed. The weight of Big 6 groups in Japan's overall economy has greatly declined. Whereas in 1970, Big 6 member firms accounted for almost 19 percent of the country's total corporate capital, this had fallen to 13 percent by 2000. Likewise, Big 6 firms used to control 17 percent of assets and account for 15 percent of the total in 1970, but these have dropped below 11 percent. So small had this impact become that in 2000, the Japan Fair Trade Commission terminated its surveys of the economic impact of horizontal groups (JFTC 2001).

Regular JFTC surveys between 1977 and 2000 provide trend data on the decline, as presented in figures 5.1 through 5.3. A first challenge in studying keiretsu is to identify a group's core members. An often-used separator has been whether the chief executives of a company participated in the regular presidents' council meetings, either as a full member or as an observer. For its survey of 2000 the Japan Fair Trade Commission found that the six groups had a total of 180 members (192 if double memberships were counted).

5.1. *Intra-Group Shareholding Ratio, 1977–1999 (in % of all group shares outstanding, for 181 member firms, not including life insurance companies)*
Source: JFTC (2001).

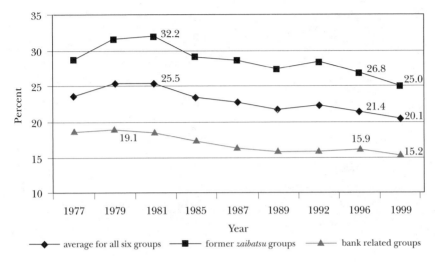

The fall in cohesion of these six groups, as expressed in the most important bond of intragroup shareholdings, is shown in figure 5.1. The chart shows the percentage of all members' shares outstanding that were held by other group members. Although one company's ownership in another was typically quite small, in sum the group became a sizable voting block at the shareholders' meeting. Yet, by 1999 intragroup shareholding averaged only 20 percent, down from about 25 percent in 1981. The cohesion of the old *zaibatsu* groups (Mitsubishi, Mitsui, and Sumitomo) had dropped from 32 percent to 25 percent over the two decades. This is all the more remarkable because Mitsubishi is still highly cohesive, meaning that the Mitsui and Sumitomo groups have lost more in interrelatedness than figure 5.1 suggests. The three bank-related keiretsu groups of Fuyō, Sanwa, and Dai-Ichi Kangyō, which have always been less tight, by 1999 had further reduced their intragroup shareholdings to an average of 15 percent. Thus, the group is no longer a major shareholder for most firms.

The second measure of group cohesion is preferential trade. The measurable portion of this trade has been in significant decline (see figure 5.2), as the percentage of purchases from group firms of the total purchases has roughly halved, from an average of 12 percent in 1981 to 6.4 percent in 1999. For the three bank-related groups, it has dropped to below 5 percent.

5.2. *Within-Group Procurement Ratio, 1981–1999 (in % of responses by 163 firms, not including financial institutions)*
Source: JFTC (2001).

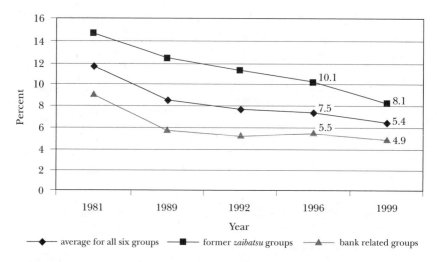

Percent

| Year: 1981 | 1989 | 1992 | 1996 | 1999 |

10.1

7.5 — 8.1

5.5 — 5.4

4.9

——◆—— average for all six groups   ——■—— former *zaibatsu* groups   ——▲—— bank related groups

These two main categories of group cohesion are mapped in figure 5.3 into a two-axis repositioning chart from 1981 to 2000, which shows that the cohesiveness of all six groups has waned significantly. The longest distance, reflecting the biggest loss in cohesion, was covered by Sumitomo, and the smallest by Dai-Ichi Kangyō. By 2000, the Mitsui group was no longer more cohesive than the bank-anchored DIK group, and Fuyō and Sanwa were least cohesive. The Mitsubishi group, always the tightest, remained in that spot, and the decline is more in terms of purchasing than it is in shareholding.

Perhaps the ultimate insurance derived from group membership was support in hard times, based on group governance. One way in which this was cemented was through the exchange of directors to the boards of other firms in the groups (e.g., Nakatani 1984; Lincoln and Gerlach 2004). Here, too, group activities have been greatly diminished. The JFTC survey revealed that personnel exchange at the executive level was halved between 1981, when almost 9 percent of group senior executives were dispatched to other group members, and 1991, with an average of 4 percent of all senior executives.

Insurance against failure was directly tied to the role of the main bank. As we will see in more detail below, this bank was the largest lender and shareholder, and also assumed responsibility to rescue its clients from failure (Hoshi and Kashyap 2001; Sheard 1989, 1994). However, data show a decline in intragroup lending, as measured in the percentage of member firms

5.3. *The Combined Effect of Declining Cross-Shareholdings and Declining Preferential Trade in the Six Keiretsu Groups, 1981 versus 2000*
Source: JFTC (2001).

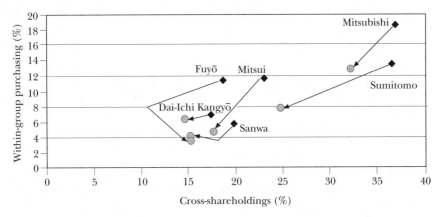

that borrowed from a keiretsu financial institution. This ratio dropped from 98 percent in 1989 to 73.5 percent in 1999 (JFTC 2001). Although this may still sound high, recall that the main motivation behind business groups was said to be the financial setup and insurance, so that this downward trend signals important change. Measured in terms of total loan volume, the role of group financial institutions has always been more limited, because the main bank was rarely the only provider of funds. Expressed as the percentage of group lending to total loans, intragroup loan provision dropped from 7 percent in 1981 to only 2 percent in 1999. Clearly, lending is no longer a main aspect of group membership.

In its last survey conducted in 2000, the JFTC also asked member firms of the Big 6 what they thought would happen to their groups in the future. Only one third of the member firms thought their groups would continue in its 1999 shape, and 20 percent believed that the functions of the group would change. One third of the members of the DIK and Fuyō groups had an inkling that their groups would dissipate. Given mergers among banks that used to be at the core of separate groups, such as Sumitomo and Mitsui, it is not surprising that 43 percent of group firms believed that their groups would merge. The only exception was the Mitsubishi group, where 91 percent of members believed that the group will continue in its current form (JFTC 2001, 17).

The survey also asked core group members what they considered the biggest benefits derived from keiretsu membership. In 2000, roughly 85 percent listed the "exchange of information" as their primary benefit, followed by brand name benefits and the sharing of know-how. Supporting the impression from figures 5.1 through 5.3, long-term trade relations and insurance through stable shareholdings only came in fourth and fifth. Less than 10 percent thought that keiretsu membership facilitated shareholder policies, and less than 5 percent felt that the group any longer offered effective insurance against crisis (JFTC 2001, 13).[2]

Perhaps the biggest impact on the evolution of business groups was corporate reorganization and restructuring. To the extent that group ties remained robust, these could help with efforts at mergers between group firms to increase efficiency. New boundary-crossing bank ties were supportive of matchmaking, too. For example, given global pressures for consolidation in the pharmaceutical industry, Mitsubishi Pharma merged with Tanabe Seiyaku, a second-tier company whose previous merger attempts had failed. Tanabe's main bank was UFJ, and UFJ's merger with Tokyo Mitsubishi Bank in 2001 created new ties between the two companies that resulted in an arranged marriage, with the creation of Mitsubishi Tanabe Pharma in 2007.

A much more frequent phenomenon in the early 2000s, however, was for firms to establish new companies that straddled group boundaries and made previous affiliations immaterial. One popular way of exiting a noncore business without completely severing ties to that industry was for a firm to establish a joint venture with a competitor, which almost by definition meant going into business with a firm from a different group. Recall the examples of Elpida Memory Inc., founded in 1999 by Hitachi of the Fuyō group and NEC of Sumitomo, as well as Renesas, a joint venture between Hitachi and Mitsubishi Electric. In 2006, Renesas Technologies was the seventh largest chip maker in the world.[3] Another case was the 2002 spin-off of the silicon wafer business by Mitsubishi Materials Corporation into SUMCO, a joint venture with Sumitomo Materials. Takeda Pharmaceuticals' 2002 joint subsidiary with Kirin, which provided both companies a chance to exit the food business, cut across Sanwa and Mitsubishi lines.

Thus, restructuring has led to the creation of new, large corporations in Japan. Although these may operate in low-margin, commoditized industries such as DRAMs or LCDs, they provide critical supplies. They are focused, competitive players in important niche markets of their industries. And they cut across the former keiretsu boundaries as well as the newly formed financial groups. For these companies, former group ties are largely irrelevant.

2. See Lincoln and Gerlach (2004) for advanced statistical research on group relations that support the findings represented in this survey.

3. See the special feature "Denki Kaitai" (The dissolution of Japan's electronics industry), *Shūkan Daiyamondo*, March 10, 2007.

Cross-Shareholdings

Cross-shareholdings were the glue that kept business groups together. The majority of ownership stakes were held for the long run by companies of the same business group or by companies that maintained long-term trade relations. They were based on an understanding that they would not be sold, in particular in times of market downturn, to insure companies against the inherent instability of stock markets. However, a reduction in cross-shareholdings and the new composition of Japan's shareholders have brought great forces for change.

Unraveling of the Postwar System

Throughout the postwar period, the majority of shareholdings between companies, and those between banks and companies, were stable. This became such an important phenomenon that detailed data were collected beginning for 1987, through two annual surveys that collate corporate annual reports with survey responses on large shareholders, one from Nihon Life Institute (NLI 2004), and the other from Daiwa Institute of Research (DIR 2004, 2005). NLI also takes credit for introducing the distinction between "stable shareholders" (*antei kabunishi*, long-term ownerships that may be one-sided and serve to cement trade relations), and the two-sided "mutual shareholders" (*mochiai kabunishi*, reciprocal commitments, even if unbalanced). In a way, reciprocal shareholdings constituted the superglue of group cohesion. The last survey of this type was conducted in March 2004, when NLI found that the phenomenon had become too small to be measured accurately.

The percentage of stable and reciprocal shareholdings of total stocks outstanding at all Japanese stock exchanges for the period 1987 to 2003 is shown in figure 5.4. The top line indicates that whereas stable ownership remained fairly unchanged at over 45 percent of all shareholdings until 1995, it dropped significantly to a level of under 25 percent in 2003. The bars in figure 5.4 show that the percentage of firms that identified themselves as having at least one stable stock in their portfolio also dropped sharply. Based on a separate survey, table 5.1 takes a more detailed look at this development, by showing the percentage of firms engaged in cross-shareholdings by investment target. The left portion of the table reveals that in 1993, 88.9 percent of all listed companies held stable shares in banks, and 72.2 percent held stable shares in other companies. By 2003, these numbers had dropped to 59.4 percent and 45.4 percent—that is, less than half of the listed companies in 2003 held cross-shareholdings in other firms.

Leading explanations for the corporate sell-offs in this period were the bank mergers (reducing the number of friendly shares a company needed to hold),

5.4. *Stable Shareholdings and Reciprocal Shareholdings, 1988–2004*
Source: adapted from NLI 2003, 16–20; as of March of the indicated year.

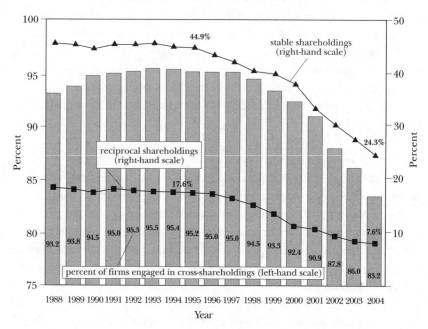

TABLE 5.1. *Number of Banks and Companies Involved in Cross-shareholding*

Year	Number of Firms that have cross-shareholdings (% of all firms)					Average number of firms in which shares are held				
	1993	1998	2001	2002	2003	1993	1998	2001	2002	2003
Companies owning banks	88.9	87.5	62.7	66.1	59.4	3.5	3.0	2.3	1.9	1.9
Companies owning other companies	72.2	72.8	41.7	45.3	45.5	5.4	4.9	2.2	2.3	2.5
Banks owning companies	83.8	90.7	92.5	94.6	92.4	79.8	81.9	57.0	50.0	46.0

Source: Adapted from DRI 2004: 3.

the recession, and the shift to mark-to-market valuation of cross-shareholdings in 2001. The 1998 crisis caused a huge drop in the stock market, and by 2002 the Nikkei Index had fallen to its level in 1982. Depressed stock prices greatly affected corporate earnings data, and when Japan shifted to mark-to-market accounting rules even for cross-shareholdings in 2001, companies began to sell shareholdings they had bought during the bubble period to avoid having to report losses (Kuroki 2003). The increase in the percentage of banks owning companies can be explained with consolidation, as the number of banks decreased by more than half.

The right-hand side of table 5.1 reverses the angle of this analysis, by showing the number of stable shares invested in by one firm. In 2003, the average Japanese company engaged in cross-shareholding relations with 1.9 banks, as compared to 3.5 in 1993 (again, in part due to bank mergers). But companies also limited the number of other firms they invested in, from an average of 5.4 to 2.5. Banks were most active in cutting their ties, from almost 80 companies in 1993 to only 46 in 2003.

Before we consider the banks' motivations, a brief mention is warranted of the more restrictive reciprocal (*mochiai*) shareholdings, because the loosening of ownership ties is most pronounced in this "superglue" segment. Data suggest that banks and companies have been equally active in dissolving these positions. The lower line in figure 5.4 shows that whereas in the 1980s and early 1990s more than 17 percent of listed firms were intertwined in mutual ownership, this ratio fell to 7.6 percent in 2003. Expressed in absolute terms for the year 2002, of a total market valuation of ¥237 trillion for all 2,674 listed firms, ¥17.6 trillion was identified by survey respondents as being mutual. This not only represented a decline of ¥10 trillion over a one-year period, but 2003 was also the 17th year in a row in which the percentage of *mochiai* declined (Kuroki 2003; NLI 2004; Suzuki 2005).

Are Cross-Shareholdings Really on the Decline?

Even though these data indicate a great reduction in cross-shareholdings, there is some debate whether they are in fact dissolving. One reason is that data may be influenced by accounting rule changes, for beginning in 2000 small shareholdings may be lumped together and thus not be fully captured in recent data.[4] Moreover, Suzuki (2005) argues that while the decline rates may be eye-opening, most listed Japanese firms still had at least one cross-shareholding arrangement as of 2004. According to a 1999 survey (CAO 1999), while 10 percent of companies saw no merit in sustaining stable ownership stakes

---

4. Beginning with the FY 2000 annual statement (*Yūka shōken hōkokusho*), Japanese firms switched to consolidated accounting. Because this allows lumping small intragroup holdings together, exact data on stable shareholdings are no longer declared. Likewise, firms only have to list their largest 10 shareholders and banks, and all loans are lumped together. As a consequence, the standard source for the research on corporate groups, the *Kigyō Keiretsu Sōran* (published annually by Tōyō Keizai), was discontinued in 2001.

and 41 percent were concerned about having to declare losses on their stock portfolio should stock prices fall, about half of respondents still thought that long-term holdings would reduce the variance in their stock prices.

In 2007, there was also evidence of a trend reversal. According to the Nomura Research Center, in March 2007 a combined 12 percent of the market value of listed firms' outstanding shares was owned by other listed firms. This compared to 33 percent in 1990, but it also marked a 1 percent increase over the previous year.[5] Some observers suggested that at least some portion of this increase was driven by attempts to protect against hostile takeovers. Indeed, this had been the original motivation for cross-shareholdings in the 1950s and 1960s, when even a very small ownership stake of, on average, 2 percent by several friendly firms was effective because at that time Japan had no rule that obligated minority owners to surrender their shares to a hostile bidder.

In 1999, Japan changed this rule such that minority owners must now sell at a fair price to a hostile bidder once a majority position has been established. Therefore, if stable shareholdings are to protect a friendly company, this has to occur through different mechanisms. As discussed in more detail in chapter 6, new takeover rules allow for poison pills, that is, defense mechanisms that make a hostile bid prohibitively expensive. Japan's most popular pill is the issuance of new, restricted warrants (bonds that can be turned into stocks) that are granted only to friendly owners, thereby diluting the raider's share. Management must receive a two-thirds majority vote from shareholders before it can issue such warrants.

Under this new rule, group-based cross-shareholdings no longer offer a guarantee for success—unless group members became majority owners. This was rare even in the postwar period, as it is undesirable for most CEOs to give potentially unanimous corporate shareholders that much power. Alternatively, the company can be very specific in lining up a few select shareholders that are trusted not to abuse their increasing power when allotted new warrants.

The new cross-shareholdings of 2007 fell in this second category, and, importantly, these were often unrelated to business groups. One new type was between companies in the same industry, such as steel. As the global steel industry was undergoing consolidation, fear of foreign bidders led Nippon Steel to forge tie-ups with competitors Sumitomo Metal and Kobe Steel. These three companies are increasingly considered as one new steel group. Nippon Steel

5. "Cross-shareholdings See First Rise since '90s." *Japan Times*, September 2, 2007. The 12% figure represents a subset of total corporate shareholdings, which stood at 21% in 2007 (cf. figure 6.1).

president Akio Mimura was quoted as saying "cross-shareholdings today are different from those in the past."[6] Another example was the reported cross-investment between Toyota and Matsushita Electric (MEI), with the stated goal of enhancing business ties, as MEI had emerged as a critical supplier of batteries for hybrid cars.

Thus, the new poison pills work without cross-shareholdings, and not all shareholdings are aimed at guarding against takeovers. And finally, the up-take in corporate stock investments in 2007 can be explained by the fact that Japan's takeover premium at that time was at about 35 percent. Investing in a company that could become a takeover target could be a wise move. The company could launch a turnaround or it could be acquired; in either case, the stock price was bound to go up. In sum, as of 2007 it was too early to evaluate the newly forming cross-shareholdings, or to judge whether the new shareholders would remain loyal even when offered a high takeover premium. However, it was already very clear that cross-shareholdings had become much more strategic.

Banks Selling Out

Another important difference in cross-shareholdings from the postwar pe-riod is that banks, to all intents and purposes, are no longer part of the equa-tion. Data that break cross-shareholdings down by industry show that the 16 large commercial banks were most active in dissolving their stakes. In 1991, they held about 11 percent of total stock market capitalization, but reduced their holdings to 3.6 percent in 2003 (DIR 2004).

Some banks may have had idiosyncratic reasons to reconsider their share-holdings. But the most important trigger of the mass sell-off after 2001 was the new Law Limiting Banks' Stock Ownership. Designed to improve the stability of the banking system, this law limits a bank's total shareholdings to its size, strictly defined as "own capital."[7] In fiscal year 2001, the largest four banks alone were estimated to face a shareholding overhang of about ¥7 trillion, which created immense pressure to reduce stakes. By way of reference, in

6. "Analysis: Cross-Shareholding Re-Emerging as Takeover Defense Step," *Nikkei*, July 13, 2007.

7. The law is the Ginkō-tō no kabushiki-tō no hoyū no seigen-tō ni kan suru hōritsu. The new limit is a bank's "Tier 1 capital." Based on BIS regulation, which requires a capital ad-equacy ratio for internationally operating banks of at least 8%, there are two types (tiers) of capital, of which Tier 1 refers to the bank's paid-in capital, shareholder's equity, and retained earnings not yet appropriated at the end of the fiscal year. Tier 2 capital consists of 45% of the estimated value of unrealized gains of the bank's stock portfolio, plus loan-loss reserves and subordinated debt issued by the bank. The new law says that Tier 2 capital (ownership in other firms) must not exceed Tier 1 (the bank's own equity).

March 2001 city banks and other banks (excluding trust banks) held ¥35.7 trillion worth of shares at current market value, but this declined to ¥18.2 trillion in March 2003. During this time, the stock market moved largely sideways. Thus, banks truly halved the value of their stockholdings within a two-year period. The fact that banks were required by law to unravel their holdings makes this unwinding largely irreversible.[8]

A law forcing banks to dissolve ownership stakes is in and of itself another indicator that postwar industrial policy has ended. The banking crisis and capital infusion thwarted all resistance against a law that aimed to increase the stability of the banking system at a time of new bank strategies, global bank mergers, and pressures on the banks' own refinancing costs in international financial markets.

The Main Bank: From Lender of Last Resort to Specialized Financial Adviser

Between 1949 and 1994, the business model of Japanese banking was straightforward. The Temporary Interest Rate Adjustment Law of 1949 regulated basic interest rates such that there was a fixed spread between rates to be paid on savings accounts and rates to be charged for loans. To guide the flow of funds into targeted growth firms, the government regulated the issuance of bonds and stocks so as to make bank loans easier and cheaper, leading firms to rely on banks for most of their financial needs.[9] Given the fixed spread (price), banks had to compete for volume: the more loans, the higher the banks' interest income. So easy was this business model, and so regulated the market for financial innovation, that banks engaged in few fee-income activities.

The largest banks became central figures in horizontal business groups, whose large members included the targeted growth champions. Ever eager to lend more, banks soon found themselves with many highly leveraged large borrowers as main clients. As this was potentially very risky, the banks were

8. Banks reduced their shareholdings in a planned process that lasted until September 2006. To facilitate the sell-off, in 2002 the "Banks' Shareholdings Purchase Corporation" (Ginkō-tō hoyū kabushiki shutoku kikō) was established as a government-backed entity with a lifespan of 10 years and funds of ¥2 trillion. In 2002, the Bank of Japan (the central bank) began absorbing another ¥1.7 trillion worth of banks' shares (FSA 2001 White Paper at www.fsa.go.jp; Kuroki 2003). Because of the strong performance of the Nikkei index, by 2006, the Bank of Japan had earned estimated capital gains of ¥1.8 trillion, and the purchase corporation another ¥1 trillion, making up for some of the banking system's losses in the previous years (*Nikkei*, May 22, 2006).

9. On interest rate regulation and how the banks' lending behavior was influenced through administrative guidance, see Patrick (1962), Calder (1993), Schaede (2000b). Weinstein and Yafeh (1998) describe capital market regulations, and argue that the bond underwriting committee (*kisaikai*) was a cartel designed to make firms dependent on banks.

very keen that their clients maintain a secure stream of income so that they could pay interest on their loans. Banks hedged against the threat of failure in two ways. First, the banks pushed their clients to diversify into multiple business areas, to stabilize the companies themselves. This was also good for business, since diversification required more loans. From the banks' perspective, the profitability of the client was much less important than a steady flow of revenues, so they encouraged companies to diversify into business segments where they would compete not to win but simply to be represented.

The second way banks hedged their risk was to diversify their own loan portfolios, which they did in two ways. It was already built in to the logic of "one-setism" of the business group, as these groups straddled many industries. In addition, banks arranged joint lending with other banks. Rather than being the only lender, the main bank assumed the role of the largest lender to its main clients, but it also became a secondary lender in nongroup companies. In a system of delegated monitoring, the main bank assumed the lead role in monitoring its own clients but piggybacked on other banks' monitoring of their clients. To bolster its credibility, in case of distress the main bank would assume additional responsibility and carry a share of the financial burden exceeding its loan share.[10] In return, other large banks would lend to group companies without much further credit analysis.

Bailing out a highly leveraged company was exceedingly expensive. Yet, while case studies on bank rescues abound, we know of no case during the postwar period in which a large company with a clearly defined main bank was closed down.[11] In addition to maintaining their credibility in the delegated monitoring system, this can be explained by economics and politics. In economic terms, as Stiglitz (1990) and Greenwald and Stiglitz (1992) have shown, for a highly exposed bank it is usually favorable to support a failing debtor, because the rescue creates at least a chance of partial recovery of the loans, whereas closure does not. The government was supportive of the main banks' role as rescuer of last resort, because it feared unemployment due to large corporate failures at a time when the country's unemployment insurance

10. Wallich and Wallich (1976, 273); Hodder and Tschoegl (1985, 1993); Sheard (1989, 1994); Aoki and Patrick (1994).

11. Sheard (1994) and Hoshi and Kashyap (2001) offer accounts of main bank bailout processes during the postwar period. Hoshi, Kashyap, and Scharfstein (1990a) present evidence of the disproportionate responsibility for bad debts carried by main banks. Kaplan and Minton (1994), Kang and Shivdasani (1995), and Morck and Nakamura (1999) show that the dispatch of bankers to the failing company preceded the replacement of management, and that poor earnings and low cash flow predicted bank appointments of senior management.

and public assistance programs were still being developed. Thus, when a bank had to rescue a large employer, the Ministry of Finance would usually be involved and see to it that the bank was rewarded—through new licenses to open branches, through special tax write-offs, or through extra business from the government.

Bailouts were the culmination of an ongoing process of management monitoring by the main bank. Although monitoring ensured superior information on the company, it was expensive, as it often required personnel dispatches. High loan exposure gave banks an incentive to do this. Moreover, they developed a mechanism that enabled them to charge higher than prescribed rates through so-called compensating balances: a bank requested a borrower to take out a bigger loan than needed, but placed the excess portion in a low-interest checking account with the same bank (Suzuki 1980). In this way, the bank increased both its deposit base and its loan volume, seemingly increasing size and market share, plus earning interest income on the excess loan amount. One result of the compensating balances was that we cannot be sure what interest rates were charged during the postwar period (this was the banking equivalent to relational pricing; see chapter 8). The bank was also at liberty to adjust compensating balances to needs, so one can surmise that when asked by the business group to bail out an important group member firm, it might have asked all group companies to open additional savings accounts. Although data on effective interest rates do not exist, some studies have shown that main bank clients faced higher costs of borrowing than firms without a main bank, with the premium representing membership dues.[12] Thus, the bank was compensated through increased interest income from the client firm and its trading partners. This further increased the emphasis on volume in lending in the banks' business model.

Changes in Corporate Finance

The banks' business model was greatly affected by financial deregulation, which began in the mid-1980s with the onset of a piecemeal process of lifting the formal and informal restrictions on the issuance of bonds. During the bubble period, disintermediation accelerated when more and more large firms stopped borrowing altogether. They relied instead on retained earnings and the capital markets (bonds and stocks). The large banks therefore directed their attention to small- and medium-sized firms, but continued to secure loans

---

12. See Caves and Uekusa (1976); Suzuki (1980); Hodder and Tschoegl (1985, 1993); Aoki (1988); Weinstein and Yafeh 1998. See also Lincoln and Gerlach (2004) on redistribution within business groups.

simply through collateral. Risk evaluation in project financing was rare. When the bubble economy burst in 1991, it became painfully obvious that chasing loan volume with just the face value of real estate as collateral was not good business. The banking crisis in 1998 led to a reorganization of the banking system and a reorientation of the surviving banks toward businesses that yield fee income.

This disintermediation is shown in figures 5.5–5.7. Figure 5.5 highlights that in the decade between 1993 and 2003, and in particular after 1998, total loans outstanding shrunk by 30 percent, and small-firm loans accounted of over 63 percent of business. Part of the overall decline was attributable to the banking crisis and the banks' struggles to maintain their 8 percent capital-adequacy ratio. Recession also dampened demand for bank loans throughout the 1990s. And even though normalization of the banking business in the early 2000s led to an increase in lending after 2006, loans to large firms clearly accounted for a decreasing fraction of commercial banking.

Figures 5.6a and 5.6b tell this story from the borrowers' perspective, by presenting data on financing of large firms for the period 1960–2004. These figures break corporate finance into three components: (1) internal, through the use of retained earnings; (2) external, through bank loans; and (3) external, through the issuance of bonds or equity. Finance research on the "pecking order" suggests that firms prefer to use internal funds. If they have to use external funding, they prefer low-risk debt, and will issue equity only when leverage becomes so high that the costs of potential financial distress spike interest rates over the costs of issuing equity.[13] In Japan, especially in the early postwar

5.5. *Bank Loans Outstanding, by Size of Borrower, 1993–2003*
Source: METI 2003a.

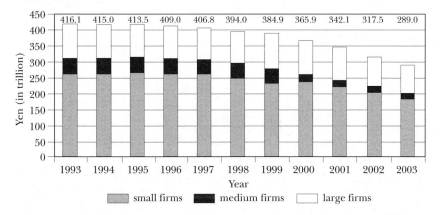

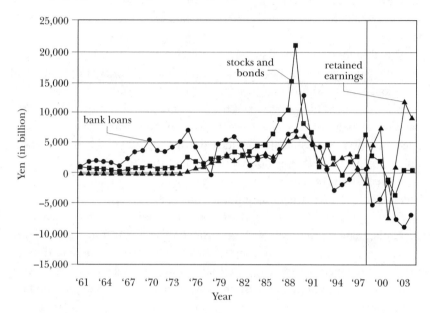

5.6a. *Flow Data for Corporate Financing, 1960–2004: Retained Earnings, Bank Loans, and External Financing*
Source: calculated from *Hōjin kigyō tōkei;* for all large firms with capital exceeding ¥1 billion, all industries (n=5,275).

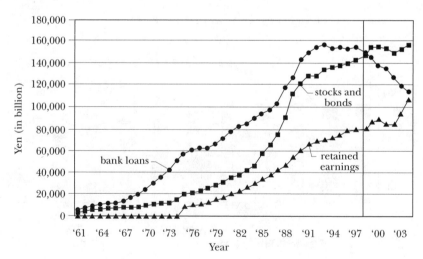

5.6b. *Stock Data for Corporate Financing, 1960–2004: Retained Earnings, Bank Loans, and External Financing*
Source: see 5.6a.

period, firms had limited retained earnings to use, and therefore were highly dependent on external funding. Interest rate regulation paired with strict rationing of bond issues interfered with the pecking order logic in that it made bank loans the cheapest and easiest form of debt, and in that the risks of high leverage for banks were partially socialized by the government's support of bank-led rescue operations.

In annual terms, after 1998 retained earnings became the most important source of corporate finance (figure 5.6a). By 2004, in cumulative terms internal financing equaled the level of outstanding bank loans (figure 5.6b). Moreover, stocks and bonds have become more important than bank loans in external financing of Japan's largest firms, both in terms of annual flow and accumulated stock.

These changes in the capital structure of Japan's large corporations translate into a normalization of debt-equity ratios. The exposure of banks to corporate loans is highlighted in figure 5.7. At its height in 1975, the debt-equity ratio for all industries stood at over 600 (and 900 for the steel industry)—meaning

5.7. Normalization of Leverage: Debt-Equity Ratios, 1960–2004
Source: Calculated from *Hōjin kigyō tōkei;* "large companies" refer to firms with capital exceeding ¥1 billion.

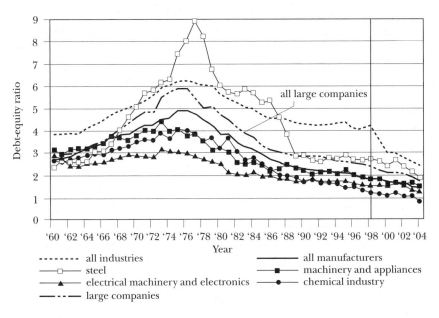

13. Myers (2001) provides an overview article on capital structure; Hodder and Tschoegl (1985) present an early application to the Japanese situation.

that the average large firms had six times as many loans outstanding as it had equity capital. Between 1998 and 2000, however, leverage dropped precipitously to below 300 and it has been on a downward trend since. Looking only at the large firms (with capital exceeding ¥1 billion), we see that from a peak of 590 in the 1970s, their leverage has fallen to below 200. It is even lower for those industries that shifted to a "choose and focus" strategy early, such as the chemical, electronics, and machinery industries.

A New Business Model for Banks

These changes in corporate finance have triggered a complete reorientation of the banking sector. The collapse of real estate prices beginning in 1991 brought an abrupt end to the land myth of the bubble period, when the strange notion that land in an island country is somehow more limited than in countries with manmade borders was debunked. In the New Japan, large banks can no longer successfully compete by vying for market share in corporate lending. The introduction of financial holding companies in 1997 wiped out the last remnants of business segmentation in banking, making the commercial bank just one part of a financial group. This has allowed greater variation in business pursuits, and banks have begun to broaden their income streams by developing fee income businesses, such as syndicated lending, specialized advice on capital structure (as opposed to simply pushing for more loans), the planning and financing of mergers or acquisitions, or advanced financial services for firms of all sizes and individuals, such as middle-market lending, credit cards, leasing, and consumer finance.

The results of a 1999 government survey of large, listed companies as to what they considered the greatest merits of having a main bank in the past and of having such a relationship in the future are shown in table 5.2. The previous reliance on banking activities relating to stability, access, and long-term relations has begun to be replaced by services, support in credit rating (to lower the cost of external funding), and global competitiveness. Whereas in this questionnaire, 98 percent of respondents still saw merit in having a main bank, the main benefit was seen in support in domestic M&A and international business transactions. In a smaller survey conducted by the magazine *Shūkan Daiyamondo* in 2006, 30 percent of the CEOs of Japan's 100 largest firms felt that the main bank system was a thing of the past (November 18, 2006). However, what is meant by these responses is not so much that the institution of a main bank per se will disappear but that its offerings will have to become more multifaceted and advanced in order for the banks to be of true help with their clients' new business strategies.

TABLE 5.2. *Survey on Benefits from the Main Bank System*

Merits of having a main bank (up to three answers)	Important in the past	Important for the future
Having stable access to funds	59.7	50.3
Having main bank as a stable shareholder	**49.5**	**27.6**
Existence of a long-term trade relationship	**32.4**	**16.4**
Financing at conditions and interest rates that meet the firm's needs	28.6	35.1
High level of service in settlements and other transactions	24.9	23.4
High level of information and help on financial management	20.2	30.7
Rescue and support in times of crisis	18.0	17.4
Higher credit rating and financial health due to bank's reputation	9.8	**20.6**
Information and support in corporate strategies, such as M&A	5.2	**18.0**
High level of support in international business needs	5.2	**11.2**
Support through dispatch of executives	3.3	1.6
High level of management monitoring on fiscal and risk management matters	2.8	5.6
No merit	1.6	2.1

Source: CAO (1999).
Note: Numerals in bold signify response with the deepest drops or increases. Total n=1,361 listed companies, up to 3 answers allowed.

Evaluation: Banks and Business Groups in the New Japan

The foundations of Japan's industrial architecture have shifted. In the New Japan, calculations of the value of main banks, business groups and cross-shareholdings are based on new needs. No longer crucial as lenders for large firms, Japan's large banks have reacted to ongoing financial deregulation by merging into four financial holdings and acquiring expertise in financial services other than lending. These new banks are no longer simply interested in a client's longevity, but in performance and profitability. New accounting and disclosure standards have undermined the banks' erstwhile monopoly on corporate financial information, and made personnel dispatches redundant. With their ownership stakes in firms reduced, banks no longer benefit from monitoring clients closely. New bankruptcy legislation has introduced viable alternatives to informal bank restructuring, reducing the banks' erstwhile pivotal role in orchestrating bailouts. Thus, the main bank of the postwar period is fast becoming history. In the New Japan, financial intermediaries must aim at fee income through offering specialized services. This makes Japan's banks more similar to house banks in other countries. The old main bank was the largest lender and shareholder. The new main bank is the bank with which a company chooses to conduct most of its financial business. This choice is no longer preordained by business-group ties, but is based on expertise and determined competitively.

Similar to other countries, for small- and medium-sized firms close bank ties continue to be important because smaller firms face greater obstacles in securing access to credit. However, here too we can observe changes under the heading of relationship banking (e.g., Tago 2003; Ono and Uesugi 2005; Ono and Noda 2006). Unlike the previous long-term relations between a smaller firm and a bank based on relational pricing and characterized by almost automatic loan rollovers, Japan's new relationship banking refers to a system of credit scoring augmented by in-depth and ongoing inspections to evaluate smaller businesses where credit scoring can be only one aspect in determining creditworthiness. The breakup of Japan's rigid interest rate structure and waning political influence in the small-firm-loan market have finally allowed banks to price loans commensurate with risk. Even for Japan's smaller firms, pressure to increase profitability has become real.

Business groups have also greatly changed. Perhaps most important, the bank mergers have cut across previous group boundaries, such as in the case of Sumitomo-Mitsui. This has ended the previous logic of "one-setism," because competitors in one industry may now share the same main bank. For example, when Fuji Bank, DIK, and IBJ merged into Mizuho, the new bank suddenly had six construction firms as clients. For companies to be part of such an arrangement makes sense only to the extent they can differentiate into market segments and do not compete head-on. Therefore, if two companies in one industry remain group members, the merging groups increase pressure toward differentiation and specialization.

The steep decline in within-group trades underscores the fact that sales regardless of costs are no longer pursued. Profitability has become so important strategically that high-charging Japanese firms are no longer willing to bail out group firms to maintain overall group stability. As a consequence, many firms do not expect their groups to continue, as many react to the new competitive environment by opting for less insurance with the benefit of greater strategic flexibility. Groups known to be competitive in nature, such as Sanwa or Sumitomo, are most likely to see this evolution. Even the Mitsubishi group, considered the most conservative, has reduced preferential trade and group ownership, because this type of insurance is no longer meaningful to many firms. Instead, a viable business group has to increase members' performance.

Although it is too early to identify how this will happen, the pooling and strategic deployment of group resources will have to play an important role. This might include pooled labor and the exchange of specialized knowledge in new technologies, or joint subsidiaries that facilitate longer-term technology bets at shared costs. Whatever it will be, the value proposition of keiretsu and main banks will be about forward progress and the ability to compete in dynamic and fast-changing global markets.

Newly created firms that combine spun-off business units, sometimes jointly owned by former companies, are emerging as industry leaders in a variety of intermediate product markets. Founded after 1998, these firms are not members of a group and do not have one predetermined main bank. Nor do they carry postwar-period baggage in terms of employment practices, loyalty to established trade relations, or other constraints from the previous century. As a result, the percentage of leading firms that describe themselves as group members is falling rapidly in industry after industry.

The decline in main bank and group relations is immediately visible in the reduction in cross-shareholdings. The banks' withdrawal was prescribed by law and therefore is not reversible. The ratio of listed firms' shares owned by other listed firms fell from 33 percent in 1990 to 10 percent in 2006. When this ratio showed a small uptick to 11 percent in 2007, some observers were quick to judge that this was Old Japan reemerging in a desperate search for protection from hostile takeovers.

However, in many instances these new tie-ups serve strategic business purposes unrelated to takeover defense. To the extent they are used as defense mechanisms, these are no longer predicated on business groups, and much more strategic than the old "no questions asked" stakes, and may occur in one industry, that is, across business groups. It is also important to recognize that defense mechanisms against takeovers are part and parcel of the move toward the market. The United States is widely regarded as having the most developed market for hostile takeovers, and yet it is also known for its leadership in developing legal technologies to defend against raiders. The two are really two sides of the same coin: a market for takeovers begets a market for takeover defenses. And as the market for hostile takeovers develops in Japan, there are fewer and fewer guarantees that corporate owners, especially of the Old Japan type, will always remain loyal and friendly.

6

OWNERSHIP: INSTITUTIONAL

INVESTORS, MERGERS AND ACQUISITIONS,

AND CORPORATE GOVERNANCE

The decline in business group relevance, the unwinding of cross-shareholdings, and the changing role of banks have greatly affected the composition of shareholders. Moreover, the wholesale changes in legal structure included the strengthening of shareholder rights, legal recourse, and the introduction of internal management control obligations through J-SOX. The emergence of a vibrant market for mergers and acquisitions, as well as for hostile takeovers, has fundamentally altered the incentives and management goals of Japanese business executives. Together, these developments have completely changed the mechanisms and processes of corporate governance in Japan.

The New Shareholders

Perhaps the most important development for New Japan finance and governance was the emergence of institutional investors in the form of Japanese trust banks, foreign trust accounts, and foreign and domestic buyout funds and private equity funds. For corporate governance, these are important because they hold big stakes, are professionally managed, and compete through returns on investment. Rarely are they stable shareholders, for when they find a company underperforming, they either sell their stock or assume an active role in influencing management to increase profitability. First sightings of such institutions in Japan were reported in the mid-1990s, when banks began to sell off the collateral underlying nonperforming loans at a discount, and they have become increasingly prominent since. Whereas at the height of the postwar system in the mid-1980s, corporations and banks together owned about 70 percent of the shares listed at the Tokyo Stock Exchange, by 2007 institutional investors had more than 40 percent of total holdings.

This remarkable shift is shown in figure 6.1. As of June 2007, foreigners represented the largest groups of investors at the TSE with 28 percent

6.1. *Ownership Percentages, by Type of Investor*

Source: TSE (2007), in % of total market capitalization, as of March of each year.

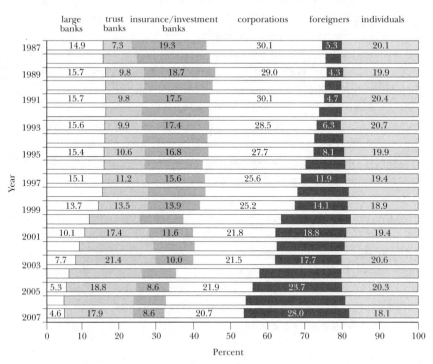

	large banks	trust banks	insurance/investment banks	corporations	foreigners	individuals
1987	14.9	7.3	19.3	30.1	5.3	20.1
1989	15.7	9.8	18.7	29.0	4.3	19.9
1991	15.7	9.8	17.5	30.1	4.7	20.4
1993	15.6	9.9	17.4	28.5	6.3	20.7
1995	15.4	10.6	16.8	27.7	8.1	19.9
1997	15.1	11.2	15.6	25.6	11.9	19.4
1999	13.7	13.5	13.9	25.2	14.1	18.9
2001	10.1	17.4	11.6	21.8	18.8	19.4
2003	7.7	21.4	10.0	21.5	17.7	20.6
2005	5.3	18.8	8.6	21.9	23.7	20.3
2007	4.6	17.9	8.6	20.7	28.0	18.1

Year

Percent

(in comparison, the share of foreign investors at the New York Stock Exchange was less than 10 percent at the time). Industries in which foreign investors held more than 30 percent in 2005 included pharmaceuticals (37%), insurance (35%), precision machinery (34%), electronics (33%), nonbank financial services (32.5%), and automobiles and real estate (both at 31%) (TSE 2006). In March 2006, 11 large listed companies had foreign ownership exceeding 50 percent, including Orix, Yamada Denki, Hoya, Rohm, Fujifilm Holdings, Canon, and Sony (*Nikkei,* June 19, 2006). Majority purchases of Japanese firms by foreign entities, such as by Renault of Nissan and Ford of Mazda in the automobile industry, further pushed this development. The April 2007 acquisition of 61 percent of Nikko Cordial by Citigroup was the largest foreign acquisition of a Japanese firm on record to date, worth $7.7 billion. Citigroup subsequently acquired the remaining 39 percent through a triangular merger.

Foreign Investors

Japan became attractive to foreign investors in the late 1990s for several reasons. The 1998 revision of the Foreign Exchange Law removed lingering vestiges of postwar cross-border financial controls, including restrictions on foreign direct investment, by abolishing all prior permission and notification requirements as well as the system of specialized foreign exchange banks, so that cross-border financial transactions became unrestricted for everyone, regardless of residency or status. To increase disclosure for monetary policy and statistical purposes, an ex post facto reporting system was introduced. This meant that foreign-based funds could freely invest in Japan, and Japanese households could open bank accounts abroad. Together with other legal and institutional reforms Japan had become a much easier financial market to invest in.

In the late 1990s, foreigners were also attracted to Japan for economic reasons. Some foresaw a steep loss in value of the dollar, caused by the growing U.S. trade and budget deficits, just when Japan's stock market looked undervalued. Indeed, the Nikkei 225 doubled from closing at 8,600 in 2002 to 17,200 in 2006. As the leading Japanese companies began their refocusing and restructuring, foreign investors sensed an opportunity.

A large portion of foreign investments were held as so-called street names. These were foreign trust administrators, led by State Street Bank & Trust Co. and Chase Manhattan Bank, London. These were mainly custodian holders for global institutional investors. However, not all investors labeled "foreign" by the Tokyo Stock Exchange represented foreign money, as some foreign trusts attracted large amounts of Japanese money. In addition to wealthy individuals, Japanese banks in particular were interested in such indirect investment, because they were cash rich during a period of zero-interest rates in which they had curbed their lending due to capital adequacy constraints and the nonperforming loan crisis (*Diamond Weekly* 2005).

The success of foreign private equity funds in Japan also spawned a domestic fund industry through start-ups headed by former bank employees. Although located close to the Tokyo Stock Exchange, these new firms were typically registered in tax havens such as the Cayman Islands and placed their trades out of low-fee locations such as Singapore. Although these funds were run by Japanese and invested Japanese money, they entered the TSE statistics as foreign investors (*Nikkei Weekly*, December 11, 2006). Regardless of who was behind the money, however, new investment methods had arrived, as these new investors aimed to maximize return on investment and would not suffer quietly through long episodes of subpar management.

Domestic Institutional Investors

A second important shift was the emergence of so-called megatrusts. As we can see from figure 6.1, all financial institutions (large commercial banks, trust banks, insurance companies, and others) reduced their holdings from a 41.5 percent in 1986 to 31.1 percent in 2007. Within that group, the shrinkage in bank and insurance company holdings was counterbalanced by a substantial increase in the role of trust banks, from less than 10 percent in the 1980s to 18.4 percent in 2006. Breaking this number down into subcategories reveals that mutual funds (*tōshi shintaku*) accounted for 4.4 percent of total shareholdings in 2006, whereas pension funds made up 3.6 percent (TSE 2007). This means that 10 percent of total shareholdings were so-called investment trusts, that is, pooled investments by corporations, banks, and others that are administered by trust banks.

During the postwar period, trust banks enjoyed special status within Japan's banking system, as they were banks (collecting deposits) that were also allowed to offer pooled securities investing (mutual funds), thus straddling the commercial and investment banking businesses that were separate in Japan until the 1990s. Although the seven postwar trust banks suffered badly after the collapse of the stock market bubble, they caught a second wind after merging into the newly established financial holdings in the early 2000s, when fund investing became popular. This partly was for the same reason that banks and corporations invested in foreign funds, that is, anonymous investments, and partly it was a reflection of shrewder investment by companies realizing that under zero-interest rates it was more advantageous to have retirement benefit reserves managed professionally.

Trust banks are mostly custodians for pooled investments. To streamline this administration, three megatrusts were founded. In 2000, the Japan Trustee Services Bank, Ltd. (Nihon turasuto saabisu shintaku ginkō) was established jointly by Sumitomo Trust and Banking, Resona Bank, and Mitsui Trust Holding. Referred to as a trust of trusts (*sai-shintaku*), this bank specializes in securities processing by administering the trust businesses of two of the four main banking groups. Although it also manages its own fund, 75 percent of its revenues were from fee income as of 2006. Assets under management stood at ¥75 trillion in 2002, and grew to ¥144 trillion (roughly $1.3 trillion) by March 2006. With this size, Japan Trustee Services now appears as a major shareholder for most large listed firms, often replacing the previous main banks as lead shareholder.

Similarly, the Master Trust Bank of Japan (Nihon masutaa turasuto shintaku ginkō) was founded in 2002 as the specialized trust investor of the Mitsubishi UFJ financial group. In addition to Mitsubishi UFJ Trust and Banking, Nippon

Life Insurance, and Meiji Yasuda Life Insurance, this bank also counted Nōchū Trust, the trust arm of the umbrella bank for all agricultural cooperatives, as a shareholder. With ¥106 trillion (almost $1 trillion) to invest, this bank became the second ubiquitous shareholder in the early 2000s, and 84 percent of its revenues in 2006 were generated through fee income.[1]

These trusts have begun to affect corporate management and the workings of the stock market. As custodians, trust banks vote on proxy, that is, as determined by the owner. However, it is typically not the investors but the retail institutions that determine votes, such as an investment bank, asset management firm, or a financial adviser.[2] These intermediaries compete for clients by offering high returns. And unlike some individual investors or corporations owning shares in certain companies, institutional investors care about the overall short-term return on their portfolio.

The differences with Japan's previous major shareholders could not be starker, because the new foreign and institutional investors have an opposite interest in corporate performance to that of Japanese banks in the postwar period (Ahmadjian 2007). Whereas banks pushed their clients toward diversification, professional investors diversify their portfolios themselves. To do this most successfully, they demand transparency and simplicity, and ideally want companies to be in one business only, easily comparable to its competitors. They then pick the most profitable or promising companies, and invest across a large number of industries. To appeal to these new investors, companies have to self-identify their core businesses and impress with performance. Rather than diversified and stable, companies have to become focused, nimble, and profitable. In 2007, Japan's Pension Fund Association announced that it would oppose the reappointment of directors at companies whose return on equity had stayed below 8 percent for three consecutive years (*Nikkei Weekly,* June 18, 2007). In the New Japan, companies that fail to attract and keep investors by showing performance face the risk of stocks being sold rapidly, making them potential takeover targets.

Mergers and Acquisitions: The Buyout Wave

At the turn of the century, corporate reorganization triggered, and in turn was propelled by, unprecedented activity in Japan's market for mergers and

1. See www.japantrustee.co.jp. Moreover, in 2001 the Mizuho Financial Group established Trust & Custody Services Bank, Ltd. (Shisan kanri saabisu shintaku ginkō, www.tcsb.co.jp). Owned by Mizuho (54%) and four life insurance companies that belong to that financial group, as of 2006 this company was investing assets of ¥94 trillion (roughly $900 billion).

2. Interviews with a Japanese asset management company, September 2006, and a Japanese buyout fund, February 2007. Both pointed out that shareholders interested in influencing management are unlikely to invest through funds, but rather hold their shares directly.

6.2. Mergers and Acquisitions, by Number of Deals, 1986–2006
Sources: Nomura (2005, 2006); *Japan Times*, April 28, 2007.

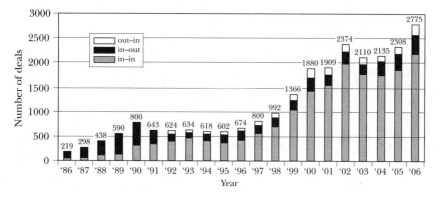

acquisitions (M&A). The steep increase in the number of deals after 1998, which tripled to reach almost 2,800 in 2006, is shown in figure 6.2. In addition, the chart bespeaks of a qualitative shift in M&A. Differentiating between types of deals, we see that until 1990 the majority of M&A in Japan were "in-out" deals (Japanese acquisitions of foreign firms). In contrast, by 2006 the ratio of those deals had shrunk to 15 percent, while so-called out-in deals, whereby foreigners purchase Japanese assets, climbed to 7 percent. The main reason for the increase in activity is clearly the upsurge in domestic deals, from a level of roughly 600 per year in the mid-1990s, to almost 2,200 in 2006 (as discussed below, this includes deals by foreign private equity funds operating in Japan). In terms of value of these transactions, data are available only for public deals, which account for 20 percent to 40 percent of total transactions. These data exhibit a similarly dramatic rise: whereas until 1997 the annual value of domestic M&A was less than ¥2 trillion, it jumped to the ¥10 trillion level in 1999, and reached ¥15 trillion (roughly $130 billion) in 2006 (Nomura 2006; *Nikkei*, January 9, 2007).

The bars in figure 6.3 differentiate between types of M&A between 1993 and 2005. The lowest bar shows that mergers (a marriage between equals) account for only a small portion of all deals and have not increased much. The growth in activity is attributable to takeovers (dark-gray bar), the purchase of assets from another company, and the purchase of minority stakes in other companies. Survey data that break down M&A deals by objective support this notion, as almost two thirds of deals in the early 21st century were made to strengthen an existing business by purchasing either assets or entire organizations from competitors. In contrast, entering a new business, which accounted for a quarter of domestic deals until the mid-1990s, has become negligible (Nomura 2006).

6.3. Domestic M&A Deals, in Number, by Type of Deal
Source: Nomura (2005, 2006).

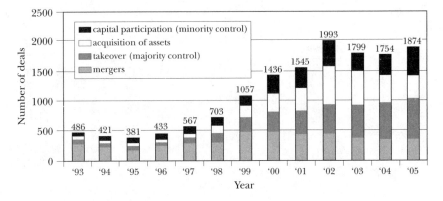

A more critical view of Japanese M&A is that the recent growth notwith-standing, the market remains small. In 2004, total global mergers topped $2 trillion, but Japan accounted for only 4.3 percent of that total (Dhaliwall 2005; Rowley 2005). And Japan's 2,775 deals in 2006 compared to almost 13,700 in the U.S. and over 14,700 in Europe during that year (*Japan Times,* April 28, 2007). However, observers expected the Japanese M&A market to quadruple in the coming decade, once remaining barriers to that market are removed. These barriers include: (1) human capital (building of expertise in analysis and information brokerage); (2) corporate knowledge of M&A strat-egies; (3) infrastructure that supports new business creation (ranging from ease of starting a new firm to societal bias against failure); (4) legal infrastruc-ture; and (5) related services such as law firms specializing in M&A (ESRI 2004). Since the Japanese government offered this analysis in 2004, great strides have been made in all of these areas. Therefore, even though Japan's M&A market may still be comparatively small, it is growing rapidly, and the infrastructure—supporting industries such as litigation and financial lawyers, securities analysts, and the legal environment—is evolving to accommodate a growing market.

Foreign Private Equity Funds

The fast growth of Japan's M&A market was fueled by the happy en-counter of rising demand for Japanese companies with the supply of objects in great variety and at low prices. In the early 2000s, financial intermediaries that had first surfaced on Wall Street in the 1980s reemerged globally in the form of hedge funds and private equity funds. The discounted sale of collateral for nonperforming loans made Japan an investment opportunity, just at a time when the United States was reaching the peak of a real estate cycle, so that properties in Japan were comparatively cheap. As Japanese banks switched to direct bad-loan disposal methods after 1998, and with added emphasis in 2002, they either liquidated companies and sold the collateral in a fire sale, or they restructured the client by selling off the least profitable businesses. In other cases, banks structured debt forgiveness and swapped debt into equity shares, which they sold off at only a few cents for each dollar of bad debt. Suddenly there was a market for real estate and buildings, shares in turnaround projects, and business units that were being spun off. For 2006 alone, the Bank of Japan estimated that of ¥5.26 trillion ($45 billion) worth of foreign direct investment in Japan, 95 percent occurred through mergers and acquisitions (*Nikkei*, April 4, 2007).

Buyout funds pool private investments and specialize in buying up companies or assets at a discount price, to restructure these for sale at a higher price. Perhaps the first contemporary buyout fund that attracted general interest to this industry in the United States was Kohlberg Kravis Roberts & Co. with its takeover of RJR Nabisco in the 1980s (KKR also contributed to the industry's image as vultures for breaking RJR Nabisco into pieces). In the 1990s, these funds once again caught attention for their large and bold deals, at a time when high-wealth individuals, pension funds, and other institutional investors were in search of more aggressive investments. Funds differ by area of specialization. Hedge funds may focus on derivatives that promise arbitrage opportunities, while others aim at one particular type of investment, such as real estate.

Among the first foreign investors with a keen interest in Japan's renewal were financial firms (such as GE Capital), insurance companies, and investment banks, followed by private equity funds. Ripplewood's 1999 purchase of Long-Term Credit Bank, followed by Lone Star's acquisition of Tokyo Sowa Bank, and Cerberus's investment in Aozora Bank were important early examples. A bit more quietly, Goldman Sachs and Lone Star began to purchase resort hotels and golf courses. These initial investments were aimed at the depressed real estate market as well as at mismanaged firms whose asset value was clearly above market valuation. The foreign funds buying these bargain assets came to be known as "vulture funds" (*hagetaka fando*). According to one estimate, between 1997 and 2002 the vultures bought more than ¥30 trillion ($250 billion) worth of distressed assets (Kawakami 2002). A 2007 TV drama series titled *Hagetaka* ("Vultures"), featuring a former Japanese banker returning to Japan as an employee of a Wall Street firm to buy up Japan, turned into an unexpected hit, as it discussed the pros and cons of market discipline on management versus business based on long-term trust relationships. The TV soap even came with a booklet and a website explaining technical terms such as "golden parachute," "proxy fight," or "white knight."[3] Japan's emerging market for corporate control, and the need for Japanese firms to restructure to defend against unwanted raiders, had made its way into Japanese living rooms.

A second wave of foreign fund activities beginning about 2006 resulted from Japan's economic recovery. Rather than seeking dud leftovers from the bubble period, the new focus was on identifying viable yet underperforming companies to launch a management turnaround through reorganization funds. In early 2007 KKR launched a new Asia fund worth $4 billion, of which $2 billion was said to be directed at healthy subsidiaries of major Japanese firms undergoing "choose and focus" reorganization. In its 2007 White Paper on the Japanese Economy, the government lauded M&As as an efficient way to address Japan's lingering structural inefficiencies. As if on cue, Morgan Stanley's April 2007 purchase of 13 hotels from the airline All Nippon Airways, which was undergoing "choose and focus," marked the largest real estate deal on record in Japan to date.[4]

This second wave of foreign investments was sustained by ongoing legal revisions, in particular the 2006 Corporation Law. In addition to the early entrants, by 2007 the leading foreign investment funds in Japan were CVC Capital Partners, Permira, the Texas Pacific Group, and the Carlyle Group. Fueling the fund growth was a new interest by Japanese institutions such as life insurance companies and pension funds in higher investment yields. In early 2007 funds were estimated to have almost tripled their capital earmarked for Japan over 24 months, to ¥4 trillion ($34 billion). Of these, more than half were raised by foreign funds, even though according to one estimate foreigners provided barely more than 10 percent of total fund capitalization.[5]

Domestic Funds

The success of U.S. funds naturally also attracted Japanese players. The first independent Japanese buyout fund, Advantage Partners, was established in 1997 and continues to be one of the industry leaders. At the turn of the century, it was joined by some of Japan's more aggressive venture capital firms,

---

3. www.nhk.or.jp/hagetaka/keyword/keyword01.html.
4. *Nikkei Weekly,* April 16, 2007; *Japan Times,* July 12, 2007, *Japan Times,* July 8, 2007.
5. See *Diamond Weekly* (2005); *Nikkei,* May 16, 2006; *Nikkei,* November 22, 2006; *Nikkei,* January 15, 2007; *Nikkei,* March 28, 2007.

such as JAFCO and Tokio Marine Capital, which, with the burst of the IT bubble, identified new opportunities in corporate reorganization.[6]

As of late 2006 more than 230 domestic funds were estimated to operate in Japan, with ¥2.8 trillion ($23 billion) under investment. This was a significant increase over 2005, when 108 funds were estimated to have raised ¥1.8 trillion (roughly $15 billion). Many of these funds were subsidiaries of banks, insurance companies, general trading companies and corporations, such as Aozora Investment Co., Hirogin Capital Co., Millennia Venture Partners, Nikko Antfactory, ORIX Capital, Sojitz Private Equity, or Mitsui Ventures. Banks used affiliated buyout funds to accelerate the reorganization of deadbeat clients: by buying out the assets underlying their own nonperforming loan portfolios, they created an upside potential with these restructurings through debt-equity swaps (Kawakami 2003; MRI/Chikusei 2004). Beginning in the late 1990s independent investment funds also became prominent, such as MKS Partners and Unison Capital. The introduction of the limited liability partnership as a legal organization in 2006 allowed funds to reward partners according to their own track record, which has attracted new funds as well as new talent.

The industry received a further push through a government infusion in 2001, when in support of the government's revitalization program the Development Bank of Japan (DBJ) received a special budget of $900 million to invest in "corporate revival funds," which were geared toward pushing reorganization of smaller firms in rural Japan. This triggered the formation, in 2002, of Phoenix Capital, a joint venture between Tokyo Mitsubishi Bank and DBJ that became an industry leader with ¥172 billion ($1.4 billion) invested in 2007 (*Nikkei,* January 15, 2007).

One reason for the fast growth of fund investments was the rise in management buyouts (MBOs), whereby investors and management cooperate to take the firm private and structure a turnaround. The advantage is that restructuring can be accomplished without ongoing stock market pressure on performance. In 2006, 80 MBOs valued at ¥687 billion (about $5.7 billion) were recorded, which was three times their value in 2005.[7]

The sudden surge in M&A activities and MBOs has also greatly benefited the banking industry by opening new business opportunities in financing highly leveraged deals. According to one industry estimate, buyout funds borrowed three to five times the size of their funds. In early 2007, investment funds reported to have earmarked funds of ¥4 trillion for Japan, meaning that they

---

6. Interview, Tokio Marine Capital, January 2005, Tokyo. See chapter 10 on Japanese venture capital.

7. *Nikkei,* January 15, 2007.

were ready to invest ¥20 trillion (about $160 billion), of which ¥16 trillion (about $130 billion) would be raised from the banking sector. Japan's banks had cleaned up their nonperforming loan portfolios and were once again willing to engage in high-risk, high-return lending, especially as corporate loans remained sluggish in the early 2000s (*Nikkei,* January 15, 2007). Meanwhile foreign banks, led by Citigroup, HSBC, and Merrill Lynch, saw crisp demand for bridge-bank operations and LBO financing as a brilliant opportunity to position themselves as leading players in Tokyo.

Perhaps the clearest indication of the banks' new risk attitude was the fast growth of very highly leveraged management buyouts. The number of such deals—which use the assets of the takeover target as collateral—quadrupled, from less than five in 1998 to over 20 in 2006, reaching almost ¥2.5 trillion ($20 billion). In 2006, the leveraged financing market was forecast to grow to over ¥10 trillion within a decade (about $800 billion). The first leveraged deal exceeding ¥1 trillion was Softbank's 2006 financing of its purchase of J-Phone from Vodafone. In 2007, Japan Tobacco's acquisition of Britain's Gallaher Group for $15 billion marked Japan's biggest takeover of a foreign company to date.[8]

Hostile Takeovers

In 2005, one third of all M&A (or 690 deals) were majority acquisitions (see figure 6.3). These come in two flavors: friendly and hostile. In a friendly acquisition, the target agrees with the deal, a fair price is agreed on, and executive management of the target may remain involved in running the business. In contrast, hostile takeovers typically involve fierce battles which often end in price run-ups and even lawsuits.

Traditionally, Japan has had very few hostile takeovers. One reason may be an element of "saving face"—by no means singular to Japan but possibly more pronounced there—that entices parties to label an acquisition friendly even when it is not. More important, until 1999 minority shareholders were not obligated to surrender their shares to a bidder, and extensive cross-shareholdings often made it impossible for the bidder to gain complete control. Even where stable shareholdings were not a factor, capital-gains taxes applied to the sale of shares even in a hostile takeover bid, making many minority owners unwilling to surrender their shares voluntarily (Higashino 2004b, 2004c). The 1999 revision of this system undermined the role of cross-shareholdings as a powerful

---

8. See *Nikkei,* January 9, 2007; *Nikkei,* January 15, 2007; *Nikkei,* April 20, 2007; *Nikkei,* April 27, 2007.

takeover defense. It has also invited unprecedented takeover activity, as well as new defense mechanisms against hostile raids.

Uninvited yet successful takeover bids increased from 14 in 1998 to 79 in 2006 (see figure 6.4), when the total estimated value reached ¥3 trillion ($24 billion). If deals reported as "mergers" in order to save face were included, these numbers would be higher still. The majority of these hostile takeovers were launched by Japanese corporations acquiring competitors. Following Livedoor's 2005 bid for a broadcasting station, the first openly fought-out battles within one industry occurred in 2006. The August bid by Oji Paper to acquire Hokuetsu Paper for its advanced production facilities was a true "choose and focus" bid in that Oji attempted to acquire a direct competitor in order to establish dominance of the domestic paper market. In the same month, menswear retailer Aoki launched a hostile bid for Futata, a competitor with a presence in Kyushu that Aoki lacked. Both battles occupied headlines for a long time, though neither was ultimately successful. However, both resulted in a reshuffling of their industries, as the targets then tied up with another competitor to strengthen their market positions. The high profile of the two concurrent intraindustry battles caught the public's attention. The fact that both battles were fought by very traditional companies in mature industries signaled that hostile takeovers had reached Old Japan, and that new competitive positioning was likely to trigger an even bigger hostile takeover wave (*Sankei Shinbun*, August 9, 2006).

In reaction to this sharp increase in takeovers, the 2005 Takeover Guideline expanded management choices in defending against hostile bids, by validating a poison pill in the form of new warrant issues that dilute the raider's

6.4. *Successful Hostile Takeovers Bids, 1995–2006*
Sources: Fujioka (2006); *Nikkei*, April 1, 2007.

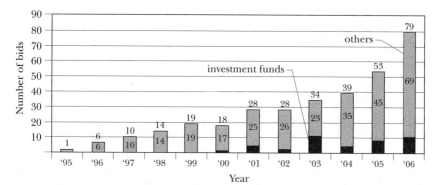

stake.[9] The 2006 Corporation Law made these rules binding, and also clarified the role of shareholders in the process of building and executing defense mechanisms. Shareholders now have a choice of issuing a carte blanche for such mechanisms or of insisting on ratification each time new defense schemes are crafted. This means that over time Japanese companies will come to differ in the extent to which shareholders can affect takeover battles (Miyazaki 2006; *Nikkei,* June 27, 2006).

Some observers feared that these new rules would lead to a plethora of defense tactics. However, as of October 2007, only 10 percent of listed Japanese companies had either adopted or decided to adopt poison pills. More than half of these adopters showed below-average performance, with return on equity well below the average 8.3 percent at that time. Among those that decided against the adoption of poison pills, many felt that they were ineffective. Rather than structuring legal mechanisms, these firms aimed to attract long-term shareholders by improving their performance.[10]

One subject of heated debate in 2006, was a one-year ban on so-called triangular mergers by foreigners that was to be lifted in May 2007. Foreign journalists had interpreted this one-year ban as a sign of Old Japan clamping down against foreign investors. In reality, triangular mergers are not ordinarily used for hostile takeovers. This is because rather than using cash to buy out a company, in a triangular merger the foreign company establishes a local unit that purchases the Japanese firm by swapping ownership shares, so that Japanese investors receive shares in the foreign parent. Such swaps are predicated on a friendly exchange. Indeed, the lifting of the ban in May 2007 did not trigger hostile foreign bids. The only side effect of allowing such international stock swaps was renewed interest by foreign firms in being listed on the Tokyo Stock Exchange, to facilitate friendly mergers of this type (*Nikkei,* April 17, 2007).

As of 2007 the main defense mechanism against a hostile bid was to issue warrants with special rights only to friendly shareholders, thereby diluting the raider's stake and making the bid much more expensive if not impossible. Issuing such warrants can be decided by the board of directors if the shareholders

9. Milhaupt (2005) and Milhaupt and Pistor (2008) discuss the adaptation of Delaware takeover rules in Japan. See MOJ and METI (2005) for the "Guidelines for Corporate Value Protection" (Takeover Guidelines) and CVSG (2006).

10. *Nikkei,* April 19, 2007; *Nikkei Weekly,* June 18, 2007; *Japan Times,* March 19, 2007; *Nikkei,* October 15, 2007. Some industries were more aggressive in seeking defense mechanisms; for example, 17.5% of Japan's steel companies had adopted antitakeover measures (in addition to rapid industry consolidation), followed by 13.6% of companies in land transportation (i.e., railways).

agreed at the annual meeting; otherwise, the board has to call an extraordinary meeting. The main difference between Old Japan and New Japan are the shareholders' incentives as they vote on this proposal. In Old Japan, the lead shareholders were the main bank and other members of the business group, and they were in a quid-pro-quo deal not to sell in time of crisis. In New Japan, the lead shareholders are funds, foreigners, individuals, and corporations. They may have idiosyncratic reasons to side with the target, but they also face a new temptation: the takeover premium. There is a significant body of research for the United States that shows that almost all stock market gains in an acquisition accrue to the owners of the target firm. For example, Andrade, Mitchell, and Stafford (2002) report a three-day abnormal gain of 16 percent after the merger announcement in the 1980s and 1990s.[11] For the 79 hostile takeovers in Japan in 2006, the average premium earned by target firm shareholders was 25.8 percent (meaning that the stock price increased by that much over the firm's average stock price for the three-month period before the bid). For 2005, this premium stood at an average 19.3 percent (*Nikkei*, April 1, 2007). At a time when profitability and returns on investment are valued highly by banks, companies, and individuals alike, it could be delusional for the target firm to count on shareholders to be stable in the event of a hostile takeover. The only way to ensure stable shareholders in this new setting is to improve operations so as to promise higher long-term returns on the stable investment than the short-term gain through selling out.

The increase in hostile takeovers has affected Japan's business organization in important ways. Obviously hostile bids for competitors increase industry consolidation if successful, but even if fended off they can lead to new alliances or even mergers among competitors, enabling them to resist the industry leaders' forays. This has already happened in Japan's paper, clothing, and confectionary industries, among others. But more important, the threat of hostile takeovers has greatly sharpened the sensitivity of Japanese business executives to their financial performance and the necessity to compete more strongly. The objective of a hostile takeover is typically to purchase an underperforming company, replace its management and business model, and improve the company's performance. The best defense against such a takeover is for management to undertake these reforms by itself, to ensure that its stock price is not underperforming. Therefore, whether or not a hostile bid is launched or is eventually successful is not as relevant to managerial discipline as is the constant potential threat of a hostile bid, and this threat has arrived in Japan.

11. See also Bruner (2001), Moeller, Schlingemann, and Stulz (2005).

Bull-Dog Sauce vs. Steel Partners

Following on the heals of Livedoor's Horie receiving a jail sentence for accounting fraud after his 2005 takeover bid of a broadcasting station, in June 2007 the Bulldog-Sauce Company's defense against Steel Partners, a U.S. hedge fund, caused great furor. Over a period of several years, Steel Partners had bought stakes in more than 30 mostly medium-sized companies that had been identified as underperformers with high turnaround potential. In some of these, Steel Partners worked with management to improve operations, but where it met resistance the fund attempted to assume control and replace management. On May 18, 2007, Steel Partners launched a hostile bid for Bull-Dog Sauce Co., based on a 10.52 percent ownership stake. Bull-Dog Sauce had a 28 percent market share of condiment sauces, and after the successful acquisition of smaller rival Ikari Sauce Co. was posting slow profit increases. As of May 2007, the company did not have any approved defense measures.

In response to Steel Partners' bid Bull-Dog declared it would ask shareholders for permission to issue special rights warrants to all shareholders, except the raider, at the shareholders' meeting on June 24, where it needed 66 percent of the votes. Steel Partners filed for a provisional injunction in the Tokyo District Court, and increased its offering price by 7 percent, to ¥1,700. When the injunction was not granted, Steel Partners sued for discrimination. Meanwhile, the shareholders approved the defense and rejected the bid, diluting Steel Partners' stake to below 3 percent. On July 9, the Tokyo High Court ruled that the issuance of warrants only to some shareholders did not violate shareholder equality, and characterized the U.S. fund as an "abusive acquirer" and therefore unequal to other shareholders by nature. On August 7, 2007, the Supreme Court upheld this decision. However, this poison pill cost the company an estimated ¥3 billion ($25 million). On July 11, the day of "victory," Bull-Dog's share price plummeted to ¥725 and trading was discontinued as shareholders rushed to sell their shares before they were diluted by the new warrant issues. By August 2007, the stock had fallen 62 percent, to ¥630.[12]

Although the court's ruling made it easier for other companies to activate defense mechanisms, the irony of the tremendous losses incurred by the target did not go unnoticed by the public. The case brought to a boiling point the trade-off between financial indicators of success and the human elements of small firm management. Opponents of Steel Partners' bid argued that Bull-Dog was doing just fine and offering secure employment to its workforce. Supporters claimed that Bull-Dog could be doing even better. In March 2007, the

---

12. These events were widely chronicled in the Japanese press. For an English-language source, see *Japan Times* between June 30, 2007, and August 9, 2007.

business magazine *Ekonomisuto* published an in-depth report on Steel Partners' Japanese investments since December 2003, and concluded that these were all long term and focused on firms with a high equity ratio but very low return on equity. Disagreeing with the courts, the article saw Steel Partners as a value investor (Kikuchi 2007).

The public debate was complicated by the fact that the majority of hostile bids in 2007 were launched by Japanese firms, so that the equation of foreigners equaling vultures could not be upheld. Even as the Bull-Dog battle raged, the IT start-up firm Rakuten attempted, eventually in vain, to raise its stake in Tokyo Broadcasting System to over 20 percent in April 2007. The very fact that takeover battles made it to the front pages of the daily newspapers for most of the summer was yet another sign that the market—for companies, for ideas, and for the law—had arrived.

Corporate Governance: From Contingent to Continuous Oversight

The growing market for corporate control has also brought great changes in Japan's system of corporate governance. This refers to the processes by which shareholders (owners) can incentivize and monitor management such that executives will employ their informational advantages about the firm fully in the interests of owners. One way to structure an analysis of system change in corporate governance is to assume a functional perspective that posits that there are three core objectives to corporate governance: (1) to protect providers of capital (financial and human); (2) to manage asymmetric information; and (3) to monitor management. Different countries, at different points in time, have different institutions to fulfill these three functions, such as a market for takeovers as opposed to a house bank. From this perspective, when systems change, the attention of analysis is directed at identifying old and new key actors in the process of performing the three main functions of governance (Crane and Schaede 2006).

Japan has typically been described as a bank-centered type of corporate governance, comparable to Germany, in contrast to more market-oriented systems such as the Anglo-Saxon varieties. As we saw in the previous chapter, in this system the bank's exposure as a large investor and shareholder induced efforts at oversight of management. Other investors trusted the bank's superior corporate information. Few independent agents monitored companies, and hostile takeovers were rare. When a company fell into distress, the main bank assumed the lead role in protecting the providers of capital, by restructuring debt and ensuring survival. This system led Sheard (1989) to argue that the main bank is a functional equivalent to the market for corporate control. However, the difference between the two has great implications for the incentives posed to managers. Whereas the market evaluates performance in relation to potential, the main bank looks at long-term growth but intervenes only when a company is in serious trouble. However, the strategic inflection point has changed Japan's system, by replacing the main bank as the leading governance institution with the market.

Using the functional perspective, such system change is analyzed by looking at three areas: reforms that affect the providers of capital, changes in the flow and dissemination of corporate information, and new processes of monitoring the activities of management. Although these three are ultimately interrelated—for example, good management monitoring serves to protect the providers of capital—analysis is helped by looking at these three separately.

Protecting the Providers of Capital

The critical providers of capital in this context are financial investors (owners and lenders).[13] These face two main challenges: how to trust the pricing mechanism of the stock and bond markets, and how to ensure that they can extricate their investment whenever they want to. In Japan, both of these have greatly changed with the strategic inflection point.

Before the unraveling of stable shareholdings after 1998, the Tokyo Stock Exchange was often considered a thin (i.e., illiquid) market. Stocks could be subject to price manipulations, while exit was not always immediately possible. However, the decline in stable shareholdings, advances in trading technologies, and new regulation of insider trading greatly improved access to and the flow of stock trading. Brokerage fee deregulation and Internet-based trading have undermined the erstwhile dominant role of investment banks. In combination, all this has made the Japanese market much more liquid, improved the integrity of the market and afforded investors new protection. New bankruptcy legislation set another milestone for investor protection. In informal main bank workouts loss allocation used to be uncertain. The new laws have introduced cut-and-dried rules on process and court procedures. The risk of investing or lending in Japan can now be estimated with much greater precision.

Dissemination of Accurate Corporate Information

Before the 1998 Big Bang and its new accounting and disclosure rules, access to accurate corporate information was a challenge in Japan. However,

---

13. Another important provider of capital is labor, and Japan has long been cited as a case of "stakeholder" governance, whereby the concern of stakeholders such as employees or suppliers are considered more critical than those of owners. The shift within Japan toward the strategic relevance of profits has greatly affected this system, for rather than being an end in itself, labor has become a means to achieve overall corporate strategic goals.

since 2000 consolidated accounting has ruled out old habits of hiding un-profitable businesses in privately held subsidiaries. When the accounts of the failed Hyogo Bank were opened in 1995, regulators were stunned to see that the actual losses were a multiple of what the bank's books had led them to believe, because in addition to accumulating its own losses, 15 affiliated financial institutions had served as depositories for the bank's nonperforming loans (Schaede 1998). Under the new rules, this is no longer possible. Moreover, mandatory quarterly earnings reports have greatly improved the timeliness of Japanese corporate information.

A further push toward transparency came with the introduction of mark-to-market evaluation of corporate stockholdings in 2001. Whereas previously banks and companies were allowed to declare their extensive shareholdings at book values (i.e., the purchase price), these now have to be valued at the current stock price. Throughout the postwar period, Japanese banks and corporations had claimed to look poorer than they were because the market had increased so much since they had bought their portfolios. This situation reversed itself with the 1990s reduction of the Nikkei index by half, causing many stocks to fall below the purchase price of the bubble period. The 2001 shift has eliminated uncertainty over the value of a company's shareholding portfolio.

The "sunshine laws" of accounting and disclosure requirements of the early 2000s were pushed further with the 2007 introduction of J-SOX, Japan's version of U.S. rules on internal controls to ensure full and accurate provision of financial information. Triggered by a series of accounting scandals, including those of Livedoor Co., Seibu Railway Co., and Kanebo Ltd. in 2004, as well as Nikko Cordial and Sanyo in 2006, these new rules were written into the 2007 Financial Instruments and Exchange Law. Listed companies and their consolidated subsidiaries now have to certify the accuracy of their financial statements. With that, managers can no longer claim ignorance or blame lower-tiered employees for inaccuracies. The reliability of the financial information of Japanese companies has been greatly improved.[14]

In addition to the quality of information, a second aspect to the asymmetric information challenge in corporate governance is the dissemination of information to all investors. Japan's securities industry has been truly transformed in this respect, as there is now an open market for corporate financial information. Competition with foreign rating agencies such as Standard & Poor's has made Japanese rating institutions more credible. Competition among TV

---

14. See, for example, the January 2007 special issue of *Shūkan Daiyamondo* titled "Naibu tōsei jigoku: Nihon-pan SOX-hō ga kaisha o osou" ("Internal Control Hell: How J-SOX Is an Challenge for Companies"); also Shimizu (2006).

stations and magazines has turned features on investing from simple sales pitches into more meaningful analysis. Competition for investors has driven most Japanese companies to provide ample investor relation information on their corporate websites. All in all, both quality and accessibility of information have been greatly enhanced.

Management Monitoring

The third functional category of corporate governance is the oversight of management. Here, system change relates to the role and rights of shareholders vis-à-vis corporate executives, as well as rules and regulations on means of compensation (e.g., stock options), the composition and tasks of the board of directors (e.g., inside vs. outside directors), and the accountability of the management team for its actions.

In the postwar period, most Japanese boards of directors consisted exclusively of insiders, as the promotion of an employee to the level of director (e.g., head of a business unit or function) automatically meant promotion to the board. To what extent these directors exercised governance is unclear, but we know of only one case, Mitsukoshi, in the entire postwar period where a president of a large firm was ousted by his board. Although directors were not compensated nearly as highly as executives elsewhere, perquisites were bountiful. There was no outside market for senior managers, and the chief executive was instrumental in selecting his successor from among the directors. Extending one's tenure as a director by being promoted to advanced levels of directorship was lucrative, as it meant collecting multiple lump-sum retirement payouts.

Shareholders came in two flavors, stable owners and general shareholders. Stable owners, as we have seen, were often group member firms and banks. The group may have engaged in informal oversight, as the Presidents' Council of the Big 6 keiretsu met regularly. In times of crisis, the group bank brought in a turnaround team, and eventually replaced management. Although there was some turnover at the top related to performance, the successor to the president was ordinarily another in-house executive.

General shareholders had only limited voice. Shareholder rights were narrowly prescribed by law, and except for approving dividend payments shareholders had little say about financials. Neither were they typically asked about decisions to diversify into new businesses; dating back to a 1950 revision of the Commercial Code, they did not even have to approve changes in a company's bylaws (Wakasugi 2006). Their main function was to agree with the promotion of a set of executives to the director level, which they would usually do due to lack of information about these or other internal candidates.

This system worked, by and large, because in-house executives had been screened over their lifetime careers to pursue the interests of their organization. Moreover, the ex ante nature of the Commercial Code limited management's freedom to devise new schemes. For example, stock swaps to affect a merger or acquisition were not allowed, and there were tight rules on equity and bond issues. Managers could not outrageously overpay themselves. Thus, although shareholders were given little influence, management was also constrained.

Still, occasional managerial mishaps and even wrongdoings could have triggered discontent among general shareholders. To curb potential interference, in the early postwar period many companies hired special "professionals" related to the *yakuza* (mafia), paying them to deny activist shareholders access and intimidate those who still dared to speak out at the annual meeting. Over time, these *sōkaiya* turned the table on management and extorted money by threatening to publish embarrassing information. To further diminish access for noisy attendees, companies began to hold annual meetings on the same day in late June, so that activist shareholders—who were thought to own shares of more than one company—could attend only one meeting. At the peak of this custom, in 1997, 2,350 companies held their annual meeting on the same day; by 2004, the number had declined to 1,500. In a country known for slow deliberation processes and seemingly endless ceremonial gatherings, shareholder meetings came to last less than 45 minutes, with an average of 25 minutes reported in the early 1990s (*Nikkei*, June 22, 2006).

The postbubble recession and the nonperforming loan disaster brought inescapable pressure to change all this (Ahmadjian 2003; Itami 2005). The first reforms, in 1990, targeted the internal corporate auditing system. Soon thereafter, some of the leading multinationals, led by Sony, moved to reduce the size of their boards of directors, simply by not automatically promoting every senior manager to the board. Instead, some of these managers became "corporate executive officers" (*shikkō yakuin;* i.e., a head of a business unit or a function who is not a member of the board). Distinguishing different types of directors was an easy way to reduce the size of boards that had grown tremendously (with aggressive diversification, some boards had 70 directors), and this was a first step toward placing greater responsibility onto the board.

Another move in the late 1990s was to appoint outside directors—board members that had never been employed by the company or one of its subsidiaries. In general, the idea is that outside directors can provide unbiased strategic advice because of their distance from the nitty-gritty details of daily management routines. Although it was applauded as a major change in Japanese corporate governance at the time, in reality the effects remained limited.

In a 2000 survey of 1,310 large firms, fewer than 20 percent had outside directors, and this represented no change from 1990 (Ahmadjian 2003).

More substantial reform occurred with the Commercial Code revision of 2002, when a committee system was introduced. A company adopting this system has to establish three board committees—audit, nomination, and compensation—with at least half of the committee members being outside directors. This system is even stricter than in the United States where a company may establish one or all of these committees. Together with the simultaneous introduction of different types of shares, stock options, and increased possibilities for corporate reorganization through mergers and acquisitions, these changes opened the door to new processes of governance. The committee system was written into the 2006 Cooperation Law and adoption has increased since then (Hashimoto 2002; Wakasugi 2006).

Yet again, although celebrated as a major breakthrough, the effects remained negligible, as only 5 percent of large firms adopted the committee system within the first three years. Even for those few firms, the committee system did little to change the role of general shareholders in monitoring management. Moreover, critics voiced doubts as to whether the nominating committee would be co-opted by the company leadership, that is, it would be chosen to reflect executive interests.[15]

Real system change, however, came with the 2006 Corporation Law. As outlined in chapter 2, this law completely reworked the established legal logic, and no company was offered a choice on this. In turn for new managerial flexibility, the law greatly empowers shareholders. Managers can now be held liable for their actions through derivative lawsuits brought by a shareholder on behalf of the company. The processes for such suits have been streamlined and shareholders have standing to sue even if a company were to engage in stock transfers or other tactics to curtail shareholder rights. As a result, the number of derivative suits jumped from 31 cases for the 1950–93 period to an annual level of over 160 in the early 2000s.[16]

Perhaps the most important of the new shareholder powers is that any change in the company's bylaws now requires a two-thirds majority vote at the annual shareholders' meeting (also stricter than in the United States,

15. See Itami (2005). This has also been shown for the United States: in about 80% of Fortune 500 companies in the 1990s, the chief executive officer was also the chairman of the board, and thus in charge of assembling nominating and compensation committees (Belliveau, O'Reilly, and Wade 1996).

16. West (2001) and Milhaupt and West (2004) analyze the role of derivative lawsuits in changing managerial incentives. Data from Nipponkoa (2006) and NKK (2003) show that the combined number of regional and high court cases reached a high of 220 in 1999 and 206 in 2000, and has stayed at over 160 a year since then.

where a simple majority suffices). Other important decisions now also require shareholder approval, including (1) approval of the budget and balance sheet; (2) executive compensation and stock options; (3) mergers and acquisition, both as raider and as target; (4) hostile takeover defense mechanisms, and (5) the appointment of directors. Although this may look fairly standard, except for the last all these had previously been decided by management itself (Fujita 2006).

The Corporation Law also tightened rules on auditors, whose responsibilities were expanded from the previous accounting audits to include operational audits. In large companies, auditors have to be true outsiders, and they are responsible for reporting also on corporate activities that could be detrimental to the firm (e.g., introducing takeover defenses, merging with or acquiring another company, or expanding into new businesses) (Takehara and Nihei 2006). Thus, the previous internal approach to corporate governance based on consensus and an overlap of board and management has been replaced by much clearer processes. The FSA also strengthened its stance as a watchdog, as became evident during the Livedoor accounting fraud case of 2005 and the subsequent criminal prosecution of related instances of insider trading.

In addition, pluralist shareholder interests and the arrival of a market for corporate control have greatly changed the incentives for corporate executives. New voting rights for owners are expected to fuel shareholder activism. One indication of change is the much increased voting at annual shareholder meetings. In 2006 the Tokyo Stock Exchange expanded e-voting to institutional investors. In the past, these had often been overburdened with paper ballots given that so many firms scheduled their annual meetings at the same time. An analysis of 2006 annual shareholder meetings found that more institutional investors voted, and fewer engaged in carte-blanche proxy voting (*Nikkei,* June 26, 2006). E-voting was also expected to curb the influence of *sōkaiya* by undermining their ability to coerce votes.

From Contingent to Continuous Monitoring

Japan's new market for corporate control has replaced the main bank as a major monitoring agent of large Japanese corporations. This marks a reversal in the logic of corporate governance in Japan that is best described as a shift away from contingent monitoring to continuous oversight. In postwar Japan, monitoring was activated only by a true crisis event. The main bank, relying on its information gathered over years of repeated interactions with the company, intervened in management only if a client went up in flames. A bailout was contingent on failure. A company performing below its potential, in contrast, would not trigger a monitoring response. In the strategy terminology introduced in chapter 4, a company that was "stuck in the middle" and did not operate along the competitive frontier would not have triggered an intervention by the main bank.

In contrast, continuous monitoring occurs through constant, proactive sampling by a plurality of interested parties that are constantly checking whether the firm is operating on the competitive frontier. Monitoring agents in New Japan include institutional investors whose interests are diametrically different from those of postwar-period banks. These shareholders have no tolerance for "stuck in the middle" and are activated at the earliest indication of subpotential performance. Rarely are these owners loyal, for they practice exit or voice with immediacy.

Both systems of corporate monitoring have their strengths and create their own costs and disadvantages. Next to legal and consulting expenses, perhaps the biggest cost of continuous monitoring is the waste created when a corporate raider tears apart a firm even though it is operating close to full potential—as Steel Partners was accused of in the Bull-Dog Sauce case. The biggest downside of contingent governance, such as Old Japan's, is the opportunity cost incurred when mismanaged firms are allowed to operate suboptimally for long periods of time until they hit a true crisis, and when "zombies" are created by supporting companies without viable business models. Both financial and human capital could have been put into more productive use in the meantime. Kaplan and Minton (1994) and others have shown that overall economic performance is not necessarily compromised if bank oversight substitutes for a market for corporate control. Still, the biggest challenge with contingent monitoring is that banks typically only worry about the weakest firms, and when they step in their biggest concern tends to be debt holders rather than shareholders.

Regardless of how one judges these trade-offs, New Japan is moving toward continuous governance, with the main bank becoming just one of several monitoring agents. As a result, managers now face more pluralistic pressures from shareholders, and are pushed toward focusing on performance and profitability.

Evaluation: Competition for Investors in the New Japan

For companies, the shift in shareholder structure and the declining role of the main bank has enormous implications. During the postwar period the management of large firms aimed to increase sales, almost at any cost, not just because size meant power and prestige but also because it pleased shareholders. The typical process for rectifying mismanagement was for the business group to advise on improvements first; only when the company faced the brink of bankruptcy did the main bank step in to orchestrate an informal debt restructuring. Improvements on overall corporate strategy were often a secondary concern. The main bank had an information monopoly on the firms, and the full details of the restructuring were rarely made public. Shareholders other than banks and corporations were typically too small or too pluralistic to intervene. Their rights and access to information were limited, and annual shareholder meetings were too short to allow activists to speak out.

All of this has become a thing of the past. Companies are now concerned with the cost of external financing, which is priced according to corporate performance. The new dominant shareholders, institutional investors, are driven by returns. Low-performing companies will either face some intervention or be dumped from the portfolio. The dumping of shares may invite a new potential threat to management: hostile bidders. Considered by some for their potential negative effects as "vultures" or "raiders," hostile bidders nonetheless work to keep management on its toes. Because this is a recent development, data are still too limited to analyze whether mergers and acquisitions in Japan have served to increase the performance of the buyout targets. However, the effect for the overall economy is to increase large firms' sensitivity to efficiency and competitiveness.

The legal reforms between 1998 and 2006 enabled the M&A market in Japan to take off, and they also reflect a shift in corporate strategic thinking. Much more than before, Japanese firms now pay attention to measures such as return on equity, return on investment, and profit margins. Accounting rules are no longer ambiguous, and auditors and senior management can be held liable for irregularities. Disclosure requirements and the Internet have greatly opened access to corporate information. Japan's senior executives have been incentivized toward the market.

SUBCONTRACTING: GLOBALIZATION AND SUPPLIER RELATIONS

One prominent feature of Japanese manufacturing in the postwar period was a system of sourcing from long-term, stable, and affiliated smaller firms. Created from necessity in the early 1950s and turned into a virtue with the introduction of the Toyota Production System in 1963, Japan's subcontracting system had mitigated problems of asymmetric information and uncertainty by turning suppliers into collaborators with a keen interest in a long-term relationship through knowledge infusion. Thus, stable subcontracting offered a solution to the problems associated with either arm's-length sourcing or full vertical integration.

However, globalization and technological changes in production processes referred to as modulization have led to a reconfiguration of Japan's subcontracting system. Beginning in the 1990s, the location of production abroad accelerated greatly, while price competition arrived in Japan as large buyers realized cost savings from sourcing low value-added parts globally. The arrival of global competition in parts procurement, further fueled by e-commerce that allowed for global price comparison, enabled buyers to be more strategic in their choice of suppliers, while also necessitating "choose and focus" among Japan's many small- and medium-sized manufacturing firms.

The Subcontracting System

Subcontractors are mostly small firms. Japan's Small- and Medium Enterprise Basic Law defines a small- or medium-sized manufacturing firm (SMM) as one with capital of less than ¥300 million or fewer than 300 employees.[1]

---

1. In wholesale, a "small and medium-sized enterprise" has capital of less than ¥100 million or fewer than 100 employees, in services these limits are ¥50 million or 100 employees, and for retail outlets ¥50 million or 50 employees. There is no legal definition of a "very small" firm, but in most statistics this refers to firms with fewer than 20 employees in manufacturing, and fewer than 5 employees in other industries. Few countries have a legal definition of "small firms," but in Japan this was necessitated by numerous postwar small-firm-support policies that required an eligibility standard.

Japan's SMMs fall broadly into three categories: (1) independent firms with a strong technology base that sell to multiple buyers; (2) suppliers that are exclusive subcontractors to one large buyer; and (3) very small firms with a weak technology base. The Law on the Promotion of Subcontracting Small Firms defines a subcontracting relation as one where "a larger company contracts out production, repair, creation of information deliverables, or provision of services" from a smaller company over an extended period (SMEA 2005, 34). In statistics, a subcontractor (*"shita-uke,"* lit. "lower-level order taker") is sometimes defined as one that sells more than 50 percent of its output to one larger buyer.

Subcontracting in the Postwar Period

In the immediate postwar years, manufacturing firms had limited production capacity at a time when capital was scarce and labor rambunctious (due to a newly introduced labor law that was tightened in the early 1950s). For newly founded or fast-growing firms (such as Toyota, Honda, Matsushita, or Sony) outsourcing was the only option, as it reduced the need for investments, transferred labor problems to other firms, and provided speed in development as it reduced the need to build in-house expertise in a wide range of areas (Smitka 1991). By the time these constraints were alleviated in the 1960s, many companies had turned their subcontracting system into long-term arrangements offering additional advantages, and therefore continued and refined the practice.

In the stable arrangements from the early 1960s through the early 1990s, suppliers formed hierarchies, led by first-tier suppliers (usually medium-sized firms with a clear core competence) that outsourced from second-tier suppliers, which in turn bought from third-tier suppliers, who relied for very low-value-added parts on very small-sized family businesses. The relationship with the buyer differed depending on the tier of the hierarchy. First-tier firms would often cater to more than one buyer and possessed significant bargaining power due to their technological know-how, whereas fourth-tier firms were low-tech, easily interchangeable, and thus at the mercy of their buyers for survival.[2]

Subcontractors to one buyer often formed associations that facilitated the exchange of product specifications and know-how. Personnel exchange with the buyer bolstered cooperative agreements. In some cases, subcontractors built cities around the main buyer, in a setup referred to as *jōkamachi* ("castle

---

2. Most of the research on subcontracting focuses on the relation between the buyer and first-tier suppliers, such as Asanuma (1989), Dyer (2000), McMillan (1990), and Nishiguchi (1994).

towns")—as in the medieval period, the warlord (main assembler) attracted suppliers who made co-location their first weapon of competition against other suppliers. Toyoda City in Aichi Prefecture is a prime example (Bernstein 1997). By 1981, two thirds of small manufacturing firms identified themselves as subcontractors to specific large firms. There were great differences across industries, however, and in electric and transportation equipment, the ratio exceeded 85 percent (see below, figure 7.1).

Initial research on subcontracting, mostly generated within Japan, centered on the potential for exploitation of small firms in this system. This line of research was congruent with the policy view, especially in the 1950s and 1960s, of small firms as weak and needy of government support. In the 1970s, the fast growth of subcontracting as a dominant mode of production led to more nuanced analyses, when economists identified stable subcontractor relations as a source of efficiencies that helped large firms save on supplier selection and bidding, while also enhancing product quality through technological cooperation with suppliers. Risks could be shared yet dependencies reduced when buyers procured from more than one supplier. Cultural values of trust, loyalty, risk aversion, and saving face were sometimes invoked as contributing to close relations between buyers and suppliers (e.g., Smitka 1991). Relations were often cemented through shareholdings, either based on reciprocity or on the buyer owning majority stakes in core suppliers. This led to the so-called vertical keiretsu, business groups led by the assembler with a clear line of control from the top down.

In the 1980s, insights into how this worked were enhanced by studies in game theory and transaction cost economics. These attributed the stability of Japan's subcontractor arrangements to the logic of repeated games and reputation in preventing opportunism. Moreover, mutual investments in specific production technology and joint R&D coupled companies' interests and thus mitigated the threat of holdup and resource dependence. Bargaining power, according to these insights, was equilibrated because of complementary knowledge and joint R&D. Taken together, Japan's subcontracting ties were held as an example of successfully dealing with the problems of asymmetric information and cheating that often destabilize outsourcing relations (e.g., Aoki 1988; Asanuma 1989; Asanuma and Kikutani 1992; McMillan 1990; Kimura 2002).

Sociologists added an analysis of the value of interfirm networks (e.g., Lincoln, Ahmadjian, and Mason 1998; Ahmadjian and Lincoln 2001). These studies emphasize the system's benefits in terms of speed, flexibility, and efficiency that result from mutual learning. Mutual investment and R&D, as well as the custom of *shukkō* (dispatching employees to related firms) allowed cross-fertilization, which was otherwise limited due to lifetime employment. Sometimes, these dispatches were used to support smaller suppliers in trouble, by sending managerial talent, or as an important buffer during a temporary decline in demand, when the large firm suffered from excess labor. Rather than laying off workers, they were sent to smaller suppliers (or even car dealers, in the case of automobile companies), where they could perhaps prove useful at a lower salary.

Importantly, these analyses apply best to first-tier suppliers and perhaps some second-tier firms, that is, those with proprietary capabilities critical to the final product. The smallest manufacturing firms, which typically engaged in mundane assembly out of a shed or even a living room, enjoyed much less stability, cooperation, or positive network effects (Miwa and Ramseyer 2000). This difference in levels became more pronounced over time, as the benefits from close collaboration with the large firm accrued for first-tier suppliers. Subcontractors could increasingly be divided into innovative, competitive, and fast-growing medium-sized manufacturing firms on the one hand, and stagnant lower-tier firms on the other. Many first-tier firms, such as Denso, have graduated from their supplier role and sell to competitors (Lincoln, Ahmadjian, and Mason 1998). Lower-tiered firms, in contrast, became ever more dependent on the buyer. Although the buyers rarely demanded that small suppliers be exclusive, many remained so in order to achieve economies of scale. According to a 1987 survey, more than half of the small manufacturers were subcontractors, and 81.5 percent of these depended on only one buyer (Aoyama 2001; Kimura 2002). It was these latter suppliers that were weeded out by global competition in the 21st century, and were part of the record bankruptcy rates in the late 1990s.

Dependency also meant that the buyer could control prices and therefore margins for their exclusive subcontractors. During recessions buyers were known to squeeze their suppliers by reducing price and delaying payment. In the 1950s, the government outlawed exploitation or the extension of bill payments beyond 180 days.[3] In the 1970s, small suppliers that organized in cooperative supplier groups (*kyōryoku-kai*) became eligible to receive government support. After buyer transgressions intensified during the recession of the 1990s in what was labeled "subcontractor bullying" (*shita-uke ijime*), in 2003 the government introduced stricter rules and expanded coverage to more firms and industries. Along with proactive supportive measures, the new law

---

3. This was accomplished through the Subcontracting Charges Law (Law to Prevent Extension Etc. of Payments to Subcontractors), and the Law on the Promotion of Subcontracting SME, revised in 2003.

increased the penalties and prohibited a larger range of actions, including forced "contribution monies" to be paid by the supplier, forced dispatching of redundant workforce to the supplier, and denying that a delivery had been received and refusing to pay for it.[4] In contrast to the glamorous account of collaboration and technological progress achieved between first-tier suppliers and assemblers, these policy measures point to the negative side of low-level supplier relations.

Regardless of these challenges, however, the majority of small manufacturing firms engaged in subcontracting. For some, the relationship helped economize on advertising, sales promotion, and R&D. For others, they had little choice but to join a supplier hierarchy, given that the predominance of subcontractor hierarchies had greatly truncated the arm's-length market. Over time the system fed on itself, leading to a tight and impenetrable arrangement for input parts, repairs, and services that excluded new entrants.

Changes in Subcontracting

The percentage of small- and medium-sized manufacturing firms that identify themselves as belonging to a stable hierarchy of subcontractors is shown in figure 7.1, based on survey data collected by METI.[5] The average for all industries is presented in vertical bars, while the lines show industries with above-average subcontractor rates. In 1966, when the system was still forming, about 53 percent of all SMM identified themselves as subcontractors, and in 1981 this ratio hit a high point with over 80 percent in the automobiles, textiles, electronics, and general machinery industries. The fall in the ratio since 1981 is remarkable, and by 1998 it had shrunk to 48 percent overall and below 70 percent in automobiles.

Information on the opposite perspective—the degree to which buyers rely on outsourcing—is more difficult to gather, as it differs by industry, product category, and the size of the buyer. For example, Ahmadjian and Lincoln (2001) show that Toyota used to outsource almost all its electronics—from electronic fuel injection systems to air conditioning—from Denso, often at a rate of 100 percent. The automobile industry has long been considered the poster child for subcontracting in Japan, as car parts account for about 70 percent of the value

4. *Nikkei*, February 9, 2003, "*Shita-uke* Protection to Include Services Industries." In 2003, subcontracting in the service industries (such as software development, shipping, building maintenance), were included in the rules, which extends the total coverage of these policies to over one million small firms.

5. Every six years between 1966 and 1987, METI has conducted a Basic Survey on the Manufacturing Industries (*Kōgyō jittai kihon chōsa*); and this chart combines these with the 1998 Manufacturing Industries Survey (*Shōkōgyō jittai kihon chōsa*).

7.1. *Trends in Subcontracting, 1966–1998*
Source: SMEA 2003, fig. 2–4–1.

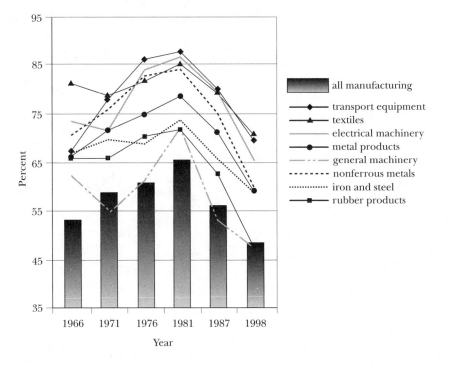

added in car manufacturing (Kobayashi 2003). However, across all industries, METI's Basic Survey of Business Structure and Activity (*Kigyō katsudō kihon chōsa*) suggest that in the early 21st century, the percentage of outsourced input of total sales by manufacturing firms decreased from 17 percent to 12 percent. This annual survey covers roughly 26,000 companies with more than 50 employees.

Table 7.1 details survey results for all manufacturing industries, as well as for the high outsourcing industries of automobiles, electronics, and precision machinery. A significant drop in the value of outsourced parts of total sales, especially in transportation equipment, was accompanied by a marked increase in the percentage of outsourcing from affiliated firms (i.e., subcontractors in which they have an ownership stake). Although these data are only available beginning in 2001, they point to a decline in outsourcing overall, yet more outsourcing from core subcontractors. That is, outsourcing of core parts is reduced by moving it in-house, but those parts that continue to be outsourced are purchased from a smaller set of closely affiliated firms. This interpretation is backed by field research reported by Lincoln, Ahmadjian, and Mason (1998) who in interviews with three large companies (Toyota, Matsushita, and Hitachi)

TABLE 7.1. *Changes in Outsourcing Intensity*

	2001	2002	2003	2004
Total manufacturing				
% of firms that engage in outsourcing	80.8	81.1	81.9	82.2
% of outsourcing purchases from affiliated firms	20.1	26.3	25.0	24.1
% of outsourcing in total sales value	16.8	12.8	12.1	11.9
Number of respondents	13,486	13,247	12,946	12,450
Transport equipment				
% of firms that engage in outsourcing	92.0	92.5	92.2	92.1
% of outsourcing purchases from affiliated firms	13.0	14.9	14.1	14.4
% of outsourcing in total sales value	23.7	10.9	10.9	10.2
Number of respondents	1,121	1,117	1,108	1,088
Electronics				
% of firms that engage in outsourcing	90.5	91.1	90.4	91.1
% of outsourcing purchases from affiliated firms	15.9	10.8	12.7	13.0
% of outsourcing in total sales value	18.0	14.8	13.5	11.1
Number of respondents	2,032	890	890	846
Precision machinery				
% of firms that engage in outsourcing	85.0	84.8	85.7	86.2
% of outsourcing purchases from affiliated firms	8.4	13.5	12.0	10.1
% of outsourcing in total sales value	14.0	11.5	10.8	10.2
Number of respondents	354	348	370	354

Source: Compiled from 2002–2005 editions of the Basic Survey of Business Structure and Activity, METI.

observed a qualitative shift in subcontracting toward a more strategic identification of main suppliers and a focus on learning from these suppliers. They also report an increased in in-house production of parts central to current and future technological leadership in the final product, such as electronics in cars.

In contrast, at the lower levels of the hierarchy the shift is toward price competition and independence from supplier networks. Surveys attest to a significant rise in the number of lower-tier subcontractors per buyer, and a clear shift toward cost reduction. The ratio of suppliers selling to more than 10 buyers has also grown, and in 2004 half of the survey respondents reported further efforts to reduce the proportion of sales directed at the largest buyer (Aoyama 2001, 124; SMEA 2005; SMEA 2006, section 2–3–1). The Small and Medium Enterprise Agency, in its 2006 White Paper, refers to this shift as a meshing of trade relations, away from the previously fairly orderly, hierarchical "one buyer–one supplier" structure to a multifaceted "multi-buyer multi-supplier" system.

This meshing is associated with new processes of bidding and spot pricing, in what is called *open kompe* ("open competition"). One question asked in a 2005 survey on changing subcontractor relations was what buyers valued more in 2005 than they did in 1995, and 64 percent of suppliers and 52.5 percent of buyers answered "cost." In contrast, the long-hailed virtues of Japanese subcontracting—such as speed of delivery, flexibility in product design, joint R&D, co-location of production facilities, and joint financial or business group affiliation—were among the features considered least critical for competing in the New Japan (SMEA 2006, fig. 2–3–8/9).

The reason that first-tier level supplier relations are becoming more critical is a global change in product design and manufacturing toward modulization. This refers to a change in outsourcing toward ordering a complete module containing all parts already preassembled from one lead supplier, as opposed to outsourcing one part, such as shock absorbers, from one supplier and other parts of the suspension system from another. Modulization reduces the number of parts to be outsourced, as well as complications at the final assembly stage, thus reducing costs for the assembler. Importantly, modulization also includes the delegation of product design to module suppliers.

Modulization has great ramifications for Japan's subcontracting system. By delegating product development and design, it requires the first-tier supplier to assume responsibility for a much larger product. Only suppliers that can upgrade their technologies and capabilities can compete at this advanced level. At the same time, owners are loath to become dependent on certain suppliers and have to build more of the critical components in-house, while also making the connection to critical suppliers even closer. Meanwhile, there is no longer a need to sustain a network of separate part makers. This development is particularly evident in the electronics, precision machinery, and IT-related equipment industries that led the shift to modulization and "design-in" (SMEA 2005). Thus, modulization has turned the logic of Japanese subcontracting on its head, by making first-tier collaborators more exclusive, yet opening up procurement of lower value-added parts to arm's-length, price-based bidding.

Globalization and "Hollowing Out"

The main engine for the shift to a cost emphasis was globalization, both in terms of production abroad and of increasing import competition in Japan. In 1999, for the first time Japan produced more abroad than it exported: total foreign production amounted to ¥50 trillion while exports stood at ¥48 tril-lion (Kobayashi 2003). Underlying this reversal was the longer-term trend of moving off-shore, that is, the relocation of production abroad that began in the 1980s and culminated in the "China Boom" of the early 21st century.

By 2003 more than one quarter of investments in production facilities oc-curred overseas (see figure 7.2). The ratio of manufacturing abroad climbed from roughly 7 percent in 1995 to 17 percent in 2004, meaning that every sixth product made by Japanese firms was no longer made in Japan. Import

7.2. *Outward-Bound Investments, Overseas Production, and Import Penetration, 1986–2003*
Source: Adapted from CAO (2004), fig. 3–2–1.

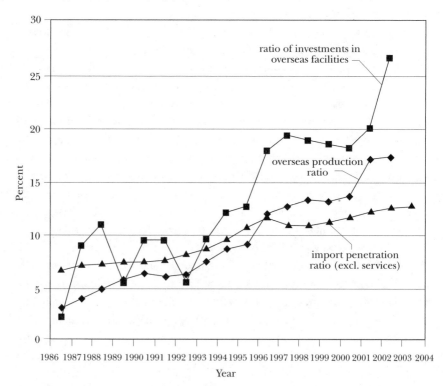

penetration of manufactured products (including reimports of Japanese goods) has more than doubled, from about 5 percent in the early 1980s to 13 percent in the early 2000s. This has forced Japan's small manufacturers to increase their competitiveness, either by going abroad with their buyers or by becoming more differentiated in order to sell to several domestic buyers in the face of competition from low-priced imports. Leaving the previous protection of subcontractor hierarchies required upgrading facilities and building independent marketing and sales competencies. The increase in global competition, in particular in automobiles, electronics, IT equipment, and precision machinery, has forced suppliers to "choose and focus" by identifying new strategies of how to assume a differentiated position in a rapidly changing market.

Three Waves of "Hollowing Out"

Japan's multinationals first began to locate production abroad in the 1970s, initially to Southeast Asia for low-cost assembly of original equipment manufacturer (OEM) products for sale in the United States and Europe. This was followed by expansion abroad in reaction to trade frictions and local content rules, mostly into the United States. Relocation was further pushed in the mid-1980s, when the exchange-rate realignment based on the Plaza Accord of 1985 led to the so-called High Yen Recession, and producing outside Japan became one way to hedge against increasingly volatile exchange rates. Trade data reveal the results of this first wave of global production: in the late 1980s roughly 30 percent of Japanese exports were directed at the United States, but in the early 2000s this ratio had shrunk to about 22 percent. Over those two decades, however, 61 percent of Japan's cumulative outward-bound foreign direct investment (FDI) had been in the United States, indicating that trade with the United States had been replaced with production there.[6]

This first wave of investments in overseas plants led the media to coin the phrase *kūdōka*, the hollowing out of Japan's industrial base. The second wave of hollowing out occurred in the mid-1990s, and especially after the yen appreciated to record highs against the U.S. dollar in 1995 (thus decreasing yen-based returns of sales denominated in dollars). Unlike the first wave, the 1990s saw a turn toward Asia in search for locations with cheap labor. Trade with Asia had also become increasingly important, growing from less than a fifth of total Japanese exports in the late 1980s to 44 percent in 2004. Small firms, in particular, directed 69 percent of exports to East Asia, but only 15 percent to

6. Based on CAO 2005; *Trade Statistics of Japan;* www.customs.go.jp/toukei/suii/html/time_e.htm; and Ministry of Finance web site, "Statistics," www.mof.go.jp. See also Schaede (2007).

the United States in 2004 (SMEA 2006, fig. 2–1–9). At the same time, cumulative Japanese FDI into Asia had jumped to 17 percent, signaling the arrival of Japanese plants in Asia.

The third wave of hollowing out was the China boom of the early 21st century. While Japanese exports into China were cited as a major contributor to the economic recovery of Japan after 2002, between 1998 and 2003 China's exports, too, grew by 77 percent, and in 2002 alone they jumped by 22 percent. Japan was a major buyer of these exports. In 2002 Japan registered its first trade deficit with China, as imports of $62 billion from China were no match for exports worth $40 billion. The imbalance also showed in FDI: in 2001 alone, 69 major Japanese firms shut down 120 factories in Japan, and 70 percent of these were moved to China (Ryan 2003). Whereas Japanese FDI into China accounted for a mere 5 percent of total FDI into Asia in 1990, this share grew to 48.6 percent in 2004 (SMEA 2006, fig. 2–1–12). These developments caused a "China fear" in some Japanese circles, triggering everything from government "hollowing out deliberation councils" to protectionist policy proposals.

Opponents of the China angst argued that half of China's exports were produced by overseas firms (e.g., Lincoln 2002). In the case of Japan, 60 percent of its imports from China were reimports from Japan's electronic, car, textile, and other manufacturers (Ryan 2003). Even if China occupied only a small piece of Japan's cumulative global production map, however, the new imports from China were critical in reshaping competition within Japan, both in finished consumer products and intermediate input materials. Whereas the first two waves of hollowing out had not challenged domestic pricing structures or the retail distribution system, the China boom brought competition in choice and price to Japan.

The Effects of Hollowing Out

Over the course of these three waves of hollowing out, doomsday prophecies abounded. In 2002, the Fuji Research Institute estimated that between 2002 and 2010, domestic production would fall by ¥8.8 trillion (roughly $73 billion), GDP would fall by 1.7 percent and employment by a further 1.25 million (*Diamond Weekly* 2002; see also figure 7.3). In the same year, a government council warned, not entirely tongue in cheek, that if the current rate of overseas FDI by Japanese firms were to continue, no manufacturing plants would be left in Japan by 2018.[7] By 2004, two positive trends appeared on the horizon to alleviate overdrawn fears. It became clear that a large portion of the production located abroad was indeed in lower value-added activities,

---

7. Interview with a government official, Tokyo, Spring 2003.

while advanced production and R&D remained in Japan. Data also pointed to a reversal in domestic investment with ongoing economic recovery, especially by electronics firms (SMEA 2006).

Short-term shifts in the location of production investments do not negate the larger trends of globalization. This is threatening to some, because hollowing out curtails value-added production and employment in Japan, and has the potential to erode R&D capabilities if it involves the transfer of research to the locale of production. And while corporations engage in this relocation based on profitability calculations, greater societal interests may be overlooked (Nakamura and Shibuya 2002). The discussion parallels that of moving off-shore in the United States, albeit with the important difference that the United States is a large recipient of FDI in manufacturing, such as for car and electronics plants by Japanese and Korean companies, whereas Japan is not. Japanese outbound FDI is concentrated in manufacturing, while inbound FDI has traditionally been in the finance and telecommunications industries, which create fewer, and more specialized, jobs than manufacturing.[8]

However, not all observers agree that hollowing out is necessarily negative. Kwan (2002) differentiates between "good" and "bad" hollowing out. The former refers to investments abroad aimed at increased economic efficiency that raises productivity and profitability in the industry, thus contributing to economic growth and the necessary reorientation of economic activities to higher-value-added activities. Japan's FDI into China, with the goal of reducing labor costs by relocating simple assembly processes while reinvesting the profits into R&D centers in Japan, would be an example of such good FDI. In contrast, bad hollowing out refers to FDI abroad in reaction to trade barriers and other market-disturbing mechanisms; an example is a car plant abroad that serves the single purpose of adhering to local content rules and avoiding tariffs. Little macroeconomic gain is reaped from such an investment.[9]

The biggest impact of hollowing out is on employment and subcontracting. Because labor is not perfectly mobile, especially for very small, low-value-added part producers in rural areas, the shift of production abroad poses a great social challenge. Nor are losses in employment and wages compensated at the individual level by cheaper import prices. Figure 7.3 shows trends in

8. Cabinet Office, 2004 Annual Report on the Japanese Economy and Public Finance, at www5.cao.go.jp/zenbun/wp-e/wp-je04/04-00302.html.

9. This view is not shared by all economists. Bailey (2003, 4) describes the "tariff-preventing" FDI as less harmful for Japan's economy than the labor-cost-reducing FDI into Asia. This view is echoed by Itami (2004) who suggests that "tariff-hopping" investments are complementary (being mere extensions of existing production), whereas labor-cost-reducing FDI threatens to deindustrialize Japan.

7.3. Total Employment vs. Employment in Manufacturing, 1960–2004, and the Three Waves of Hollowing Out
Source: Compiled from *Hōjin kigyō tōkei*.

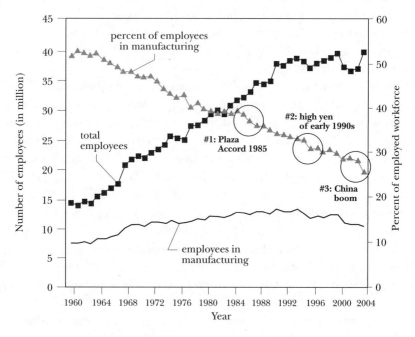

overall employment (all regular employees including part-timers, but not including day laborers and other contracted help), and the proportion of manufacturing jobs in total employment (in %, right-hand scale). The percent of manufacturing in total employment has decreased from over half of the private sector workforce in the 1960s to one quarter in 2004. Figure 7.3 underscores the significant impact of the three waves of hollowing out on employment in manufacturing, reducing the ratio by roughly 4 percentage points each. In absolute terms, the first wave of the mid-1980s had little effect on the total number of manufacturing employees, but the following two episodes combined to cause significant job loss, reducing the number of manufacturing employees from 12.8 million in 1994 to 10 million in 2004. This shift presented a new challenge to Japan's government, since it created structural, long-term unemployment (Nakamura and Shibuya 2002).

However, it is difficult to separate the effects of hollowing out from those of the recession of the 1990s. Perhaps the job losses in manufacturing in the 1990s were not caused by hollowing out, but were rather the combination of depressed Japanese consumption and increased labor productivity (Itami 2004). Moreover, production abroad has triggered exports of specialized plant and equipment, parts and materials. Increased imports from Asia have also created new jobs ranging from longshoremen to trading company employees, so that hollowing out needs to be appreciated for the spark it has given non-manufacturing jobs in Japan (Ryan 2003). This interpretation is supported by the increase in total employment during the first two waves of hollowing out, as shown in figure 7.3.

Whatever its effects on employment, hollowing out has greatly affected the subcontracting logic in Japan's industrial architecture. The push into Asia, in particular, has undermined production processes in many industries, led by precision machinery, textiles, and household appliances. Figure 7.4 shows that, on average for 11 leading industries, 14 percent of production is now located in Asia; for precision machinery and textiles, the ratio is almost one quarter, up from 7 percent before the onset of the China boom.

Locating production in Asia is by no means restricted to large firms. By 2003, 43 percent of Japan's multinationals operated production facilities outside Japan, as compared to roughly one third of all large companies. At the same time, the ratio of small manufacturers with subsidiaries abroad increased

7.4. *Percent of Total Sales Produced in Asia, by Industry, 1994–2004*
Source: SMEA (2006), fig. 2–1–14.

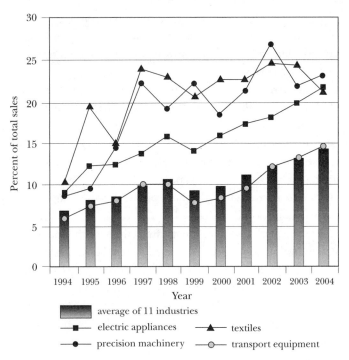

from 7 percent in 1992 to 13 percent in 2004, with a steeper growth trend than for large firms (SMEA 2004, figure 2–2–2). These differences in growth trends are explained, again, by the different waves of hollowing out. By 2002, 30 percent of Japanese overseas subsidiaries were located in the United States, 25 percent in Southeast Asia, 18 percent in China, and 15 percent in the NIEs (the newly industrialized economies of Asia). Survey data indicate that two thirds of the subsidiaries in North America and Europe were established to cater to that market (and to circumvent trade regulations, such as local content rules and tariffs). In contrast, more than 60 percent of subsidiaries in China and the NIEs were explicitly operated in order to reimport cheaper products into Japan. In particular, in Southeast Asia the main role of foreign subsidiaries was seen as providing parts to the local Japanese affiliates (SMEA 2004, 136).

Being embedded in large subcontractor hierarchies and dependent on co-location for just-in-time delivery, Japan's auto parts industry was long hesitant to locate production abroad for cost reasons. In the early 21st century, however, investment in Asia accelerated from the previous level of about ¥65 billion per year to ¥250 billion in 2004 (SMEA 2006). This jump in auto-parts-related investments has turned what used to be a domestic affair into perhaps the most global of all Japanese manufacturing industries. In 2001, more than 38 percent of Japanese cars were produced outside Japan (METI SKS 2001). As for car parts, by 2002 imports into Japan had reached ¥145 billion ($1.2 billion), which represented an increase of 19 percent over 2001 (in particular, car part imports from China increased by 45 percent in that one year; Kobayashi 2003).

In 2004, Japan reported the first signs of a reversal, in what was labeled a "return to home" (*kokunai kaiki*). Data comparing domestic investments with those in Asia reveal that electronics and IT-related industries saw a spike in domestic investments between 2002 and 2004, while foreign investments declined. One reason for this reversal was the final correction of the so-called three excesses of the 1990s: debt, labor, and capacity. With capacity levels reduced to production needs and a booming economy, companies moved to establish new production facilities in Japan. Near-zero interest rates in Japan made the financing of new investments attractive. Furthermore, the leveling off in locating production abroad was partially explained by the fact that one third of large Japanese firms already produced abroad, so that potential gains from relocation had already occurred. Finally, protecting intellectual property continued to be difficult, capping the type of production that can safely be moved abroad; what could be moved abroad was already there, so that investments into the region slowed down.

Price Competition in Subcontracting

Although globalization has greatly affected subcontractor relations in all industries, the best-known example comes from the automobile industry. With its numerous global alliances and ownership ties, the world automobile industry is perhaps the most global manufacturing industry. Compared with their competitors, for many years Japanese carmakers forged only a few strategic alliances abroad, but in the late 1990s this changed dramatically, when Ford acquired a majority ownership stake in Mazda (dating back to the 1970s but now increased to over 30%), Renault and Nissan structured a cross-ownership alliance, and DaimlerChrysler temporarily controlled Mitsubishi Motors. Global consolidation among major car companies was driven by the simultaneous goals of addressing cost pressures while building economies of scope and scale to offer all types of models in all major markets.

The alliance between Nissan and Renault is a well-chronicled turnaround success story, but it also represented a major force in reconfiguring supplier relations in Japan. One of the first measures by Renault executive Carlos Ghosn upon arrival at Nissan in 1999 was to cut the supplier base by half, which meant severing ties with 600 long-term suppliers. This initially caused great resistance and posturing by Keidanren (big business's umbrella organization, at the time headed by the chairman of Toyota), citing the detrimental effects of Nissan's actions on Japan's social fabric. Nissan could not be deterred, and the episode underscored Ghosn's reputation as "Le Cost Killer." It also highlighted one aspect of subcontractor-based production largely ignored in the literature—its potential to invite slack over time. While Toyota has long been considered a master in disciplining its suppliers, Nissan had been much less effective at keeping suppliers on their toes. Yet, within two years Nissan succeeded in reducing parts costs by 30 percent by modifying its supplier system, cutting investments in suppliers, and sourcing lower value-added parts from China, while also pushing core suppliers toward increased efficiency.

Once such drastic steps had become possible, however, there was no turning back. When Ford took over Mazda, it launched its own "C30" program, slashing prices on all parts by 30 percent. Subcontractors that refused to go along were cut off (Ghosn and Ries 2005). Meanwhile, the electronics makers, such as Hitachi, Matsushita, and Mitsubishi Electric, quietly underwent similar transformations beginning in the late 1990s. In industry after industry, employment and subcontractor structures were reconsidered.

Global price competition, in all industries, meant that the subcontracting system had become too expensive, all its benefits notwithstanding. Many large buyers terminated their subcontractor cooperatives in attempts to drive hierarchies apart. In an attempt to break open their circle of suppliers and open the door to new firms, some buyers were even said to have issued "orders against *settai*," the clubby drinking outings aimed at human bonding to cement long-standing business relations (Aoyama 2001).

Evaluation: Subcontracting in New Japan

During the postwar period the logic of Japanese subcontracting was built on the notion of long-term, protective relations based on risk sharing, network arrangements geared to mutual learning, and the reduction of holdup risk by aligning several suppliers in each category and managing a subcontractor hierarchy. The price for this insurance against dependency was efficiency losses in scale of production. In the 1990s this price became too high, and many assemblers began to search for economies of scale with fewer suppliers. In the early 21st century, all this changed again when outsourcing of generic, low-value-added parts shifted to arm's-length deals. Started by electronics makers in the 1980s, price-based procurement is now integral to part procurement even in the car industry, where subcontracting remains substantial. According to one analysis, the open pricing system (where suppliers submit bids, and the lowest bidder wins the contract) can lead to cost savings of 3–4 percent if existing suppliers are used, and savings of 15–30 percent if new firms enter the market. Internet-based procurement processes, moreover, allow carmakers to procure from whoever is cheapest around the globe (Aoyama 2001; Kobayashi 2003).

After Nissan successfully implemented its first round of cost cutting, Toyota shifted to "open competition" for robotics and cut the number of its suppliers by dismissing or consolidating inefficient firms and encouraging suppliers to work with more than one buyer.[10] In a November 2004 survey of small manufacturers, half of the respondents had experienced a significant reduction in domestic sales and unit price due to competition from foreign products. Price competition was felt particularly strongly in the metal industries, where suppliers engaging in pressing, polishing, and other intermediate metal-processing steps faced great difficulties competing (SMEA 2005, 32–33; SMEA 2006, 2–3–2).

These shifts have presented suppliers with three options: (1) follow the buyers to the new locations, to compete globally; (2) stay in Japan but upgrade to compete through differentiation; or (3) muddle through and eventually exit. At the macroeconomic level, these options have caused a simultaneous weeding

---

10. Newspaper and magazine articles describing these qualitative changes in the automobile industry abound. See, for example, *Ekonomisuto*, February 3, 2004, 4–5; July 29, 2002, 28–30; *Tōyō Keizai*, March 13, 2002, 9–12; *Nikkei*, May 15, 2002; July 12, 2002; August 22, 2002; June 25, 2003; May 14, 2004; and November 9, 2004.

out of inefficient small parts makers and a leveling up of first- and second-tier suppliers.

Suppliers that followed their buyers abroad were confronted with new management challenges, including the development of skills in international management, marketing, and branding. What is more, since Japanese firms are unlikely to beat competitors in China on cost even if producing there, they also had to develop their own, superior R&D and production processes to differentiate against local suppliers (SMEA 2002). As a result, hollowing out has forced many suppliers to develop their own, independent business strategies.

Likewise, suppliers staying in Japan must compete forcefully against imports, by becoming more cost-competitive and by differentiating with high-value-added products. Import price competition has forced them to become more efficient to win arm's-length bids. To address reduced order volume, these firms also had to develop new domestic sales channels and exporting abilities. Their new aggressiveness explains the increase in the number of customers per subcontractor reported earlier. Thus, these firms have been forced to "choose and focus." As a result, even the increase in domestic investments is unlikely to lead to a return to postwar subcontracting relations, because the combination of stronger, more independent suppliers and global competition for lower-level products has already altered the previous logic of subcontractor hierarchies.

For many lower-tiered suppliers, however, the exit option was the only choice at the turn of the century. A large subgroup in this category were founder firms established in the early postwar years, which faced succession issues when their children were uninterested in running a low-value-added parts shop at a time when competition was increasing. Most of the record-high bankruptcies of small firms between 1998 and 2004 occurred in manufacturing and can be attributed to changing subcontractor relations. This also altered Japan's industrial geography, because many of the castle towns that grew around new greenfield plants in various regions of Japan in the 1960s (such as in Yamagata, Aomori, Iwate, and Kyushu) have turned into ghost towns (*Diamond Weekly* 2002). Meanwhile, new Japanese castle towns have sprung up around the globe, from Ohio to Shanghai. Once there, these suppliers compete with local small firms, and the best are courted by several competing Japanese firms in the area, which in turn increases their bargaining power. The bifurcation between strong, first-tier suppliers and left-behind local firms has grown further.

Among the remaining, competitive suppliers, roles and assignments have also changed. Historically it was the first-tier suppliers that had the most diversified client base, whereas the smaller suppliers were often exclusively tied to one subcontracting hierarchy. Globalization and modulization have turned this on its head. Whereas smaller firms sell to more buyers, larger suppliers with strong technological capabilities are getting closer to their buyers and cooperate even more with a specific buyer. In their role as core suppliers, they contribute to the buyer's product design, and in some cases new cross-shareholdings cement this relation, such as between Toyota and Matsushita Electric in 2007.

From the large firm's perspective, the postwar logic of stable subcontracting hierarchies is history. In global markets, long-term "wet" (close, personal) relations with a complete lineup of parts makers, painstakingly arranged for all to contribute to just-in-time delivery no longer supports efficient, global mass production. Production processes have been altered to support efficient production in a variety of locations around the globe. Modulization has made the lower tiers of subcontractors more interchangeable, thus allowing sourcing from the cheapest global bidder.

Another ramification of modulization is the increase in in-house production by the assemblers themselves. Throughout the postwar period Japanese firms competed mostly with low-priced products known for reliability and clever commercialization of new features, but not for cutting-edge technological innovation. The strategic inflection point has made differentiation through technological leadership imperative. This has elevated the role of proprietary innovation. Many large firms are reconfiguring their outsourcing strategies, not just from whom they buy but also what they buy and in what areas to focus and build their own core competencies to compete through innovation and differentiation.

PRICE COMPETITION:

THE BUSINESS-TO-BUSINESS

AND RETAIL PRICE REVOLUTIONS

During the postwar period, in many Japanese markets prices were not set by market clearance. For many intermediate products they were often renegotiated post hoc, and in many consumer product markets they were set through retail price maintenance. This does not mean there was no competition, only that it was often not based on spot pricing. Nor was the system necessarily inefficient. It was simply different, and thus corporate strategies were directed at different goals.

All this has begun to change with the arrival of price transparency and price competition to Japan. Accordingly, corporate strategies are being reoriented to address this new type of competition, with competitors and their prices better known. In intermediate products, globalization, Internet-based trading, and the reorganization of business groups and supplier networks have undermined the previous relational contracting; i.e., long-term trade relations where joint progress concerns often overrode price considerations. The erstwhile widespread practice of "after-sales price adjustment" (*ato-gime*) has been replaced with declaring nonnegotiable prices upfront. For this common method, Japan has a special word—"pre-sale pricing" (*saki-gime*). In consumer products, the retail revolution of the 1990s, which brought new competing retail formats such as discount stores as well as Internet-based price comparisons, together with a rapid increase in imports, have undermined previous patterns of maintaining retail prices through specialized retail chains.

The arrival of price transparency and price competition has greatly affected the structure of domestic markets, as trade-restricting practices and barriers to entry through relational contracting have been removed. This has also affected the global business tactics of Japanese firms, as the previous sanctuary strategy, whereby some Japanese firms competed through aggressive pricing abroad while earning an extra profit cushion in their restricted home markets, is no longer a viable approach. The strategic inflection point is also marked by a change in the nature of competition within Japanese markets. As an executive of Asahi Glass put it, "From now on we will not sell only to push sales volume up; we will sell only if it is profitable and we won't if it isn't—we are switching to normal trade" (*Nikkei*, December 1, 1993).

After-Sales Price Adjustment

Business-to-business (B2B) transactions in the postwar period in many industries were often not based on spot transactions but on differential, post-hoc pricing influenced by long-standing trade relations. In this peculiar pricing mechanism, the price for the product was set only tentatively at the time of the transaction, often as a range, only to be renegotiated afterward—between six to twelve months later—based on the changing market situation for both parties. This was different from contingent pricing known elsewhere, where the price may be altered post hoc based on clearly stipulated conditions, such as quarterly changes in input costs or a competitor offering a lower price for the exact same product within a prespecified time period (e.g., Biyalogorsky and Gerstner 2004). Until the 1990s, in Japan the very conditions for price changes, too, were often situational and determined post hoc.

A variety of after-sales price negotiations were practiced, differing by industry and over time.[1] In some petroleum-based industries the price was adjusted post hoc, largely depending on the price of naphtha (Tilton 1994). More commonly, input material costs were but one of several considerations, next to changes in supply and demand during the quarter, the size of inventory accumulated, the final product price that could be negotiated, and thus, overall, the gross margins earned by both sides. That is to say, in trades governed by after-sales price adjustment, the final price of the product was often related less to the cost of the product and more to the revenue situation of both trading partners. To understand why companies would engage in this relational contracting, it is helpful to distinguish between two underlying motivations, risk reduction and system stability through welfare distribution.

Risk Sharing and Mutual Insurance

The first rationale for after-sales price adjustment lies in its function as a mutual insurance scheme between two companies to smooth out revenues over time. One trading partner would not make a windfall gain at the expense of the other; instead, both would earn stable income over time, and accomplish their most important strategic goal of the postwar period, which was to stay in business in rapidly growing and changing markets.

---

1. Several terms exist in Japanese to describe the practice: *atogime* (decide afterwards), *ato-shikire* (adjust inventory afterwards), *ne-modoshi* (return to pricing later), or *jigo-chōsei* (after the fact adjustment).

Townsend (1994) developed an equilibrium framework for risk reduction by risk-averse entities in a study of Indian villages, by combining five dominant ways in which members of a network can reduce the risk of exogenous shocks to their income. These are (1) diversification (spatially separated holdings); (2) storage to smooth supply over time; (3) purchases and sales of assets; (4) borrowing from lenders or trading partners; and (5) transfers and gifts among group members. In combining these five approaches, Townsend shows that insurance agreements allow group members to exclude idiosyncratic risk for each entity so that the volatility of income is the same for all group members. Thus, all group members are insured, and exogenous shocks hit all in similar fashion.

The features of Japan's postwar political economy (including high dependence on bank loans, underdeveloped bankruptcy legislation, and lifetime employment) made Japanese firms highly risk averse, in particular those that had already self-selected to be members of business groups or trade circles with long-term relations. Risk aversion made them willing to pay to ensure that everybody would be equally well off over time, with shocks suffered jointly rather than wiping out one firm. If variation in the income of all members of a trade circle was equalized so that a firm's income variability was the same as all members' income variability, then market hierarchy and corporate survival were assured.

Townsend's theory of risk sharing helps us understand Japanese after-sales price adjustment in the postwar period. We have already seen that diversification was a widely adopted means of risk spreading, but it left companies with the risk of variance in sales over time in each market segment. Storage to smooth out quarterly revenues may not have been an option in some industries, such as steel, chemicals, or other perishable items. Purchasing and selling assets (such as business units) to counterbalance income variation over time was inhibited by rules of lifetime employment and limitations on repurchasing a company's own stock. However, equalizing income streams across the network could be done through relational pricing with trading partners.

The insurance that these risk-averse firms bought was an agreement to adjust prices after the fact such that profits were divided according to some measure of fairness between trading partners. After-sales adjustment was a mechanism to hedge against price volatility and smooth out the effects of price or demand shocks on earnings over time.[2] Not surprisingly, the practice

---

2. Japan has long had commodities futures exchanges, and boasts the first organized futures markets with extensive records, dating back to 1730 (Schaede 1989). In the postwar period, however, these markets remained small. A 1993 *Nikkei* article suggests three main

was most widespread in industries with potentially highly volatile prices. It is said to have been omnipresent throughout the postwar period in the chemical industries, as well as in plastics, glass, paper, cement, aluminum, semiconductors, and tires. Congruent with theory, not all trades in one product would be governed by after-sales adjustment, which coexisted with spot trades (Townsend 1994). This is because, naturally, companies would engage in mutual insurance schemes only with their closest allies. After-sales pricing was reinforced by the existence of business groups, where the one-set approach required ensuring that all members remained viable. Since the well-being of the group was paramount, and corporate profits were less relevant than sales volume, profit sharing across group members was a reasonable thing to strive for. Of course, companies often also engaged in cross-shareholdings, which from the group perspective further reduced the meaning of profit as compared to the relevance of longevity.[3]

Unfortunately, data limitations disallow a more detailed study of risk sharing and insurance through variable pricing in postwar Japan.[4] Although we may never truly know whether the system worked as an insurance scheme as predicted by theory, the strategic inflection point has undermined this logic by making many Japanese firms risk neutral such that the willingness to pay for this type of insurance has greatly declined.

Bargaining Power and Welfare Distribution

The second, more mundane, rationale for after-sales pricing was more frequently observed in vertical setups, either in business groups or distribution keiretsu: here, companies did it because they could. In industries where either the basic input seller or the final product buyer (or both) had stronger bargaining power than the intermediate product manufacturers or wholesalers, the middle was squeezed to a point where margins were just sufficient to remain in

---

reasons: a lack of product standardization, administrative guidance in many basic materials industries that interfered in market pricing, and after-sales price adjustment (*Nikkei*, January 13, 1993, 27). Financial futures were introduced into Japan in the late 1980s but these were also inhibited by "customary trading practices" and regulatory intervention (Schaede 1990).

3. Post-hoc adjustments may also have been used to help a trading partner facing losses: by receiving a huge "rebate" just before the end of the fiscal year, the suffering company could report figures in the black and return the favor in the future (*Nikkei*, May 8, 2000). On welfare sharing within business groups, see Lincoln and Gerlach (2004).

4. After-sales price adjustment is, in fact, a brilliant example of no-fee insurance, that is, it might be actuary-fair. To test whether this presumption holds would require data to show that price negotiations between trading partners were mean zero (evened out) over time. Partially because after-sales pricing was characterized in U.S-Japan trade negotiations as cartel pricing, such records are not available.

business. This power differential scenario also applied to subcontracting, where the assembler would adjust prices according to changing demand. A large car company, for instance, would stipulate a price for parts for a particular model, but adjust it after the demand for the finished car had been observed for a few months.

The stereotypical example comes from the distribution system in paper or glass. Japan's sheet glass industry for many years was an oligopoly consisting of three large firms, and the largest two buyers of sheet glass were the construction and automobile industries, both also rather powerful. Each glass manufacturer had structured its own distribution system, often with four or more layers, in which each wholesaler added some value, such as cutting the sheet to the right size, framing it, or shipping it to a smaller wholesaler. The glass company would stipulate a price range at the initial sale (and often make an actual payment), and the wholesalers would each stipulate a price at each step of the process. Only when the construction or car company bought the final window pane, however, would the price be negotiated in earnest, in this case directly between the power brokers at both ends. Should they eventually agree on a lower price than initially stipulated, the glass company would demand money back from each wholesaler. If the price was higher, the glass company would distribute a bonus to each.[5] In slow markets, rather than pressuring each other too much in the post-hoc negotiations, the large companies would both squeeze the distributors' margin.[6]

Why the power brokers at both ends would squeeze the middle to increase their own gain is obvious. In contrast, why a large buyer would distribute post-hoc bonuses can be understood as welfare distribution through profit sharing, and it was a common practice with wholesalers and subcontractors to cement long-term relationships. In the above example, the glass company had a keen interest in a stable distribution hierarchy because it typically insisted that the wholesalers be exclusive. This was an important tool in creating effective barriers to competition from other glass companies or new entrants. Moreover, since glass was processed in the distribution system and often stored for several months, prices were likely to change during that time period. Wholesalers were important contributors to the final product, and the glass company had

5. *Nikkei,* July 22, 1993, 11; January 5, 1993, 25; *Nikkei Business,* October 4, 1993, 21–24; Kawagoe 1997; Schaede 2000; interview at the Ministry of International Trade and Industry, Tokyo, Summer 1995.

6. This type of behavior has frequently been chronicled. For example, in 1993 the paper industry raised prices but publishers refused to pay more, so rather than alienating their important clients, the paper companies leaned on the distributors in between, using them as a buffer to dampen distortion between upstream and downstream prices (*Nikkei,* January 5, 1993, 25).

an interest in keeping the distribution hierarchy stable, so subsidizing whole-salers for price erosion during a recession was the price to pay for not miss-ing out on fast-climbing prices during construction booms. Since there were more construction booms than busts in the postwar period, the calculation was often positive for the glass company.

The interests of the intermediate wholesalers or subcontractors overlapped with those of the powerful firms, as both strove for longevity, certainty, and stability of income. The benefits of technology and information sharing in the subcontractor system have already been discussed. In the distribution of manu-factured intermediate products, wholesalers and value-added intermediate manufacturers were similarly tied to large buyers, either due to self-selection as they were risk averse, or because they had no choice as there was no open market. For example, leaving the exclusive hierarchy of the oligopolistic sheet glass industry would have meant being without a supplier of glass, and thus exiting the industry.

Examples abound for after-sales price adjustment during the postwar pe-riod, both in reaction to changes in supply (input prices) or demand (to main-tain the distribution system). Cement and steel were priced after the bridge had been spanned; the price of paper was renegotiated after all that quarter's newspapers had long been delivered; and aluminum and plastics renegotiated after the car had been sold. Adjusting for demand swings, gas stations used to receive "support money" should gas prices fall after they took on inventory. Car dealerships would receive post-hoc rebates on slow-moving models. For the largest electronics firms, the price for DRAM was adjustable through the 1990s. And we cannot be sure what price a bargaining powerhouse such as Toyota used to pay for its steel.[7]

Economic Implications of After-Sales Pricing

Although after-sales price adjustment served important functions in Japan's postwar economic system, in the late 1990s its negative repercussions began to dominate the positive efficiency consequences, leading to great changes in price-setting mechanisms. One obvious positive effect was the built-in stabi-lizer of the economy and employment, by helping companies and their whole-salers and suppliers smooth out revenues over time.

A second advantage of flexible price adjustment lies in its dampening of business cycles. Imagine a sudden, unexpected demand spike for a new car

---

7. On DRAM, see, e.g., *Nikkei*, December 1, 2000, 29; February 2, 2001, 29; May 2, 2001, 24; on gas stations, e.g., *Nikkei*, July 22, 1993, 11.

model. If prices for parts had been fixed upfront, the carmaker would order more parts at the preset price and keep all the windfall profits. Meanwhile, parts makers had an incentive to invest in more capacity (plants, people) to increase revenues through volume production while demand lasted. When demand slowed down, parts makers would suffer from excess capacity. Under flexible pricing, in contrast, the carmaker could raise the price of the model and pass on some of the profits to its subcontractors. Parts makers therefore could partake in the suddenly generated profits even without increased capacity, simply through higher margins, making them much more circumspect in their plant and equipment investment decisions. During the postwar period, in many of the regulated or officially cartelized industries that had access to low interest rates, such as steel, Japan suffered from periods of excess investment, when declining demand left manufacturers with surplus inventory (e.g., Yamamura 1982). Without the dampening effect of post-hoc price negotiations in the supplier industries, these business cycles might have been even more pronounced.

On the negative side, perhaps the biggest downside of after-sales price adjustment was nontransparency. This is not only a nuisance for the researcher, but also posed a challenge for government economic policies. For example, in its regular announcement of wholesale prices, the Bank of Japan had to use "stipulated" prices, missing out perhaps on exactly the adjustments described above to dampen business cycles.[8]

Another problem with nontransparent pricing was that it inhibited competition by erecting strong entry barriers. First, if the competitor's prices are not known, it is difficult indeed to compete on price. Thus, competition was on product differentiation, and where that was impossible (e.g., in commodity markets), by access to long-term relations. After-sales pricing also reinforced exclusive distribution setups. A wholesaler who had received post-hoc price concessions from a manufacturer in the past, on condition that he refuse to deal with other manufacturers, would consider very carefully whether profits in the open markets promised to be sufficiently high to give up on this insurance. For example, new entrants in sheet glass found it impossible to identify distributors, and new entrants in distribution could gain access to domestic products only with great difficulty. This was a particular challenge for foreign manufacturers in the glass and paper industries, which were a centerpiece of trade negotiations with the United States in the mid-1990s.

---

8. For example, see Bank of Japan, "Proposal for Revisions in Wholesale Price Statistics" (*Oroshi-uri bukka-sū no minaoshi ni kan suru saishūan*), September 2001, at www. boj.or.jp.

A final way in which after-sales price adjustment inhibited competition was by inviting cartels by the industries that were squeezed between powerful sellers and buyers. These companies attempted to increase their bargaining power by setting industry-wide prices, in the hope of resisting pressures to renegotiate. For example, the vinyl wrap plastics industry was one of the longest-standing cartels, having been reprimanded for suspicious activities for 17 years in a row before the Japan Fair Trade Commission finally took stricter action in 1991 (Schaede 2000a). The case study below of the petroleum-based chemical industry will highlight this point further.

At the micro level, too, after-sales pricing over time had negative consequences. The time span of post-hoc pricing could vary depending on the business cycle and relative bargaining power. In a recession, a buyer (e.g., the construction firm) with power over the seller (the glass company) may have pushed for after-sales downward adjustment almost immediately. In other settings, the downward negotiations could be drawn out for over a year. As a result, companies could be certain only about sales volume, whereas revenues and other measures of business performance could not be attained with certainty until a year later. Again, because market share was so much more important than profitability during the postwar period, this was not widely considered a problem. So important were sales that prices may at times have been settled so low as to leave the seller with no profit, or even a loss. In addition to being costly in terms of time and manpower expended on negotiating, after-sales pricing thus had negative effects on corporate cost sensitivity. The insurance against price fluctuations meant that management did not have to concern itself with costs, for their main buyers would adjust margins on a need basis. Moreover, the very time lag itself led to a "softening of management" ("*keiei ga amaku naru*," *Nikkei*, January 5, 1993). A lack of price discipline eroded cost consciousness in many industries.

Change: The End of the *Atogime*

Over time, multiple concurrent developments combined to reduce the original merits of after-sales price adjustments and eventually make the practice undesirable or untenable in most industries. Moreover, the strategic inflection point has altered the setting in which Japanese firms operate, thereby shifting their stance from what economists call "risk averse" to "risk neutral." Being risk averse means a reluctance to accept a bargain with uncertain payoff, and a preference for a bargain with a certain but lower payoff. Being risk neutral, in contrast, refers to making a rational calculation of the expected return on investment in each bargain, multiplied by the probability of its success. In Japan, the decreased role of banks, increased labor mobility, and new bankruptcy laws have reduced the relevance of longevity at all costs. Fewer firms are willing to participate in an insurance scheme that is costly and no longer valuable (or where it is useful, it can be bought on global futures markets). At the same time, business groups are no longer as concerned with stable trade relations, while investors have a keen eye on profitability. Rational companies will prefer the option of assessing each trade for its own merit over the low-payoff insurance.

A further trigger for change was globalization. When Japanese firms moved into Asia beginning in the late 1980s, they found their requests for after-sales price adjustments flat-out refused by their new suppliers overseas. Some of these firms switched to spot pricing in Asian markets even with their Japanese suppliers, while continuing post-hoc pricing with the same firms in Japan. This was not sustainable, and when the rapid appreciation of the yen in the early 1990s led to an increase in parts imports, the subcontractor pricing system began to be undermined in the electronics, precision machinery, and textiles industries. Moreover, market opening has put stress on the exclusive distribution system, because ambitious wholesalers can now leave their exclusive relationship for a competitor.[9] As Japanese firms globalized their operations, they began to switch to global pricing standards.

Although globalization affected mostly the exporting industries, several developments in the early 21st century changed the business model even in the domestic markets. One important pressure point was the revision of accounting rules, and in particular the 2003 stipulation by the Tokyo Stock Exchange that all listed companies submit quarterly earnings reports (turned into law with the 2007 Financial Instruments and Exchange Law). These quarterly reports were fiercely debated in the course of 2002, precisely because after-sales pricing made it impossible to declare earnings each quarter. Using the "stipulated price" would not only be misleading but also not feasible in industries were the initial price was expressed as a range, such as in PVC pipes. In industries offering volume rebates to retailers (a price discount after a certain sales volume had been reached), quarterly statements posed a similar challenge. As a result, quarterly earnings reporting began in 2003 with only bare-bone statements. However, beginning April 1, 2004, all listed companies were required to provide quarterly information on sales, operating profits, net profits, total assets, shareholders' equity as well as balance sheet data including loans and losses, all on a consolidated basis.[10]

---

9. *Nikkei,* November 10, 1994, 29; January 14, 1995, 23; *Nikkei Business,* October 4, 1993, 21–24.

10. *Nikkei,* October 3, 2002, 17. For details on quarterly reporting, see the TSE website under *shihanki kaihi,* at www.tse.or.jp.

Another big push toward transparency has occurred through the Internet and the growing role of e-commerce. In the early 2000s several trading companies invested in the creation of Internet-based markets for products such as paper, chemicals, and steel. Although bulk chemicals and steel pipes are fairly homogeneous products, Japan's after-sales price adjustment system had made these "one item, one hundred prices" markets, and nontransparency had made price comparisons difficult. Internet-based markets are for spot transactions, and they allow buyers and sellers to know the identity of their competitors and their prices. Some of Japan's e-commerce sites were slow to catch on, and post-hoc pricing was listed as the biggest impediment to their growth. As Japanese firms switch to e-commerce globally, however, the domestic websites, too, are becoming more important. This has increased product and price information, and has put downward pressure on domestic prices by inviting spot price bidding.[11]

The move away from after-sales pricing was further helped by an unlikely ally—the extended recession of the 1990s. Insurance through after-sales pricing requires that both parties give up something, but in the 1990s some industries, such as construction, were unable to offer anything in return for favorable treatment. While pushing down prices on past deliveries, builders were not placing new orders. Moreover, as bankruptcies became more common, forward-looking insurance was suddenly fraught with uncertainty. As the recession continued, the mutual insurance became unsustainable. For suppliers, selling at a high price suddenly became more valuable than insurance against lower prices in the future.

Meanwhile, companies that had suffered from being squeezed in after-sales pricing moved aggressively to set spot prices. This was becoming easier with ongoing industry consolidation due to "choose and focus" mergers. The newly merged, larger companies had stronger bargaining power, and naturally faced fewer domestic competitors. In some industries, this turned price takers into price setters—as happened in the chemical industry, the last stronghold of widespread after-sales price negotiations.

Case Study: Plastics—The Petroleum-Based Chemical Industry

The plastics industry represents a prime example of after-sales pricing in an industry squeezed in the middle, and it is also one of the last strongholds of this practice. The chemical industry that uses petroleum (naphtha) as a main ingredient can be divided into two large groups. The first are the makers of

11. *Nikkei,* May 8, 2000, 2; May 18, 2000, 13; May 20, 2001, 1; June 18, 2002, 27; June 19, 2002, 26.

chloroethylene resins, known to most people by its main product, PVC, and sold to various suppliers of the construction industry. The second are polyolefins (polypropylene and polyethylene), used for a large variety of plastics of varying degrees of sophistication, of which the main buyers include the packaging industry (from vinyl wrap and shopping bags to ketchup bottles), the automobile industry (from interior panels to brake pads and fenders); the health-care industry (equipment, instruments, drug packaging), the electronics industry (computers, connectors, switches, casings), the building and engineering industries, the agrochemical industry, the textile industry, and the paper industry (disposable food trays, filters, heat sealing paper, tea bags).

This industry is huge and characterized by powerful suppliers and buyers. On the supply side, the price volatility of naphtha is a major factor, whereas the buyers represent Japan's most important final-product industries. While R&D allows for competition through differentiation at the cutting edge of technology, many of the chemicals and the products such as vinyl wrap are standardized and homogeneous.

In 2002, shipments of petroleum-based products totaled ¥7.5 trillion (roughly $62 billion). At the time the market leaders in polyolefin chemicals were Mitsubishi Chemical (18.2% market share), Mitsui Chemicals (15.5%), Idemitsu Kosan (13.4%), Marubeni Chemical (11.9%), and Shōwa Denkō (8.7%). Competitors in polystyrene products included Asahi Kasei and Sumitomo Chemical. The industry was stagnating and suffered from excess capacity equaling roughly 25 percent of total output. Slumping domestic demand was not yet being offset by increasing exports to China, and the sharp increase in naphtha prices since 1999 had depressed profits (Nikkei 2005; DBJ 2004).

Traditionally, prices had been determined post hoc for most trades. The chemical companies stipulated a price at the beginning of a quarter, which had regularly been adjusted downward, considering "market conditions, etc." In periods of high price volatility, the negotiation period would be extended from the usual one quarter to up to one year.[12] If, at the end of twelve months, the initially stipulated price was too high by whatever standard, the buyers pushed powerfully for reimbursement. Loathing this constant post-hoc discounting, beginning in the early 1990s the plastics companies had repeatedly attempted to fix prices in order to stand up to discount requests, but this had proven unsuccessful because the industry suffered from excess capacity, which invited cartel members to cave in to buyers' demands for post-hoc rebates. Even the

12. See, e.g., *Nikkei Business,* August 30, 1993, 25.

establishment of joint sales companies did not empower the chemical firms. By 1993, all chemical companies reported annual losses in the polypropylene segment averaging several billion yen.[13]

Throughout the 1990s, repeated announcements by the chemical companies that they would no longer engage in after-sales pricing went without effect. Because post-hoc pricing had become a major thorn in U.S.-Japan trade negotiations, and because it was detrimental to the plastics industry, beginning in 1995 even METI (then still named MITI, in charge of the chemical industry) pushed companies to resist post-hoc price negotiations and launched annual surveys of the PVC and vinyl wrap industries. According to these surveys, in 1995, roughly one third of the vinyl wrap trade (representing all types of plastic packaging) was governed by post-hoc pricing, but this ratio declined rapidly thereafter and by 2006 it seemed that the practice had been terminated. For PVC, the ratio stood at 75 percent in 1995, at 63 percent in the early 2000s, and was eventually abolished after 2004 (DBJ 2004; MITI 1997; METI 2002b, 2003b).

A big push for spot pricing in vinyl wrap came through the strategic repositioning by the oil companies. In June 1994, Mitsubishi Oil announced a switch to "upfront pricing" for two of its base products, arguing that it was easier to pass on sharp jumps in crude oil prices if the company's processed products were only tied to crude oil, rather than complicated and uncertain contingencies. Besides, the company claimed, it needed to develop cost consciousness, which was impossible if prices were decided a year after the fact. Other oil companies followed suit.[14] This had immediate ripple effects, as smaller buyers of these chemical firms were also in favor of ending the squeeze. The switch to spot pricing was also helped by consolidation. In April 2005, Mitsui Chemicals and Idemitsu Kosan formed Prime Polymer, the new polyolefin industry leader with a market share exceeding 25 percent in Japan and also the third largest in Asia. Industry consolidation increased the bargaining power of the chemical companies, such that requests for post-hoc negotiations could be more easily rejected.[15]

The PVC industry took until 2004 to finally reform. Again, the recession of the 1990s was a big obstacle, as industry attempts not to yield to price pressures were regularly undermined by suffering chemical companies happy to sell at whatever price buyers would offer. As the industry began to consolidate,

---

13. *Nikkei Business*, March 18, 1993, 29; *Nikkei*, June 11, 1994, 25.
14. *Nikkei*, September 12, 1990, 24; *Nikkei*, June 11, 1994, 25.
15. *Nikkei*, May 12, 1995, 11; *Nikkei*, July 31, 1996, 11; *Nikkei*, March 29, 2000, 29; *Kagaku Kōgyō Nippō*, April 27, 2006.

however, it strengthened its bargaining power: Mitsui Chemicals, Idemitsu Kosan, and Denki Kagaku Kōgyō founded a joined subsidiary, Taiyō Enbi, to lead the PVC industry, while Shin-Etsu Chemical focused on becoming the leading developer of cutting-edge PVC resins for use in IT-related industries and semiconductor wafers. Between 1998 and 2005, the number of firms in this industry shrank from 15 to five.

In the early 2000s, the new demand from China coincided with a 21 percent capacity reduction and ongoing consolidation. The resulting price hike invited a dramatic recovery by the PVC industry and in 2004 the two industry leaders (Taiyo Enbi and Shin-Etsu Chemical) revolutionized trade practices by posting a nonnegotiable quarterly spot price on their websites. Most important, beginning in 2004 these companies managed not only to raise prices twice but to resist requests to lower them post hoc. "Choose and focus" had greatly increased the bargaining power of the chemical firms, as well as its profitability and transparency.[16]

Thus, the transition away from after-sales-price adjustment was triggered by industry consolidation, capacity reduction, and rising demand and prices, including in global markets. It was further pushed by the regulatory stance toward the market and new disclosure requirements in the form of quarterly earning reports. The strategic inflection point had changed the logic of how to compete even in this last stronghold of relational pricing.

The Retail Revolution

Unlike business-to-business pricing mechanisms, Japan's postwar distribution system for consumer end products has been the subject of extensive research.[17] The system stood out as multilayered, complicated, exclusive, seemingly duplicative, and, in the eyes of some, highly inefficient. During the 1990s all this began to change, as new retail formats and price competition have become the dominant themes.

Multiple Layers of Distribution

At the end of the postwar period, Japan boasted twice as many wholesalers and retailers per capita as most other industrialized countries, with one wholesaler per 261 people and one retailer per 77 people in 1991. This

16. *Nikkei*, January 12, 2004, 22; January 27, 2004, 27; March 9, 2004, 27; *Kagaku Kōgyō Nippō*, January 1, 2005; May 26, 2005; January 1, 2005; April 27, 2006; May 31, 2006; www.shinetsu.co.jp/j/news/s20031222.shtml.

17. The following is based on studies on the postwar distribution system, by, e.g., Larke (1994), Miwa, Nishimura, and Ramseyer (2002), Kubomura (1996), Flath (1989, 1990, 2003), and Maclachlan (2002).

compared to 565 people per wholesaler and 166 per retailer in Germany (as of 1987), and 535 per wholesaler and 169 per retailer for the United States (as of 1994). However, by 2004 Japanese layers of distribution had been reduced by a third, falling to one wholesaler for every 340 and one retailer per 103 people.[18]

Multiple reasons have been advanced to explain Japan's high distribution density, which can be grouped into four main sets of explanations. A first reason is geography. Japan is difficult to traverse, requiring various modes of transportation. In addition to remote villages, distributors have to service high-density areas characterized by limited storage room, narrow streets, and very small shops that necessitate small-lot deliveries on a daily basis. Over time this triggered multiple stages in wholesaling, such as in shipping and intermediate warehousing. Moreover, Flath (2003) argues that the early development of logistical arteries was contributive to a large number of stores because they could easily be stocked.

The wholesalers were often under exclusive arrangements with one manufacturer, in a setup sometimes labeled "distribution keiretsu." Similar to the vertical keiretsu of subcontractors and the vertical lineups in intermediate goods markets, exclusive retailers would deal only in the products of one manufacturer who determined margins throughout the distribution hierarchy. After-sales pricing in consumer end products came in the form of rebates tied to sales volume or display; these rebates were measured on a half-annual basis when prices were readjusted backward through the distribution chain. These *toku-yakuten* (special contract stores) became a hot topic in U.S.-Japan trade negotiations, as their exclusive allegiance obstructed new entry into Japanese retailing. For incumbents, the main long-run effects of distribution keiretsu was that many retailers, especially the smaller ones, developed neither cost consciousness nor much expertise in marketing, pricing and markups, product selection, or inventory management, since all these were effectively prescribed by the manufacturer (Ekonomisuto 2001).

Wholesalers supplied many small retail outlets, which existed for social and political reasons. In the early postwar period, urban dwellers usually lived in very small houses with small kitchens, and accordingly small refrigerators (if any at all). Even after refrigerators became standard, few people had cars. Japanese cuisine required daily shopping (especially fish), and this high-frequency shopping was done by bicycle and in small lots from nearby places.

18. Japanese retail data are accessible at www.meti.go.jp/statistics/syougyou/2004niji/index3.html; population data were sourced from www.stat.go.jp. German and U.S. data are based on MITI materials, received during an interview in Tokyo, summer 1995.

Many women went grocery shopping twice a day, and the trips also fulfilled a social function by allowing housewives to catch up on local gossip.

Many of the small outlets were mom-and-pop stores, run by an elderly couple that tended to vote for the Liberal Democratic Party as long as they received a tax write-off on their house by turning the entrance into a store-front to sell sundry nonperishable goods such as cigarettes, potato chips, and instant ramen, and offer access to a pink or green pay phone. Liquor stores typically also fell into the mom-and-pop variety, as liquor licenses were strictly controlled by the Ministry of Finance, which was in charge of collecting the very high liquor taxes. Stationery stores and the ubiquitous greengrocer selling three tomatoes or two cucumbers, arranged in little plastic baskets on cardboard boxes on the sidewalk, were all examples of this postwar retail format. A main reason that these stores continued to remain in business was that they were protected. To entice the "moms" and "pops" to vote for the LDP, they received supportive legislation. Most important, small stores benefited from the Large-Scale Retail Law that made it enormously difficult, and often prohibitively expensive, to open a supermarket or other store with scale advantage in neighborhoods served by many small stores (Upham 1993, 1996; Larke 1994). Even where such a store opened, it would not receive a liquor license, a rice license, or other such entry requirements that granted some of the mom-and-pop stores a local monopoly.

What held all of this together throughout the postwar period was that the small stores also served the economic interests of Japan's manufacturers. Next to the neighborhood greengrocer, pharmacy, stationery and liquor stores, there would typically also be a Shiseido store, selling exclusively Shiseido soaps and lotions, as well as a specialized electronics store, such as those franchised by Matsushita Electric, selling all items produced under the brands of National and Panasonic. The local shopping area would be rounded out by a few other specialty stores, such as for sporting goods, toys, and books.

These specialty stores existed because of their critical role in retail price maintenance. Throughout the postwar period, many manufacturers engaged in price setting, and their suggested retail price, which was often printed on the end product, was upheld through controlling margins in the distribution system and by tying retail stores directly and exclusively to the manufacturer. Volume rebates, the no-cost return of unsold goods, or even outright pressure and bullying kept retailers from selling these products at a discount.[19]

19. Progressive rebates enticed a store to carry only one brand. The "return of unsold goods" policy explains the mom-and-pop store business model. Not only did the storefront greatly reduce property taxes for a retired couple, but they also faced little inventory costs. It also ensured that stores would be well stocked. Small bookstores operated on a similar logic.

To the extent a local store offered discounts, these too were suggested by the manufacturer. In the very early postwar years, retail price maintenance had been officially sanctioned when everyday household goods were exempted from antitrust rules. Once established, the practice was difficult to stop given the legal interpretation of what constituted a violation of antitrust statutes through the 1990s.

As a result, prices often were set uniformly for products in the same category and choice was often limited, especially in the local stores. Imported goods were difficult to find, since the exclusive retailers carried only one brand. For large city dwellers, an excursion to larger stores often revealed that prices were somewhat lower compared to the neighborhood store, but the same as those at the direct competitor. Retail price maintenance applied to all kinds of specialty stores, from tires to travel agencies. Competition for many of these products was on product specification and access to a store, rather than on price.[20]

Naturally, high prices invited mavericks. The earliest of these was Daiei, a general merchandise discount chain, built on a drugstore founded in 1957 to sell "good stuff at cheap prices." Daiei introduced white label (no brand name) and private label products to Japan. The company's founder, Nakauchi Isao, became a member of the core group of early mavericks who managed against all odds to introduce new choice and lower prices in rigidly regulated markets. Reckless diversification during the bubble period eventually led to Daiei's collapse and restructuring in 2004, but its impact on Japan's distribution system cannot be exaggerated. Perhaps the most famous aspect of the Daiei challenge came to be referred to as the "30-Year War" with Matsushita Electric, which refused to sell National and Panasonic household electronics through Daiei for fear that the discounter would destroy its pricing structure.

In the early 1990s, more attempted to break loose and set discount prices for items usually governed by retail price maintenance, such as cosmetics. Many of these became subject to coercion, threats of having the store closed down, and other *ijime* (bullying) by manufacturers (e.g., Fukunaga and Chinone 1994). In 1993, Fujiki, an independent retailer, sued Shiseido for stopping shipments to his chain as punishment for his discounts. The Japan Fair Trade Commission (JFTC), in a move it came to regret, looked into the case

---

20. Even in Tokyo's electronics district Akihabara, lower price caps existed for most products. In 1983, it was said that prices in Akihabara were set by the local trade association. This sounded dubious, because price tags suggested differences across stores. In a two-day field research, I attempted to negotiate the lowest price for three different makes and models of a Walkman by bargaining with 20 different stores. All stores were willing to offer a small price break of varying percentages. In the end, however, adjusting for different sticker prices, these discounts resulted in all 20 stores offering the exact same price for each model and make.

but found insufficient evidence of wrongdoing. Fujiki persisted, filing another suit claiming that Shiseido's insistence on the importance of face-to-face consulting—allegedly critical for consumer protection—was simply a cloak for suppressing discount stores. What began as a contract dispute had suddenly become a major antitrust case. Consumer groups jumped in and brought the case into the headlines, as they had long been pushing for a breakup of vertical restraints in retailing, to no avail (Taylor 2003; Maclachlan 2002).

Eventually, the Supreme Court upheld the previous sentence in 1998 on the grounds that face-to-face sales were a critical part of the sales strategy of cosmetics, as consumers benefited from guidance by trained consultants. But even though Fujiki lost the battle, he ultimately won the war. Concerned that the JFTC, sharply criticized inside and outside Japan for its initial punting, would reopen the case and investigate vertical constraints, Shiseido announced that it had changed its sales strategy and now differentiated between luxury cosmetics and lesser categories and everyday items. The latter were shipped to all retail formats, with no pressure on retail price maintenance. For luxury items, Shiseido crafted new contracts with special outlets, such as department stores, who committed to face-to-face sales and no discounting (Taylor 2003). Price competition had arrived in drugstores, and this in turn spawned the emergence of new discounting chains, such as MatsumotoKiyoshi.

Also in the midst of the 1990s recession, the 100 Yen Stores experienced a boom. Selling imported and domestic goods that were explicitly cheap at a sticker price of ¥100, they offered an alternative to hardware and basic household goods stores. Their growing popularity undermined the marketing myth that Japanese consumers loved high prices because they loved high quality. Given the choice, Japanese consumers were just as happy or as cautious in considering lower-priced options as consumers elsewhere.

Retail Price Competition

These developments paved the way for what was labeled Japan's "retail revolution" (*ryūtsū kakumei*). The four main contributors of the postwar multilayered, multistore setup—geography, society, politics, and economics—were all simultaneously undermined. Advances in transportation technology (packaging, cooling trucks) made many of the wholesale middlemen superfluous. Urbanization and affluence led many households to switch to one-stop, once-a-week shopping in large suburban stores, as most households now had cars, more women were in the workforce and less interested in chatting with their greengrocer, and houses (and refrigerators) were getting larger as suburbs grew. A change in diet away from the previous dominance of fish allowed for less frequent shopping. Moreover, the mom-and-pop stores often had no successors and attrition reduced their frequency. The decline in their political power combined with foreign pressure to result in repeated revisions of the Large-Scale Retail Law. In 2000, this infamous law was replaced by the new Large-Scale Retail Store Location Law that grants the authority to limit large stores to prefectures and municipalities, based on considerations of noise or traffic; the input of small stores in this decision was curtailed to but one voice.

The emergence of new retail formats also challenged the traditional system. In the 1970s, Itō Yōkado, a leading supermarket chain, had ventured into building small 24-hour convenience stores in urban areas, strategically located between subway stations and apartments. As subsidiaries of larger supermarkets, they enjoyed bargaining power in purchasing that translated into lower prices than those offered at other local stores. Over time, extensive use of information technology, advanced stock-keeping processes, and smart business strategy made these stores the most successful and cutting-edge retail outlets in Japan. Between 1974, when Itō Yōkado opened its first Seven-Eleven, and 2002, the number of convenience store chains grew to ten, with total stores exceeding 41,000.[21]

Another big push toward the reform of traditional Japanese retailing came with the arrival, beginning in the mid-1990s, of foreign competition through American and European large-scale retailers, such as Carrefour, Toys-R-Us, Office Depot, Wal-Mart, and Tesco. In spite of the 1990s recession, these retailers were attracted to Japan because deregulation afforded access while the ongoing recession had made Japan comparatively cheap. Even though not all of these retailers were ultimately successful, their new business practices had a huge impact on Japan's market. The foreign chains refused retail price maintenance or rebates but instead relied on standard practices of spot pricing and discounting. Their business model was also much advanced compared to the older retail formats in Japan as it built on global merchandise sourcing, efficient logistics and point-of-sales stock-keeping information systems, and effective marketing in the selection of goods and product category management. All this began to challenge Japan's existing system of exclusive wholesalers and price markups determined by the producer. Thus, these stores brought what one observer labeled the "Carrefour Wedge" to Japanese retailing (Ekonomisuto 2001).

The breakup of rigid retail structures invited discounters in all specialty areas. In electronics, Big Camera and Yamada Denki undermined the former

---

21. Japan has been the chain's most successful market, and with the formation of the Japanese Seven & i Holdings Co. in 2005, the U.S. 7-Eleven, Inc. became a wholly owned subsidiary of Seven-Eleven Japan.

grip on the market held by Yodobashi and Sakura, which had already greatly challenged the local National Stores. In clothing, the men's clothing store Aoyama paved the way for new discount chains such as Mujirushi and Uniqlo (the brand names of Ryōhin Kaikaku and Fast Retailing, respectively), which source predominantly outside Japan.[22]

To remain competitive in light of these developments, Japan's traditional retailers such as department stores and supermarkets began to consolidate. Whereas at its peak in 1982, Japan had 1.72 million retail stores, by 2002 this number had dropped to 1.3 million stores, a 24 percent reduction. In international comparison, however, Japan's retail system remained fragmented: whereas in the United Kingdom, the top five retailers accounted for more than half of all sales, and in the United States the top ten retailers combined had over 20 percent of total sales, in Japan the top ten retailers had a meager market share of less than 8 percent (as of 2000).[23] Combined with the breakup of previous vertical constraints, these numbers suggest that Japan's retail market is now more competitive than those in other countries. New Japan retailing is fundamentally different from its postwar form.

At the onset of the 21st century, retail price maintenance received yet another blow from the Internet, which facilitated price comparisons through transparency. The first wave of discounting, through Daiei in the 1960s and 1970s, had been triggered by Japanese tourists who realized that products (often including those from Japan) were cheaper abroad than they were at home. The second round of price transparency has been propelled by the Internet, in particular companies that provide price comparisons, such as Kakaku. com (see case study in chapter 11).

The End of the Sanctuary Strategy

The final contributing factor to the end of retail price maintenance was changes in global competition and business strategies by Japanese multinationals that negated the role of domestic price and distribution controls. As the exclusive retail chains began to disappear and the large independent discounters took over, imports could flow more freely into Japan, simultaneously introducing price competition and choice. Equally important, globalization had begun to undermine the previous sanctuary strategy pursued by some exporting industries. In such a strategy, the manufacturers cooperated at home

22. See, e.g., Larke and Causton 2005; Meyer-Ohle 2003; Sakamoto 2004; Minakata 2005.

23. *Nihon Shokuryō Shinbun,* November 13, 2000; Japan Retailers Association, www. japan-retail.or.jp/english/p4.htm.

by establishing a price cartel and pushing high prices through their exclusive retail chains and then used the resulting profits for aggressive price competition in foreign markets. The issue was first raised in the TV case of the 1970s, when U.S. electronics firms sued their Japanese competitors for dumping. It resurfaced during the U.S.-Japan trade negotiations on semiconductors in the 1980s and the 1995 WTO case of Kodak vs. Fujifilm. A sanctuary strategy is a variety of multimarket competition, where the same companies cooperate in one market but compete in others. This was possible because of the exclusive and segmented nature of Japanese retailing and the ineffectiveness of antitrust policies against retail price maintenance during the postwar period (Dewey Ballantine 1995; Schaede 2004; Schwartzman 1993).

The strategic inflection point and the arrival of global competition have made the sanctuary strategy no longer viable. Market share through low-priced, high-volume global sales is no longer the strategic focus. Increased labor costs in Japan (as compared to the 1960s and 1970s) have eroded all Japanese cost advantages. The newly emerging global competitors can be outdone only through differentiation by innovation. Moreover, with increased production abroad, either in the target market itself or in locations with low labor costs, the difference between the home market and third markets is no longer as easy to establish. Overall, the sanctuary strategy, as practiced by Japanese industries, is a late-developer strategy exercised in a closed country with labor cost advantages. For Japan, it was a 20th century strategy that is neither profitable nor executable in the global economy of today.

With the sanctuary strategy a thing of the past, the exclusive chain stores lost their relevance to the manufacturers, and therefore they are now being phased out. Together with the increasing imports, this has greatly opened up choice for Japanese consumers. Whereas previously consumers basically bought what was offered by the local store, new megastores compete on price and product selection. One indicator of more choice was the shortening of hit product life cycles. Through the 1970s, 60 percent of hit products in Japan had a life span of over five years, whereas in the early 2000s only 5 percent of hit products stayed on top that long. Conversely, whereas only 1.6 percent of all hit products had a life cycle of less than one year in the 1970s, this ratio increased to 19 percent in 2003. Asked for the reasons why products were replaced so much faster, 40 percent of survey respondents in the 1970s cited a change in consumer taste. In contrast, in the early 2000s, 35 percent of products were replaced by cheaper products of the same type, 25 percent by change in taste, and 16 percent by substitutes (SMEA 2005). In short, imports had joined price competition to provide more competition, shortened product life cycles, and greatly enhanced consumer choice to Japan.

Evaluation: The Changing Nature of Rivalry

Price transparency is the basic facet of market competition. Throughout the postwar period, Japanese firms engaged in numerous efforts to stabilize their business environment by designing insurance mechanisms, including limiting the variability of prices for the individual firm, in order to shift the risk of exogenous shocks to the system as a whole. A critical component of this insurance system was after-sales price adjustment, in addition to price agreements at the industry level and retail price maintenance in end markets. In New Japan, however, this type of insurance has become either too costly, by constraining strategic options, or impractical due to import competition. Spot pricing has become the norm, and retail competition has shifted to price. Trade has turned toward the market.

For the foreign observer, the nontransparency and situational handling of contingencies may have looked mysterious, but it worked because it was tied into other Old Japan mechanisms ensuring stability, such as long-term trade relations within business groups and banks and highly organized supplier relations. Competition with other companies in the same industry was for stable customers, which one attracted and kept through careful management of long-term reciprocal give-and-take. At the retail end, competition focused on the availability and location of retail outlets, service, and product features such as quality or appearance. It was no accident that Japanese household appliances were offered in all colors of the rainbow at a time when consumers elsewhere thought of these strictly as "white goods."

Increased price transparency—the prerequisite of price competition—goes together with increased corporate disclosure. Statutory quarterly earnings reports all but rule out extended after-sales price adjustments. These reports are intended for the newly empowered shareholders that include active traders. Rivalry has extended to those shareholders as well, as companies try to not only produce better products and sell those at higher margins than their competitors but also to attract cheaper external capital due to higher credit ratings. Price competition has arrived in Japan.

9

LIFETIME EMPLOYMENT:
CHANGING HUMAN
RESOURCE MANAGEMENT

The implementation of strategic change depends critically on a change in human resource practices. Success in corporate renewal hinges on the alignment of new strategic tasks with formal organization, people, and corporate culture. As companies shift toward focus and differentiation, they must reorient corporate culture toward efficiency and promote people for contributing to profitability. To turn from diversified goliaths to nimble and lean competitors they must restructure. Human resource management is at the center of a successful strategic reorientation.

Recognizing the importance of increased labor mobility for corporate reorganization, in the early 2000s the Koizumi government pushed for a revision of the previously rigid rules on lifetime employment, as well as for new laws that give more structure to the market for nonregular workers. New court interpretations regarding dismissals and a 2004 revision of the Labor Standards Law turned the previous "lifetime" obligation toward a regular employee into a long-term commitment that can be terminated if performance is lacking. In the next step, companies have begun to make qualitative changes to how they manage long-term employees, putting greater emphasis on individual performance and career goals. Long-term employment has turned from a rigid, automated process into a strategic tool in the war for talent, especially given a looming labor shortage. That is, the concept of long-term employment per se is not disappearing, but rather it is being restructured to serve new goals that have less to do with steady training of loyal generalists, and much more with competing through specialization.

Demographic changes in Japan's workforce, changes in the value system as pertaining to work-life balance, and the strategic inflection point have combined to challenge the postwar system in ways that echo the experience of the United States and Europe beginning in the 1970s and 1980s. Strategic repositioning has translated into a rise in the proportion of external labor, as companies pursuing a focus strategy benefit from externalizing noncore tasks. In light of these changes, Japan's government, too, has changed its stance, no longer viewing labor market rules as social regulation but as an important tool in allowing the flow of workers from declining industries to competitive businesses, thus accelerating economic recovery and reorganization. Labor mobility, including in the white collar world, has arrived in Japan.

The Postwar System of Lifetime Employment

One of the well-studied facets of postwar Japanese business organization is the practice of lifetime employment and the associated system of seniority wages, which together with in-house labor unions formed the "three treasures" of Japan's employment system. However, not all that we know about these three treasures stands undisputed, and neither long-tenured employment nor the wage system may have been as unique as sometimes suggested. Rather, the Japanese "salaryman" represented an extreme version of the "organization man" in Europe and the United States in the 1960s and 1970s.

Under postwar-period lifetime employment, companies hired their core workers straight out of college with an open-ended contract that stipulated a retirement age (*teinen*).[1] Until the early 1980s this was set at 55 in most companies, but has been raised to 60 during the 1980s, and by 2006 was stipulated by law to be raised again to 65 over the following decade. The employment contract of regular employees was fairly standardized across companies, and although it contained stipulations regarding the termination of employment, court decisions over time had made dismissal increasingly difficult.

The origins of lifetime employment are debated in the literature. While some trace it back to the late 19th century when trade associations established strict rules on poaching (stealing trained apprentices from another company), others see the first signs in the labor controls introduced before World War II (Kikkawa 1988). Still others date the beginnings to the early 1950s, when the government strove to pass on to companies some of its responsibilities put forth in the new Constitution of 1949, which obligated the government to provide livelihood with dignity and to protect labor rights. Both would be ensured if companies could not easily lay off workers. Whatever its roots, the postwar system came into full force as an institutionalized practice with the onset of fast economic growth in the late 1950s and the labor shortage of the 1960s (Gordon 1998; Mizumachi 2002).

During this labor shortage, an important tool to tie workers to the corporation developed in the system of seniority wages, which is a misnomer as it

1. For detailed analyses of Japan's postwar employment system, see, e.g., Abegglen and Stalk (1985); Aoki (1988, chap. 3); Araki (2002); Clark (1979, chaps. 4–6); Dore (1986, 1987); Dore and Sako (1989); Ito (1991, chap. 8); Lincoln and Kalleberg (1990); Odagiri (1992, chap. 2); Rebick (2005).

was partially based on ability (expressed in rank and determined by education degree), and determined not by seniority as expressed in age but by length of tenure with the company. For the first 15 years with the company, the employee was comparatively underpaid, and for the second 15 years he (rarely she) was comparatively overpaid. A stylized visualization of this system is in figure 9.1. An employee leaving his company after a decade would have to start back at the very low entry-level at another employer (similar to firefighters or airline pilots in the United States). This established strong incentives for employees to stay with one company, regardless of how unhappy the working relationship or how frustrating the frequently unpaid overtime. In turn, the company felt quite assured that it would reap the benefits from employee training, such as sending young employees abroad for two years of graduate study or arranging for on- and off-the-job skill development. Wages did not differ by job category (e.g., accounting versus sales), and employees were expected to rotate through divisions to learn all aspects of the corporation. Japan's education system reflected this notion of generalist knowledge and firm-specific skill development, as advanced education in professional schools such as business or law remained underdevelopment.

A second tool to tie in regular employees was the corporate pension, which, until the late 1990s, was also determined by length of service. Vesting only set in after ten years of service with one company, and pensions increased in non-linear fashion with every added year of service. This amplified the indentured character of regular workers, creating a financial double whammy for those who changed jobs in midcareer.

9.1. *Stylized Wage Curve for Postwar-Period Japan*

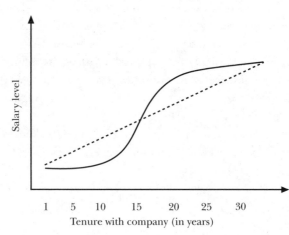

At the turn of the century, the rigidities of this system were no longer bearable. From the companies' perspective, corporate restructuring was predicated on the removal of the three excesses from the 1990s—debt, capacity, and labor—and they pushed for more liberties in layoffs. For individuals, the stereotypical life of a "salaryman" became increasingly unappealing, as younger people demanded greater work-life balance and more individualized careers (MHLW 2007). When several court decisions relaxed the criteria for dismissals in the early 2000s, many began to wonder whether lifetime employment was a thing of the past. Abegglen (2004), who first observed the practice and coined the term, insists that lifetime employment is the one tenet of Japanese business organization certain to remain. Others see a great transformation in the rights of employers vs. labor (e.g., Araki 2002). In fact, Japanese employers have constantly adapted their human resource practices according to circumstance, even though publicly they may speak out in favor of the status quo, lest they cause unnecessary union unrest or seem unpatriotic. To better see how this system is evolving, it is helpful to understand its legal foundations.

The Courts' Creation

Perhaps the biggest bone of contention surrounding postwar lifetime employment is what portion of the workforce was actually covered by it. This is uncertain because the practice was not based on any legal provisions. At the low end of estimates, some have posited that it applied to some 25 percent of the workforce, by equating lifetime employment status with union membership, or alternatively with being employed by large firms. However, Cole (1983) was one of the first to point out that long-term employment relations well described work relations in small manufacturing firms. Abegglen and Stalk (1985), likewise, were skeptical of this equation, and argue that an accurate estimation is impossible.

A look at the legal situation sheds light on the issue. In 1947, the Labor Standards Law was introduced to regulate labor aspects such as wage payment methods, working hours, annual paid leave, and work rules. The law has been amended repeatedly, but until its 2004 revision contained virtually no rules on dismissals beyond requiring the employer to give a 30-day advance notice. Strictly by the letter of the law, dismissals were extraordinarily easy in Japan (Nakakubo 2004).

The law divides employment relations into two types—those based on unrestricted, open-ended regular contracts and those based on limited-term contracts. Until the 2004 revision, limited-term contracts had a maximum duration of one year but could be extended repeatedly. Limited-contract employees were referred to as part-timers, although working hours were often the same. Neither side could change the terms of the contract during the year, but the employer could choose not to extend without a specific reason. This increased flexibility for employers who used part-timers as buffers to adjust their workforce over the business cycle. However, because wages and benefits for part-time workers were less than half of those of regular employees, this also gave rise to inequity. In 1974 the Supreme Court ruled that if a fixed-term contract had been renewed for several years in a row such that it had become indistinguishable from a regular contract, a refusal to renew was akin to a dismissal and thus governed by the same legal rules as termination of regular contracts. It is this ruling that has led some analysts to believe that in the 1980s and 1990s roughly 80 percent of the workforce could effectively not be dismissed, that is, they were thought of as regular, "lifetime" employees (e.g., Araki 2002; Nakakubo 2004).

Importantly, the provisions on dismissals were entirely the courts' making. Because the Labor Standards Law made no mention of dismissals, the courts relied on Civil Code Section 3(1) to evaluate whether or not a dismissal was reasonable. Yet, the Civil Code simply states that "rights shall not be abused." To establish a baseline, the courts developed the "doctrine of abusive dismissal" that identified four situations in which dismissals could be justified: (1) an existing agreement with the corporate union; (2) incompetence on the part of the employee; (3) violation of disciplinary rules; and (4) business necessity. The last category was also called "adjustment dismissal," and it was further informed by four conditions that would make these adjustments reasonable: (a) Was the reduction of the workforce truly needed? (b) Had the employer made efforts to avoid the layoff? (c) Were the people to be laid off selected based on reasonable grounds? and (d) Had the employer provided an explanation to the workers and the labor union in an effort to gain their understanding? (Ouchi 2002).

Each of these criteria may seem sufficiently flexible were it not for the fact that over time courts came to rule that *all* of these requirements had to be met for a dismissal to be found "not abusive." For example, the incompetence of a worker alone was not an acceptable reason for dismissal; rather, it became the company's duty to find a job for this person that suited the employee's abilities (Araki 2002). Effectively, a company could lay off workers only if it faced near bankruptcy, had already terminated all part-time contracts, could identify underperforming personnel clearly, *and* had overcome union resistance by offering generous "voluntary retirement" bonuses. Companies could not use labor policies preemptively to avoid crisis. In spite of having the most lenient labor law on paper, in a 1999 OECD comparison of 25 industrialized countries Japan ranked 25th in terms of difficulty of dismissing a worker (Kuroda 2004).

Araki's (2002) estimate that 80 percent of Japan's workforce was in lifetime employment rests strictly on the legal question of how many employees could have reasonably expected to be able to fight a dismissal as abusive in court. In this view, which is echoed in labor statistics, lifetime employment was restricted neither to large firms nor to holders of regular contracts. It is possible that large-firm employees were more likely to have the wherewithal to sue, but to the extent small-firm employees went to court they could have maintained employment. Thus, lifetime employment was much more widespread than often thought, but this system has also begun to undergo much greater change in the early 2000s than is commonly appreciated.

Toward the Externalization of Labor

According to labor survey data, as of January 2006 employment had recovered from the recession, with unemployment falling from the peak of 5.7 percent in 2002 to 4.6 percent.[2] However, the recession had greatly truncated the number of the self-employed. Whereas in 1995, self-employed and family workers accounted for almost 11.8 million workers (18% of the total labor force), this ratio was halved to 5.3 million (8.3%) by 2002. This decline is explained by the high rate of bankruptcies among very small firms, including the mom-and-pop shops examined in the previous chapter, coupled with succession problems and a low start-up rate during the 1990s.[3]

But the most important long-term trend in Japanese labor data is the decline in regular employees in the total workforce. The sharp increase in nonregular work, especially with the onset of the strategic inflection point in 1998, is shown in figure 9.2. Nonregular workers have more than doubled, from 15 percent in 1984 to 34 percent in 2006. In its 2007 White Paper on the Labour Economy (MHLW 2007), Japan's government forecast that this would be a continuing trend, because traditional mechanisms of economic growth

2. Countries differ in how they measure and calculate the unemployment ratio. In Japan, this is the percentage share of employment seekers of the active labor force, as opposed to the total working-age population (see, e.g., Ito 1991). This makes the labor force participation rate (people older than 15 years who are in the workforce or are looking for work) an important variable. Sometimes part-time workers drop out of active labor force data when their contracts expire, and family workers are often not captured in active labor force counts; neither would therefore be counted as unemployed should they lose work.

3. See chapters 10 and 11 on start-ups. Labor data are accessible at www.stat.go.jp/english/data/roudou.index.htm.

9.2. Shifts in Nonregular Work, 1984–2006
Source: MHLW (2007), based on Sōmushō Tōkeikyoku, *Rōdōryoku tokubetsu chōsa* (until 2001), and *Rōdōryoku chōsa (shōsai kekka)* (from 2002).

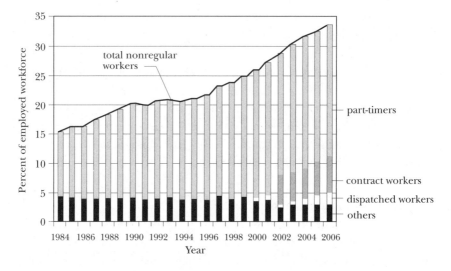

leading to lifetime employment had become "ineffective." Moreover, since 2004 the Ministry of Labor has calculated two separate job-opening ratios (measuring the availability of jobs in proportion to job applications). In 2006, the ratio for overall workers had increased to over 1, meaning that there was excess demand for labor. However, the ratio of openings for regular employees stood at only 0.6, meaning that 40 percent of job seekers were pushed into nonregular positions.

Nonregular work is divided into three separate categories. Part-timers are hired directly by companies, whereas dispatched workers are contracted through temporary employment agencies. The fastest growing category of nonregular workers is so-called contract work, introduced only in 2002. Unlike dispatched workers, these workers constitute a pool of highly specialized, outsourced labor, and they demand higher wages than other nonregular workers (Fujimoto and Kimura 2005, Saitō 2006). Contract work was initially widespread in the electronics and auto industries. Growing new areas are so-called support services, such as staffing, consulting, leasing, advertising, legal, financial and accounting. According to a METI estimate, the U.S. market for these services grew from ¥96 trillion in 1990 to ¥160 trillion (or about $1,280 billion) in 2000. In Japan, it expanded from ¥53 trillion, and 4.6 million employed in 1990 to ¥76 trillion (roughly $680 billion) and 6.3 million workers in 2000, with a 4 percent annual growth forecast for the coming decade (JETRO 2005b).

The development portrayed in figure 9.2 is informed by a study on the externalization of labor in the United States beginning in the 1980s.[4] Pfeffer and Baron (1988) observed a growing proportion of labor being outsourced and engaged on a temporary or part-time basis, often working outside the firm (e.g., from home), and increasingly handled administratively by an agency other than the firm. In the early postwar period, the "corporation man" in the United States was not unlike his Japanese equivalent in terms of long-term tenure and pride of affiliation, that is, identification with and commitment to the organization.[5] A first shift in the United States to an increase in part-time work in the 1970s was followed by a fast rise in contract work, temporary employment, and home work at piece rates throughout the 1990s (Pfeffer and Baron 1988; Segal and Sullivan 1997).

The analysis of the costs and benefits of long-term employment versus out-sourcing begins with transaction cost economics (Williamson 1975, 1980). The benefits of building a long-term labor force in-house include the increased loyalty of the worker through tie-in. This translates into more effort, dedication, and willingness to work long hours. The buildup of firm-specific skills through on-the-job training as well as intergenerational skill transfers without fear of replacement benefit organizational learning. Increase in experience over time allows the company to move down the learning curve and produce more efficiently. Perceived equity and limited fear of losing the job boost morale and teamwork among workers. Enhanced information on workers facilitates grooming for executive positions. Finally, the company saves greatly with low labor turnover. These benefits have also been well chronicled for Japan.

However, contracting workers in the market offers its own advantages—and it is these advantages that have begun to weigh more heavily in New Japan. Contract work is cheaper, because no reserves for benefits have to be accumulated, and often no benefits are offered at all. Recruiting mistakes are much less costly, and lawsuits for dismissals unlikely. Contracting will increase measures of profitability or productivity, such as sales per employee, as these measures are typically calculated with only core workers in the denominator. Outsourcing affords flexibility in workforce adjustment. In companies pursuing a focus strategy, externalizing a part of the workforce allows the company to concentrate on its distinctive competence and make a greater push for differentiation,

4. The claim here is not that the two countries have similar human resource management practices overall, or are necessarily converging to the same set of practices (Jacoby 2005). Rather, the theoretical model developed by Pfeffer and Baron (1988) is a helpful tool to analyze ongoing changes in Japan.

5. On commitment and changes in U.S. labor relations, see also O'Reilly and Chatman (1986); Jacoby (1997, 2005); Capelli (1999); Pfeffer (2006).

while leaving peripheral tasks to contract workers. Where wage parity is high (as is common in Japan), outsourcing allows an isolation of the wage structure, which is beneficial when a company is in temporary need of highly skilled labor. Finally, for the United States at least it has been shown that temporary or contract workers may sometimes work harder, thus introducing competitive pressure into the workforce.[6]

Taken together, externalization increases flexibility and allows for more adaptive strategies, at the loss of skill formation and morale. These advantages were not important in postwar Japan, when stability was an important strategic goal, but they became critical with the strategic inflection at the turn of the century. To implement "choose and focus" strategies, companies needed flexibility in labor, and therefore increased their proportion of external labor to regular workers.

Resource dependence theory predicts that companies lower their dependence on critical resources in periods of high uncertainty, economic recession, increased competition, or other changes in the environment that make the future unpredictable (Pfeffer and Salancik 1978). Accordingly, the more tumultuous the environment, the more likely is a shift away from lifetime and toward limited-term employment. However, the increase in external labor is not simply a reaction to the recession of the 1990s. To see why this shift toward nonregular work is strategic, we also must look at longer-term trends affecting this shift.

Supply Side Factors That Increase Nonregular Work

In addition to the economic trade-off between "hierarchy" (permanent employees) and "markets" (outsourcing), Pfeffer and Baron (1988) discuss how long-term changes in the labor market and the firm's environment trigger changes in employment practices. While they observed these changes for the United States and parts of Europe in the 1970s and 1980s, Japan underwent similar shifts in the 1990s.

The biggest supply side change is demographic, in particular the increased participation of women and elderly in the workforce. When these enter the

---

6. Pfeffer and Baron (1988) also show that externalization helps companies resist unionization, both by introducing potential competition to main jobs and simply because it is difficult to organize workers that work from home or are only present for limited hours. In the early 2000s, the role of unions was also changing rapidly in Japan. As of 1997, 95.6 percent of all unions were enterprise unions representing regular workers only; because their main concern was maintaining jobs, these unions were usually pragmatic when considering revisions in changes in work conditions and wages. A 2004 revision of the Trade Union Law, together with changes in the 2003 Labor Standards Law, paved the way for new representation, also in light of a fast-declining unionization rate that had fallen to 19.6 percent in 2003. How nonregular workers will be represented remains an open issue (Araki 2005).

workforce at a time of slow economic growth, they have little bargaining power and therefore will have to take what they can get—which is typically part-time or temporary work. Thus, the influx of new labor translates almost directly into an increase in nonregular workers. Because lifetime employment in Japan extended only to age 55 (and later on to 60), a large number of the elderly rejoined the workforce as nonregular workers after they retired. In a fast-ageing society such as Japan's, their number naturally increases quickly. In the early 2000s labor analysts in Japan warned of the "2007 problem," referring to the year when baby boomers began to retire in record-high numbers (Mitani 2006).

The limited role of women in Japan's workforce has been well chronicled.[7] Labor participation over the life cycle of women has shown a distinct "M" shape, with age plotted on the x-axis. The first spike of the "M" was due to women in their 20s joining the workforce, typically in general track jobs (as opposed to the men's management career track). In these positions, women were expected to work for several years—often as "office ladies" preparing copies or tea—and resign upon marriage. The second spike was caused by women reentering the workforce in their 40s, after their children had entered college, and as midcareer entrants all they could receive were nonregular appointments. In 2005, 18 percent of males but 53 percent of females found themselves in nonregular positions (Saitō 2006).

Although the number of women in management career tracks began to grow in the 1990s and was further pushed by stricter enforcement of equal opportunity legislation in the early 2000s, their number in the management ranks remained low. According to a 2001 survey by the Ministry of Labor, Health and Welfare, 12 percent of assistant managers (*kakarichō*) were female, but only 5.5 percent of managers (*kachō*) and 3.2 percent of general managers (*buchō*). More than one third of survey respondents said that males with a university degree were promoted through these ranks much faster than women, principally because males were assigned tasks requiring more skills and knowledge so they had more opportunity to prove themselves. Temporary relocations used to constitute a crucial factor in promotions in Japan, but whereas men and women were said to have been offered similar opportunities, the frequency of transfers was twice as high for males (JLB 2003b, 2). The government added to the bias by offering tax breaks on monthly income below a certain amount and, until the pension reform of 2003, by not collecting social security contributions from part-time workers. Thus, unless highly skilled, women reentering the workforce in their 40s were financially better off working in part-time jobs.

---

7. See Abegglen and Stalk (1985); Rebick (2005); Schoppa (2006).

It is important to note that some of this has begun to change, including government incentives for part-time workers. With ongoing changes in society and a looming labor shortage, many companies turned to hiring female career employees, as foreign companies in Japan have already done for years.

In addition to women and the elderly, in the 1990s a third source of term-limited labor was young people. Given the constraints on large firms dismissing workers at the time, during the recession of the 1990s firms downsized partially through attrition. Therefore, the cohort born in the early 1970s that graduated in the early 1990s ended up with limited opportunities for regular employment. Some of these came to be known as *freetas* ("free-timers"), typically with a negative connotation of laziness and noncommitment.[8]

It is sometimes assumed that part-timers choose to work in nonregular positions with no career opportunities or skill development. However, studies for the United States, where similar assumptions were made in the 1970s, show that this was often out of necessity for there was no choice. Attributing the trend in temporary work to the desires of women or the young is misleading at best (Pfeffer and Baron 1988). In Japan, in a 2003 Ministry of Health, Labor and Welfare survey, more than half of respondents cited personal reasons for choosing temporary work (such as reduced working hours), but 26 percent said they found no opportunities to work in regular employment.

In contrast, the highly paid, specialized contract workers make a positive choice to work on a nonregular basis. The explanation for this phenomenon, also observed in the United States in the 1970s, is a change in social norms about work. In Japan, this has been expressed in workers turning down requests for transfers to other cities, an increasing social acceptance of working for temporary staff agencies, and higher acceptance of midcareer job changers. The 2002 White Paper on Labor reported that two thirds of workers in their 20s, half of those in their 30s, and one third of those in their 40s thought that it was more important to tip the work-life balance toward "life" (MHLW 2002). That this became a pressing matter in Japan is evidenced by the subtitle of the 2007 White Paper of the Ministry of Labor, "Work-Life Balance and Employment Systems" (MHLW 2007). Still, not all companies were willing or able to change work norms and processes as fast as their younger workers demanded. As a result, in the early 2000s a growing

8. Yamada (1999) labeled them "parasite singles," based on his discovery that about 60 percent of single men and 80 percent of single women between the ages of 20–34 were living with their parents (allegedly carefree, spending their income on holidays and leisure). Although this may describe a subgroup of young workers in the 1990s, Genda (2002) attributes the phenomenon to the rapid increase in unemployment and low-paid temporary work among young people.

number of workers with specialized skills chose to work on a consulting or contract basis.

Demand Side Factors

The shifts in the labor force are met by changes in corporate demand. The most obvious is that permanent employment is expensive. This is not only so in terms of benefits but also in recruiting, training, and socializing permanent workers, and in the inflexibility associated with permanent work over the business cycle. And even as layoffs of regular workers are getting easier in Japan, there are direct costs associated with layoffs ranging from severance pays and the potential of lawsuits, to the cost of goodwill in the community.[9] To avoid these costs, companies are becoming more selective in the types of positions they fill with regular employees.

The cost trade-off between permanent and externalized labor becomes more critical as a company finds itself under pressure to become efficient and flexible in its reaction to a changing business environment. The strategic inflection point did just this to Japanese firms. Uncertainty has greatly increased due to competition and globalization, making more flexible human resource practices a strategic necessity. New accounting rules and disclosure requirements have increased pressures to increase profitability. Japanese companies became more concerned about the built-in rigidities of the system relative to its virtues and began to push for changes in the courts' interpretation of the labor laws.

With the continuing recovery and the looming labor shortage, at around 2007 circumstances changed yet again and the growth in nonregular work as shown in figure 9.2 showed signs of slowing down. In 2007, some companies were reportedly offering regular positions even to workers usually hired on a part-time basis, such as sales staff in clothing stores. But rather than as a return to Old Japan, this development can be the explained precisely by the greater ease with which companies can now terminate such contracts. Therefore, in addition to the quantitative decline in regular work over the previous decade, legal reforms have also affected the qualitative standing of regular workers, by turning them from "lifetime" to less-binding long-term employees. Overall, the system has become more flexible.

New Labor Laws

In 2002, in its push for economic revival and a turn to the market, the Koizumi government began a series of labor reforms to increase flexibility in

---

9. Ahmadjian and Robinson (2001) find that the increase in layoffs, transfers to lesser jobs, and voluntary retirements in the 1990s in Japan can be explained by safety in numbers—because all companies were doing it, the competitive loss in reputation evened out.

employment practices, following a reorientation in legal doctrine regarding dismissals. The Labor Standards Law was revised, as were laws governing temporary work. To ensure fairness, the greater liberties of employers were counterbalanced by more transparent and clear-cut processes of labor dispute resolution. As of 2007, the new system was still developing, with a further revision of the main labor law under review. The transition to more market-driven processes in labor relations had begun.

The Labor Standards Law

In addition to new competitive pressures, changing demographics and so-cial norms, specialization and increasing individualism, a main trigger for legal revision was the extended recession of the 1990s. The threat of bankruptcy had given credibility to large firms' demands, and layoffs began to be consid-ered not so much as an abuse by large firms but also as a means for companies to survive and compete. In a series of highly controversial legal cases around 2000, the Tokyo District Court repeatedly found dismissals just for economic reasons to be reasonable. This was remarkable, because with these findings the court deviated from the postwar doctrine of the four conditions and instead argued that these four were not so much necessary requirements as simply important elements to consider in a given case. The most publicized of these decisions was the case of National Westminster Bank in which a dismissal was considered reasonable because the employer was in the process of restructur-ing and had offered to pay a lump-sum retirement bonus (Yamakawa and Araki 2001; LAAJ 2000).

The Tokyo cases marked a transition from a requirement doctrine to an ele-ments doctrine and caused great furor. Some claimed that the rulings spelled the end of the lifetime employment system. The Labor Attorney Association of Japan challenged the legality of the rulings (LAAJ 2000). Employers and econ-omists pushed for reform to clarify existing rules that were obscure and overly restrictive. Rulings in several cases between 2001 and 2005 suggested that courts were increasingly leaning toward the elements doctrine, repeatedly find-ing it no longer necessary that all four conditions be fulfilled.[10]

As these discussions unfolded, in 2004 the government revised the Labor Standards Law itself. Whereas previously the law had said nothing about dis-missals, it now contains a new Section 18(2) titled "Dismissals" that summarizes the existing legal interpretation by stating that a dismissal is null and void "if it is not based on objectively reasonable grounds and may not be recognized as socially acceptable." Although some were disappointed that this sounded like

---

10. See, e.g., Araki (2002); Noda (2003); Okuno (2004, 2005).

a statement of the status quo, the inclusion of dismissals in the law in and of itself defined a watershed shift and paved the way for further reforms.[11]

Although it is still not easy to terminate regular workers in Japan, it is no longer as prohibitively expensive or difficult as it used to be. This has reduced the cost of hiring mistakes and has increased the willingness of firms to offer regular contracts to more employees, as the trade-off between inflexibility costs and the benefits of attracting talent has shifted. Japan's regular employment is switching from a rigid lifetime pact toward a long-term commitment that, although based on expectations of extended tie-in, can be ended if employee performance is unsatisfactory or if the company needs to restructure or reposition strategically.

The second important change in the amended Labor Standards Law was to increase the rights associated with limited contracts. The maximum duration of a part-time contract was extended to three years, and only the employee may terminate a contract before it expires. For employees older than 60 and specialized contract workers, the maximum duration of a limited contract was raised to five years. The Ministry of Labor was tasked with crafting guidelines to limit abuse by employers, including rules on contract extensions, advance notice, and reasons for terminations (Nakakubo 2004). Thus, in a reflection of the increasing relevance and social acceptance of limited contract work, the law has clarified the rules and facilitated the administration of these workers.

Laws Structuring the External Labor Market

One main reason why Japanese companies could rely more extensively on outsourcing in the late 1990s was the emergence of a structure for the external labor market that greatly reduced the transaction costs of searching and contracting. As shown in figure 9.1, the fastest-growing portion of nonregular work was specialized contract work, followed by dispatched temporary workers (*haken*). This rise in both was greatly pushed by the emergence of temporary staff agencies that acted as brokers for nonregular workers as well as for job changers. As in other countries, private employment agencies had begun to complement government job placement offices by offering services ranging from screening, hiring, and payroll administration in the 1980s, but they were hampered by remaining legal restrictions on their scope of services. A series of legal reforms paved the way for a breakthrough growth period for staffing agencies,

11. See Kuroda (2004) and Nakakubo (2004). The revision was hotly debated between the progressive Council for Regulatory Reform, the more cautious Ministry of Labor, and unions and opposition parties that pushed for greater worker protection. The revised law is based on compromise and leaves critical issues open to legal interpretation, and it still does not include punitive provisions. As of 2007, a further revision was in preparation.

and in the late 1990s global players flocked to Japan's fast-growing market. As of 2007, there were more than 10,500 temp agencies in Japan, and the industry was growing at more than 10 percent per year. Adecco Japan increased the number of people registered for placement from 320,000 in 2000 to over 700,000 in 2005. Headhunters have also become a boom industry, and by 2006 there were 3,744 head-hunting firms actively pursuing midcareer job changers in Japan.[12] One of Japan's successful IT start-ups in the early 2000s was "en-japan," a website listing openings and applications for job changers. The relevance of this new outsourcing and matchmaking industry lies in its contribution to economizing the search process, often guaranteeing quality, thereby reducing the costs of recruiting and administration for companies and increasing the speed of finding new employment for job changers as well as for nonregular workers.

Japan's temp workers are governed by the Employment Security Law (which initially allowed only the government to provide job placement services) and the Worker Dispatching Law. In 1999 and 2004, the government revised the latter to specify 26 job categories in which staffing agencies could operate freely. In addition to removing limitations on scope of business, the 1999 revision gave staffing agencies new rights to represent their staff and increased their leverage over corporate clients that previously could violate contract rules almost with impunity. Dispute resolution processes were also clarified (Araki 1999). The 2004 revision further increased the scope of temp agency services by allowing "temporary-to-permanent service," that is, the introduction of temp workers to companies with an eye toward turning this into a regular appointment. The 2004 revision allowed worker dispatching also in manufacturing jobs, which opened up a new market for private temp agencies. The dispatching period was extended to a maximum of three years, to be congruent with new Labor Standard Law limits (Mizushima 2004).

These legal revisions reflect two main changes. First, they underscore the government's new stance that for companies to compete and reposition strategically they need greater flexibility in hiring. At the same time, giving new structure to the external labor market also recognized the growing diversity in Japan's workforce, which reflected broader trends in society. The 2007 TV hit series *Haken no hinkaku* (The Dignity of Temp Workers) contrasted the stereotypical clueless female without skills with a new type of powerful, skilled, and strong-willed temporary worker that chose not to become a regular employee in order to maintain her own lifestyle and freedom to travel, while working according to her

---

12. "Temporary Worker Law," *Mainichi Shinbun*, May 20, 1999; Oscar Johnson, "How to Get Ahead," *Metropolis Magazine*, October 2006, Tokyo; www.jassa.jp. However, Weathers (2002) reports continuing problems, such as discrimination, in temp work in Japan.

own conditions. The TV show created new aspirations for nonregular workers who not only increased in numbers but also began to change qualitatively.

As already observed, women and the elderly have long been most likely to find themselves in part-time positions. In the early 2000s, the looming labor shortage made many observers predict that Japan had to greatly increase the role of women in the workforce. The government launched new programs to increase the availability of day care, and 1999 revisions of the Child Care and Family Care Leave Laws were aimed at further opening the labor market to women (Weathers 2005; Schoppa 2006). Some companies began to structure in-house day-care facilities, and even if those initially remained the exception they attracted media attention and began to be copied.

In terms of the law, an Equal Employment Opportunity Law was first passed in 1985, but it had long been criticized as a "lame duck" (e.g., Hanami 2000). The law's biggest shortcoming by far had been that it only stipulated a "duty to endeavor" not to discriminate, but it contained neither an outright prohibition of discrimination nor any sanctions or redress. Interestingly, the old law concerned itself explicitly with the rights of women only, but not with equal opportunity in regards to disability, age, race, religion, or other personal characteristics. Around the turn of the century, this too began to change. The 1999 revision of the Equal Opportunity Law prohibited discrimination, of any kind, in recruiting, assignment, and promotion, and clarified dispute resolution mechanisms (Araki 1998).

Elderly workers are governed by the Law concerning the Stabilization of Employment of Older Persons. Perhaps motivated by the government's interest in extending the overall lifetime work span in order to reduce its pension responsibilities, this law offers financial support to companies that reemploy older workers. A revision that became effective in April 2006 ties rules on elderly workers to the ongoing pension reforms and stipulates a new retirement age of 65, to be phased in until 2013. Companies can choose whether they want to raise the retirement age stepwise, introduce continuing, flexible employment until age 65, or jump to the new retirement age immediately but not pay a lump-sum retirement payment because at age 65 the worker can switch directly into the pension system. Likewise, retiring workers now have a choice in how to draw their pension payments.[13]

13. Pension reforms of 2006 offered a retiree a choice to receive his pension beginning at age 65; to receive a partial pension while working part-time into his early 70s; or to defer receiving a higher monthly pension until a later age. A 2003 survey revealed that corporations were ready to increase the retirement age to 65 on condition that a new wage system be introduced together with terminating retirement allowances based on years of service. See, e.g., Iwata (2003) and Rebick (2005).

Although there was still ample room for improvement as of 2007, these legal revisions all point to great changes in labor mobility, and a better structuring of nonregular work. The emerging labor market has increased hiring flexibility for companies and employment options for job seekers.

The New Demand for Law: Labor Disputes

Another indication of Japan's turn to market mechanisms in employment relations is the rapid rise in labor-related lawsuits. Throughout the postwar period, Japan had relied mostly on collective bargaining through corporate unions, but lacked a well-defined system for individual disputes. Employment litigation remained limited, with only about one thousand lawsuits a year in all courts (Sugeno 2006). This began to change in the early 1990s, when labor-related lawsuits rose sharply. Between 1993 and 2002 the number of cases in Japan's district courts (not counting smaller courts and arbitrations) doubled to a level of almost 2,500 a year (see figure 9.3). More than half of these lawsuits revolved around wage disputes (in particular, unpaid overtime) and retirement allowances. Roughly a quarter, or 500 cases a year, concerned dismissals.

9.3. *Labor-Related Lawsuits, 1993–2002*
Source: JLB (2003).

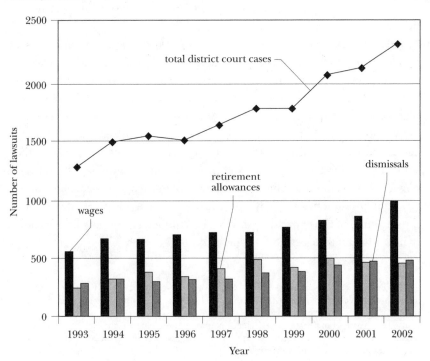

A study of labor law cases in the second half of the 1990s had revealed that in 80 percent of cases judges had ruled in favor of employees (Ouchi 2002). However, when this began to change in 2000, more employers opted to fight cases in court. Courts also changed processes to reduce the average time of labor lawsuits to twelve months, as opposed to the past when disputes could extend over several years (JLB 2003a). Previously, if the employer lost, past wage payments accrued for the entire period, making legal cases expensive. If the employee lost, legal fees could be devastating. Clarification of rights as well as streamlined processes have greatly increased access to the legal mechanisms of dispute settlement for both sides.

In many countries, such as Germany, labor disputes are addressed in the first instance in out-of-court arbitration. This has proven cost efficient and effective in reducing court overload and speeding up the decision. Following this model, the 2001 Law for Facilitating the Resolution of Individual Labor Disputes established 250 counseling offices throughout Japan. Within the first three months after the introduction of the law, these mediation offices handled 121,000 consultations, and by 2004 the number of consultations had increased to 820,000. Almost one third of these cases related to layoffs due to restructuring, followed by wage cuts (17%). Of the total, 82 percent of claims were filed by employees, and half of these were regular workers (JLB 2002b; Sugino and Murayama 2006).

The popularity of this new process underscored a need for further improvements in handling worker grievances. In April 2006 the new Labor Tribunal Law outlined a new process for employment disputes in district courts. Under this system, a tribunal consisting of one career judge and two part-time labor experts attempt mediation. If they fail, the tribunal makes a nonbinding decision for review in a civil court (Sugeno 2006).

These increases in employment arbitration and lawsuits indicate new disputing behavior in Japan, a society often considered not to be litigious. There is a long-standing debate over whether a limited number of lawsuits during the postwar period is to be explained by Japanese behavioral or cultural traits or simply by exorbitant costs, convoluted processes, and a lack of lawyers. The rapid increase in lawsuits with legal reform may support the latter argument, or it may reflect changes in society and behavior.[14] To investigate the new disputing behavior, Sugino and Murayama (2006) conducted a national survey on the use of the 2001 labor dispute facilitation system. By extrapolating

14. The concept of the nonlitigious society dates back to Kawashima (1967). It was challenged by Haley (1978) who pointed to a lack of means and processes to sue effectively. See also Yoshida (2003) for a recent reassessment.

from survey results, they estimate that 3 percent of the population experienced employment-related problems (roughly 500,000 persons a year), mostly concerning unpaid overtime, nonpayment of wages, harassment, unfair dismissal, and unfair relocation. Only 5 percent of affected employees contacted a lawyer, and even fewer pushed for a court procedure, but 21 percent sought help at the newly established local arbitration offices. Not surprisingly, the higher the educational level and the more understanding of the costs and procedures of arbitration, the more likely employees were to seek such help. Overall, the authors conclude that there has been an increase in willingness to seek legal processes, and that the 2006 introduction of labor tribunals also has opened access to the law to workers unable to afford attorneys or unwilling to sue.

Changing Human Resource Practices

Partially in response to ongoing social changes, and partially because of the looming labor shortage, human resource practices for lifetime employees are also being adjusted qualitatively, particularly in pay and promotion and in work content.

Toward Performance-Based Wages

Even though often portrayed as fairly monolithic, Japan's wage system has undergone several changes throughout the postwar period. Fujimura (2003) describes how, in the immediate postwar period (1945 to the early 1950s), the predominant notion was that of providing livelihood. Once the economy began to grow, the priority shifted to ability determined by the level of education. Ability was assumed to increase over time with experience, so that wages would be raised annually. Although bonuses became an important part of the annual income—they could be as high as six monthly salaries—they were based on the performance of the company, not that of the individual.

By the 1980s the system had evolved to be based on ability, determined by education, and experience, measured in number of years with the firm. There was some room for individual adjustments through paying monthly "handouts" (*te-ate*) separate from salary that differed from employee to employee. Therefore, while nominal wage parity persisted within age cohorts and base salaries remained predictable for each cohort, some employees effectively began to earn more than others. But the most important means of rewarding high performers in the 1970s and 1980s was promotion to more important positions. Two employees with the same rank could receive lighter or more demanding assignments, and as companies grew and diversified into new businesses at a rapid pace, high performers were put in charge of new business units or promoted within headquarters as opposed to being sent to peripheral branches (Takahashi 2006). The ultimate promotion was into senior management, which occurred upon official retirement from the original labor contract with a lump-sum pension payout, and rehiring into the executive level at a new salary scale.

In the 1990s, large companies began to revise their wage system to make greater room for rewarding performance. This shift was based on several motivations, the most important of which was, initially, to reduce overall payroll cost. Obviously, seniority wages increased wage pressure as the workforce got older over time. Downsizing during the recession of the 1990s was partially accomplished by not hiring young workers. One way to scale back payroll further was to determine a higher portion of wages based on performance and instruct evaluators to be very strict in their evaluations (Takahashi 2006; Arakawa 2005; Fujimura 2003).

Although the switch to performance pay addressed a temporary need, it also was motivated by longer-term considerations. A first was, again, the looming labor shortage. To retain and motivate high-performance employees, companies had to adapt compensation and career paths to individual performance and achievement. At the same time, the switch to performance pay made retention much more difficult, because it straightened out the S-curve of figure 9.1 and removed the indentured nature of lifelong employment. That younger workers were serious about the work-life balance was revealed by a fast-rising ratio of job quitting within the first few years of employment (MHLW 2005, chap. 3–2).

The implementation of reforms began with performance-based pay at the executive level. According to one estimate the portion of variable pay (e.g., stock options, bonuses) of total compensation increased from 21 percent to 33 percent between 1996 and 2003 (Komoto 2004; Milhaupt 2005). The pioneers in introducing performance pay were Japan's global leaders, in particular the automobile and electronics firms. Fujitsu, Honda, Toyota, NEC, Takeda Pharmaceuticals, as well as Nissan, Mazda, and IBM Japan were forerunners in a trend that, by 2002, had spread to 80 percent of white-collar jobs at large firms (Arakawa 2005; ESRI 2005). In a 2004 survey by the NLI Research Institute, only one quarter of respondents intended to maintain their current pay structure, whereas 29 percent had already switched to performance pay for all employees, and 35 percent were in the process of making this switch. The larger the firm, the more likely it was to have already switched.

Just how companies paid performance-based pay differed widely. In a study of Canon, Fujimura (2003) shows that performance metrics were added to the existing system. Monthly wages were determined by job group ranking (roughly 80%), and performance and improvement by the individual (20%).

Bonuses were no longer uniformly handed out to all employees. At Orix, the performance pay system has already been changed twice. In the early 1990s, the company adopted a three-pronged evaluation of performance (duties, creativity, and leadership), attitude, and demonstrated ability (knowledge, skill). Of these, performance was most critical for promotion and individual bonus considerations. By 2003, the system became based on the three aspects of performance, ability, and accomplishment. Accomplishment referred to efficiency, creativity, information utilization, and customer relations, but the highest weight was attached to "getting things done" (negotiation skills, development of business relations). Salary raises depended entirely on accomplishment and getting things done, whereas the bonus rested 100 percent on performance. Promotion was based on a combination of accomplishment and ability at 50 percent each (Beaulieu and Zimmerman 2005).

Appraisals and performance evaluations are a challenge everywhere, and it is not surprising that Japanese firms encountered problems with implementing their new processes of individual performance appraisal in a society marked by high collectivism, group-oriented management, and concerns about saving face. In the early 2000s, employee discontent with the fairness and transparency of evaluation was high. Previously, appraisals had been based on easily observable measures such as punctuality, hours spent at work, days of sick leave taken, politeness, and dependability. So strong were existing norms against differentiating among subordinates that in the 1990s many companies failed to achieve the goal of payroll reduction (JILPT 2005). However, a 2001 Japan Labor Institute survey showed that half of the respondents thought meritocracy was a good system, 60 percent found that it increased personal motivation, and 49 percent felt that it boosted overall corporate performance. One thing all observers agreed on was that it would take several more years for the change in wage system to be fully implemented.[15]

Challenges in implementation notwithstanding, data show that wage differentials (measured as the highest wage divided by the lowest wage of regular employees in an age group) are becoming more pronounced. In a comparison of 1999 and 2004, figure 9.4 shows that the wage gap for employees up to 30 years old has increased from 1.57 to 1.69 in all companies, but from 1.7 to 1.91 in companies where at least 50 percent of employees are on performance-based pay. The gaps are similar for the age groups of "40s" and "50s and older." Although these differentials may look small in comparison with other

---

15. Tatsumichi and Morishima (2007). See also Arai (2005); Arakawa (2005); Fujimura (2003); and Morishima (2002). For a detailed analysis of recent changes in human resource management, see JILPT (2005).

9.4. *Wage Differentials by Age Group, 1999 vs. 2004*
Source: ESRI (2005).

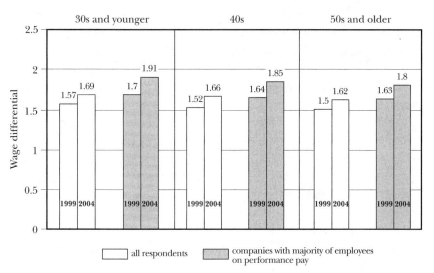

countries, the increases in each age cohort are substantial and likely to expand as performance-based pay is implemented more widely and more effectively.

Another emerging trend that is bound to contribute to intrafirm wage differentials and to push meritocracy is the arrival of market wage comparisons. One challenge faced by highly innovative and highly specialized companies in particular was that traditionally Japanese firms did not engage in market comparison for wages. Instead, each firm set base levels for all jobs according to the size and reputation of the company, and the larger the company, the higher the base wages. This introduced wage parity across the entire organization. It also greatly facilitated the rotation-on-the-job practice of training white collar employees in a variety of divisions and subject areas. In the 1990s, the downside of training generalists became painfully obvious in many industries that could not compete with specialists in areas such as finance. In many firms, rotation-on-the-job was limited to related business tasks, or phased out altogether. Although in-house training remained important, it became more specialized.

This move toward individual specialization was also evident in the emergence of market rates. These first appeared in banking where the mergers caused some employees to quit and move to other firms, including foreign investment banks. As of 2002, 2.3 percent (over one million employees) of the workforce were employed by foreign firms in Japan (Beaulieu and Zimmerman 2005). These employees often had MBA degrees from the United States and were hired based on skill and knowledge, demanding market rates.[16] As this began to occur in other industries, Japan's wage system was pushed further in the direction of individual achievement and meritocracy. In 2006, Takeda Pharmaceuticals was among the companies that introduced a "wage by job category" system. Instead of paying universally by rank, Takeda introduced wages by type of job (depending on specialization) and performance. This allowed a differentiation among long-term employees between high-charging, top-notch people and standard rank and file. This new trend was also expected to lead to a narrowing of wage differences between regular and part-time workers (Arakawa 2006). Moreover, wages by job category increase the individual value component of wages, as it builds on individual job qualifications that are transferable to other employers, thereby further boosting job mobility.

As a result of these shifts, the age-related S-curve of wages, as depicted in figure 9.1, has begun to straighten, thereby reducing the incentives of an employee to stay with one company. Another huge boost to individual career planning was provided by the 2001 introduction and 2005 revision of the "Japanese 401(k)" system of individually portable defined pension contributions.[17] This reduces an employee's dependence on one company's defined benefits and reduces the lifetime income hit incurred with midcareer job changing.

Changing Working Conditions for White Collar Employees

The stereotypical image of the Japanese salaryman of the postwar period is not very flattering. In addition to being a "corporation man" who identifies himself not by occupation but by employer, the concept evokes images of a man who works very long hours and socializes with co-workers after work, has no hobbies, is eternally sleep deprived, and may be in danger of dying from overwork (karōshi). Although this image is not entirely fair, it points to some of the side effects of pay by rank, appraisal based on the hours of work put in, and seniority promotion. The shift toward more fluid labor markets, meritocracy in pay and promotion and perhaps even by occupation rather than employer, and the changes in societal values as pertaining to work-life balance all augur a shift in the content and requirements of work, away from the focus on process and toward a focus on results.

In the late 1990s, the popular Japanese term for the growing number of people leaving a lifetime employment contract was das-sara (lit., "extricating

16. Interviews with Japanese venture capital firms, Tokyo, January 2005.
17. Even though the term "401(k)" refers to the U.S. tax code detailing the exemption, Japan's Defined Contribution Pension Law (Kakutei kyoshutsu nenkin hō) introduced a similar system under the same moniker, pronounced as "Nihon-ban yon-maru-ichi-kee puran." For details, see Endo (2000).

oneself from the life of a salaryman"). A *Nikkei* survey of large Japanese firms revealed an increase in the number of positions earmarked for midcareer hires of 15 percent in 2006 and another 6 percent in 2007 (*Nikkei,* April 30, 2007). The more people in their 40s changed jobs, the more the *das-sara* phenomenon paved the way for a normative reorientation of what constitutes a successful career.

For those that remained "organization men," work content also began to shift. Not only did performance appraisal begin to consider efficiency and effectiveness but the shift toward more individualized careers and the specialization of knowledge all augured changes in work content for large-firm white-collar workers. Morishima (2003) conducted a survey to identify changes in work intensity, replacement fears, changes in work conditions due to IT developments, as well as increasing individualization and competition among white collar workers. Although a low response rate begs for caution, the results nevertheless point to three trends. In companies that have shifted toward meritocracy, the differences based on performance are more visible in wage differentials than in promotion differentials; that is, many companies have upheld their rank system and automated promotion up to the *kachō* (section chief) level, but monetary rewards are becoming more differentiated. Moreover, while individualism and competition are on the increase, regular workers—at least as of 2002—did not seem to fear being replaced by external labor such as highly specialized contract workers. However, respondents reported that work content was becoming more demanding, as goals were set higher and more clearly, attaining goals became more important, and competition at the higher ranks had grown fierce. These shifts have led to work reorganization, as employees are trying to become more efficient and effective to succeed in the promotion tournament. These results are reinforced by data showing that the proportion of employees working less than 35 hours per week is increasing (given the rise in external labor), but the proportion of employees reporting working 60 hours or more is also on the rise (MHLW 2005, chap. 3–1).

As companies match their aggressive efforts at cost reduction and profitability with an emphasis on work efficiency and effectiveness, the increase in nonregular work and the adoption of performance-based pay have invited a division among Japan's white collar workforce into professionals and routine workers. According to the 2005 White Paper on Labor, more than two thirds of Japanese firms plan to engage in more skill development of their regular workforce, yet at the same time to rely more extensively on older workers for standard tasks (MHLW 2005, chap. 3–1). Therefore, on one end, highly coveted star performers receive long-term contracts and are offered skill development opportunities. They face competition from highly skilled contract workers that have received external graduate training and introduce new energy into the midcareer job market. On the other end, more clerical and standard assignments are given to lower-paid employees with limited career prospects. These may be nonregular workers, but because performance pay allows differentiation, and because layoffs due to underperformance are becoming easier, firms are more willing to offer these lower-level employees regular contracts as well. Most certainly, the stereotypical "salaryman" of the postwar period, the loyal soldier and paper shuffler, is a relic of Old Japan.

Evaluation: Employment in the New Japan

The strategic inflection point has been accompanied by moves to make Japan's employment system more flexible, transparent, and efficient. The recession brought to the fore the postwar system's negative consequences. In macroeconomic terms, limited labor mobility created opportunity costs, as talent could not easily transfer to the economy's growth sectors. At the corporate level, labor rigidities greatly impeded restructuring and the exit of nonperforming businesses. Constraints on layoffs made firms cautious in hiring, and therefore contributed to skyrocketing youth unemployment in the late 1990s. Rigidities in the labor market made it almost impossible for middle-aged unemployed workers to find new employment. Large firms began to ask not for a complete shakeup of the system—as many still value the positive aspects of low turnover, skill formation, and the social norms in which Japan's work rules are embedded—but rather for a qualitative change, by introducing more flexibility in order to refine the system to exploit its advantages while removing its greatest constraints.

The 2004 revision of the Labor Standards Law marks a first step away from the binding rigidities of lifetime employment. Although it is still not easy to terminate regular contract employees, it has become possible if one good reason can be provided. With this, Japan is shifting from lifetime employment to long-term employment, similar to some European countries. This increased flexibility has reduced the fear of hiring and given a boost to the overall job market. It has also allowed companies to restructure, and it has made mergers and acquisitions a viable tool for reorganization. Whereas in the postwar period, mergers automatically meant increasing the size of the workforce, New Japan mergers have come to be associated with a reduction in the number of employees.

In 2004, Japan's average payroll costs stood at about 70 percent of what they were at the peak in 1990 (MHLW 2005). This was accomplished by shifting to performance-based pay to stop automated pay raises and an increased reliance on nonregular workers. But cost reductions were only one objective behind the ongoing change in labor relations. Firms have begun to use external labor strategically, by developing specialized capabilities in-house in core business areas while outsourcing noncore tasks. Staffing agencies have facilitated a greater reliance on external labor by reducing search costs. The emergence of contract workers—professionals with highly specialized knowledge—has not only raised the status of temporary work in society but has offered a viable alternative to hiring highly paid regular staff. This has enabled moves toward "choose and focus" through the outsourcing of labor in noncore business aspects (Morishima 2003; JETRO 2005a).

One important implication of these shifts for Japan's political economy overall is that it spells the end of the postwar-period corporate welfarism. A decreasing portion of Japan's workforce finds itself in regular employment situations where the company provides benefits, in-house healthcare, pensions and de facto unemployment insurance by an implicit understanding of long-term employment. As of 2006, the majority of Japan's workforce (which also includes the self-employed, family workers, and day laborers) was without most of these benefits. This has increased pressure on the government to expand social security programs, in particular by introducing long-term unemployment insurance. The only way to finance this expansion is through raising individual and corporate contributions. We can expect a shift away from corporate provision of benefits and social support toward a greater reliance on tax-financed public pensions as well as individually portable defined contribution plans. As popularity of the new "Japanese 401(k)" plan increases, this will further increase job mobility and individual career choices.

Studies of the implementation of corporate renewal point to the critical role of reorienting people and corporate culture toward the new strategic tasks of the company (Tushman and O'Reilly 1996, 2002; O'Reilly and Tushman 2004, 2008). In organizations with a strong corporate culture, such as Old Japan's where strong norms and values govern ingrained company processes, this is often the hardest part, and it may take a generational shift in middle and upper management to take root. The strategic inflection point implies a shift from socialized risk and work toward individual meritocracy and efficiency increases. In this shift, lifetime employment is not replaced, but it is undergoing a qualitative change toward serving greater work productivity.

IV

NEW

MARKETS

AND

NEW

ENTRY

VENTURE CAPITAL:
OPENING ACCESS
TO FINANCE

Throughout the postwar period Japan's large firms were little concerned about either the threat of new entry or of being replaced by disruptive substitutes. The government structured R&D policies, such as research consortia, with the stated goal of diffusing new technologies to several incumbents and upholding market hierarchies. Patent policies likewise were oriented toward ensuring large firms' access to innovation. The focus of the financial system on bank loans, combined with regulated interest rates, all but precluded start-up firms from access to credit, as banks were unwilling to provide risk capital at low rates. Meanwhile, ongoing diversification of large firms meant that new technologies were developed in-house, while outsourcing of critical technologies was limited. To the extent outsourcing occurred, it was structured in hierarchical and often exclusive subcontractor relations. Therefore, in the rare cases where an innovator managed to find financing and develop its own technology, it often faced insurmountable difficulties finding buyers. Moreover, the high status associated with being a bureaucrat or lifetime employee meant that talent was attracted into ministries and large companies. Entrepreneurial inventors were rare, and they were usually unable to profit from technological innovation.

During the recession of the 1990s, this issue was picked up by the Ministry of Economy, Trade and Industry (METI). A survey dating back to the 1970s revealed great obstacles to innovative new firms, and most new firms were in the traditional service sector, such as restaurants. In the 1990s, bankruptcies of small firms hit a postwar high, as the rate of new firm formation continued a long-term downward trend (figure 10.1).[1] METI was concerned about these developments because it was also in charge of overall small firm policies through its affiliated Small and Medium Enterprise Agency (SMEA). Created immediately after World War II, the SMEA operated on a perceived

1. For detailed data, by industry and size of company, as well as the method of calculation, see SMEA (2006) Statistical Appendix, chart 11.

10.1. *"Births" and "Deaths" of Business Places, 1964–2004*
Sources: 1966–1980: Aoyama (2001, 59); 1981–2004: SMEA (2006), in %, not including agriculture.

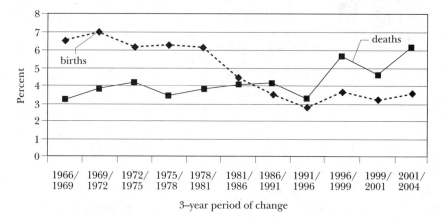

need to support and protect small firms, which were considered, by definition, as weak. Postwar small-firm policies came to pursue a strongly socialist objective, soon hijacked by the conservative LDP (Liberal Democratic Party) in its attempt to appease large numbers of small-firm voters.

The story of how this changed begins with one man, Hideaki Kumano. During the early 1970s Mr. Kumano worked in the Machinery Insurance Division of the Machinery and Information Industries Bureau at MITI (Ministry of International Trade and Industry). It was mostly personal curiosity that made him join a discussion group of small-firm managers in the late 1960s, and he was soon convinced that Japan had no future without new entrepreneurship. He also realized that existing small-firm policies were counterproductive to nurturing new firm formation in high-technology areas. Kumano succeeded in creating a New Industries Section (Shinki sangyō shitsu) within his ministry. After several reorganizations, including of the ministry itself in 2001, this is now the New Industries Section of the Economic and Industrial Policy Bureau, of METI. It is this initiative that created an initial bias in Japanese venture-capital policies toward IT-related start-up firms.[2]

Mr. Kumano's contribution was his insight that in every economy, there are two types of small firms that benefit from fundamentally different policies— the high-charging entrepreneurs and the low-tech self-employed (or, in the

2. Hamada (1999, 99). The story was confirmed by Mr. Kumano in interviews in 2001 and 2003. Mr. Kumano became administrative vice minister of MITI in 1993, and after retirement from the government in 1994 became the president of Tokyo SBIC, a government-related VC. He was instrumental in shaping new firm policies throughout the 1990s.

words of a sociologist, the "caterpillars" and the "worms"; Rona-Tas 2002). The former are entrepreneurs with new ideas and a hunger for success. More often than not they fail, but when they succeed they may make economic history. These are Schumpeter's "captains of industry" who contribute to creative destruction by overthrowing existing business models or technologies. Policies supportive of their activities are access to markets (finance, products, buyers, and so forth) and a social safety net to cap the risk of failure for personal livelihood.

The second type of small firm is self-employed small shop owners whose main goal is to secure a stable clientele to make a living. They contribute in important ways, by producing low-technology parts, distributing goods to consumers, or providing everyday services, such as the fourth-tier suppliers in Japan's production networks, the greengrocers around the corner, the dry cleaners or the local soba restaurants. These firms may benefit from policies that protect them from competition, such as Japan's rules on minimum distance between bathhouses, special liquor licenses for mom-and-pop stores, or the blanket exemption from antitrust rules (Schaede 2000a).

Japan's challenge in the 1990s was that small-firm policies had been exclusively geared toward supporting this second type of small firm, while the "caterpillars" had been stifled by industrial policy priorities that favored large firms. Although small firms account for the majority of companies in all countries, Japan stands out among industrialized nations in that 99.3 percent of companies are small, but employ 80 percent of the workforce and contribute more than 50 percent to GDP. What is more, "very small firms" (with fewer than 20 employees) account for 73 percent of all firms and 26 percent of employment (SMEA 2006).

In the 1990s, humming the mantra of creative destruction, METI made high-tech start-ups a main concern. A series of legal revisions aimed at opening access to credit and markets. The global Internet and IT bubble around the turn of the century brought a first truly market-driven start-up boom. Success stories of Internet start-ups altered competition in many industries and society's evaluation of entrepreneurship as well as of the moral integrity of becoming rich fast. As of 2006, the Japanese venture-capital (VC) industry may still have looked small in comparison with the United States, but it was by no means negligible or marginal. New entrepreneurs with sufficient ideas and willpower were no longer at the mercy of the old system dominated by banks and large firms. New market opportunities have sprung up, and new entry is possible. Meanwhile, the private VC industry has evolved in its own process of "choose and focus" to become more strategic, specialized, and result driven.

Venture-Capital Policies in the 1990s

The fact that it was government industrial policies that thwarted new firm formation meant that it took government measures to jump-start Japan's venture capital market. Similar to European countries such as Germany and France, the ex-ante constraints of the legal system limited new opportunities, so that the laws needed to be revised first for a new industry to emerge. This began to happen in Japan in the second half of the 1990s.

The most important policy measures taken in regard to venture firms and financing are highlighted in table 10.1.[3] In combination with the concurrent major revisions of the Commercial Code and the 2006 Corporation Law, these policy measures have reshaped the business environment for venture capital financiers and start-up firms in Japan. Although the details may seem a bit tedious, a brief overview is warranted here to underscore the breadth and depth of reforms that have opened a rapidly growing and vibrant private venture capital market in Japan.

Easing Entry: Start-up Enabling Laws

In line with industry policy thinking in the postwar period, the policy approach to small-firm finance under interest rate regulation was to insert the government as an agent, by offering subsidized loan programs and loan guarantees through public banks. These loans were earmarked for the "modernization" or "rationalization" of weak small firms, until the 1989 New Businesses Law (Shinki jigyō-hō) introduced special measures for newly founded firms. However, given the dominant evaluation of small firms as needing protection, during the 1990s recession these programs were quietly rerouted to all small firms in trouble, including companies that had been in business for decades (Hamada and Asai 2001, 35; Schaede 2005).

True venture support measures materialized in 1999. A first attempt to foster high-tech business creation with the 1995 Small Firm Creation and Support Law was boosted by the 1999 Venture Business Support Law (Benchaa kigyō shien hō). This law stood out for its ambitious goal of doubling the number of start-up firms over a five-year period, through a complete makeover of the environment for entrepreneurship, ranging from financial subsidies to education programs and management consulting, and even including a "people's movement" to change the social acceptance of start-up firms.[4] The revision of

---

3. Details on these programs can be found in the final section of the annual SMEA White Paper, titled "SME Policies"; see http://www.chusho.meti.go.jp/hakusyo/index.html.

4. See Hamada and Asai (2001, 36). The Sōgyō/Benchaa Kokumin Undō (People's Movement Toward Start-up and Venture Businesses) consisted of public hearings and seminars on the necessity of supporting small firms in high-tech areas. For a full list of measures based on this law, see SMEA (2003).

TABLE 10.1. *Venture Capital Policies in Japan*

Year	VC-related Laws	Finance measures	Tax/investment measures	Technology-related measures
1963	SBIC law; establishment of 3 SBIC			
1975	VEC established			
1982		First investment cooperatives (civil code based)		
1983		OTC listing requirements lowered		
1986	SBIC privatized			
1988		VEC debt guarantee program for start-ups		
1989	New Business Law (Shinki jigyō-hō); debt guarantees for firms specified by MITI			
1990	VC singled out in SME Agency "Vision" for the 1990s			
1994	Government Policy Plan (first explicit mention of VC) Revision of antitrust rules to exempt VC from rules on personnel exchange			
1995	Small Firm Creation Promotion Law (Chūsho kigyō sōzō katsudō sokushin hō); basic law for VC support	Relaxation of OTC listing requirements	Stock option system for firms identified under the 1989 New Business Law	Science and Technology Basic Law

(Continued)

TABLE 10.1. Continued

Year	VC-related Laws	Finance measures	Tax/investment measures	Technology-related measures
		Creation of "2nd OTC Market" Japan Development Bank introduces "New Business Development Loans"		Venture education programs
1997		Relaxation of investment rules for pensions and mutual funds	Special tax incentives for Angels; introduction of stock options	
1998	Limited Partnership Act for VC, LP funds allowed effective 4/99	Holding companies allowed (revision of Antimonopoly Law)		SBIR (*Chūsho kigyō gijutsu kakushin*) started
	New Business Formation Promotion Law (Shinjigyō zoshutsu sokushin-hō); abolition of MITI license requirement for start-up support	"Big Bang" laws implemented; revision of Foreign Exchange Act; deregulation of Securities and Exchange Act; Banks, insurance companies allowed to enter the mutual fund business		Technology Licensing Office Law; local education programs (*akinai* initiative); Incubator equity program and entrepreneurship seminars launched
1999	Revision of Commercial Code: stock transfers allowed	Complete deregulation of brokerage fees	JASMEC allowed to invest in rivate VC funds; invests in SBIC	Relaxation of "Bayh-Dole" system; to allow university professors to be interlocking executives at private firms
	Revision of SME Basic Law	Relaxation of IPO requirements	Investment funds allowed to invest in DBJ "Basic Fund"	

Year				
	Industry Strength Revitalization Law (Sangyō katsuryoku saisei-hō)	TSE opens MOTHERS market; JASDAQ turned into an exchange		
2000	Revision of Commercial Code to facilitate spin-outs	OSE opens NASDAQ Japan market; Revision of Investment Trust Law; stock exchange reforms	Relaxation of rules on stock option transfers	Reduction of fees etc. on patents filed by SME; regional clusters program
2001	Revision of Commercial Code: accounting, rules on stocks (class voting rights)	Stock options completely liberalized		2nd S&T Basic Plan (independence of national laboratories), "University-based Start-ups 1000 Plan"
2002	Revision of Commercial Code: stock transfers, auditing rules, different types of stocks	NFLC start-up loan program (non-collateralized)	Federation of Angels Forum	
2003	5-year suspension of minimum capitalization requirement for new firms ("¥1 Company System"); Formation of LPs for specific buyout funds allowed	Hercules stock exchange opened (reform of NASDAQ at OSE); Tax reduction on stock transfers	Further extension of angel tax incentives (front-end)	Venture Capitalist Education Program; Intellectual Property Basic Law; Dream Gate Project
2004				Reform of national universities (allowing VC business)
2005	LLP for General PE funds			Revision of Patent Law
2006	Corporation Law: LLP officially introduced			Intellectual Property Strategy Program (Phase 2)

the SME Basic Law, also in 1999, underscored the reorientation in small-firm policies. Small firms were no longer considered "losers" in need of help; they were considered to be growth engines for the economy.

Perhaps the biggest boost to new company formation came with the so-called One-Yen System of 2003. In an exemption from existing Commercial Code provisions, a start-up no longer needed to have a minimum capitalization of ¥10 million minimum, but could be founded with paid-in capital of ¥1. Within a year, almost 12,000 companies were founded under this system, and the measure was made permanent in the 2006 Corporation Law.

Finance: VC-Enabling Laws

Deregulation of financing small firms through private venture investments came about in the annual revisions of the Commercial Code between 1998 and 2006, as well as tax system reforms to make risk investments more attractive. Reforms regarding innovation processes included measures ranging from changing the patent system to privatizing national universities, thus fostering commerce-oriented research.

A pathbreaking legal change occurred in 1999 with the introduction of investment funds through the Limited Partnership Act for Venture Capital Investment (Tōshi jigyō yūgen sekinin kumiai-hō). Until then, a VC fund had to be based on the Civil Code and was fraught with problems, not the least of which was that liability could not be limited. The new law, based almost literally on the U.S. model, finally allowed for the easy pooling of investments in a fund. This paved the way for a larger-scale participation of institutional investors in the VC market as limited partners, with the VC firms assuming the role of general partner. The Corporation Law in 2006 and separate legislation for funds in 2006 finally introduced the limited liability partnership (LLP) as an organizational form, thus removing the greatest obstacle to market-based fund management.

The Commercial Code revisions between 1998 and 2006 that aimed at streamlining large firm restructuring also greatly assisted the growth of venture capital. This included the transfer of stocks between companies, which facilitated shifts in ownership stakes by venture capitalists in subsequent rounds of financing; the introduction of different classes of stock with different voting rights; and new ownership rules on spin-offs that attracted new money to the industry. In the area of taxation, the stepwise deregulation of stock options opened the door to new vehicles of VC payment. Taxation of venture investments was clarified, and taxes reduced, both for stock transfers and the provision of angel (very early stage) financing. These measures were adopted between 1997 and 2003, and have reached a point where the Japanese system, on paper, is largely at par with the U.S. system, although as of 2007 differences how the various instruments could be used persisted.

An important concern of any venture capitalist is the choice of exit options. In the United States by far the most commonly used option is to sell the small firm to a larger firm, particularly in the biotechnology, medical instruments, telecommunications, and software sectors. In Japan, acquisitions had long remained limited, partially due to a lack of legal infrastructure and partially due to a propensity to resist "selling out."[5] The legal revisions together with new ways of thinking about start-up success have spurred the growth of M&As as exit options. The second option, listing on an exchange after an initial public offering, saw a first boom with the IT bubble at the turn of the century. Initial public offerings (IPOs) require the functioning of so-called junior markets that list stocks of firms with no existing profit record. Since 1999, Japan has established several such markets, including JASDAQ, MOTHERS, and Hercules. After an initial flurry in 2000, these exchanges had to retrench and reorganize, but they have picked up again since then. Whatever these markets' initial challenges, their more stringent disclosure requirements and quarterly earning statement rules have eventually also reformed the rules of the main segments of the Tokyo and Osaka stock exchanges.

Entrepreneurial Environment and Management Education

In the research area, the most important reforms of the early 2000s pertained to university reform, the provision of incubators, and patent policy revisions, all of which were aimed at facilitating R&D by small firms. Perhaps the most drastic change was the privatization of national universities in 2004. As professors are no longer civil servants, they are at greater liberty to become company founders, corporate directors, or heads of research projects with an eye to commercialization. It also allows universities to establish their own venture capital outlets, such as UTEC, the University of Tokyo Edge Capital Co., which launched its first fund in 2004. Together with measures to support technology licensing offices (TLO) that began in 1998, the policy goal is to tap universities as sources for cutting-edge R&D, offer support to academics and researchers with innovative ideas, and create linkages between innovators and entrepreneurs.

Even with these structural changes, however, a great challenge was to reorient the content of research at Japanese research universities that are not as well funded or oriented toward commercialization as their U.S. counterparts.

5. Interviews with Japanese VC executives, Tokyo, 2002, 2005. One executive referred to this phenomenon as the "my company syndrome."

To entice movement in this direction, the government made funds available to so-called incubators, in the form of impressive research facilities to support R&D and economic activity. With a few exceptions, such as the private Kyoto Research Center, these incubators have yet to create major new business breakthroughs. However, by creating opportunity for research and interaction between researchers and aspiring entrepreneurs, the tangible results of these incubators may be less relevant than their long-term effects on structuring exchange fora and a market for innovation.[6]

Another area identified by METI as needing support was management education. Unlike the United States, where MBA programs and job mobility have created a vibrant market for managerial talent, Japan's management curricula remain limited. Moreover, postwar human resource practices curtailed the mid-career market for managers. To address these social impediments and change the ways in which society regards the *das-sara* (leaving the salaryman existence behind), the government and prefectures launched education and consulting programs. For example, the city of Osaka opened an entire building dedicated to small firm management support, with the Japanese-English-German name of Akinai-Aid Platz, Osaka. *Akinai* (help) consultants offer advice on management and finance, and, in addition to seminar rooms and lecture halls, the building also makes cubicles and secretarial services available to start-up firms at highly subsidized rates.

Overall, then, Japan's government was sending out clear signals that it is supportive of new company formation. In one program, METI even ventured into education, by developing textbooks and CDs for use in elementary, middle, and high schools to explain the virtues of investments over savings, of entrepreneurship over employment, and of being wealthy. While the effectiveness of cartoon-based education about capitalism remains unexplored, these measures indicate an important shift in policy thinking away from government intervention to structuring a market for competition.

Government Venture Capital Firms

In addition to crafting policies, Japan's government also helped jump-start the VC industry by establishing three so-called small business investment companies (SBIC) in Tokyo, Osaka, and Nagoya. Unlike their U.S. models in the 1950s and 1960s, which were private VC companies that benefited from preferential tax treatment, the Japanese SBIC were funded by the government with the task of supplementing the equity base of small firms. Given industrial

---

6. Interviews, UTEC 2005, Kyoto Research Center 2002; site visit, Tamagawa Research Center 2003.

policies at the time, the SBIC were not initially tasked with funding start-ups, but with improving small firms' access to funding, regardless of firm age or industry.[7] Run by former government officials, their investment attitude was rather conservative, as they distributed small amounts of investments across a large number of recipients to reduce risk, in what is sometimes referred to as "salaryman type portfolio investment." Although the SBIC were privatized in 1986, a government flavor persisted and funding remained partially government backed. Moreover, the SBIC business model remained anchored in dividend income resulting from the equity positions in small firms, underscoring a basic lending rather than investing approach. Even as of the early 1990s, the SBIC invested in small firms with a certain profit record over the past few years, thus supporting growth companies rather than early stage start-ups. It was only after Mr. Kumano assumed leadership of the SBIC Tokyo in the 1990s that it began to explicitly nurture the fledgling VC market by engaging in true venture investments.[8] The SBIC Tokyo is the most successful of the three SBIC and most resembles a private VC firm, both in strategy and appearance.

Perhaps the best sign of success of the SBIC in jump-starting a VC industry is an increasing complaint by private VC firms that they are no longer needed. Private VC firms have emerged and claim that the SBICs distort the market as they compete for the best start-ups with subsidized refinancing through government backing.[9] As industry data below will show, the SBICs were still among the largest VC investors in Japan in 2006, and the three firms have consistently represented between 7 percent and 8 percent of the market. From a startup's perspective, SBIC funding may be easier to obtain, and an initial round from an SBIC may provide the imprimatur needed to raise additional private funds.

Japan's Private Venture Capital Industry in 2006

Japan's private VC industry has undergone enormous change since the turn of the century. Until the late 1990s, the image of Japanese venture capital was that of an unspecialized, slow market dominated by subsidiaries of banks and insurance companies, with investment decisions made by people on a two-year rotation with little in-depth industry knowledge. The market was small

7. Interview, SBIC Osaka, May 2002.

8. Mr. Kumano's second major impression on Japan's VC industry was to transform the SBIC Tokyo into a true VC firm. He was instrumental in pushing through a legal revision in 1999 that allowed the SBIC to invest in firms without a profit record. In the same year, JASMEC, a public corporation for small firm policies, was allowed to contribute to venture funds. Interview with Mr. Kumano, 2001; see also Hamada (1999) and Hamada and Asai (2001).

9. Interviews with Tokyo-based VC executives, 1998, 2003, and 2005.

and unexciting. All of this has changed. New Japan's leading VC firms are hard-charging independent investors with professional staff. While the market remains small in comparison to that in the United States, it is growing in leaps and bounds, both quantitatively and qualitatively.

Market Overview

As in other countries, disclosure rules for VC are limited, and the industry's evolution must be traced with survey data. Two separate annual surveys have been collected since 1996, one by the *Nikkei Financial Daily* (*Nikkei Kinyū*), the other by the Venture Enterprise Center (VEC). Most reports on Japan's VC industry in the past have relied on VEC data, which contains more exhaustive questions. However, some large VC, notably industry leaders Softbank Investment, CMC, and Orix Capital, do not regularly respond to the VEC survey. The following analysis therefore builds on a database constructed from the more representative *Nikkei* survey, published in early June in the years 1996 through 2006. Unfortunately, these surveys have not received responses from foreign VC, so that the important role of foreign funds during the IT bubble of 1999–2001 and the subsequent turn to management buyout (MBO) funds remains unexplored.

Nikkei's annual survey has enjoyed a fairly stable response rate from over 90 firms, and to the extent there has been turnover in the data, this was mostly caused by mergers between VC that in turn were often triggered by mergers between their parent financial firms. The largest 30 VC firms in Japan, as of March 2006, in terms of outstanding and annual investments, average investment amount per target firm, global exposure, and operating profits, are shown in table 10.2.[10] Industry concentration is high, as these thirty firms represent 91 percent of total estimated domestic VC investment. Table 10.2 shows that, on average, only 8 percent of investments are made abroad, and only a few firms like JAFCO and Japan Asia Investment are big international players.

The annual and total outstanding VC investments for Japan between 1996 and 2006 are shown in figure 10.2. During the global technology bubble of 2000–2001, VC investments topped the ¥1 trillion mark for the first time, and new annual investments topped the ¥400 billion mark in 2000. A recovery has materialized since 2004, and the market grew by almost 30 percent in 2005–06 to reach ¥1.26 trillion (more than $10 billion). In spite of this aggressive growth, in absolute volume this market is dwarfed by the U.S. market by orders of magnitude. A METI calculation showed that as of March 2002,

10. Advantage Partners, an important shaper of the industry, is not included in this table because it shifted into buyout funds in 1998.

TABLE 10.2. *The Top 30 VC Firms in Japan, as of March 2006 (in million Yen, %)*

Rank	Name of VC	Affiliation	Total investments	# target firms	Average investment per firm	% of investments abroad	New annual investments FY 2006	Operating profits
1	Softbank Investment Holdings	publicly traded	249,220	304	820	5	62,578	51,365
2	JAFCO	publicly traded	172,209	959	180	26	48,993	17,302
3	NIF SMBC Ventures[1]	publicly traded	117,569	1,083	109	19	25,061	4,604
4	CMC (Chuo Mitsui Capital)[2]	bank	85,630	72	1,189	0	74,332	n/a
5	Japan Asia Investment	publicly traded	67,205	762	88	25	18,081	5,709
6	Mizuho Capital	bank	49,641	1,149	43	6	8,901	6,556
7	Mitsubishi UFJ Capital[3]	bank	43,948	1,200	37	9	9,698	10,488
8	SBIC Tokyo	government	38,536	912	42	0	3,999	3,184
9	Nikko Antfactory	securities	36,596	336	109	16	17,732	1,211
10	SBIC Osaka	government	35,942	767	47	0	2,521	2,318
11	Tokyo Marine Capital	insurance	29,447	25	1,178	0	5,110	885
12	Orix Capital	corporate	28,015	709	40	4	7,825	n/a
13	Resona Capital[4]	bank	27,409	1,026	27	1	4,481	2,152
14	SBIC Nagoya	government	24,010	494	49	0	949	1,735
15	Yasuda Enterprise Development[5]	insurance	21,913	378	58	22	5,621	1,211
16	Nihon Venture Capital	independent	18,135	272	67	24	4,444	990
17	Future Venture Capital	independent	11,471	183	63	0	4,270	35
18	Nissei Capital	insurance	9,426	401	24	4	2,364	1,171
19	Tsunami Network Partners	independent	8,854	59	150	18	2,871	5
20	Globis Capital Partners[6]	independent	8,623	32	269	5	1,951	n/a
21	Millenia Venture Partners[7]	corporate	7,521	60	125	5	602	34

(Continued)

TABLE 10.2. *Continued*

Rank	Name of VC	Affiliation	Total investments	# target firms	Average investment per firm	% of investments abroad	New annual investments FY 2006	Operating profits
22	Aozora Investment[8]	bank	7,370	218	34	3	1,585	n/a
23	MU Hands-On 14[9]	securities	7,276	97	75	10	1,142	69
24	Biofrontier Partners	independent	7,253	33	220	29	747	n/a
25	Meiji Capital	insurance	7,109	302	24	0	1,741	89
26	New Frontier Partners[10]	corporate	6,808	169	40	6	1,374	−229
27	Nihon Technology VP	independent	6,199	23	270	0	1,912	n/a
28	Hokuriku Capital	bank	5,836	88	66	0	265	86
29	Kankaku Investment Co.	securities	5,717	124	46	1	0	290
30	Shinko Investment	securities	5,521	238	23	0	1,266	495
	Total / Average		1,150,409	12,475	184	8	322,416	111,755

Source: Nikkei Kinyū Shinbun, Annual VC Survey, July 7, 2006.
Notes:
1. NIF Ventures merged with SMBC Capital in October 2005.
2. CMC was founded in 2000 as the venture arm of two trust banks; heavily engaged in MBO funding.
3. UFJ Capital = merger of Sanwa Capital, Central Capital, and Toyoshin Capital in 2000; merged with Diamond Capital in 2005.
4. Resona Capital = merger between *Daiwagin kigyō-tōshi* and *Asahigin jigyō-tōshi* as of 2003.
5. Yasuda Enterprise Development merged with NED in 2000.
6. Globis Capital Partners = merger of US VC Apax/Patricof and Globis (formerly Apax Globis Partners).
7. Millenia Venture Partners = 100% subsidary of Mitsubishi Corporation.
8. Aozora Investment = Formerly Nippon Credit Bank Private Equity.
9. MU Hands-On = formerly UFJ Tsubasa Hands-On.
10. New Frontier Partners = Owned by Aiful (formerly Kokusai Capital).

10.2. Annual and Total Venture Capital Investments Outstanding, 1996–2006
Source: Calculated from *Nikkei Kinyū Shinbun*, Annual Venture Capital Surveys, 1996–2006.

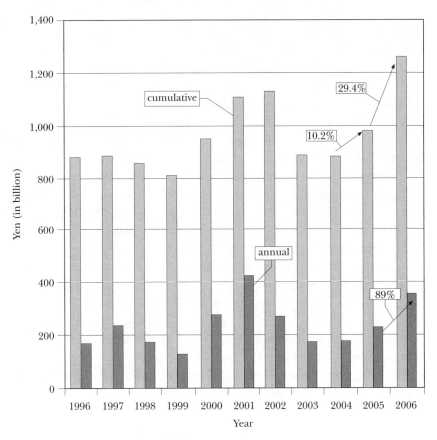

annual VC investments in Japan represented 0.06 percent of GDP and 1.8 percent of R&D expenditures, whereas in the United States these numbers were 0.41 percent and 15.6 percent, respectively (METI 2005). According to one estimate, in the early 2000s there were about 600 VC firms in the United States, as compared with perhaps 200 in Japan, and Japan's market was about one-tenth the size of the U.S. market.[11]

Venture Capital in Old Japan

The widely held image of Japanese venture capital until the late 1990s was that in addition to being small, the industry was underdeveloped, focusing on

11. Interview, Ignite Japan, Tokyo, 2005.

loans rather than investments. Indeed, the industry started out as a lending business during the postwar period, when interest rate regulation and restrictions on the stock market made VC a means to circumvent interest rate caps on loans for banks. The loan orientation was reinforced by the fact that some 80 percent of Japanese VC firms were subsidiaries of larger financial institutions. In comparison, in the United States about 20 percent of VC firm were thought of as affiliated, mostly with investment banks (DIR 2001).

Financial system reform and interest rate deregulation have brought the end of lending by VC firms. In particular, JAFCO's shift in business model in 1993 is credited as a main impetus for moving toward a stronger investment orientation.[12] Whereas in 1997 almost a fifth of venture finance occurred as loans, by 2006 this ratio has dropped, for all intents and purpose, to zero. Still, in some bank-affiliated VC the attitude remained, as investments were sometimes treated as functionally equivalent to loans, and some start-up firms reported fears that the VC could withdraw funds should they encounter trouble.[13]

Table 10.2 shows that only ten firms on the list are independent, while six of the thirty largest VC firms are related to banks, three to investment banks, and four to insurance companies. It is also noteworthy that four of the top five firms—Softbank Investment Holdings, JAFCO, NIF SMBC Ventures, and Japan Asia Investment—are listed companies. While this has been commented upon as an unusual arrangement that creates conflicts of interest between fund investors and shareholders, it may be a precursor of new industry developments, even in the United States.[14]

Another characteristic of Old Japan venture capital was high industry concentration. This has continued into the 2000s, when the ten largest firms still accounted for more than 65 percent of market share, and for as much as 71 percent of all investments outstanding in 2006 (calculated from *Nikkei* Survey). The main reason for this high concentration was the dominance of the top four independent firms, which combined for 49 percent of the market. The market shares by category of VC firm for the largest 30 firms in the *Nikkei* Survey are shown in figure 10.3. Between 1996 and 2006, the large four

12. Hamada and Asai (2001). JAFCO started out as "Ace Finance" in 1973, as a joint venture of Nomura Securities, Daiwa Bank, and Nippon Life. It is considered Japan's first venture capital firm. Although initially tightly connected to Nomura Securities, the company became increasingly independent, and when the banking portion of the business was spun off into Nomura Finance in 1993, JAFCO became a specialized venture investment firm. It was listed on the Tokyo Stock Exchange in 2001.

13. Interviews with start-up firms, Tokyo, 2002.

14. Interview with Japanese VC executives, 2005. In March 2007, the largest private equity fund at the time, the Blackstone Group, announced plans to go public in the United States.

10.3. *Market Share of the Top 30 Venture Capital Firms, by Affiliation,*
1996 and 2006
Source: Calculated from *Nikkei Kinyū* annual surveys.

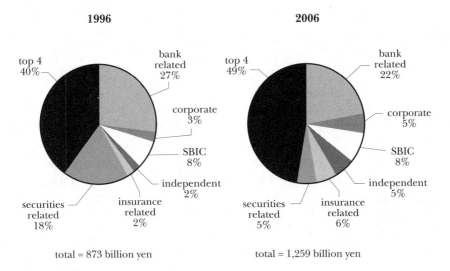

total = 873 billion yen   total = 1,259 billion yen

players have increased their dominance, whereas firms related to investment
and commercial banks have reduced their share. The largest increases are visible for insurance-related VC and independent VC.

The affiliation effect has influenced the development of Japanese VC in
important ways. Given restrictions on funds and limited liability partnership
until 1999, the affiliated VC firms used to invest mostly "own money" (i.e.,
mother company's assets). Even as of 2005, only about half of the VC investment in Japan was based on third-party funds (VEC 2006). This reliance on
own money reinforced a conservative bias in investment strategies. Bank- and
insurance-related VC, in particular, invested small lots into many firms, thus
engaging more in portfolio diversification than in venture financing. Only a
few firms offered hands-on guidance, with the exception of advice on financial procurement, which was usually tilted toward the interests of the mother
company (e.g., bank-VC would praise the virtues of borrowing, investment
bank-VC of IPOs).[15]

Partially because of the conservative investment bias, and partially due to
the 1990s recession, rates of return reported by Japanese VC used to be paltry,

15. The affiliation was also visible in staffing, as the mother companies often rotated staff
into the VC subsidiary. During the time an employee was sent to the VC subsidiary on a two-
year rotation, his main ambition was not to incur losses. One survey found that in fiscal year
2000, 60% of bank-related venture funding was in very-late-stage firms (Fujita and Matsuno
2001). Interviews, Tokyo, spring 2003 and January 2005.

with an annual average of 5.05 percent since 1982 (as compared with the Tokyo Stock Price Index at 4.34%). Needless to say, variance in the reported VC internal rate of return was much higher than the stock market, and in stellar years funds averaged returns of 38 percent (1994) and 21 percent (1997, 2003) (VEC 2006).

Venture Funds and Management Buyout Funds in New Japan

The growing market share of insurance-related and independent VC, as shown in figure 10.3, is evidence of a shift from own money investments toward third-party funds. Moreover, the introduction of limited liability funds for VC in 1999 and of LLP for private equity funds in 2005 have allowed more aggressive fund-raising and easier entry, and numerous new boutique VC have opened up, usually under the radar of the surveys. Combined, these factors have greatly changed the industry.

During the aftermath of the burst of the IT bubble in 2000, large VC firms realized that Japan's wave of corporate renewal had opened new, promising investment opportunities in management buyouts. As reorganization through spin-offs gained full speed after 2000, a market for small yet viable businesses sprung up. It was further nurtured by the so-called succession problem faced by the founders of the immediate postwar period, whose children were often not interested in continuing the family business. Both offered opportunity, if a fund could identify underperforming enterprises, turn them around, and sell them off. MBO investments are inherently less risky than venture investments, and the turnaround time is shorter, producing faster results. It also did not go unnoticed that foreign funds were earning very high returns with MBOs in the early 2000s. Both factors combined to help in raising third-party funds.

The emergence of successful MBO funds has in turn greatly propelled Japan's venture capital industry. It has allowed more aggressive VCs to gain independence from the mother company by raising outside funds. The rapid growth of third-party funds has diversified investment interests and increased transparency. Above all, MBO funds have attracted new liquidity to the market, thus also contributing to the growth of VC.[16]

Constraints that used to hamper fund-raising are starting to be lifted. For example, Japanese VC have long faced difficulties in attracting pension funds, which were said to be more risk averse than in the United States. A 2001 SMEA survey revealed that only 1.6 percent of all Japanese pension funds had ever invested in venture capital. The main reasons cited for this reluctance were

16. Interview, Tokio Marine Capital and Ignite Japan, Tokyo, 2005.

the lack of information and a lack of in-house expertise in evaluating these investments (Fujita and Matsuno 2001). However, the great success of turn-around funds in the early 2000s, and the shift toward professionalism in the industry in terms of industry knowledge, management guidance, and business strategy consulting, has invited sizable investors such as the Japan Pension Association.

Legal reforms have paved the way for new VC funds to enter the market. For example, the 2006 introduction of LLP allows VC partners to earn returns based on individual performance. New competition coincided with fundamental changes in the banking sector, where many midcareer employees found themselves discouraged and could more easily be tempted to join a cutting-edge, high-paying fund or venture firm. Tokyo now has a booming headhunting industry for finance professionals.

The new competition, including from foreign funds, has led the leading Japanese VC firms to change their investment strategies toward specialization. Even though, at $500,000 on average, funds remained much smaller than those in the United States, third-party money has brought a shift away from portfolio diversification to targeted investments in industries where the VC firm has specialized industry knowledge and engages in hands-on management guidance. Human resource policies, likewise, have evolved to place emphasis on specialized knowledge. Thus, the venture capital industry has embarked on its own move toward "choose and focus" and can be expected to grow further in the future.

Start-up Firms and Initial Public Offerings

The combination of legal revisions and supportive policy measures along with the growth of private funding geared toward innovative start-ups has greatly effected new company formation. Although figure 10.1 at the beginning of this chapter showed that the overall rate of exits (bankruptcies, liquidation) still exceeded that of new entries as of 2004, one explanation for the "death" overhang was a continued weeding out of inefficient, Old Japan firms. In contrast, many of the new entrants were drawn into new, fast-growing market segments. In absolute numbers, in the period from 2001 through 2004, Japan recorded an annual average of 290,000 exits but 168,000 new entrants. As a result of this continuing trend since the 1980s, the total number of companies operating in Japan shrank by one fifth, from 5.35 million in 1986 to 4.34 million in 2004 (SMEA 2006).

The majority of exits were recorded for sole proprietorships. About 40 percent of exits were by companies whose owner was older than 60 years, and the majority were in the manufacturing and services industries, some of which were themselves fading out (e.g., public bathhouses). In contrast, 52 percent of the new company formations were Internet-related, perhaps reflecting METI's jump-start role, with biotech gaining ground in the mid-2000s. The main target markets of these new firms were information and communication (10%), services for the elderly (6.4%), and diversification of modes of employment such as temporary staffing (6%).

The creative destruction element of these start-ups stands out when looking at the age of the company founders: as of 2002, 44 percent of new founders were younger than 40 years old, and an additional 20 percent were in their 40s (SMEA 2006). A separate survey, dating back to the IT bubble year 2000, revealed two separate types of entrepreneurs. The first were middle-aged founders that left their regular employment, either because of layoffs or job dissatisfaction. The second type were the young founders drawn into the fast expanding new Internet-based markets of information provision, services, or shopping (NLFC 2001).

As elsewhere, in-depth research on Japanese start-up firms is difficult because these are usually not captured in the statistics. Anecdotal evidence bespeaks of a new subculture emerging, in particular in human resource practices, in Bit Valley (a start-up cluster in Shibuya, Tokyo). Some start-ups, as well as VC boutiques, attract some of the brightest risk takers and independent thinkers who loath rigid hierarchies of large firms (see case studies in chapter 11). Just as for Silicon Valley, data analysis of this fast-moving market has to confine itself to the upper layer, the IPO segment.

The IT bubble at the turn of the century provided a much-needed push for the development of a market for young companies and initial public offerings. Between 1998 and 2006, Japan recorded 1,332 new company listings, of which 171 were on the Tokyo Stock Exchange, and 1,161 were IPOs of start-ups. After the IT bubble in 2000, which saw 204 IPOs in that year, 2006 was the second most active IPO year in this period with 188 new listings.

There are six exchanges in Japan with junior markets, the largest of which are JASDAQ, MOTHERS, and Hercules.[17] JASDAQ was founded by Japan's Association of Securities Dealers as an over-the-counter market in 1963, but was turned into a securities exchange in 1999. As figure 10.4 shows, it was Japan's largest IPO market, with 653 IPOs between 1998 and 2006, and 979 listed companies in 2007. It posts the J-Stock index, which is based on the stock prices of companies over a certain threshold of earnings and profits.

17. The others are Centrex (Nagoya Stock Exchange, established in 1999), Ambitious (Sapporo Stock Exchange, 1999), and Q-Board (Nagoya Stock Exchange). These cater to local start-up firms aiming to attract local investors. Between 1998 and 2006, these three exchanges attracted only 97 new listings.

10.4. *Initial Public Offerings in Japan, 1998–2006, by Stock Exchange*
Source: Compiled from data on www.jasdaq.co.jp and www.tse.or.jp.

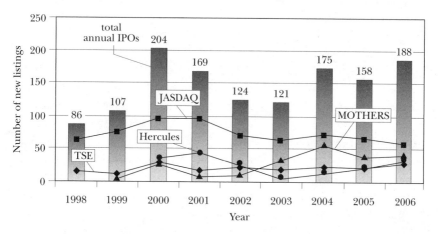

The second largest market for new company listings is MOTHERS ("Market of the High-Growth and Emerging Stocks"), which was established as a section of the Tokyo Stock Exchange in November 1999. As of early 2007, 210 companies were listed on this exchange, of which 99.7 percent were actively traded, with an average monthly trading value per stock of ¥12 billion (roughly $100 million). In other words, the market was reasonably liquid and attracted increasing attention.

Reflecting the dominance of IT- and health-oriented service businesses, 36 percent of MOTHERS companies are in the information and communication sector, 26 percent in services (including health care), and another 15 percent in distribution and retail.[18] A look at the largest companies, by market capitalization, listed on MOTHERS in February 2007 provides a flavor of this market. These included Access Co. (a software company), DeNa (an e-commerce website perhaps best known for its *Mobaoku,* "mobile phone auction," site), mixi.Inc. (Japan's wildly successful version of MySpace.com), ARDEPRO (a Tokyo-based remodeler of condominiums), and Takara Bio (a biotech firm).

Japan's third largest IPO exchange is Hercules, located at the Osaka Stock Exchange. As of early 2007, 164 companies were listed (of which one was foreign), and flagship stocks included Starbucks Japan, BB-Net and Gungho Online Entertainment (as well as other Softbank affiliates), En-Japan (a web-based matchmaker for midcareer job changers), and the Osaka Stock Exchange itself. The roots of this exchange are in NASDAQ Japan, which opened in May 2000

18. Calculated from the list of MOTHERS companies downloadable at www.tse.or.jp/listing/mothers/list.html.

with backing from Softbank. However, NASDAQ-J attracted less than 30 IPOs in its first three years of operation and suffered from lack of trading. It was closed down and revamped into "Nippon New Market—Hercules" in December 2002. Liquidity has greatly improved since then, making this market a viable alternative to the Tokyo-based exchanges.

Several reasons explain the renewed activity on these three junior markets. On the supply side, economic recovery and a general uptake in stock prices in the early 2000s made IPOs once again a potentially prosperous investment. Of the 158 listings in 2005, 82 traded above their first price after one year, and half of these traded more than 50 percent higher. Similarly, of the 175 listings in 2004, 95 traded above the IPO price, and 58 had increased by 50 percent or more in evaluation. In 2006, GCA, an M&A advising firm, gained 186 percent over its IPO price within two months of listing (Teramoto, Yamamoto, and Tomisawa 2006; *Japan Times*, April 28, 2007).

Moreover, the investment banking industry was undergoing its very own reorganization and restructuring, and as we will see in the next chapter, deregulation had allowed numerous new entrants, in particular in web-based trading. Easy Internet and mobile-phone access to stock price information, price competition in brokerage fees, and a sense of financial liberation and independence by younger investors disappointed by their retired parents' savings account yields have created an active market for individual investors and day traders. Whereas individuals account for less than a third of trading value at the Tokyo Stock Exchange's main sections, they generate about 70 percent of trading volume on JASDAQ, MOTHERS, and Hercules.[19]

Evaluation: New Money for New Markets

A policy shift away from market involvement by the government and toward enabling small firms to compete in open markets has brought about a sea change in new company formation. Deregulation, privatization, and corporate reorganization have opened markets, both for the funding of start-ups and for entrepreneurs. In the early 2000s Japan's VC firms underwent their own transition to "choose and focus," by becoming less dependent on their mother companies through raising third-party funds and positioning themselves in those markets where they have resident knowledge to evaluate the underlying technologies and can offer meaningful hands-on advice.

Until recently, perhaps the biggest obstacle to VC development in Japan was a dearth of promising start-up firms. "Many fishermen, too few fish" was an often-heard phrase in the 1990s, describing the mismatch between available

---

19. www.tse.or.jp/english/listing/companies/statistics_12.pdf.

VC funds and the lack of investment targets. Obstacles to start-up formation and funding included a lack of networks among entrepreneurs, of fora
for entrepreneurs and financiers to meet, and of a more structured exchange
of ideas among researchers and aspiring entrepreneurs. Government policies
to alleviate these shortcomings have shown some effect, and a network for
VC firms has begun to build. For start-up firms, the strategic inflection point
also promises to bring greater opportunities to sell, as former business groups
and vertical hierarchies are breaking open and markets for new technologies
develop. For example, a new development in 2007 was the emergence of a
viable biotech industry within Japan, attracted by newly structured collabora-
tions between universities and companies and a sudden keen interest by large
pharmaceutical companies in breakthrough innovations.

Thus, in industry after industry, new domestic entrants are knocking on
the door. The following chapter will highlight four industries—telecommunications, Internet shopping, pharmaceuticals, and investment banking—that
exemplify how previously rigidly regulated or otherwise tightly controlled
markets are breaking open and are being driven to new competition by emerging entrepreneurs.

11

NEW COMPETITORS:

SOFTBANK, KAKAKU.COM,

ASTELLAS, AND SBI E*TRADE SECURITIES

The development of a venture capital industry, the information technology bubble at the turn of the century, the creation of new stock exchanges, as well as privatization, deregulation, and the arrival of foreign competition all have resulted in the emergence of New Japan companies. These have created new markets, and have brought new competitive pressures even to some of the most notorious Old Japan markets, such as telecommunications. At the same time, reorganization and "choose and focus" mergers have led to the rise of new firms that challenge their erstwhile stuffy and restricted industries, such as in pharmaceuticals. It is this shift in competitive paradigm in industry after industry, brought about by new entry and new ways to compete, that cements Japan's strategic inflection point. In this chapter I showcase four companies that have transformed the ways in which their industries compete: Softbank and its global leadership as a cross-media digital information company; kakaku.com and its contribution to the retail revolution; Astellas and the changing pharmaceutical industry; and SBI E*Trade Securities and the makeover of Japan's investment banking industry.

Softbank and the Telecommunications Industry

In the early 2000s, the United States fell from fourth to 13th place in global rankings of broadband Internet use, and even further behind in mobile-phone-based Internet access. In its stead, Japan picked up world leadership. By 2005, nearly all Japanese households had high-speed broadband that was, on average, 16 times faster than that in the United States and, at roughly $20 a month, half as expensive. More than a quarter of phone calls were through VoIP (voice over Internet). Within less than a decade, Japan had propelled itself from one of the most expensive and limited Internet nations to the world's leader in telecommunications pricing, technology, and application (Bleha 2005).[1]

1. Industry data for 2007 showed that average speed, in megabytes per second, was 61 for Japan, compared to 46.6 in Korea, 18 in France, and 5 in the United States. In contrast, the

By 2006, 80 percent of Japan's population had a mobile phone, translating into 90 million phones, and 85 percent of these had active Internet access (Osaki 2006a). While Americans were still making the transition from using cell phones for voice to perhaps using it for data transmission, Japan was approaching the third stage in this evolution, where the mobile phone offered video-streaming capabilities and became a central piece of "lifestyle infrastructure" (NTT DoCoMo website). The theme of the year of the government's 2006 White Paper on Information and Communications was the "ubiquitous economy." In this vision, to be reached in Japan by 2010, ubiquitous networks allow seamless and universal person-to-person, person-to-goods, and goods-to-goods communication. Information communication technology, it was forecast, would penetrate all social and economic activities (MIAC 2006).

The story of this enormous development is one of deregulation, competition, and entrepreneurship. The biggest engine behind it was the emergence of Softbank, a 1980s start-up in computer peripherals that exploited Japan's strategic inflection point to establish itself as the world's preeminent digital information provider. Initially shaped by regulation and Japan's slow embrace of the Internet, Softbank's strategic moves in the 21st century have in turn shaped the evolution of digital information provision in Japan—so much so that Softbank CEO Masayoshi Son was considered "the leader of a new generation of Japanese risk takers" (Wehrfritz 1999).

Evolution

Softbank was founded in 1981 by Masayoshi Son, considered by some as "Japan's Bill Gates" (Economist 1996). During the 1980s, Son built his start-up into Japan's largest software distributor and computer magazine publisher. He was one of the first to realize that the computer would eventually be simply one of several media, and in the 1990s his business model shifted from "having everything to do with computers" to one anchored on the Internet. He sparked e-commerce and venture capital in Japan, and by 1998 had positioned himself as "one of the world's biggest investors in cyberspace" by putting roughly $1 billion into Silicon Valley start-ups (Bremmer 1998). In the early 2000s, Softbank single-handedly transformed Japan from the world's most expensive and comparatively backward to the world's cheapest and most advanced broadband market. His entries into fiber optic networks in 2004 and the mobile phone market in 2006 provided Softbank with the platforms to offer

---

price per monthly service, for one megabyte a second, was $0.27 in Japan, $0.45 in Korea, $1.64 in France, but $3.33 in the United States. See *New York Times*, October 3, 2007. The following analysis has benefited greatly from joint research with Robert L. Sei.

voice, data, and video, both fixed and mobile, and positioned the company to push the industry's envelope into mobile Internet video. As of 2007, Softbank was well on its way to become the world leader in cross-media digital content provision, and Japan was at least five years ahead of the United States in these developments.

Perhaps the biggest contributor to the initial success was Son's knack for introducing new U.S. developments in computer and Internet-related commerce to Japan, where the industry developed at a different pace due to lingering telecommunications regulation favoring the erstwhile monopolist NTT (Nippon Telephone and Telegraph). Son introduced Japanese versions of many U.S. IT concepts, beginning with *PC Magazine* in 1986. His entry into telecommunications also dated to 1986 when the first measures of telecom deregulation in Japan allowed competition in fixed-line, long-distance telephony. Softbank provided a small gadget dubbed "least-cost routing device" that greatly reduced the hassle of dialing additional prefix numbers to capture cheaper rates. The device automatically calculated the cheapest service at that time and dialed the necessary prefixes without user action. This head-on challenge to NTT was to be repeated in all new market segments developed thereafter.[2]

In the 1990s, Softbank was primarily a VC firm, investing heavily in emerging Internet businesses. With enormous foresight, Son purchased a $100 million equity stake in Yahoo! Inc. in the United States, at a time when that start-up was still a directory company and portals had yet to be conceived. Softbank itself went public in 1994, with Son retaining a 31.47 percent stake. In 1996, Softbank's stake in Yahoo! had reached 37 percent, and Son founded Yahoo! Japan, with a majority ownership. By 1998, Softbank owned 35 percent of GeoCities (a home page website), and 27 percent of E*Trade, among others. Softbank was directly involved in the creation of Novell Japan and Nihon Cisco System, and in 1999 it had established GeoCities Japan, E*Trade Japan, and E*Loan Japan. Although some of these were superbly successful, not all of the IT bubble-period investments panned out as expected. For example, Softbank acquired 49 percent of the defunct Nippon Credit Bank, but later sold its stake in the renamed Aozora Bank to U.S. hedge fund Cerberus when synergies with the digital information business failed to materialize. In 2001 Softbank's market value dropped precipitously and Son was forced to write off investments in over 600 IT-related firms. Softbank's alliance with NASDAQ to form NASDAQ Japan in December 2000 likewise did not survive the IT bubble burst, and it was reformed into Hercules in 2002.

2. See www.answers.com/topic/softbank-corp-usa.

Of Softbank's various investments of the 1990s, Yahoo! proved to be the golden egg. The Internet arrived in Japan late, but it did so with a vengeance. When this shift occurred, Yahoo! Japan became Japan's dominant portal, with 86 percent of page views in late 2006 (see table 11.1). In the 1990s, Internet access was accomplished by telephone dial-up through a modem. At the time, the fixed-line market in Japan was still dominated by NTT, which charged very high prices and offered no unlimited local calling plans, thus limiting the time spent online and greatly stalling Internet acceptance.

A full-force move toward the market in Japan's telecommunications policy during the strategic inflection point greatly helped Softbank's cause. In 1998, the government announced a three-year program of deregulation that turned Japan into one of the most competitive telecommunications market in the world. Its main ingredient was the 2000 revision of the Basic Information Technology Law, which required incumbent telephone providers (i.e., NTT) to grant competitors access to its fixed-line network for a fee of about $2 a month (Vogel 2006; Bleha 2005). Such a line-sharing mandate is unknown in the United States. In Japan, it immediately opened the market for new entrants offering broadband services through ADSL (asynchronous digital subscriber lines). Many of these were small firms jockeying for local subscribers.

TABLE 11.1. *Japan Internet Property Ranking, as of September 2006*

Rank 2006	Rank 2005	Property	Unique audience (in millions)	Page views (in millions)	Year-on-year change (in %)
1	1	Yahoo! Japan	38.49	23,620	14.2
2	2	Rakuten	25.73	4,310	10.3
3	8	Microsoft	25.53	1,540	n/a
4	7	NTT Communications	24.18	1,494	n/a
5	3	GMO internet	23.31	1,344	13.3
6	4	Nifty	21.50	996	8.9
7	6	NEC	19.72	827	13.1
8	—	FC2	17.88	1,005	35.2
9	10	Amazon	17.47	566	21.9
10	15	Google	17.38	1,981	43.4

Source: Nielsen (2006).
Note: Following its acquisition of YouTube in October 2006, Google climbed from rank 13 to 6. FC2 is a hosting server that also maintains blogs. Rakuten and Amazon are e-shopping malls. The other entries are portals.

. Recognizing this new opportunity, in 2001 Softbank moved to become a "comprehensive digital information infrastructure provider" by entering the broadband business. Son greatly reduced his Silicon Valley holdings, including in Yahoo! Inc., and bet the farm on rolling out a new ADSL-based broadband service called "Yahoo! BB." In a highly aggressive marketing, pricing, and branding campaign in early 2003, broadband modems in Yahoo-red were given away at subway stations together with trial subscriptions. The monthly rate was set at less than $20 a month, significantly below NTT's services, which remained stodgy, slow, and unexciting. Yahoo! BB captured one third of the Internet provider market in 2003. As early as 2002, Yahoo! BB had also launched Japan's first VoIP service with "BB phone." So attractive were these offerings that in 2004 Japanese broadband penetration greatly surpassed that of the United States. Whereas only 43 percent of U.S. households using the Internet had broadband in 2003, 70 percent of Japanese users were connected through broadband. By 2005, overall PC penetration in Japan had reached 67 percent of household, including 90 percent for households with annual income exceeding ¥7 million (roughly $65,000) (MIAC 2006, 12; Nielsen 2004; Kimura 2004).

While Softbank was eyeing industry behemoth NTT with its entry into telephony, it also realized that a perhaps bigger competitive threat to its ADSL-based broadband service would emerge from high-speed fiber optic cable providers. In 2004, Softbank acquired Japan Telecom, then the country's second largest international telecommunication business. Although initially pooh-poohed by securities analysts as a sign of Son finally succumbing to hubris, the coup with this acquisition was to provide the new Softbank Telecom with 12,000 kilometers (7,500 miles) of fiber optic cable, based on which Yahoo! BB Fiber Optic was launched. Cable TV played a much more limited role in Japan than in the United States, and household broadband access through cable TV accounted for only 15 percent of total access in 2005. Softbank's fiber optic network acquisition was critical not only because it allowed entry into the lucrative corporate broadband and Internet platform provision businesses. Son was also highly prescient in realizing that ADSL would eventually be too slow for future Internet use, which he saw as anchored on video streaming. A 2007 industry forecast finally caught up with Son and predicted a drop in ADSL-based household broadband access from 62 percent in 2005 to 32 percent in 2011, when at least 58 percent of households were expected to access the Internet through fiber optic broadband.[3]

3. Nomura Research Institute data, reported in *Shūkan Daiyamondo*, March 3, 2007, 139.

Mobile Phones and the Internet

In addition to the growth in the fixed-line segment, a concurrent development that greatly boosted Internet penetration in Japan was mobile-phone-based Internet access, beginning with the 1999 launch of i-mode by NTT DoCoMo. DoCoMo, the mobile phone subsidiary of NTT, had developed a proprietary technology that offered extraordinary ease of use in accessing the Internet using a cell phone. To begin with, i-mode was revolutionary in that it was based on HTML-based websites, as opposed to requiring content providers to create special sites for phone users. This meant that even though DoCoMo signed up a set of official sites with joint pricing schemes (such as traffic, maps, or news), virtually all websites were accessible through the phone. Moreover, i-mode was "always-on," such that a user could receive phone calls and e-mails while surfing the net. And finally, e-mails through i-mode were based on "push" rather than "pull" access, so that there was no need to log in to check whether there was new mail; instead, like text messages, the e-mail automatically appeared. In contrast to the United States, Japanese cell phone–service providers purchased and then sold their own phones, which afforded them control over phone specifications. Soon, DoCoMo sold only i-mode phones, bringing the technology to the consumer immediately. It helped that replacement rates of phones in Japan were much higher than elsewhere, with the phone often being a fashion accessory (JETRO 2004; Bradley et al. 2006).

Developments in Japan's mobile phone industry picked up a frantic speed thereafter, as consumers realized the great advantages with accessing Internet information for maps, restaurants, or price comparisons on the go. In 2002 DoCoMo introduced FOMA, followed by KDDI's competing service, both based on their respective next-generation technology platforms, 3G/W-CDMA and CDMA 2000.

The third large player, J-Phone, was acquired by Vodafone in 2001 for $5.34 billion. Yet, in spite of aggressive investments exceeding $16 billion, Vodafone failed to attract market share due to clunky phones and poor service. When Vodafone was up for sale in early 2006, Softbank bought it for $15.4 billion, in a novel highly leveraged financing scheme that insulated the investment in Softbank Mobile such that failure would not threaten other aspects of Softbank.[4] In launching an all-out war with DoCoMo and KDDI, Softbank knew it would be aided by continuing deregulation, in particular the introduction of number portability in November 2006. Throughout 2007, DoCoMo was

---

4. http://archives.cnn.com/2001/BUSINESS/asia/05/02/tokyo.vodafonejphoneupdate/ and *Financial Express,* March 18, 2006; Merrill Lynch, *Japan Credit Weekly,* October 2006.

most affected by number portability, as it lost customers to both KDDI and its popular "au" service as well as to the fast-growing and exceedingly cool Softbank Mobile. As these three competed for new customers, an all-out price war began that made comprehensive mobile phone service prices in Japan much lower than in other OECD countries.

In response to the surging demand for Internet-based data and image exchange, in October 2007 Japan's government allotted new 2.5 gigahertz licenses for next-generation high-speed data communications, in order to spur technological competition in the domestic market. The new licenses were to increase competition in price and quality of cell phone services, and possibly invite a reorganization of the industry through mergers between incumbents and newcomers. Compared to 1999, Japan's telecommunication market had been completely transformed.

Softbank's Strategy: The Cross-Media Leader

In the next step, Softbank developed a vision of how to commercialize the new concept of a "ubiquitous society." Son's goal was to create unparalleled synergies across various media that all resulted in digital information provision. In 2007, Softbank reorganized into a pure holding company (with 113 employees) with subsidiaries in five business areas: broadband infrastructure, fixed-line telephony, mobile telecommunications, Internet culture, and e-commerce. SBI Holdings, the financial management and domestic venture capital arm, had already been spun out in 2006 as it was no longer considered a core operation. However, Softbank retained Softbank Capital, its venture capital firm in the United States that acts as a crystal ball on emerging technology trends.

The entry into comprehensive digital information began with the Internet culture segment, centered around Yahoo! Japan, the dominant portal, which had become much more advanced than the U.S. version. Yahoo! Japan's offerings of blogs, social networking (with MySpace.com), auctions, shopping, and banking were all among the leaders in their categories. As table 11.1 showed, in 2006 Yahoo! commanded roughly twice the audience as Google in Japan.

Next, Softbank built the infrastructure underneath, by aggressively assuming a dominant position in provider services through Yahoo! BB. Together with Softbank Telecom, Softbank BB operated broadband infrastructure services and also offered ADSL or fiber-optic connections, wi-fi hotspots, IP telephone (VoIP), and IP broadcasting. In each of these segments, Softbank competed powerfully against a set of competitors, but no one company could challenge Softbank in all of these areas. Softbank Mobile Communication provided domestic and international voice services, including a mobile Internet portal and services such as Yahoo! Auctions Mobile, e-mail, and music downloads. These offerings fed into each other. For example, after the launch of Yahoo! Keitai, the phone-based Internet portal in July 2006, Softbank Mobile page views shot up by 45 times within six months.

With this infrastructure in place, Softbank moved to address the upper layer, which was content provision. Perhaps most consequential for the next step in the industry's evolution was how Softbank executed the broadband triple play of voice (IP telephony), data (ADSL, fiber optic) and video (IPTV), and how it then extended this into a grand slam by offering the same three services over the mobile phone. The broadband triple play came to consumers by adding to the broadband subscription a telephone service for a low-priced $5 a month. By 2005, NTT had lost one quarter of its erstwhile fixed-line clients to VoIP. Internet-based TV was offered with the launch of BB-TV, a ¥2,280 (about $20) subscription service using a TV set top box similar to cable boxes. As of 2007, BB-TV featured primarily foreign content with Japanese subtitles, such as Fox, CNN, Bloomberg TV, MTV, the Discovery Channel, or Disney. Because cable had remained underdeveloped and most Japanese households still used antennas for TV reception, this was a true upgrade over existing TV options.

The focus on foreign content was necessitated by a peculiar Japanese regulation that granted copyrights to a TV show to the producer rather than to the TV station. This regulation was the reason why Japanese TV stations typically did not air reruns. Only their current news content (news, talk shows, sports) could be freely reused, including for video streaming on the Internet. Understanding that the next step in the Internet evolution was video content, Softbank invented new technology to cleverly circumvent broadcasting regulations—and in turn triggered further deregulation in the copyright segment. The TV Pack was a ¥990 a month ($9) service based on proprietary Softbank hardware and software. The TV Pack gadget hooked up to the TV antenna in the house and digitized analog broadcast services. The digital signals were then transmitted to the personal computer within the house. Because private broadcasting was not covered by the copyright rules, the user could watch the show on the PC at a later point. Thus, TV Pack allowed for video-on-demand as well as repeated use. For 21st century laptop multitasking, this service could also be tied in to wireless, to allow concurrent activities such as checking the Yahoo! e-mail account while watching the MySpace chat room and bargain shopping on Yahoo! Auction.

The next step in this evolution was IPTV, that is TV-streaming over the Internet. In March 2006, Softbank launched Yahoo! Doga, a free-of-charge portal with over 100,000 TV programs for on-demand video streaming on the PC.

Softbank partnered with TV Asahi and Fuji TV, two of the largest TV stations, as initial providers of news and sport content. As other broadband providers began to copy Softbank's moves, this type of service was bound to challenge Old Japan broadcasting, copyright, and telecommunications regulations, and all three industries were expected to continue their fast-paced change.

The strategic brilliance of Softbank's positioning in the IPTV segment becomes apparent in the next step, the marriage between IPTV and mobile phones. The high Internet penetration through mobile phones, the fierce competition for customers, and the providers' ability to control their cell phone specifications combined to create an enormous push for mobile TV. Japan has allocated 13 frequency band segments for digital terrestrial content distribution to mobile terminals, and in April 2006 one of these became official, labeled "one-seg." By mid-2007, ten million one-seg-equipped mobile phones had been sold. And even though KDDI was the market leader initially, Softbank posed a formidable threat when it tied up with Sharp to create brisk demand for one-seg TV phones with a rotating Aquos LCD screen (Osaki 2006b; *Nikkei,* July 17, 2007).

Softbank also forged additional alliances with TBS and NHK for news provision, and used Yahoo! Doga to showcase (and sell tickets for) the Softbank Hawks, the baseball team formerly known as the Fukuoka Daiei Hawks. It had become clear that the 2006 purchase of Vodafone afforded Softbank unparalleled synergies for the next step of digital media evolution, which as of 2007 promised to be video-based Internet communication.

Reflecting the fast evolution of this industry and Softbank's risky bets in shaping its developments and taking on regulation, the company's stock price experienced a remarkable roller-coaster ride throughout the decade. Market evaluation dropped precipitously every time Softbank made a bold, large-scale investment, and rose several hundred percent when analysts began to understand just how this investment created synergies. Figure 11.1 shows how the end of the IT bubble and the acquisition of Japan Telecom both resulted in stock price fluctuations by several hundred percent. Part of the volatility of Softbank's stock was due to the fact that it was Japan's most actively traded stock in the mid-2000s, and that most of the owners were individuals, often trading the stock on their cell phones following rumors. This was a new phenomenon Softbank itself had helped create, as we will see below on SBI E*Trade.

The story of Softbank, then, is both the story of an entrepreneur with an enormous instinct for foreseeing market evolution and a story of how the strategic inflection point and deregulation have allowed new market entry that shapes Japanese competition in new ways. Always pointing into the future,

11.1. Year-on-Year Percentage Changes in Softbank's Stock Price, Profits, and NASDAQ, 1998–2006
Source: Company data from annual reports, NASDAQ.

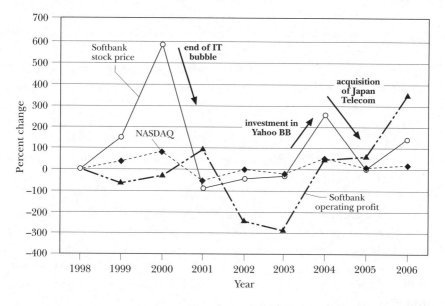

Softbank also provides a glimpse of the next evolution in corporate strategy in Japan. In contrast to the often unrelated, and often uncoordinated, diversification of Japanese firms in the postwar period, Softbank pursued very targeted diversification around a well-defined core, with an eye toward creating synergies that cannot be challenged by competitors with only partially overlapping business portfolios.

Moreover, by challenging NTT at every juncture, Softbank not only contributed to breaking open the former quasi monopolist but it arguably also made NTT a fiercer and stronger competitor. The success of NTT DoCoMo in pushing mobile phone use from simple voice exchange to lifestyle infrastructure in a matter of a decade is also a story of new competition, and new entrants reshaping Japan. And finally, Softbank has influenced Japan's IT industry not just by showing that Japanese markets can be cracked open but also by setting the stage for derivative industries in the Internet and communications sectors.

Kakaku.com and E-Tailing

The combination of the fast adoption of the Internet and its accessibility through mobile phones further propelled the retail revolution of the 1990s, by finally offering consumers full access to market and price information.

Throughout the postwar period, Japanese consumer groups had protested in vain against a lack of transparency in pricing and product information (Maclachlan 2002). The Internet, as it arrived to consumers with i-mode in 1999, undermined the retailers' grip on product knowledge in one fell swoop. In turn, the enthusiasm with which Japanese consumers embraced the new access to information and their new ability to compare prices and hunt for bargains opened a huge market opportunity for Internet-based commerce. Innumerable companies sprouted up to provide context and services for new business processes.

At the core of this shift toward price transparency was Kakaku.com (literally meaning "price.com"), which emerged as Japan's largest website for product, price, and satisfaction comparison of consumer goods and consumer-oriented services. The company's early business model took advantage of the arrival of price competition in electronics retailing. When previously rigid structures suddenly broke open, it was difficult at first to identify the newly emerging low-price leaders in any given product segment (unlike in the United States, where price leaders had been established in a more incremental process over time). Kakaku exploited this opportunity by providing consumers with detailed information on 220,000 products and services and links to participating stores. Thus, it was an Internet shopping portal offering product ratings and product information—in some ways similar to "pricegrabber.com" or "pricescan.com" in the United States, but with more in-depth product research and nifty price comparison tables. As of 2007, the company prided itself on its comprehensive user feedback system, with more than five million comments online, and it also offered independent evaluation reports and news articles on new product releases.

Kakaku.com's website sorted its offerings into nine categories, ranging from electronics, telecommunications (including an interactive site for mobile phone pricing plans), and cars (including used cars and car insurance) to everyday life products (entertainment, health and health insurance, pets), shopping and restaurants, travel and reservations, and money (including securities firms, commodity futures, loans, and foreign exchange investments). A consumer interested in purchasing an electronic piano, for example, was presented with a list of products, quality rankings, and reviews, and the cheapest price at which each of these was available. The consumer could then follow a link to a store that provided complete information on price and fees as well as consumer reviews of the vendor. Price information was updated in real time through direct feeds by participating stores. Over time, Kakaku.com increased its product categories, such as through the October 2004 purchase of a specialized website for last-minute discount deals at exclusive Japanese hotels called yoyaQ.com (a clever turn on *yoyaku*, "reservation"). Also in 2004, it entered price comparisons for funeral services, a market estimated at ¥2 trillion ($16 billion) a year. In 2007, the company acquired eiga.com, for movie and movie theater price comparisons, and in March 2007 it launched investment trust comparisons (www.kakaku.com).

Kakaku's main impact stemmed from its "pro-consumer, pro-user" stance that brought price transparency and competitive pressure to virtually every consumer product and service. In launching what the company called a reverse auction through exposing sellers, Kakaku induced sellers to bring down prices to the lowest possible level. Unlike some of its competitors, such as Livedoor and Rakuten, which soon began to branch out, the company stayed focused on building on its first-mover advantage as a reliable information provider. Its revenues derived from participant merchant fees and advertisements, making it neutral to the sales generated by its services.

Kakaku.com was also a Cinderella story of hands-on VC involvement, fast triumph during the IT bubble, and successful stock exchange listing. The company was founded in 1997 under the name of "Core Price" by 23-year-old Mitsuaki Makino, who was then working for a store selling PC accessories in Akihabara. The retail revolution had caused confusion about who was the price leader in this district of electronics stores in Tokyo. Makino was put in charge of scouting competitors' prices, and at busy times he had to visit competing stores several times a day to tally prices. It occurred to him that if he could simply stand in front of the Akihabara train station with a sign guiding people to what he had identified as the cheapest store, he could make a lot of lives easier.[5] Thus was born a website that listed prices for PC accessories by competitor; as more stores joined, the website branched out into other products and a full-fledged price comparison information center had been created.

In 1999, Kakaku became one of the first official websites for the i-mode Internet service. In 2000, the company changed its official name to Kakakukomu and began the expansion of product categories registered on its site, with the help of venture funding received from ICP. Founded as a boutique VC in 1999, ICP exerted proactive, hands-on management guidance at a time when other VC firms were still largely portfolio investors. ICP's founder, Yoshiteru Akita, became co-CEO at Kakaku.com. Only 31 at the time, Akita had several years of work experience with VC powerhouse JAFCO, as well as in direct marketing at another start-up company. In 2002, Akita introduced an additional investor, when Digital Garage acquired 45 percent of Kakaku and made it a

---

5. See interview with Mitsuaki Makino, http://pc.watch.impress.co.jp/docs/2002/0701/gyokai31.htm.

subsidiary. In 2003, the company went public on MOTHERS.[6] The company's steady growth and continuing success enabled a switch to the First Section of the Tokyo Stock Exchange in March 2005. Kakaku founder Makino continued to be an adviser to the company but is no longer involved in day-to-day management.

Digital Garage (DG) was also a product of the Internet revolution. It was founded in 1995 to create new business contexts in communication, marketing, and finance based on IT. Its initial claim to fame was to have posted Japan's first individual home page in 1994. The company started out with search engines, launching Infoseek Japan in 1996 and Ultraseek in 1997. Today it is also known for its specialized blog search engine, Technorati. The company was listed on JASDAQ in 2000.

To increase the usability of the Internet for e-commerce, DG had attempted to develop a value comparison site, without success, which led to the acquisition of Kakaku in 2002. In 2005, Digital Garage reorganized into the "DG Group," a holding company with four main businesses: Solutions (media, creative solutions, marketing); Portal and Weblog (Kakaku.com, including its 4Travel site, Technorati, DG Mobile, Web 2.0 Inc.); Incubation (venture funding through Joi Itos' Lab); and Finance (Kakaku.com Insurance, Kakaku.com Financial).[7] Of these separate businesses as of 2007, Kakaku was one of the DG Group's main businesses and revenue generators.

Kakaku.com relied on two main sources of revenue: a flat monthly fee of ¥100,000 (about $900) from the over 2,000 participating merchants and advertisement revenue. Growth was created mainly through increases in advertising, which in turn hinged on growth in use. Between March 2004 and March 2006, page views of the website almost doubled, as did ordinary profits, from ¥475 million to ¥814 million (roughly $6.5 million). By February 2007, kakaku.com had reached ten million unique users, and about 13 million page views per day. As seen in table 11.1, this compared to roughly 38 million unique users for Yahoo! Japan and about 25 million for Rakuten, Japan's largest e-shopping mall. In 2006, Amazon.com, having greatly expanded its product categories, was beginning to catch up with Rakuten with more than 16 million unique users.

Rakuten was perhaps Kakaku's greatest competitor. Rakuten was founded in 1995 as an Internet shopping mall that offered small- and medium-sized merchants an easy way to sell online at a time when PC penetration and the

6. See http://japan.cnet.com/column/nils2004/story/0,2000559I9,20078624,00.htm.

7. See Digital Garage website at www.garage.co.jp. Joi Ito is one of Japan's early successful start-up entrepreneurs that turned to VC finance.

Internet were still slow in developing. By offering software support and a central website that attracted visitors, Rakuten targeted merchants that did not otherwise have the capability to engage in e-tailing (McFarlan et al. 2005). Thus, unlike Kakaku, Rakuten's value proposition was directed at merchants. Initially, Rakuten was concerned neither with product evaluation nor direct comparisons, but the success of Kakaku led to new ideas, as users obviously valued price and product information. Conversely, Kakaku benefited from Rakuten's concept of offering direct links from price comparison to direct shopping at participating merchants. In the late 1990s, the two companies fed off each other, as both benefited from increased demand for ubiquitous, on-time price and product information.

E-tailing has introduced epochal changes to Japanese shopping behavior. In 2007, Kakaku.com's user profile—thought to be similar to the other e-shopping sites—was 70 percent male, and 50 percent of users were in their 30s and 40s. In other words, the website attracted exactly the market segment that new superstore category killers as well as specialty stores were vying for. What is more, because the participating merchants at Kakaku.com and Rakuten were mostly small- and medium-sized retailers, these websites brought new competition to Japan's leading stores through the long tail of retailing. Their emergence and success has not only brought price transparency to what used to be one of the world's most opaque retail markets but it has also begun to challenge some of the industry's structural inefficiencies, as witnessed in the restructuring by Japanese department stores and the multilayered wholesale and distribution system. Japan's previously ironclad consumer markets have opened up.

Astellas Pharma Inc. and the Fast-Changing Pharmaceutical Industry

Similar to telecommunications, Japan's pharmaceutical industry in the post-war period was known as highly protected and slow moving. However, deregulation and health care reforms beginning in 1998 have brought a true strategic inflection also to this prime example of Old Japan. While a viable start-up sector in the biotech field was still beginning to emerge in the 2000s, the industry itself was swept by an enormous wave of "choose and focus" that opened access to innovation and new ideas. The process of consolidations through mergers, spin-offs of noncore businesses, and repositioning of product offerings was forecast to continue for another decade. The following account offers a snapshot of one new company that has resulted from this reorganization, Astellas, to highlight the mechanisms through which Japan's pharma industry has been reformed.

The global pharmaceutical market in 2005 was estimated at $602 billion in sales, of which 11 percent were generated in Japan. Whereas Japan's pharma

industry had historically been highly fragmented, with more than 1,500 small-
and medium-sized companies, as of 2005, of Japan's $66 billion market,
three companies accounted for 38 percent. These market leaders were Takeda
Pharmaceutical Co. (with sales of about $8.5 billion), Daiichi Sankyo Co.
($8.3 billion), and Astellas Pharma Inc. ($8 billion) (Gray 2006). But this high
concentration was only the result of recent, large-scale consolidation. Astellas was born in 2005 through a merger between Yamanouchi and Fujisawa
(previously ranked number three and five, respectively). A year later, Daiichi
Sankyo resulted from the merger between the second and sixth largest firms,
and Dainippon Sumitomo Pharma Co. was the marriage of its two namesakes.
Consolidation continued into 2007, when Mitsubishi Pharma and Tanabe Seiyaku merged into the country's fifth largest drugmaker. At the second- and
third-tier levels, mergers and acquisitions were also occurring at a rapid rate.
Two main currents had unleashed this reorganization: domestic deregulation
introduced price competition and shrank the Japanese market, thereby forcing
Japanese firms to think globally just at a time when the global pharma industry
was undergoing a major wave of consolidation.

Domestic Deregulation and Global Pressure

In 1950, Japan established a regulatory regime intended to secure steady
delivery of drugs to the national health insurance system.[8] Its main aspect was
a list price system, under which all drugs of one category were reimbursed
according to a set price, which was lowered downward over time in a type of
government-enforced depreciation. This "set price" system was not conducive
to the growth of a vibrant, competitive pharmaceutical industry, because the
returns for true innovation and breakthrough ideas were exactly the same as
the returns earned on incremental improvements on old drugs in existing categories. Both the new drug and the incrementally improved drug would be put
at the top of the "set price" list, but incremental improvements were of course
much cheaper and much less risky.

Moreover, with regulated prices, sales volume was key. Market share could
be increased by diversifying into various categories of drugs, instead of specializing in a few core therapeutic areas. This preference for breadth in portfolio
was reinforced by a rigid and exclusive distribution system, in which powerful
wholesalers offered certain doctors access to drugs from certain companies
only. A wider product portfolio increased the sales of these companies. The
distribution system also greatly impeded new entry by domestic or foreign

8. www.pacificbridgemedical.com/publications/html/JapanApril98.htm. This section has
benefited from research assistance by Bryan Green and Rika Kido.

firms, so that competition was limited. Government protection of the industry through excessive drug approval procedures further put the industry into a slumber.

Added to this was the curious practice of putting doctors, as opposed to pharmacies, in charge of drug sales to the patient. Competition among pharmaceutical companies, as everywhere, was about getting a doctor to sell more of their drugs. Under fixed prices, this was accomplished by offering the doctor a discount from the government's list price—meaning that the doctor's purchase price for drugs was lower than the "set price" to be charged to the health care system. In line with postwar-period distribution practices, volume rebates would entice doctors to prescribe even more of the same drug or drugs from the same company. The doctor pocketed the differential between the list price and the discount price, which may have been as high as 30 percent.[9] Accordingly, doctors prescribed drugs with the highest spreads between list price and real price, and according to widespread observations, many doctors were tempted to prescribe more drugs than strictly necessary in light of a patient's condition (Watts 2000; Arai and Ikegami 1998).

The system became so obviously skewed and inefficient that the Ministry of Health and Welfare began deliberations about abolishing the list price system in 1997. Cost pressures on the national health insurance system added urgency to reforms, which were greatly resisted, in particular by doctors. In 2003, Prime Minister Koizumi's Council on Structural Reform placed the pharmaceutical industry squarely at the top of its reform agenda. The 2004 revision of the Pharmaceutical Affairs Law replaced the set price system with a reference pricing system that was not as binding. The revised law also opened new sales channels (distributors and pharmacies) and disallowed doctors from earning profits through drug delivery. Finally, barriers to entry and innovation by foreign and new domestic firms were greatly reduced by clarifying and speeding up the drug approval process.

This sea change created new competitive pressures for Japan's pharmaceutical firms from two ends—the aggressive entry of global megapharma companies and new rules of domestic competition. With the doctor's incentives to inflate prescriptions corrected, even Japan's ageing society and long life expectancy would not compensate for the reduction in the total available market in Japan. This meant that Japanese pharmaceutical companies had to compete in world markets. At the same time, the breakup of the distribution system and the arrival of foreign drugs within Japan meant that they had to compete with better drugs that had been produced more efficiently. The name of the game

---

9. www.okusuri110.com/yaka/about_yaka.html.

became drug discovery and approval, and the magic word was pipeline, referring to new drugs in development scheduled to reach the market at certain
future points just when older drugs were to go off patent. These new pressures
necessitated specialization on a few therapeutic areas in which to differentiate
and lead the market, and the streamlining of operations to exploit economies
of scales in R&D and marketing—that is, the industry turned toward "choose
and focus." Its repositioning bode well for growth in R&D, including through
biotech start-ups, and the clinical trial market.

Changes in the domestic environment were made even more exigent because Japanese pharmaceutical companies had historically been small. In 2006
the minimum efficient scale for R&D for a globally competitive firm was estimated to be roughly $1.2 billion, a budget that among Japanese firms only
Takeda could reach on its own. But Takeda was dwarfed by the global megaplayers, ranking only 15th in global sales in world comparisons (*Diamond
Weekly* 2007b; Gray 2006). And even as Japan was going through its own
deregulation pains, the global pharmaceutical market had undergone a series
of megamergers, including those of Bristol-Myers Squibb (1989), GlaxoSmith-
Kline (1995), Novartis (1996), AstraZeneca (1999), Sanofi-Aventis (2004),
and Pfizer with Warner-Lambert and Pharmacia (2000 and 2003). With annual sales of over $30 billion, some of these companies had R&D budgets
larger than the total revenues of Japan's leading firms. To compete in global
markets, Japanese firms had to consolidate.

A New Type of Merger

Astellas was Japan's first pharma megamerger. The two partners to the arrangement were Yamanouchi, founded in 1923 and known for an expertise
in urology, and Fujisawa, which dated back to 1894 and boasted a diverse
portfolio but was best known for the dermatology drug Protopic and the immunology drug Prograf. For the fiscal year ending in March 2006, Astellas
reported net sales of ¥880 billion ($7.3 billion), R&D expenditures of ¥142
billion ($1.2 billion, 16% of sales) and net income of ¥104 billion ($886 million). These numbers ranked it 20th in the global pharmaceutical landscape.[10]

Most remarkable about the story of Astellas is how this New Japan merger
differed from postwar instances of large-scale mergers in Japan, including
the recent ones in the banking industry. Old Japan mergers invariably were
characterized by infighting between two strong corporate cultures, great resistance to downsizing and streamlining, a continuing employee loyalty to the

---

10. See Astellas Annual Report 2006, www.astellas.com/global/ir/library/pdf/annual2006_
eg.pdf.

original firm that would only subside with the next generation, and above all a lack of rigor and vision as to how, exactly, the merger would add value and synergies.

Astellas, in contrast, was remarkable in the clarity of the company's forward-looking strategy as to what markets it would be in and how it would compete. In preparation for the merger, both companies engaged in their own housecleaning, by launching separate "choose and focus" campaigns. Noncore businesses were either sold off or structured to allow for easy future spin-offs. For example, both companies initially kept some generic drug manufacturing, which they merged into Zepharma and later sold to Daiichi Sankyo. Next, a clear vision was developed that the company was to position itself as a global category player by 2010, meaning they would compete only in certain clearly defined drug categories, as opposed to the super-scale players such as Pfizer or more specialized companies. The five categories Astellas decided to compete in, as of 2007, were immunology (Prograf), dermatology (Protopic), infectious diseases, cardiology, and urology (Flomax). In each of these, the company had a few leading drugs as well as ongoing pipeline activities.[11] Between November 2006 and April 2007 Astellas acquired drugs or licenses from eight foreign biotech start-ups, including a major investment and exclusive licensing agreement with FibroGen, to augment its pipeline. Only time will tell whether the company will succeed in executing this strategic plan, but even if it does not pan out as expected, the existence of a clear, explicit strategy was a dramatic change from previous mergers in Japan.

As Astellas moved to become a powerful player, market leader Takeda Pharmaceutical was not sitting still, as we saw in chapter 4. These companies' arrival on the global market with competitive products such as Flomax or Rozerem reflect the transformation of Japan's pharmaceutical industry during the strategic inflection point. Within one decade, Japan's pharmaceutical industry has moved from what used to be one of the world's most archaic, rigged domestic markets to a much more deregulated setting with new entry and forceful strategic positioning of the main players. These developments have also fed into the growth, however haltingly, of a domestic biotech industry. Data on acquisitions by Japanese pharmaceutical firms of Japanese biotech start-ups are not available, but METI and MHLW research on university-industry collaboration and venture funding suggest that biotech has become the second-largest category of start-up firms, behind IT. With Japan's pharmaceutical market open to innovation and competition, more of these activities can be expected.

11. www.astellas.com/global/about/news/2006/pdf/061206_eg.pdf.

SBI E*Trade Securities Co. and the Investment Banking Transformation

Similar to the pharmaceutical industry, in the early 21st century Japan's investment banks found themselves squeezed between global megaplayers competing forcefully in Japan and deregulation and great changes in the retail sector. The three main trends in this industry were the incorporation of investment banks into the four large financial groups resulting from the mergers in the banking sector; mergers and consolidations both domestically and with large foreign banks; and the emergence of individual investors as highly active traders and the arrival of new competition for these investors.

In postwar Japan, studying Japan's investment banking industry was fairly straightforward. Even as of 1996, the market was led by four companies—Nomura, Nikko, Daiwa, and Yamaichi Securities—followed by a group of about ten second-tier players such as Shin-Nihon, Kokusai, Wako, Kankoku, and Sanyo, and rounded out by roughly 200 smaller firms, often with direct ties to industrial companies. Nomura Securities was the clear market leader in assets, underwriting, and profits, and during the bubble period of the late 1980s analysts observed repeated instances of herding behavior, when even Daiwa and Nikko seemed to follow Nomura's every move. Nomura reigned through sheer power and size. Beginning in the mid-1980s, foreign competitors such as Morgan Stanley, Salomon Brothers, and Goldman Sachs rapidly expanded their offices in Japan. During the stock market bubble they recorded great success, in particular in advanced proprietary trading such as in the newly emerging futures markets where the employees of Japan's securities firms, often generalists on two-year rotations, were much less knowledgeable and experienced (Schaede 1990).

Since 1998 Japan's investment banking industry has undergone changes of revolutionary dimensions, as the strategic inflection point invalidated precisely those aspects of the business model that used to be its main sources of competitive advantage. In the old days, fixed brokerage commissions and underwriting fees had meant that profits were correlated with size and trading volume. Another advantage of size was superior information through relationships with the best clients, at a time when disclosure requirements were lenient. Herd behavior meant that size translated into power, because the largest players could move the market. And last but not the least, close relations with the regulator (the Ministry of Finance at the time) and politicians proved invaluable in further increasing the amount of business.

Change arrived with the Big Bang of 1998 and continuing deregulation, including of corporate disclosure, brokerage commissions, and entry requirements. These opened access to corporate information and invited competition.

The regulatory shift toward protecting the service user rather than the provider, as finalized with the Financial Instruments and Exchange Law of 2007, annulled the value of close relationships with regulators. And perhaps most important, traditional and standard financial products were fast becoming commodities. This reduced margins in the main areas of revenue generation for Japanese brokers.

Growth markets, on the other hand, included fee income other than brokerage commissions, earned through specialized customer-oriented services (such as M&A advice in the corporate sector or financial planning in the retail sector) and global financial services. However, in order to compete in these growth sectors, Japanese investment banks needed to specialize and develop niche capabilities that allowed an escape from commoditization and enabled them to compete through excellence (Fuchita 2006). A major challenge in making this transition was that most of these niches were already occupied by foreign investment banks, even within Japan. To compete head-on, Japanese banks had to restructure, both in terms of strategy and organization, and in human resource practices.

In less than a decade, these pressures transformed the industry. Of the old large players that had so long dominated the industry hierarchy, only Nomura Securities persisted. And even Nomura has emerged as a transformed entity, having reorganized into a holding company in 2001 to become a much more driven, focused global player (Khanna, Egawa, and Nakajima 2005). Yamaichi went bankrupt in 1997. Daiwa was restructured into a holding company and split into Daiwa (retail) and Daiwa SMBC (corporate), the latter with an investment by the Sumitomo-Mitsui Financial Group. Wako and Shin-Nihon became part of the Mizuho Group, and Kokusai merged into MUFJ Securities. In 1999, Nikko merged into Citigroup to establish Nikko Citigroup Securities (corporate), and changed its name into Nikko Cordial for retail business in 2001. In 2006, Nikko Cordial was exposed for having committed accounting fraud, and after a 62 percent investment in 2007, in January 2008 Citigroup fully acquired Nikko Cordial.

As of 2006, in the corporate business realm, the top players in Japan's securities markets by size and profits were Nomura, Daiwa SMBC, Mizuho, Mitsubishi UFJ Financial Group, and Nikko Citigroup. However, in contrast to the postwar period, there was no longer one clear power broker. Daiwa SMBC led the rankings in new company listings, measured in value, before Nomura, Morgan Stanley, Goldman Sachs, and Citigroup. In total number of IPOs including all junior markets, however, the overall market leaders were MUFG and SBI E*Trade Securities. Mizuho led the market in bond underwriting, followed by Daiwa SMBC and MUFG. When it came to M&A advising, the

Japanese market was ruled by foreign firms, as only Nomura at number four could keep up with Citigroup, Goldman Sachs, and UBS (*Diamond Weekly* 2007a). The necessity of competing against these global powerhouses caused continuing pressures for consolidation. It also pushed the newly created firms toward focusing on particular areas of knowledge and expertise. Rotation-on-the-job was replaced by specialized tracks of promotion and investment banking became one of the most active arenas for Japan's newly emerging headhunting industry.

Retail Brokerage

At the same time, Japan's securities firms also faced disruptive challenges at the retail end. During the postwar period, and in particular during the stock market bubble of 1987–91, this had been a lucrative business because brokerage commissions were fixed at high levels. Nomura had dominated this segment based on its power to move the market. However, retail brokerage received a huge blow after the stock market bubble burst in 1991 and almost all Japanese securities firms were shown to have engaged in business practices of dubious taste and integrity, in ways that were especially detrimental to small account holders. In particular, many brokers had engaged in churning—actively trading a customer's account without being so instructed, with the goal of raising commission income. The compensation scandal of 1991, one of the contributing factors in the bursting of the bubble, revealed that all but one minor firm had compensated their main clients (mostly corporations) for stock losses, while leaving individual investors with losses and fees to pay. A subsequent series of scandals greatly dampened individual investors' interest in dealing with Japanese brokers, and Merrill Lynch was able to greatly expand its Japan business in the mid-1990s.

The IT bubble of 1999–2001 brought individual investors back to the market. A transition in society was under way referred to as "save less, invest more," and although that was unlikely to counterbalance the overall decline in the savings ratio due to the rapidly ageing population, it brought a shift of business away from banks and toward brokers. Meeting this new demand by a new generation of investors were the newly emerging online brokerage houses. Complete deregulation of brokerage commissions in 1999 as well as less taxing market entry requirements translated into a start-up boom. In 2006, 35 new brokers entered the market, bringing the number of registered securities firms in Japan to 307 (*Diamond Weekly* 2007a). The number of accounts at the five largest online brokerages grew from roughly 900,000 in 2004 to 3.3 million in 2006. Of these, more than 60 percent belonged to individuals. At that time, individuals represented about one third of shareholders and 28 percent of the trading volume on the main floor of the Tokyo Stock Exchange. However, they accounted for 80 percent or more of the trading value at the TSE's Second Section and the junior markets JASDAQ, MOTHERS, and Hercules.[12]

As of 2003, Nomura still led the retail sector with 3.1 million customer accounts, and it was also the high-end broker with ¥27 trillion (roughly $220 billion) of assets under management, resulting in an average account size of almost ¥70 million ($560,000). This compared well with Daiwa's 2.8 million accounts and assets of ¥12 trillion (about $96 billion), meaning that Daiwa's average account, with $270,000, was less than half that of Nomura's (Khanna, Egawa, and Nakajima 2005). The large brokerage houses had also opened online accounts, and by March 2006 Nomura led that segment with 1.9 million accounts, before Daiwa with 1.5 million and Nikko Cordial with 1 million.

However, in an epochal upset in the first quarter of 2005, E*Trade Japan overtook Nomura as the country's lead generator of brokerage commission income from individual trading at the three main exchanges (TSE First and Second sections, and JASDAQ). By early 2006, E*Trade Japan's commission income of ¥28 trillion represented 10.7 percent of the market total. Nomura came in a distant second with ¥19 trillion (7.26%), followed by Matsui, another online broker, with ¥11 trillion (4%) (E*Trade Japan 2006). Deregulation, combined with the disruption caused by Internet trading and the slow and ineffective response by the incumbents, had allowed the specialized online brokerages to take over the individual investor segment of the industry. In March 2005, 57.4 percent of all individual investor trades were placed through the top five online brokerage houses.

The Online Brokerage Industry

With assets of ¥8 trillion and 1.4 million user accounts as of early 2007, SBI E*Trade Securities Co. was by far the largest pure online brokerage in Japan. In terms of number of accounts SBI E*Trade occupied a 34 percent market share among the pure online brokerage accounts, way ahead of its five foremost competitors: Monex (18%), Rakuten (16%), Matsui Securities (16%), and Kabu.com (14%). Competition promised to become even fiercer when Joinvest entered the market in 2006, offering the cheapest Internet trading while also impressing with its easy-to-read charts and company information (*Diamond Weekly* 2007a).

E*Trade Japan was founded as a joint investment by E*Trade Financial of the United States, with a 42 percent stake, and Softbank, with 58 percent. At that time, Softbank owned 27.2 percent of E*Trade in the United States. In

---

12. www.tse.or.jp/english/listing/companies/statistics_12.pdf.

1998, during Japan's financial crisis, the two companies bought out Osawa Securities, a small Tokyo-based securities firm, for about $20 million. In September 2000, E*Trade Japan went public and reached an initial market capitalization of ¥127 billion (roughly $1 billion). Over time, Softbank reduced its stake in E*Trade Financial, and vice versa, so that E*Trade Financial of the United States is no longer involved in the Japanese company. Whereas the financial business had been a core of Softbank's portfolio in the late 1990s, in 2006 it was spun off into SBI Holdings, the venture capital and investment firm. As of late 2006, SBI Holdings owned slightly over 52 percent of SBI E*Trade, followed by six institutional investors. To reflect this change in ownership, the online brokerage was renamed SBI E*Trade Securities in 2006.

In spite of offering the lowest commissions, SBI E*Trade was one of the few online brokers to earn profits from the beginning. Figure 11.2 shows a sevenfold increase in customer accounts, from 181,000 to 1.4 million, in just five years. The company stood out for its customer-centric orientation and ease of use. As a result, in the fiscal year ending March 2006, of total revenues of ¥60.2 trillion, two thirds were generated through commission income and another ¥13.2 trillion through financial revenues (mainly margin trading accounts) (E*Trade Japan 2006). Whereas brokerage commissions had been set at ¥2,500 per spot trade in 1999, SBI E*Trade had lowered these stepwise, until in 2007 it offered two main accounts, with fees in the standard account beginning at ¥200 ($1.60) per trade and increasing with the value of the trade,

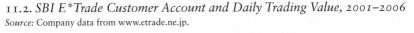

11.2. *SBI E*Trade Customer Account and Daily Trading Value, 2001–2006*
Source: Company data from www.etrade.ne.jp.

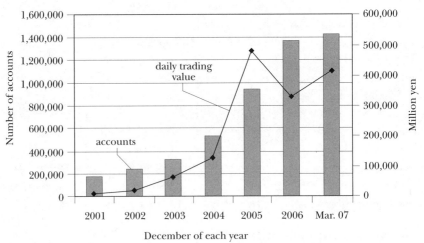

up to a maximum of ¥1,575 ($13) for a trade over ¥3 million ($24,000). Within just a few years, Japan moved from being one of the most expensive to one of the cheapest markets to trade stocks in. SBI E*Trade's sharp increase in revenues was due to the simultaneous rapid growth in both customer accounts and trading activity. The latter was enticed by real-time information provision, often through the mobile phone, special accounts with discounts for heavy traders, and Hyper E*Trade, an account geared to super-active traders.

In an attempt to diversify sources of income and create synergies with other business by SBI Holdings, SBI E*Trade also moved into the corporate market. In particular, after entering the IPO business segment in 2005, the company became the market leader in IPO placements, with 96 companies in 2006 (E*Trade Japan 2007). The company also increased efforts to become more prominent in underwriting and M&As, both for listed and unlisted companies.

Day Traders and E-Money

Meanwhile, SBI E*Trade constantly strove to offer individuals more attractive products to invest in. The company was one of the first to identify the growing popularity of mutual funds in the early 2000s, and as of 2006 offered 251 funds on its website (compared to about 150 at Monex and Kabu.com and 53 at Rakuten). In 2005 and 2006, E*Trade also noticed several trends in its customer base. The first was that 57.5 percent of account holders were company employees, which meant that trading might be increased if after-work trading hours were offered. In August 2007, SBI Holdings and Goldman Sachs Japan Co. formed a joint venture named SBI Japannext Co. to open a proprietary after-hours trading system. The second trend in customer accounts was a shift in the age distribution toward younger investors. Whereas in 2002 62.3 percent of account holders had been 30–49 years old, in 2006 22 percent were in their 20s and 35 percent were in their 30s. Moreover, 35.5 percent of new SBI E*Trade customers reported to have had no previous experience in stock investing. E*Trade responded by hosting online seminars and offering more content on its website for new investors (E*Trade Japan 2006, 2007; *Nikkei*, June 28, 2007; *Nikkei*, August 17, 2007).

These data point to another industry development—the emergence of day traders in Japan. Implicit in the user data was that 42.5 percent of account holders were not company employees, and a large portion of these account holders were assumed to be female. In the early 2000s, stories of young women who had resigned from their companies after getting married but taking on a career as day traders hit the news, and one of these women in her 20s even became a "stock idol" featured in the booming day-trading and stock investing magazine business (Fackler 2006). A more systematic observation supporting the rise in day trading was the spectacular growth of margin trading accounts, which allow leveraging positions by temporarily borrowing securities or money in order to sell or buy more than one owns. Day traders were the most active users of margin accounts. The number of margin accounts at SBI E*Trade almost quintupled within two years, from around 30,000 to 141,000 in late 2006. Again, SBI E*Trade was the clear industry leader with a market share of 34.4 percent, followed by Matsui (12%) and Rakuten (10%). As of early 2007, the margin open interest at E*Trade exceeded ¥500 billion (roughly $4 billion). In FY 2005, 33 percent of SBI E*Trade revenues were generated in this business segment (E*Trade Japan 2006).

Another important development for e-trading was the emergence of the wallet phone (*osaifu keitai,* a term trademarked by NTT DoCoMo). This refers to mobile phones that can make monetary transactions, either on a prepaid basis or tied to a credit card. Two main standards were fighting for market share in the early 2000s, of which the Sony/DoCoMo technology FeliCa seemed to be winning. Between 2005 and 2007, Japan's mobile phone companies aggressively tied up with large vendors, such as Japan Railways and convenience stores, to push their e-money service plans. In addition to convenience, the great advantage of tying e-money to a cell phone as opposed to a prepaid plastic card was that a lost cell phone could be deactivated, whereas a prepaid card could not. Credit lines were also much higher and more flexible on wallet phones. This invited tie-ups between the mobile phone providers and credit card companies. A user would swipe her phone past a reader device in the convenience store or train station, receive a receipt and balance immediately on the screen, and be billed on the next credit card statement. DoCoMo, an early mover in this field, had introduced postpayment plans tied to the phone bill in 2005, and after acquiring 33 percent of Sumitomo Mitsui Credit Card also launched service plans tied to this credit card. By April 2007, 57 million Japanese, or one in every 2.2 people, had adopted e-money, and the main draw was universally usable train and subway tickets (Bradley et al. 2006; *Nikkei,* April 30, 2007).

In addition to shaping the credit card and loan industries, mobile phones that allow always-on Internet access, as 85 percent of all phones in Japan do, and have a wallet function are also great drivers for the e-securities industry. To follow NTT DoCoMo's lead in this area, as soon as Softbank Mobile was created in 2006 it announced the launch of S! FeliCa compatible handsets and a choice of seven different service plans. By April 2007, three million of these phones were in use.[13] SBI E*Trade offered special cell phone functions for its

---

13. Press release, April 3, 2007, at www.softbankmobile.co.jp/corporate/en/news/press/2007.

Hyper account holders, such as bringing automatic stock price updates immediately to the phone. Other online brokerages offered similar services, as all were carving out their particular market niches, ranging from the premium online investment bank Monex to the deep discount broker Joinvest.

Japan's investment banking industry has been completely transformed, from the stodgy postwar-period scale and power approach into an open market based on price competition and winning through excellence, strategic positioning, and speed to market and innovation. As of 2007, further reorganization of the industry was on the horizon, as the shakeout among the megaplayers in the corporate business segment continued. Moreover, given the rapid rise of online trading, large banks were naturally interested in this market. In early 2007, Nomura began to build up an equity stake in Joinvest, and in December 2007 the financial group MUFG acquired a 51.13 percent share in Kabu.com. Among the online brokers, only SBI E*Trade and Orix were expected to remain independent in the foreseeable future.

The rise of the individual investor as an active trader has ramifications not only for the investment banking industry but also for corporate governance. In the New Japan these shareholders are a true force to be reckoned with, and their stance on issues such as hostile takeover defenses is no longer influenced by the interests of Old Japan, but rather by the stock price. In 2004, the Tokyo Stock Exchange introduced e-voting at annual shareholder meetings, which greatly facilitates shareholders in exerting their rights, if so inclined, from home or on the phone.

Evaluation: New Competition

In this chapter I have showcased industry transformations in four Japanese markets that used to be upheld as prime examples of regulation and market restrictions in the postwar period: telecommunications, pharmaceuticals, investment banking, and retailing. In all four markets, deregulation and competition have fundamentally changed the rules of the game, and new market entrants and new technologies have disrupted existing processes and market hierarchies. To compete, incumbents had to reorganize, restructure, refocus, and reposition. As a result, these companies have emerged as new, forceful competitors that find themselves jockeying for position with new entrants.

Deregulation under the "leave it to the market" policy and new entry have unleashed a new wave of competition and innovation in Japan. In many consumer-oriented markets, such as cell-phone-based e-money, the perennial laggard Japan is suddenly leading the world. In 2006, the automaker Nissan tied up with an electronics firm to explore how drivers could receive advertisements and e-discounts on their cell phones (which are also car navigation systems) as they drive through certain neighborhoods. Companies such as Softbank have begun to define global strategies of what it means to win as a cross-media information provider. Japanese consumers, at long last, are not only enjoying choice but also price competition. It is these competitive developments at the market level that cement Japan's changes in legal and corporate processes as an irreversible strategic inflection point.

12

CONCLUSION:

THE NEW JAPAN

During the 1990s, Japan was in major trouble. To most observers, the country had simply lost it. And so attention shifted to China, which was an increasingly important, new, and exciting economy to watch. Japan fell off the radar screen, and to the extent it was mentioned in the news the association was typically negative, such as reports of a banking crisis, deep social challenges, or incompetent politics. So dominant had the negative image of Japan become that even good news was delivered with a dismissive spin. When Japan announced a new record of over 50 months of consecutive growth in 2006, pundits wrote it off as no real achievement for it was all driven by exports (why Japan's exports had suddenly become successful remained unexplored). When the boom period reached 66 months in 2007, it was downplayed because growth was so small. The direct impact of Japan on U.S. business was considered so insubstantial that it was not even considered newsworthy that by 2007 large Japanese firms had shown record combined pretax profits for five years in a row.

But while we were not watching, Japanese business organization has passed a strategic inflection point, and successful corporate reorganization was the real driving force behind Japan's renewed exports and sustained growth in the early 2000s. True, overall growth rates remained small because implementing corporate renewal in large organizations requires time, and smaller firms were only just beginning to follow the large firms' lead. But more important than Japan's macroeconomic data was the rise to the top of individual high-charging large firms that became the trailblazers of Japan's corporate transformation. Some of the success stories presented globally known firms, such as Matsushita Electric, Canon, Toshiba, ANA, Konica Minolta, or Fujifilm Holdings. Other leading firms were less well known, such as JSR and Nitto Denko (LCD polarizers), Toray and Tejin (advanced materials), Tokyo Elektron (semiconductor and LCD manufacturing technology), Ibiden (printed wiring boards), or NDK (crystal oscillators, such as for the iPod)—all global leaders in high-tech, high-margin input materials. In retailing, companies such as Yahoo! Japan (Softbank),

Rakuten, Fast Retailing, Aeon, and Seven & i Holdings have pushed Japan's consumer markets past competitive levels known in most other countries. It is the new leadership by these successful companies that has brought about a Japanese turnaround that falls nothing short of a complete strategic repositioning.

Going back to the heyday of U.S.-Japan relations in the 1980s, a strong image of "how Japan works" was established. Extensive research on Japan's development in the postwar period (1945–90s) has provided us with deep insights into Japan's alternative arrangements. Criticized by some as the impenetrable "Japan Inc." and praised by others, this image has remained unchanged for several decades. However, it is now time to push our Japan knowledge into the 21st century, because Japan's postwar corporate system reached a tipping point in the late 1990s when an industrial architecture geared to stability and security no longer matched economic reality. Between 1998 and 2006, Japan has experienced a strategic reversal that has fundamentally changed the inherent logic of Japan's business organization and has turned Japan's leading companies into focused, innovative competitors.

Why This Change Is Irreversible

One maxim in strategy research is that if a change is reversible it is not strategic (Burgelman 2002). A critical question, therefore, is whether the changes chronicled in this book will stick. Was the period of 1998–2006 truly a strategic inflection point, or perhaps simply an anomaly? Would old rigidities resurface, and would Prime Minister Koizumi's successors allow vested interests to regain the upper hand? Would start-up endeavors be thwarted by a return of societal preferences for stability and large firm status? As of 2007, many aspects of system change were clearly irreversible, but there were also aspects of political leadership and corporate decision making that could push progress onto a somewhat different trajectory, and it is these aspects that will allow us to measure developments in Japan as we go forward.

Among the areas of change that are clearly irreversible, the main bank system takes the lead. There is widespread agreement that Japan's main bank system has run its course, as corporate finance has shifted to the market. The consolidation of Japan's major financial institutions into four main financial holdings has put the final stamp on the transition from a highly regulated, compartmentalized, and loan-focused banking system to one competing with global megabanks through specialized services and expertise. Even in small-firm lending, Japanese banks have upgraded their methods and have adopted scoring systems and risk evaluation techniques.

Horizontal business groups (the keiretsu), too, are revising their function within a new system. Some groups have begun to fade, such as the Sanwa group where meetings are held much less frequently and important group firms no longer consider these important. Mitsubishi group members, in contrast, expected their group to continue. What they were less clear about is what they expect the group to offer. In the New Japan, the value proposition can no longer be stability or security, so for the group to be considered important by member firms it will have to offer alternative services. With the arrival of hostile takeovers, cross-shareholdings could offer management support when a two-thirds majority is needed to introduce a poison pill. However, such backup can equally well be found in strategic alliances, without the strings of group membership. Therefore, if friendly shareholders remain the sole benefit of a group, it will not be viable. If groups persist, it will be because they have found new ways to pool resources, increase productivity, lower costs, or otherwise increase the competitiveness of their members.

Japan's subcontracting system has changed because of globalization and a shift in production processes toward modulization. Neither of these is reversible—even though they can be expected to evolve further and invite more change. Likewise, in consumer markets, globalization means import competition. The breakup of the previously rigid distribution system has invited new retail formats, including the Internet. It is inconceivable that the new power granted to consumers could be reappropriated by manufacturers. The great enthusiasm with which Japanese consumers have embraced price comparison and product choice leaves no way to return to postwar practices.

Even in corporate governance, which was still evolving into a new system as of 2007, some fundamental mechanisms have been irrevocably altered. The 2006 Corporation Law and other laws in combination have completely revised the rights and responsibilities of senior management in Japanese firms. No longer fettered by proscriptive rules, companies are at much greater liberty in designing corporate strategies. In turn, they also face greatly empowered shareholders and clearly delineated management liabilities. Shareholders have more decisions to make as to what issues to delegate to management. The new laws have also brought J-SOX, the Japanese version of the U.S. Sarbanes-Oxley Act. In addition to accounting oversight, a new internal control system has made members of the board liable for wrongdoing or for not interfering when observing mismanagement. It is inconceivable that these laws could be rewritten to reintroduce old rules of nontransparency.

However, how these laws are applied will offer insights into progress versus stalemate. In corporate governance, measures to observe in the future are the level of shareholder activism and the rate of CEO turnover in response to performance. Yet, one must be cautious when interpreting the number of derivative lawsuits (brought by a shareholder on behalf of the corporation), because if the new J-SOX internal controls work as designed, lawsuits should decline rather than increase.

Similarly, if the number of successful hostile takeovers were to plateau rather than increase further, that does not necessarily mean that Japan's move to the market has come to a halt. Rather, it may simply show that Japanese companies are better managed so that opportunities for easy buyouts have dried up. A stalemate will be indicated only if incompetently managed firms are allowed to operate below potential for extended periods of time. As of 2007 there was no evidence of this; to the contrary, it was readily apparent that management incentives had been reshaped. Moreover, as of 2007, less than 20 percent of Japan's listed firms had adopted poison pills in defense against hostile takeovers, a much smaller fraction than in the United States.

Perhaps the two most telling areas of change will be lifetime employment and white collar crime. Lifetime employment as practiced during the postwar period was a creation of the courts, and it was changes in court interpretation beginning in 2000 that began to moderate rigid rules on layoffs. The revision of the Labor Standards Law was a further step in this direction, even though it fell short of determining precise rules for dismissals. If we were to see no further developments in dismissal policies, progress in the labor market could be stalled.

White collar crime is a second tell-tale area for rigor in legal execution. Even though some regulatory loopholes remain, the laws are now clearer than ever when it comes to accounting and disclosure and the responsibilities of executives. In March 2007, former Livedoor CEO Horie received a prison term of 30 months for defrauding investors through irregular accounting and fund manager Murakami was jailed for two years for insider trading. Although some, including the defendants themselves, claimed both were set up by Old Japan to forestall disruptive start-ups, others welcomed the sentencing as a clear indication that white collar crimes are no longer rewarded with a promotion to an honorary position in the company. What remains to be seen is whether white collar crimes will continue to be prosecuted in this way, and whether these cases cover Old Japan just as much as New Japan.

Finally, the government could change its policies and turn "away from the market." To the extent that this refers to privatization, it cannot be undone. It is also implausible that Japan could unwind all processes of shifting regulation away from industry and toward market processes. However, legal interpretation is always subject to change to some extent. For example, in the United States we have seen great swings in the interpretation of antitrust statutes over time, often influenced by politics. As Japanese politics become more contested—arguably also a sign of greater choice and the market in voting—we may see more variation in legal application in Japan as well.

One big change with the 2001 government reorganization was to pull policy-making powers into the Prime Minister's Office. Now the prime minister can decide whether to delegate the discussion of a policy issue to the ministry in charge (where it may be subject to strong vested interests) or whether to task his own council, the Council on Economic and Fiscal Policy, with deliberating on the issue. A strong prime minister can use this new setup to curtail the policy-making powers of ministries. Moreover, the recent empowerment of regulatory agencies such as the Financial Services Agency or Japan's Fair Trade Commission has pushed business processes toward the market. Reversal in these areas, then, would manifest itself in limited tasks for the CEFP and a reduction in activities by regulatory agencies.

Overall, the main facets of Japan's industrial architecture have been irreversibly altered. The market has been unleashed, and it will only grow further. How fast it will grow can be influenced by politics, society, and legal doctrine. But a return to the nontransparent, relationship-dominated, risk-averse Old Japan is inconceivable.

What the Strategic Inflection Point Means for Japan

The strategic inflection point has unambiguously moved Japanese business organization toward the market. The Prime Minister's 2002 Revival Program was launched under the heading "leave it to the market" and this became the header for an all-out change in commercial laws, regulatory processes, and the access to and application of commercial law.

At the most basic level, this has turned a growing number of large Japanese companies to a more targeted pursuit of profits. The fact that listed firms reported record combined pretax profits for the five years between 2002 and 2005 is not an accident, or just a by-product of the China boom. As company after company shed unprofitable or noncore business units and focused resources on the core, they have become dramatically more profitable. Increased transparency has enabled a true market for corporate assets, and the supply of spun-off business units has invited more pluralistic shareholders and even corporate raiders, which in turn have put pressures on management to operate according to potential. Muddling through is no longer a viable long-term business strategy in Japan.

At a deeper level, the strategic inflection has altered the logic of Japan's industrial architecture, away from risk aversion and toward competition. This change has occurred mostly through transformation and repositioning, rather than extinction. Business groups are reconfiguring toward competitiveness; main banks are becoming financial service providers; the production system has adapted to changes in global supply mechanisms; and labor relations have been revised to increase strategic flexibility. We have to "unlearn" what we know about Japan, and consider the country's new business environment as we analyze competitors from Japan.

At the deepest level, the turn to the market has greatly empowered previously restricted actors in Japan—in particular consumers, entrepreneurs, and ambitious professionals, including women. The retail revolution, the turn to price transparency, and the increase in imported consumer goods have opened up choice, price competition, and new retail formats. All these benefit consumers. In the early 2000s, Japan doubters pointed to continuing deflation, but some studies within Japan suggested that falling consumer prices were driven more by the new competition than by a lack of demand.

The new market in labor relations has opened new career possibilities. During the postwar period, job choices for aspiring young people were limited, and the wish list was topped by becoming a bureaucrat that could shape the country's economic policies. Short of that, the young strove to become a long-term generalist at a large firm. The move toward the market has unleashed the forces of individual performance and career ambitions. The shift toward performance-based pay has opened, however haltingly, a market for mid-career job changers, and this will be fueled by the development of specialized job categories within firms and the adoption of market rates by job category. Working for a small firm, which used to be for "losers," is suddenly also an increasingly respected option, even if start-ups continue to face challenges. The integration of women into the workforce, which will be pushed further by the looming labor shortage beginning in the 2010s, will release a pool of highly educated but underused resources. In combination, over time and with adjustments over a generational change, these developments will invite the growth of career professionals in Japan and therefore lead to an upgrade in work motivation, management skills, and corporate performance.

Thus, the strategic inflection point has brought new creativity, innovation, and dynamism that will allow Japan's successful companies to compete globally in the 21st century. The leaders are no longer only the former goliaths—even though some of them, such as Panasonic, have reemerged as focused, highly profitable companies. The new leaders also include smaller high-tech firms, new firms, and newly merged firms with new value propositions.

Some readers will wonder what all this augurs for Japan's "system of capitalism." Is Japan converging with the United States, and is the adoption of market rules really such a good thing? A complete analysis of system change requires a discussion of change in politics, which this book does not address. When just looking at the corporate level, however, Japan has unambiguously moved toward the market. Yet, it would be simplistic to assume that this means the country is becoming like the United States—even though all the new corporate laws are modeled after the U.S. example. One reason why this is simplistic is the so-called transplant effect: when a law is positioned in a different setting, governed by different court processes, and subjected to different legal doctrine, it adapts to this setting (Berkowitz, Pistor, and Richard 2003; Milhaupt and Pistor 2008). For example, even though Japan adopted takeover rules similar to those in the U.S. state of Delaware, the use of those rules, the specifics of the Japanese poison pill, and the legal interpretation by Japanese courts of what is a "fair" price or what is "discriminatory" has already moved Japan's takeover law into new terrain. A second reason why the convergence debate may not be very fruitful is that the U.S. system itself is a moving target. To stay with the takeover example, the interpretation of the Delaware code in the United States changes almost monthly, based on the particular opportunities and constraints faced by courts in this small state. It is not in Japan's interest or power to copy these changes, as they are meaningless in Japan's own setting.

Thus, Japan's corporate system will be shaped according to its own legal and corporate trajectories. But it has without doubt become a market-based system. This has introduced new economic efficiencies as well as new social costs, such as those caused by a hostile raider causing a firm to spend its resources on legal defense. Such bids, as witnessed in the Bull-Dog Sauce case described in chapter 6, often only leave legal fees, economic losses, and a bad taste. But while negative individual examples of firms broken apart by Japan's new, aggressive investors are making the headlines, what is more important is the quiet, overall shift toward efficiency brought about by companies upgrading their management systems and improving their business strategies to avoid becoming victims of a hostile takeover. This move toward operating at potential, and correcting parts of the business model that inhibit increased performance, is unequivocally positive.

What Japan's Strategic Inflection Means for the Global Economy

As large Japanese companies reenter the global economy as reinvigorated and repositioned entities with core capabilities in leading technology areas, they once again affect the global economy in important ways. It would be a grave strategic mistake to overlook this new dynamic. Yet, it would be easy to make this mistake, because, with a few exceptions such as automobiles, Japan's new leadership is no longer about market share in consumer end products, so it is not as immediately apparent as it was in the 1980s. Companies in high-tech global industries, such as airplane engineering, already know about Japan's new capabilities, but executives there, too, may be lulled by other, discouraging stories from Japan. However, the new competitors from Japan are not an exception or an aberration—they are the harbingers of a new competitive force in the global economy.

In addition to affecting global competition, Japan's reemergence greatly shapes the competitive dynamics of Asia, and thereby Asia's role in the global economy. This happens through three interdependent processes. First, Asia is not just about manufacturing and production, as Japan's new prowess contributes, once again, to the region's leadership in technological developments. And because Japan produces about one quarter of its products outside Japan, most of which in Asia, Japan's reemergence will also have positive growth effects for the region. Companies elsewhere around the globe must reconfigure strategies to allow for technological disruptions generated in the East.

Second, Asia is not only China, and neither is it led by China. Although this may sound obvious, in the 1990s the almost exclusive attention paid to China's development among U.S. businesses and the media has distorted our evaluation of Asian economic strength. Asian countries are not monolithic, and they are becoming even more diverse in their economic positioning, each carving out special roles.

Third, Japan's successful transformation is beginning to affect corporate strategy within Asia. In particular, it has challenged the business approach of firms in South Korea. "China is catching up, while Japan continues to lead. We are sandwiched between them," is how the chairman of Samsung phrased it in August 2007.[1] Faced with the challenge of declining earning power due to depressed margins, Samsung has announced reorganization toward increased efficiency. And, since Samsung represents 20 percent of South Korea's exports and total stock market value, the new competition from Japan is already pushing Korea toward new business strategies as well. Japan's "choose and focus" renewal may just be the beginning of a larger move toward specialization by a larger share of leading Asian companies. We cannot be sure how other Asian companies will react to Japan's lead in moving from market dominance through diversified goliaths toward nimble, focused competitors. However, the success of Japan's shift toward the market has not gone unnoticed.

Japan has changed. Its change is bringing new challenges and opportunities for global competition, which will be affected by the new winds from Asia. Japan's new leading firms are spearheading this change as lean, innovative, competitive, and increasingly profitable competitors. Japan is, once again, an exciting market to watch.

1. *Nikkei Weekly,* August 13, 2007, 13.

REFERENCES

Abegglen, James C. 1984. *The Strategy of Japanese Business.* Cambridge: Ballinger.

——. 2004. *Shin-Nihon no Keiei* (21st century Japanese management). Tokyo: Nihon Keizai Shinbun-sha.

Abegglen, James C., and George Stalk Jr. 1985. *Kaisha—The Japanese Corporation: How Marketing, Money, and Manpower Strategy, Not Management Style, Make the Japanese World Pace-Setters.* New York: Basic Books.

Ahmadjian, Christina L. 2003. "Changing Japanese Corporate Governance." In *Japan's Managed Globalization: Adapting to the 21st Century,* edited by U. Schaede and W. W. Grimes, 215–40. Armonk, N.Y.: M. E. Sharpe.

——. 2007. "Foreign Investors and Corporate Governance in Japan." In *Corporate Governance in Japan: Institutional Change and Organizational Diversity,* edited by M. Aoki, G. Jackson, and H. Miyajima, 125–50. Oxford: Oxford University Press.

Ahmadjian, Christina L., and James R. Lincoln. 2001. "Keiretsu, Governance, and Learning: Case Studies in Change from the Japanese Automotive Industry." *Organization Science* 12, no. 6: 683–701.

Ahmadjian, Christina L., and Patricia Robinson. 2001. "Safety in Numbers: Downsizing and the Deinstitutionalization of Permanent Employment in Japan." *Administrative Science Quarterly* 46: 622–53.

Amihud, Y., and Baruch Lev. 1981. "Risk Reduction as a Managerial Motive for Conglomerate Mergers." *Bell Journal of Economics* 12: 605–617.

Amyx, Jennifer. 2004. *Japan's Financial Crisis: Institutional Rigidity and Reluctant Change.* Princeton: Princeton University Press.

——. 2006. "The Politics of Reform in Japanese Finance: The Relative Influence of Foreign Investors." In *From Crisis to Opportunity: Financial Globalization and East Asian Capitalism,* edited by J. Mo and D. Okimoto, 23–40. Stanford: Walter H. Shorenstein Asia-Pacific Research Center.

Anchordoguy, Marie. 1989. *Computers, Inc.—Japan's Challenge to IBM.* Cambridge: Harvard University Press.

——. 2005. *Reprogramming Japan: The High-Tech Crisis under Communitarian Capitalism.* Ithaca: Cornell University Press.

Andrade, G., M. Mitchell, and E. Stafford. 2002. "New Evidence and Perspectives on Mergers." *Journal of Economic Perspectives* 15: 103–20.

Aoki, Masahiko. 1988. *Information, Incentives, and Bargaining in the Japanese Economy.* Cambridge: Cambridge University Press.

Aoki, Masahiko. 1990. "Toward an Economic Model of the Japanese Firm." *Journal of Economic Literature* 28, no. 1: 1–27.

Aoki, Masahiko, Gregory Jackson, and Hideaki Miyajima, eds. 2007. *Corporate Governance in Japan: Institutional Change and Organizational Diversity.* Oxford: Oxford University Press.

Aoki, Masahiko, and Hugh Patrick, eds. 1994. *The Japanese Main Bank System: Its Relevance for Developing and Transforming Economies.* New York: Oxford University Press.

Aoyama, Kazumasa. 2001. *Shinpan-Kaimei Chūshō kigyō-ron* (New insights on the small firm debate). Tokyo: Dōyūkan.

Arai, Hidekazu. 2005. "Seikashugi no jittai to kadai: Chōsa deeta nado kara mita" (The reality of and challenges for meritocracy: A view from survey and other data). *Business Labor Trend* 3: 26–30.

Arai, Yumiko, and Naoki Ikegami. 1998. "An Overview of the Japanese Health Care System." *Journal of Public Health Medicine* 20, no. 1: 29–33.

Arakawa, Sōta. 2005. "Ōte kigyō no chingin seido wa kō kawatta—90nendai kara genzai made no mitōshi keika" (How has the wage system in large firms changed—Observing the trend from the 1990s until today). *Business Labor Trend* 3: 14–21.

———. 2006. "Seikashugi wa 'shokushubetsu-chingin' ni mukau" (Meritocracy will lead to pay by occupation). *Ekonomisuto*, April 11: 30–31.

Araki, Takashi. 1998. "Recent Legislative Developments in Equal Employment and Harmonization of Work and Family Life in Japan." *Japan Labor Bulletin* 37, no. 4, www.jil.go.jp/bulletin/.

———. 1999. "1999 Revisions of Employment Security and Worker Dispatching Law: Drastic Reforms of Japanese Labor Market Regulations." *Japan Labor Bulletin* 38, no. 9, www.jil.go.jp/bulletin/.

———. 2002. *Labor and Employment Law in Japan.* Tokyo: Japanese Institute of Labor.

———. 2005. "Corporate Governance Reforms, Labor Law Developments, and the Future of Japan's Practice-Dependent Stakeholder Model." *Japan Labor Review* 2, no. 1: 26–57.

Armour, H. O., and David J. Teece. 1978. "Organizational Structure and Economic Performance: A Test of the Multidivisional Hypothesis." *Bell Journal of Economics* 9, no. 1: 106–22.

Asanuma, Banri. 1989. "Manufacturer-Supplier Relationships in Japan and the Concept of Relation-Specific Skill." *Journal of the Japanese and International Economies* 3 (March): 1–30.

Asanuma, Banri, and Tatsuya Kikutani. 1992. "Risk Absorption in Japan and the Concept of Relation-specific Skill." *Journal of the Japanese and International Economies* 6: 1–29.

Bailey, David. 2003. "Explaining Japan's Kudoka (Hollowing Out): A Case of Government and Strategic Failure?" *Asia Pacific Business Review* 10, no. 1: 1–20.

Barney, Jay. 1991. "Firm Resources and Sustained Competitive Advantage." *Journal of Management* 17, no. 1: 99–120.

Beason, Richard, and David E. Weinstein. 1996. "Growth, Economies of Scale, and Targeting in Japan (1995–1990)." *Review of Economics and Statistics* 78, no. 2 (May): 286–95.

Beaulieu, Nancy D., and Aaron Zimmerman. 2005. *Orix KK: Incentives in Japan.* Case No. 9-905-013. Boston: Harvard Business School.

Belliveau, Maura A., Charles A. O'Reilly III, and James B. Wade. 1996. "Social Capital at the Top: Effects of Social Similarity and Status on CEO Compensation." *Academy of Management Journal* 39, no. 6: 1568–93.

Berger, Philip G., and Eli Ofek. 1995. "Diversification's Effect on Firm Value." *Journal of Financial Economics* 37: 39–65.

——. 1999. "Causes and Effects of Corporate Refocusing Programs." *Review of Financial Studies* 12, no. 2: 311–45.

Berkowitz, Daniel, Katharina Pistor, and Jean-Francois Richard. 2003. "Economic Development, Legality, and the Transplant Effect." *American Journal of Comparative Law* 51, no. 2: 163–203.

Bernstein, Jeffrey R. 1997. "Toyota Automatic Looms and Toyota Automobiles." In *Creating Modern Capitalism: How Entrepreneurs, Companies, and Countries Triumphed in Three Industrial Revolutions*, edited by T. K. McCraw, 398–438. Cambridge: Harvard University Press.

Bhagat, Sanjai, Andrei Shleifer, and Robert W. Vishny. 1990. "Hostile Takeovers in the 1980s: The Return to Corporate Specialization." *Brookings Papers on Economic Activity: Microeconomics*, 1–84.

Bhide, Amar.1990. "Reversing Corporate Diversification." *Journal of Applied Corporate Finance* 5: 70–81.

Biyalogorsky, Eyal, and Eitan Gerstner. 2004. "Contingent Pricing to Reduce Price Risks." *Marketing Science* 23, no. 1: 146–55.

Bleha, Thomas. 2005. "Down to the Wire." *Foreign Affairs* 84, no. 3 (May–June): 111–24.

Bradley, Stephen P., Thomas R. Eisenmann, Masako Egawa, and Akiko Kanno. 2006. *NTT DoCoMo, Inc.: Mobile FeliCa*. Case No. 9–805–124. Boston: Harvard Business School.

Brandenburger, Barry J., and Adam M. Nalebuff. 1997. *Co-opetition*. New York: Profile Books.

Bremmer, Brian. 1998. "Why Softbank Is Shouting 'Yahoo'." *Business Week* 3594: 48.

Bruner, Robert F. 2002. "Does M&A Pay: A Survey of Evidence for the Decision-Maker." *Journal of Applied Finance* 12, no. 1: 48–68.

Burgelman, Robert A., 2002, *Strategy Is Destiny: How Strategy-Making Shapes a Company's Future*. New York: Free Press.

Burgelman, Robert A., and Andrew S. Grove. 1996. "Strategic Dissonance." *California Management Review* 38, no. 2: 8–28.

Caballero, Ricardo J., Takeo Hoshi, and Anil K. Kashyap. 2006. "Zombie Lending and Depressed Restructuring in Japan." *NBER Working Paper Series* no. 12129. Cambridge: National Bureau of Economic Research.

Calder, Kent E. 1988. *Crisis and Compensation: Public Policy and Political Stability in Japan, 1949–1986*. Princeton: Princeton University Press.

——. 1993. *Strategic Capitalism: Private Business and Public Purpose in Japanese Industrial Finance*. Princeton: Princeton University Press.

Callon, Scott. 1995. *Divided Sun: MITI and the Breakdown of Japanese High-Tech Industrial Policy, 1975–1993*. Stanford: Stanford University Press.

CAO (Cabinet Office, Government of Japan). 1999. "Heisei 10nen kigyō kōdō ni kan suru ankeeto chōsa" (1998 Survey of corporate activities). www5.cao.go.jp/99/f/19990420ank/menu.html. Tokyo.

CAO (Cabinet Office, Government of Japan). 2002. "Annual Report on the Japanese Economy and Public Finance 2001–2002: No Gains without Reforms II" (translation of *Keizai Zaisei Hakusho 2002*). Tokyo.

———. 2004. "Annual Report on the Japanese Economy and Public Finance 2003–2004: No Gains without Reforms IV" (translation of the *Keizai Zaisei Hakusho 2004*). Tokyo.

———. 2005. '*Kokunai kaiki*' *to wa nani ka? Kigyō ankeeto chōsa ni miru wagakuni seizōgyō no saikin no dōkō* (What Is 'Return to Home'? Recent Developments in Japanese Manufacturing based on Survey Results.) www5.cao.go.jp/keizai3/shihyo/2005/1114/2676.html. Tokyo.

Capelli, Peter. 1999. *The New Deal at Work: Managing the Market-Driven Workforce.* Boston: Harvard Business School Press.

Carroll, Glenn R. 1984. "The Specialist Strategy." In *Strategy and Organization—A West Coast Perspective,* edited by G. Carroll and D. Vogel, 117–28. Boston: Pitman.

Caves, Richard E., and Masa Uekusa. 1976. *Industrial Organization in Japan.* Washington, D.C.: The Brookings Institution.

Christensen, Clayton M. 1997. *The Innovator's Dilemma: When New Technologies Cause Great Firms to Fail.* Boston: Harvard Business School Press.

CJEB (Center for Japanese Economy and Business). 2005. *The Role of Private Equity in Japanese Industrial Restructuring: The Case of Daiei.* www.gsb.columbia.edu/cjeb. New York: Program on Alternative Investments.

Clark, Rodney. 1979. *The Japanese Company.* New Haven: Yale University Press.

Cole, Robert E., ed. 1983. *Automobiles and the Future: Competition, Cooperation, and Change.* Ann Arbor: University of Michigan, Center for Japanese Studies.

———. 1994. "Different Quality Paradigms and Their Implications for Organizational Learning." In *The Japanese Firm: The Source of Competitive Strength,* edited by M. Aoki and R. Dore, 66–83. New York: Oxford University Press.

Comment, Robert, and Gregg A. Jarrell. 1995. "Corporate Focus and Stock Returns." *Journal of Financial Economics* 37: 67–87.

Crane, Dwight B., and Ulrike Schaede. 2006. "Functional Change and Bank Strategy in German Corporate Governance". *International Review of Law and Economics* 25, no. 4: 513–40.

CVSG (Corporate Value Study Group). 2006. *Corporate Value Report 2006.* www.meti.go.jp/policy/economic_oganization/pdf/houkoku06_eng.pdf. Tokyo: METI.

Daiwa Sōken, ed. 1993. *Nihon no kaisha to gyōkai jitsuryoku chizu* (A power guide to Japan's industry and companies). Tokyo: Nihon jitsugyō shuppan-sha.

DBJ (Development Bank of Japan). 2004. "Sozai sangyō ni okeru kakaku jōshō to sono eikyō (kagaku)" (The implications of price increases in the materials industries [chemicals]). *Kongetsu no toppikusu* (Monthly topics). www.dbj.go.jp/download/pdf/indicate/no065.pdf. Tokyo: Development Bank of Japan, Research Department.

Dewey Ballantine LLP. 1995. "Privatizing Protection: Japanese Market Barriers in Consumer Photographic Film and Consumer Photographic Paper." Rochester, N.Y., and Washington, D.C.: Report prepared for the Eastman Kodak Company.

Dhaliwall, Jag. 2005. "Merill Sets Up Japan Buyout Unit, Hires Mitsumasu." April 14, www.bloomberg.com.

Diamond Weekly. 2002. "Kūdōka hontō no kyōfu" (The real dangers of hollowing out). *Shūkan Daiyamondo*, January 12, 26–43.

——. 2005. "Hagetaka? Hakuba no kishi ka? Gaishi fando zen-kaibō" (Vultures or white knights? A thorough analysis of foreign funds). *Shūkan Daiyamondo*. April 24.

——. 2007a. "Tokushū: Shōkan Dairan" (Big turmoil in the securities industry). *Shūkan Daiyamondo*, February 24, 30–51.

——. 2007b. "Juntaku na shikin de, 'jikan o kau' ōja, Takeda Seihin mo shōrai ni kikikan" (Even industry leader Takeda in crisis mode, as it uses ample cash to "buy time"). *Shūkan Daiyamondo* March 3, 58–59.

DIR (Daiwa Institute of Research). 2004. "'Mochiai' jidai no shūen" (The end of the Mochiai era). Tokyo: Daiwa Sōken.

——. 2005. "Mochiai kaishō tsuzuku ga, hanten no kizashi mo" (Mochiai are dissolving, but reversal possible). www.dir.co.jp/research/report/viewpoint/05121401viewpoint.pdf. Tokyo: Daiwa Sōken.

Dore, Ronald. 1986. *Flexible Rigidities: Industrial Policy and Structural Adjustment in Japan, 1970–1980.* London: Athlone Press.

——. 1987. *Taking Japan Seriously: A Confucian Perspective on Leading Economic Issues.* Stanford: Stanford University Press.

Dore, Ronald, and Mari Sako. 1989. *How the Japanese Learn to Work.* London: Routledge.

Dyer, Jeffrey. 2000. *Collaborative Advantage: Winning through Extended Enterprise Supplier Networks.* Oxford: Oxford University Press.

E*Trade Japan. 2006. *E*TRADE Securities Co. Ltd. Financial Review FY Ended March 31, 2006.* www.etrade.ne.jp. Tokyo.

——. 2007. *SBI E*Trade Securities Co. Ltd. Financial Review 3rd Quarter FY 2006.* www.etrade.ne.jp. Tokyo.

Economist. 1996. "After the Party: Softbank." May 18.

Ekonomisuto. 2001. "Tokushū: Ryūtsū kakumei no hikigane" (Special topic: The triggers of the retail revolution). *Ekononomisuto,* February 12.

Endo, Tadahiko. 2000. *Kore dake wa shitte-okitai: Kakutei kyoshutsukei nenkin (Nihon-ban 401[k] puran)* (What you need to know about defined contribution pensions and the "Japanese 401(k) plan"). Tokyo: Kindai sales-sha.

ESRI (Economic and Society Research Institute). 2004. *Wagakuni kigyō no M&A katsudō no enkatsu tenkai ni mukete* (Toward a smooth development of corporate M&A in Japan). www.esri.cao.go.jp. Tokyo: Cabinet Office.

——. 2005. "Heisei 16nendo kigyō kōdō ni kan suru ankeeto chōsa yōshi: Nihon kigyō no jinzai katsuyō/chingin taikei no genjō to kongo" (Annual survey of corporate behavior in FY 2004: Human resources management and present and future wage systems at Japanese corporations). www.esri.cao.go.jp. Tokyo: Cabinet Office.

Fackler, Martin. 2006. "In Japan, Day-Trading Like It's 1999." *New York Times,* February 19.

Fama, Eugene F., and Michael C. Jensen. 1983. "Separation of Ownership and Control." *Journal of Law and Economics* 26: 301–25.

Fedenia, Mark, Adrian E. Tschoegl, and Alexander J. Triantis. 1994. "Cross-Holdings: Estimation Issues, Biases, and Distortions." *Review of Financial Studies* 7, no. 1: 61–96.

Fields, George. 1988. *The Japanese Market Culture.* Tokyo: Japan Times.

Flath, David. 1989. "Vertical Restraints in Japan." *Japan and the World Economy*
1: 188–203.

———. 1990. "Why Are There So Many Retail Stores in Japan?" *Japan and the World Economy* 2: 265–386.

———. 2003. "Regulation, Distribution Efficiency, and Retail Density." In *Structural Impediments to Growth in Japan,* edited by M. Blomstroem, J. Corbett, F. Hayashi, and A. Kashyap, 129–54. Chicago: University of Chicago Press.

French, Kenneth R., and James M. Poterba. 1991. "Why Are Japanese Stock Prices So High?" *Journal of Financial Economics* 29: 337–63.

FSA (Financial Services Agency). 2006. "New Legislative Framework for Investor Protection: 'Financial Instruments and Exchange Law.'" www.fsa.go.jp/en/policy/fiel/index.html. Tokyo: Financial Services Agency.

Fuchita, Yasuyuki. 2006. "The Outlook for Japan's Financial Services Industry and Some Strategies for Survival: Certain and Uncertain Challenges." *Nomura Capital Market Review* 9, no. 2: 2–20.

Fujimoto, Makoto, and Takuma Kimura. 2005. "Business Strategy and Human Resource Management at Contract Companies in the Manufacturing Sector." *Japan Labor Review* 2, no. 2: 104–22.

Fujimura, Hiroyuki. 2003. "Changes in the Spring Wage Offensive and the Future of the Wage Determination System in Japanese Firms." *Japan Labor Bulletin* 42, no. 5: 6–12.

Fujioka, Bunshichi. 2006. "Wagakuni kigyō no M&A katsudō: Chiiki kasseika ni mukete" (M&A activities by Japanese firms: Toward regional revitalization). www.esri.go.jp. Tokyo: Cabinet Office.

Fujita, Keizō, and Masami Takeuchi. 1998. *Chūshō kigyō ron* (Small- and medium-sized enterprises). Tokyo: Yūhikaku.

Fujita, Kenji, and Tomoyuki Matsuno. 2001. "Financing the 'New Economy' Firms in Today's Japan." *Bank of International Settlement Publications.* www.bis.org/publ/cgfs19boj1.pdf.

Fujita, Tsutomu. 2006. "Shin-Kaisha-hō shikkō de kabunushi sōkai wa issō jūyō ni" (The new corporation law is implemented: Toward a stronger general shareholders' meeting). *Ekonomisuto* 6, no. 6: 78–80.

Fukui, Yoshitaka, and Tatsuo Ushijima. 2006. "Corporate Diversification, Performance, and Restructuring in the Largest Japanese Manufacturers." *Journal of the Japanese and International Economies* 21, no. 3: 303–23.

Fukunaga, Hiroshi, and Kyoko Chinone. 1994. "Taking On the System." *Tokyo Business Today* (May): 4–12.

Genda, Y. 2002. "Don't Blame the Unmarried Breed." *Japan Echo* 27, no. 3. www.japanecho.co.jp/docs/html/270315.html.

Gerlach, Michael L. 1992. *Alliance Capitalism: The Social Organization of Japanese Business.* Berkeley: University of California Press.

Ghemawat, Pankaj. 1991. *Commitment: The Dynamic of Strategy.* New York: Free Press.

———. 2006. *Strategy and the Business Landscape,* 2nd ed. Upper Saddle River, N.J.: Pearson Prentice-Hall.

Ghosn, Carlos, and Philippe Ries. 2005. *Shift: Inside Nissan's Historic Revival.* New York: Currency Doubleday.

Gordon, Andrew. 1998. *The Wages of Affluence: Labor and Management in Postwar Japan.* Cambridge: Harvard University Press.

Goshal, Sumantra, and Christopher A. Bartlett. 1988. "Matsushita Electric Industrial (MEI) in 1987." Case No. 388–144. Boston: Harvard Business School.

Goto, Akira. 1981. "Statistical Evidence on the Diversification of Japanese Large Firms." *Journal of Industrial Economics* 29, no. 3: 271–78.

Goto, Akira, and Ruhei Wakasugi. 1988. "Technology Policy." In *Industrial Policy of Japan,* edited by R. Komiya, M. Okuno, and K. Suzumura, 183–204. Tokyo: Academic Press.

Gourevitch, Peter, and James Shinn. 2005. *Political Power and Corporate Control: The New Global Politics of Corporate Governance.* Princeton: Princeton University Press.

Gray, Nicole. 2006. "Changing Landscapes: A Special Report on the World's Top 50 Pharma Companies." *Pharmaceutical Executive* (May). www.pharmexec.com/pharmexec/data/articlestandard/pharmexec/182006/323799/article.pdf.

Greenwald, B., and J. E. Stiglitz. 1992. "Information, Finance and Markets: The Architects of Allocative Mechanisms." In *Finance and the Enterprise,* edited by V. Zamagni, 11–35. London: Academic Press.

Grove, Andrew S. 1996. *Only the Paranoid Survive: How to Exploit the Crisis Points That Challenge Every Company and Career.* New York: Currency Doubleday.

Hadley, Eleanor M. 1970. *Antitrust in Japan.* Princeton: Princeton University Press.

Haley, John O. 1978. "The Myth of the Reluctant Litigant." *Journal of Japanese Studies* 4: 359–90.

Hall, Peter A., and David Soskice, eds. 2001. *Varieties of Capitalism: The Institutional Foundations of Comparative Advantage.* New York: Oxford University Press.

Hamada, Yasuyuki. 1999. *Nihon no benchaa kyapitaru: shōrai e no senraku tōshi (shinpan)* (Japanese venture captial: Future investment strategies [new edition]). Tokyo: Nihon Keizai Shinbun-sha.

———. 2004. *VB Policy and Policy Assessment.* www.econ.hokudai.ac.jp/~hamada.

Hamada, Yasuyuki, and Takeo Asai. 2001. "Benchaa no shien seido" (The venture support system). In *Benchaa kigyō no keiei to shien* (Venture business management and support), edited by S. Matsuda, K. Yanagi, and T. Ōe, 28–67. Tokyo: Nihon keizai shinbun-sha.

Hamel, Gary, and C. K. Prahalad. 1994. *Competing for the Future.* Boston: Harvard Business School Press.

Hanami, Tadashi. 2000. "Equal Employment Revisited." *Japan Labor Bulletin* 39, no. 1. www.jil.go.jp/jil/bulletin/.

Hannan, Michael T., and John Freeman. 1977. "The Population Ecology of Organizations." *American Journal of Sociology* 82: 929–64.

Harreld, Bruce J., Charles A. O'Reilly III, and Michael L. Tushman. 2007. "Dynamic Capabilities at IBM: Driving Strategy into Action." *California Management Review* 49, no. 4: 21–43.

Hashimoto, Motomi. 2002. "Commercial Code Revisions: Promoting the Evolution of Japanese Companies." *NRI Papers* 48. Tokyo: Nomura Research Institute.

Hatta, Shinji. 2006. "Chūmoku no 'naibu tōsei' itte nan da?" (What is that new thing called 'internal control'?). *Ekonomisuto,* April 11, 102.

Henderson, Rebecca, and Kim Clark. 1990. "Architectural Innovation: The Reconfiguration of Existing Systems and the Failure of Established Firms." *Administrative Science Quarterly* 35: 9–30.

Higashino, Dai. 2004a. "The Business of Rehabilitating Companies in Japan (NPLs and Corporate Restructuring, Part 2)." *Japan Economic Monthly.* www.jetro.go.jp/en/market/trend/special/index.html/pdf/jemo405-0401e.pdf.

——. 2004b. "Corporate Reorganization Picks Up Steam in Japan (Part 1): Improved Legal Provisions." *Japan Economic Monthly.* www.jetro.go.jp/en/market/trend/special/index.html/pdf/jemo411-0411e.pdf.

——. 2004c. "Corporate Reorganization Picks Up Steam (Part 2): New Currents and Prospects." *Japan Economic Monthly.* www.jetro.go.jp/en/market/trend/special/index.html/pdf/jemo412-0411e.pdf.

Hodder, James E., and Adrian E. Tschoegl. 1985. "Some Aspects of Japanese Corporate Finance." *Journal of Financial and Quantitative Analysis* 20, no.2: 173–91.

——. 1993. "Corporate Finance in Japan." In *Japanese Capital Markets,* edited by S. Takagi, 133–63. Cambridge, Mass.: Basil Blackwell.

Hoetker, Glenn. 2004. "Same Rules, Different Games: Variation in the Outcomes of 'Japanese-Style' Supply Relationships." *Advances in International Management* 17: 187–214.

Hori, Hiroshi. 2006. "Effects of the Financial Instruments and Exchange Law." *Asia Law and Practice Japan Review.* www.asialaw.com.

Hoshi, Takeo. 1994. "The Economic Role of Corporate Groupings and the Main Bank System." In *The Japanese Firm: Sources of Economic Strength,* edited by M. Aoki and R. Dore, 285–309. Oxford: Oxford University Press.

——. 2006. "Economics of the Living Dead." *Japanese Economic Review* 57, no. 1: 30–49.

Hoshi, Takeo, and Takatoshi Ito. 2004. "Financial Regulation in Japan: A Sixth-Year Review of the Financial Services Agency." *Journal of Financial Stability* 1: 229–43.

Hoshi, Takeo, and Anil Kashyap. 2001. *Corporate Financing and Corporate Governance in Japan: The Road to the Future.* Boston: MIT Press.

Hoshi, Takeo, Anil Kashyap, and David Scharfstein. 1990a. "The Role of Banks in Reducing the Costs of Financial Distress in Japan." *Journal of Financial Economics* 27: 67–88.

——. 1990b. "Bank Monitoring and Investment: Evidence from the Changing Structure of Japanese Corporate Banking Relationships." In *Asymmetric Information, Corporate Finance, and Investment,* edited by R. G. Hubbard, 105–26. Chicago: University of Chicago Press.

Hoskisson, Robert E., and Thomas A. Turk. 1990. "Corporate Restructuring: Governance and Control Limits of the Internal Capital Market." *Academy of Management Review* 15, no. 3: 459–77.

Ichinose, T. 2001. "Tenshoku ni yoru shōgai chingin no genshō to sōki taishoku yūgū seido" (Early retirement plans and the decline in lifetime income due to job changes). *Rōsei Jihō* 3484: 27–34.

Itami, Hiroyuki. 2004. "'Nihon-sei' de katsu" (Winning with "made in Japan"): (1) "'Sangyō kūdōka' ron wa koko ga machigatte ita" (How the "hollowing out" thesis got it wrong). *Ekonomisuto,* July 27, 24–26.

———. 2005. "Revision of the Commercial Code and the 'Counterattack' of the Stock Market." *Japan Labor Review.* www.jil.go.jp/english/documents/JLR05_itami.pdf.

Ito, Motoshige, and Kazuharu Kiyono. 1988. "Foreign Trade and Direct Investment." In *Industrial Policy of Japan,* edited by R. Komiya, M. Okuno, and K. Suzumura, 155–81. Tokyo: Academic Press.

Ito, Takatoshi. 1991. *The Japanese Economy.* Cambridge: MIT Press.

Iwata, Katsuhiko. 2003. "Labor Market Policies in the Era of Population Aging: Japan's Case." www.jil.go.jp/english/documents/ageing_policy-e.pdf. Japan Institute for Labour Policy and Training.

Jacoby, Sanford M. 1997. *Modern Manors: Welfare Capitalism since the New Deal.* Princeton: Princeton University Press.

———. 2005. *The Embedded Corporation: Corporate Governance and Employment Relations in Japan and the United States.* Princeton: Princeton University Press.

Jensen, Michael C. 1986. "Agency Costs of Free Cash Flow, Corporate Finance, and Takeovers." *American Economic Review* 676: 323–29.

Jensen, Michael C., and William H. Meckling. 1976. "Theory of the Firm: Managerial Behavior, Agency Costs, and Ownership Structure." *Journal of Financial Economics* 3, no. 4: 305–60.

JETRO (Japan External Trade Organization). 2004. "Japan's Mobile Phone Content Industry." www.jetro.go.jp/en/market/trend/industrial/pdf/jem0408–0402e.pdf. Tokyo: JETRO, Japanese Economy Division.

———. 2005a. "Progressive Personnel Management Promotes Japanese Business Innovation." *JETRO Japan Economic Monthly,* October.

———. 2005b. "Business Support Sector Responds to Diversifying Demand." *JETRO Japan Economic Monthly,* December.

JFTC (Japan Fair Trade Commission). 1993. *Kōsei torihiki iinkai nenji hōkoku* (JFTC Annual report). Tokyo: Ōkurashō Insatsukyoku.

———. 2001. *Kigyō shūdan no jittai ni tsuite—Dai7ji chōsa hōkokusho* (Survey of the state of horizontal business groups: Results from the seventh survey). Tokyo.

———. 2005. *Heisei 17nendo nenji hōkokusho* (Annual report for 2005). www.jftc.go.jp/info/nenpou/h17/17top00001.html. Tokyo.

———. 2007. "Guidelines to Application of the Antimonopoly Act Concerning Review of Business Combination." www.jftc.go.jp/e-page/legislation/ama/Revised Merger Guidelines.pdf. Tokyo.

JIL (Japan Institute of Labour). 2003. "Revised Labour Standards Law Enacted." *Japan Labor Bulletin* 42. www.jil.go.jp/bulletin/year/2003/vol2042–2009.pdf.

JILPT (Japan Institute for Labour Policy and Training), ed. 2005. "Seikashugi to hataraku koto no mansokudo: 2004nen JILPT 'Rōdōsha no hataraku iyoku to koyō kanri no arikata ni kan suru chōsa' no sahenshū ni yoru bunseki" (Measuring the satisfaction of working under meritocracy: An analysis of the findings of JILPT's "survey on worker motivation and human resource management"). No. 40. www.jil.go.jp/institute/reports/2005/documents/2040.pdf. Tokyo.

JLB (Japan Labor Bulletin). 2002a. "More People Unemployed, and for Longer—Labour Force Survey." *Japan Labor Bulletin* 41, no. 8: 1–2.

———, ed. 2002b. "Number of Consulting Cases Concerning Individual Labor Disputes Sharply Increased." *Japan Labor Bulletin* 41, no. 4: 6–7.

JLB (Japan Labor Bulletin) ed. 2003a. "Number of Labor-Related Lawsuits Hits Record High, 2,321." *Japan Labor Bulletin* 42, no. 5: 5–6.

———, ed. 2003b. "Firms Reduce Opportunities for Off-the-Job Training." *Japan Labor Bulletin* 42, no. 9: 3–4.

Johnson, Chalmers. 1982. *MITI and the Japanese Miracle: The Growth of Industrial Policy, 1925–1975*. Stanford: Stanford University Press.

Kagono, Tadao, Ikujiro Nonaka, Kiyonori Sakakibara, and Akihiro Okumura, eds. 1985. *Strategic vs. Evolutionary Management: A U.S.-Japan Comparison of Strategy and Organization*. Amsterdam: North-Holland.

Kahan, Marcel, and Edward B. Rock. 2006. "Hedge Funds in Corporate Governance and Corporate Control." University of Pennsylvania, Institute for Law and Economic Research, Paper No. 06–16. http://ssrn.com/abstract=919881.

Kang, Jun-Koo, and Anil Shivdasani. 1995. "Firm Performance, Corporate Governance, and Top Executive Turnover in Japan." *Journal of Financial Economics* 38: 29–58.

Kaplan, Steven N. 1992. "The Staying Power of Leveraged Buyouts." *Journal of Financial Economics* 29: 287–314.

Kaplan, Steven N., and Bernadette A. Minton. 1994. "Appointments of Outsiders to Japanese Boards: Determinants and Implications for Managers." *Journal of Financial Economics* 36: 225–58.

Kaplan, Steven N., and Michael S. Weisbach. 1992. "The Success of Acquisitions: Evidence from Divestitures." *Journal of Finance* 47, no. 1: 107–38.

Katō, Takehiko. 2003a. "'Bōryū jigyō' ga sasaeru kono kaisha: kō-shūeki toppu 30 ni igai na kao" (Companies that support "branch businesses": A look at high performers outside the Top 30). www.nikkei.co.jp/needs/analysis/03/a031112.html. Tokyo: Nikkei Needs.

———. 2003b. "'Sentaku to shūchū' sōkō suru 6sha: Hikaru Takeda to Canon no jigyō senryaku" (Six success stories of "choose and focus": The shining business strategies of Takeda and Canon). www.nikkei.co.jp/needs/analysis/03/a031120.html. Tokyo: Nikkei Needs.

Katz, Richard. 1998. *Japan—The System That Soured: The Rise and Fall of the Japanese Economic Miracle*. Armonk, N.Y.: M. E. Sharpe.

———. 2003. *Japanese Phoenix: The Long Road to Economic Revival*. Armonk, N.Y.: M. E. Sharpe.

Kawagoe, Kenji. 1997. *Dokusen kinshihō—Kyōsō shakai no feanesu* (The antimonopoly law—the fairness of a competitive society), 3rd ed. Tokyo: Kinzai.

Kawakami, Sumie. 2002. "Doctor in the House: Buyout Funds Have Charged in Japan." www.japaninc.net/article.php?articleID=821.

———. 2003. "Make Deals or Die." April. www.japaninc.net/article.php?articleID=1058.

Kawashima, Takeyoshi. 1967. *Nihonjin no hō-ishiki* (The legal consciousness of the Japanese). Tokyo: Iwanami Shoten.

Kerr, Alex. 2001. *Dogs and Demons: Tales from the Dark Side of Modern Japan*. New York: Hill and Wang.

Kester, W. Carl. 1991. *Japanese Takeovers: The Global Contest for Corporate Control*. Boston: Harvard Business School Press.

Khanna, Tarun, Masako Egawa, and Atsuko Nakajima. 2005. *Nomura Holdings*. Case No. 9-705-427. Boston: Harvard Business School.

Kikkawa, Takeo. 1988. "Functions of Japanese Trade Associations before World War II: The Case of Cartel Organizations." In *Trade Associations in Business History,* edited by H. Yamazaki and M. Miyamoto, 53–83. Tokyo: University of Tokyo Press.

Kikuchi, Masatoshi. 2007. "Stiiru Paatnaazu no dairyō hoyū meigara ni miru 'keikō to taisaku': Nerawareru yojō shisan ga ōi seijuku kigyō" (Aiming at mature companies with lots of surplus assets: "Tendencies and measures" identified in Steel Partners' large shareholdings). *Ekonomisuto,* March 27, 22–23.

Kikutani, Tatsuya, Hideshi Itoh, and Osamu Hayashida. 2007. "Business Portfolio Restructuring of Japanese Firms in the 1990s: Entry and Exit Analysis." In *Corporate Governance in Japan: Institutional Change and Organizational Diversity,* edited by M. Aoki, G. Jackson, and H. Miyajima, 227–56. Oxford: Oxford University Press.

Kimura, Fukunari. 2002. "Subcontracting and the Performance of Small and Medium Firms in Japan." *Small Business Economics* 18: 163–75.

Kimura, Kentaro. 2004. *Internet Services Industry.* Tokyo: JP Morgan.

Kobayashi, H. 2003. *Sangyō kūdōka no kakufuku* (Overcoming Industrial Hollowing Out). Tokyo: Chūō Kōron-sha.

Kodachi, Kei. 2006. "About the Financial Instruments and Exchange Law." *Nomura Capital Market Review* 9: 2. www.nicmr.com/nicmr/english/report/backno/2006sum.html.

Kojima Law Offices, ed. 1998. "New Japanese Anti-Monopoly Law Amendment Lifts Ban on Holding Companies." www.kojimalaw.jp/HoldingCompanies.html. Tokyo.

Komiya, Ryutaro, Masahiro Okuno, and Kotaro Suzumura, eds. 1988. *Industrial Policy of Japan.* Tokyo: Academic Press.

Komoto, Keisho. 2004. "Companies Make Progress in Reforming Employment and Wage Systems—February 2004 Nissay Business Conditions Survey." *NLI Research,* May 12.

Konishi, Masaki, and Keiko Shimizu. 2006. "Japan's New Financial Instruments and Exchange Law." *Asia Law and Practice Japan Review.* www.asialaw.com.

Kotter, John P. 1997. *Matsushita Leadership: Lessons from the 20th Century's Most Remarkable Entrepreneur.* New York: Free Press.

Krauss, Ellis S., and Isobel Coles. 1990. "Built-in Impediments: The Political Economy of the U.S.-Japan Construction Dispute." In *Japan's Economic Structure: Should It Change?,* edited by K. Yamamura, 333–58. Seattle: Society of Japanese Studies.

Kubomura, Ryūsuke. 1996. *Dai niji ryūtsū kakumei—21seiki e no kadai* (The second retail revolution—challenges for the 21st century). Tokyo: Nihon Keizai Shinbun-sha.

Kuroda, Shōko. 2004. "Wagakuni no kaiyō hōsei wa kigyō ni totte dono teido kenkaku ka?" (How restricting are Japanese dismissal provisions for firms?). *Nihon rōdō kenkyū zasshi* 525: 74–77.

Kuroki, Bunmei. 2003. "Mochiai kaishō ni miru kigyō to ginkō no kankei—2002 nendo kabushiki mochiai jōkyō chōsa" (The relationship between banks and corporations from the viewpoint of mochiai dissolution). *Nissei kisōken REPORT,* October.

Kwan, Chi Hung. 2002. "Is FDI in China Hollowing Out Japan's Industry?" *RIETI Working Paper.* www.rieti.go.jp/en/china/02110801.html.

Kwon, Henry. 2004. *JFE Holdings: Merger Benefits Only Just Beginning.* Tokyo: JP Morgan Asia Pacific Equity Research.

LAAJ (Labor Lawyers Association of Japan). 2000. "Kōyōken ranyō hōri to seiri kaikōhori o henshitsu saseru Tokyo chisai rōdōbu o tadasu" (Challenging the labor department of the Tokyo district court for changing the "abuse of right to dismiss" and the dismissals provisions). Tokyo.

Larke, Roy. 1994. *Japanese Retailing*. London: Routledge.

Larke, Roy, and Michael Causton. 2005. *Japan, A Model Retail Superpower*. New York: Palgrave Macmillan.

Lawrence, Robert Z. 1993. "Japan's Different Trade Regime: An Analysis with Particular Reference to Keiretsu." *Journal of Economic Perspectives* 7, no. 3: 3–19.

Lichtenberg, Frank R. 1992. "Industrial De-diversification and Its Consequences for Productivity." *Journal of Economic Behavior and Organization* 18: 427–38.

Liker, Jeffrey K. 2004. *The Toyota Way: Fourteen Management Principles from the World's Greatest Manufacturer*. New York: McGraw Hill.

Lincoln, Edward J. 1999. *Troubled Times: U.S.-Japan Trade Relations in the 1990s*. Washington, D.C.: Brookings Institution Press.

——. 2001. *Arthritic Japan: The Slow Pace of Economic Reform*. Washington, D.C.: Brookings Institution Press.

——. 2002. "On Japan: 'Hollowing Out' in Perspective." *Newsweek Japan,* August 28.

Lincoln, James R., Christina L. Ahmadjian, and Eliot Mason. 1998. "Organizational Learning and Purchase-Supply Relations in Japan: Hitachi, Matsushita, and Toyota Compared." *California Management Review* 40, 3:241–264.

Lincoln, James R., and Michael L. Gerlach. 2004. *Japan's Network Economy: Structure, Persistence, and Change*. Cambridge: Cambridge University Press.

Lincoln, James R., Michael Gerlach, and Christina Ahmadjian. 1996. "Keiretsu Networks and Corporate Performance in Japan." *American Sociological Review* 61, no. 1: 67–88.

Lincoln, James, Michael Gerlach, and Peggy Takahashi. 1992. "Keiretsu Networks in the Japanese Economy: A Dyad Analysis of Intercorporate Ties." *American Sociological Review* 57, no. 5: 561–85.

Lincoln, James, and Arne Kalleberg. 1990. *Culture, Commitment and Control: A Study of Work Organization and Work Attitudes in the United States and Japan*. New York: Cambridge University Press.

Lucier, Chuck, Eric Spiegel, and Robert Schuyt. 2002. "Why CEOs Fall: Consequences of Turnover at the Top." *strategy + business* 28. www.chucklucier.com/pdfs/WhyCEOsFall.pdf.

Lynn, Leonard H. 1998. "The Commercialization of the Transistor Radio in Japan: The Functioning of an Innovation Community." *IEEE Transactions of Engineering Management* 45, no. 3: 220–29.

Maclachlan, Patricia L. 2002. *Consumer Politics in Postwar Japan: The Institutional Boundaries of Citizen Activism*. New York: Columbia University Press.

Markides, Constantinos C. 1992. "Consequences of Corporate Refocusing: Ex Ante Evidence." *Academy of Management Journal* 35, no. 2: 398–412.

——. 1995a. "Diversification, Restructuring and Economic Performance." *Strategic Management Journal* 16: 101–18.

——. 1995b. *Diversification, Refocusing, and Economic Performance*. Cambridge: MIT Press.

Markides, Constantinos C., and Peter J. Williamson. 1994. "Related Diversification, Core Competencies and Corporate Performance." *Strategic Management Journal* 15: 149–65.

———. 1996. "Corporate Diversification and Organizational Structure: A Resource-Based View." *Academy of Management Journal* 39, no. 2: 340–67.

Mason, Mark. 1992. *American Multinationals in Japan: The Political Economy of Japanese Capital Market Controls, 1899–1980*. Cambridge: Harvard University Press.

Matsusaka, John G. 1993. "Takeover Motives during the Conglomerate Merger Wave." *Rand Journal of Economics* 24: 357–79.

McDonald, Jack. 1989. "The *Mochiai* Effect: Japanese Corporate Cross-holdings." *Journal of Portfolio Management* (Fall): 90–94.

McFarlan, Warren F., Andrew P. McAffee, Thomas R. Eisenmann, and Masako Egawa. 2005. *Rakuten*. Case No. 9-305-050. Boston: Harvard Business School.

McInerney, Francis. 2007. *Panasonic: The Largest Corporate Restructuring in History*. New York: Truman Talley Books.

McMillan, John. 1990. "Managing Suppliers: Incentive Systems in Japanese and United States Industry." *California Management Review* 32, no. 4: 38–55.

———. 1991. "Dango: Japan's Price-Fixing Conspiracies." *Economics and Politics* 3, no. 3: 201–18.

METI (Ministry of Economics, Trade and Industry). 2001. "Enka binirukan sangyō no kadai to shōrai tenbō ni kan suru kenkyūkai hōkokusho" (Study group report on the challenges and future outlook of the PVC pipe industry). Tokyo: METI Chemical Division.

———. 2002a. "White Paper on International Trade and Investment." www.meti.go.jp.

———. 2002b. "Poriorefin jushi no shōkankō chōsa (kakaku kettei hōshiki) kekka ni tsuite" (Results on trade habits and pricing mechanisms in the polyolefin resins industry). www.meti.go.jp/kohosys/press/0002608/0002600/0020415polyo.htm. Tokyo: METI Chemical Division.

———. 2003a. "Ryūtsū/ryūdōka ko-iinkai no setchi haikei" (Background materials for the subcommittee on distribution and logistics). http://www.meti.go.jp/report/downloadfiles/ g31016b31030j.pdf. Tokyo: METI Division for Intellectual Property Policy.

———. 2003b. "Enbi jushi no shōkankō jittai chōsa no kekka ni tsuite" (Results of a survey on the situation of the PVC industry). www.meti.go.jp/policy/chemistry/ main/031111enbi.pdf. Tokyo: METI Chemical Division.

———. N.d. "Jigyō portfolio no saiteki-ka" (Business portfolio optimization). Tokyo.

———. 2005. "Japan's Innovation and Venture Capital Policy." Report prepared for the Finlombarda "Finance & Knowledge 2003" Conference; revised 2005. Tokyo.

METI (Ministry of Economics, Trade and Industry), MHLW (Ministry of Health, Labor, and Welfare), and MEXT (Ministry of Education, Culture, Sports, Science and Technology), eds. 2004. *Seizō kiban hakusho, "Monotsukuri Hakusho" Heisei 15 nendo* (The 2003 manufacturing white paper). Tokyo.

METI SKS (Sangyō Kōzō Shingikai, Shinseichō seisaku bukai). 2001. "Inobeeshion to jūjō no kojunkan no kisei ni mukete" (Report on constructing positive feedback cycles in the demand for innovation). Report of the Subcommittee on New Growth Policies, Industrial Structure Council. Tokyo.

Meyer-Ohle, Hendrik. 2003. *Innovation and Dynamics in Japanese Retailing*. New York: Palgrave Macmillan.

MHLW (Ministry of Health, Labor, and Welfare). 2002. "2002 White Paper on the Labour Economy." www.mhlw.go.jp/wp/hakusyo/kousei/02/index.html. Tokyo.

——. 2005. "2005 White Paper on the Labour Economy." www.mhlw.go.jp/english/wp/1-economy/2005/index.html. Tokyo.

——. 2007. *Heisei 19nenpan Rōdō-keizai hakusho: waak-raifu-baransu to koyō shisutemu* (2007 White paper on the labor economy: Work-life balance and employment systems). www.mhlw.go.jp/wp/hakusyo/roudou/07/index.html. Tokyo.

MIAC (Ministry of Internal Affairs and Communication), ed. 2006. *Information and Communications White Paper 2006.* www.soumu.go.jp/joho_tsusin/eng/whitepaper.html. Tokyo.

Milhaupt, Curtis J. 2005. "In the Shadow of Delaware? The Rise of Hostile Takeovers in Japan." *Columbia Law Review* 105, no. 7: 2171–2216.

Milhaupt, Curtis J., and Katharina Pistor. 2008. *Law and Capitalism.* Chicago: Chicago University Press.

Milhaupt, Curtis J., and Mark D. West. 2004. *Economic Organization and Corporate Governance in Japan: The Impact of Formal and Informal Rules.* Oxford: Oxford University Press.

Minakata, Tatsuaki. 2005. *Nihon no shō-shōgyō to ryūtsū seisaku* (Japan's small retail trade and distribution policies). Tokyo: Chūō Keizai-sha.

Mitani, Naoki. 2006. "Firms' Optimum Generational Composition of the Workforce and Human Resource Strategies: Economic Analysis of the '2007 Problem.'" *Japanese Journal of Labor Studies* 550, www.jil.go.jp/english/ejournal/2006.htm.

MITI (Ministry of International Trade and Industry). 1997. "Heisei 8nendo poriorefin jushi ni kan suru kakaku no kettai no jittai chōsa kekka" (Results of the 1996 survey of price-setting mechanisms in the polyolefin industry). www.meti.go.jp/press/olddate/industry/r70704p70701.html. Tokyo: MITI Basic Materials Bureau, Chemical Division.

Miwa, Yoshiro, Kiyohiko G. Nishimura, and Mark J. Ramseyer, eds. 2002. *Distribution in Japan.* Oxford: Oxford University Press.

Miwa, Yoshiro, and Mark J. Ramseyer. 2000. "Rethinking Relationship-Specific Investment: Subcontracting in the Japanese Automobile Industry." *Michigan Law Review* 98, 8:2636–2667.

Miyajima, Hideaki, and Ken-ichi Inagaki. 2003. *Report of the Research Committee on the Diversification of Japanese Companies and Corporate Governance: Analysis of Business Strategy, Group Management, and Decentralized Organizations.* www.mof.go.jp/jouhou/soken/kenkyu/rono63_pr20030206.pdf. Tokyo: Ministry of Finance, Policy Research Institute.

Miyazaki, Takeshi. 2006. "Shin Kaisha-hō de kawaru itsutsu no point" (The five main changes with the new Corporation Law). *Ekonomisuto* April 11, 99–101.

Mizumachi, Yūichirō. 2002. "Naze kaiko kisei wa hitsuyō na no ka?" (Why we need regulation on dismissals). *Nihon rōdō kenkyū zasshi* 510: 71–78.

Moeller, Sara B., Frederik P. Schlingemann, and Rene Stulz. 2005. "Wealth Destruction on a Massive Scale? A Study of Acquiring-Firm Returns in the Recent Merger Wave." *Journal of Finance* 60, no. 2: 757–82.

MOF (Ministry of Finance). 2005. "Current Japanese Fiscal Conditions and Issues to Be Considered." www.mof.go.jp/english/budget/pamphlet/cjfc2005.pdf. Tokyo.

MOJ (Ministry of Justice) and METI (Ministry of Economics, Trade and Industry). 2005. *Kigyō kachi kabunishi kyōdō no rieki no kakuho mata wa kōjō no tame no baishū bōeisaku ni kan suru shishin* (Guidelines for corporate value protection measures). www.meti.go.jp. Tokyo.

Monden, Yasuhiro. 1993. *The Toyota Management System: Linking the Seven Key Functional Areas*. Cambridge, Mass.: Productivity Press.

Montgomery, Cynthia A., and Birger Wernerfelt. 1988. "Diversification, Ricardian Rents, and Tobin's *q*." *RAND Journal of Economics* 19, no. 4: 623–32.

Morck, Randall, and Masao Nakamura. 1999. "Banks and Corporate Control in Japan." *Journal of Finance* 54, no. 1: 319–39.

Morck, Randall, Andrei Shleifer, and Robert W. Vishny. 1990. "Do Managerial Objectives Drive Bad Acquisitions?" *Journal of Finance* 41, no. 1: 31–48.

Morishima, Motohiro. 2002. "Pay Practices in Japanese Organizations: Changes and Non-Changes." *Japan Labor Bulletin* 41, no. 4: 8–13.

———. 2003. "Changes in White-Collar Employment from the Employee's Perspective." *Japan Labor Bulletin* 42, no. 9: 8–14.

MRI/Chikusei Partners. 2004. "Japanese Buyout Fund Boom: The Current Status of Japanese Buyout Funds." Tokyo: Mitusbishi Sogo Kenkyusho, Chikusei Partners.

Murakami, Yasusuke. 1982. "Toward a Socioinstitutional Explanation of Japan's Economic Performance." In *Policy and Trade Issues of the Japanese Economy: American and Japanese Perspectives*, edited by K. Yamamura, 3–46. Seattle: University of Washington Press.

Myers, Stewart C. 2001. "Capital Structure." *Journal of Economic Perspectives* 15, 2:81–102.

Myers, Stewart C., and Nicholas S. Maljuf. 1984. "Corporate Financing and Investment Decisions When Firms Have Information Investors Do Not Have." *Journal of Financial Economics* 13: 187–221.

Nakakubo, Hiroya. 2004. "The 2003 Revision of the Labor Standards Law: Fixed-Term Contracts, Dismissal and Discretionary-Work Schemes." *Japan Labor Review*. http://www.jil.go.jp/english/documents/JLR02_nakakubo.pdf.

Nakamura, Yoshiaki, and Minoru Shibuya. 2002. "Sangyō kūdōka wa nani ka mondai ka?" (Why is industrial hollowing out a problem?). Kenkyū Series 23. Tokyo: RIETI.

Nakatani, Iwao. 1984. "The Economic Role of Financial Corporate Groupings." In *The Economic Analysis of the Japanese Firm*, edited by M. Aoki, 227–58. Amsterdam: North-Holland.

Nielsen. 2004. "Broadband Users Reach 70% of All Home Internet Users." Tokyo: Nielsen/NetRatings Japan.

———. 2006. "Google Makes Gains: Users Up Five Million from a Year Ago to Seventeen Million." Tokyo: Nielsen/NetRatings Japan.

Nikkei (Nihon Keizai Shinbun-sha). 1991. *Zeminaaru gendai kigyō nyūmon* (Introduction to modern Japanese corporations). Tokyo: Nihon Keizai Shinbun-sha.

———. 2004. *Nikkei gyōkai chizu 2005 nenpan* (The 2005 Nikkei industry map of Japan). Tokyo: Nihon Keizai Shinbun-sha.

Nipponkoa. 2006. *Shin Kaisha-hō taiō: Kaisha yakuin baishō sekinin hoken no go-annai (Directors and Officers Liability Insurance)*. www.eiki-i.com/file_h_kigyo/nk/pdf/d_o.pdf. Tokyp: Nipponkoa Sonpo.

Nishiguchi, Toshihiro. 1994. *Strategic Industrial Sourcing: The Japanese Advantage.* Oxford: Oxford University Press.

NKK (Nihon kansayaku kyōkai Kansai-shibu). 2003. "Kansayaku no tame no kabunushi daihyō soshō dokuhon" (Handbook on derivative lawsuits for auditors). Japan Auditors Association, West Japan. www.kansa.or.jp/PDF/ns031010_dkhn.pdf.

NLFC (National Life Finance Corporation; Kokumin seikatsu kinyū kōko). 2001. *Shinki kaigyō hakusho 2001nenpan* (2001 White paper on start-up companies). Tokyo: Chūshō kigyō resaachi sentaa.

NLI (Nihon Life Institute), ed. 2000. "Torihiki kankei no minaoshi o susumeru Nihon kigyō" (The ongoing revision of trade relations by Japanese corporations). *Nissei kisōken REPORT,* November.

———. 2004. "Kabushiki mochiai jōkyō chōsa 2003 nenpan" (Survey on the state of mochiai shareholdings, 2003). *Nissei kisōken REPORT,* September.

Noble, Gregory. 1989. "The Japanese Industrial Policy Debate." In *Pacific Dynamics: The International Politics of Industrial Change,* edited by S. Haggard and C.-I. C. Moon, 53–95. Boulder: Westview.

Noda, Susumu. 2003. "Rōdō-hō hanrei no ugoki" (Recent trends in labor law cases). *Jurisuto* 1246: 197–98.

Nomura Securities. 2005. "Trends in Japanese Company Related M&As in 2004." Tokyo: Nomura Securities, Investment Banking Research Dept.

———. 2006. "Trends in Japanese Company Related M&As in 2005." Tokyo: Nomura Securities, Investment Banking Research Dept.

NPA (National Police Agency). 2003. *Heisei 14nen ni okeru jisatsu no gaiyō shiryō* (Outline statistics for 2002 suicides). Tokyo.

Odagiri, Hiroyuki. 1992. *Growth through Competition, Competition through Growth: Strategic Management and the Economy in Japan.* Oxford: Oxford University Press.

Okimoto, Daniel I. 1989. *Between MITI and the Market: Japanese Industrial Policy for High Technology.* Stanford: Stanford University Press.

Okuno, Hisashi. 2004. "Rōdōsha e no jinsen kijun teiji to seiri kaikō no kōryoku" (The criteria to select dismissees and the validity of dismissal). *Jurisuto* 1272: 160–63.

———. 2005. " 'Hannichi paato' no shokushu haishi ni tomonau seiri kaikō no kōryoku" (The validity of dismissal with regard to abolishing half-day part-time jobs). *Jurisuto* 1262: 169–72.

Ōmura, Takeo. 2006. " 'Naibu tōsei' de fushōji wa nakunaru ka?" (Will the "internal control" system prevent misdeeds?). *Ekonomisuto,* June 13: 34–35.

Ono, Arito, and Akihiko Noda. 2006. "Tayōka ka susumitsutsu aru chūkei/chūshō kigyō no shikin chōtatsu: Mizuho sōken ankeeto chōsa kara mita kuredito sukoring kashidashi, ABL, shinjikeeto roon, CLO/CBO no genjō to kadai" (Small firm funding under continuing financial diversification: Reality and challenges with credit-scoring-based loans, ABL, syndicated loans, and CLO/CBO, based on a Mizuho Research Institute survey). Tokyo: Mizuho Research Institute.

Ono, Arito, and Ichiro Uesugi. 2005. "The Role of Collateral and Personal Guarantees in Relationship Lending: Evidence from Japan's Small Business Loan Market." www.rieti.go.jp/jp/publications/dp/05e027.pdf. Discussion Paper 05-E-027. Tokyo: RIETI.

O'Reilly, Charles A. III, and Jennifer Chatman. 1986. "Organizational Commitment and Psychological Attachment: The Effects of Compliance, Identification, and Internalization of Prosocial Behavior." *Journal of Applied Psychology* 71: 492–99.

O'Reilly, Charles A. III, and Brian G. M. Main. 2007. "Setting the CEO's Pay: It's More Than Simple Economics." *Organizational Dynamics* 36, no. 1: 1–12.

O'Reilly, Charles A. III, and Michael L. Tushman. 2004. "The Ambidextrous Organization." *Harvard Business Review* (April): 74–83.

——. 2008. "Ambidexterity as a Dynamic Capability: Resolving the Innovator's Dilemma." In *Research in Organizational Behavior,* vol. 29, edited by B. Staw and A. Brief. Greenwich, Conn.: JAI Press, in press.

Osaki, Tad. 2006a. "Showdown at Dawn: On the Threshold of a New Era, It's Survival of the Fittest." *Television Asia,* May 1.

——. 2006b. "Content Distribution to Mobile Terminals." *Asia Image.* May.

Ōsono, Tomokazu. 1991. *Hitome de wakaru: Kigyō keiretsu to gyōkai chizu* (Maps of industrial groups and the business landscape: a quick guide). Tokyo: Nihon jitsugyō shuppan-sha.

Ouchi, Shinya. 2002. "Change in Japanese Employment Security: Reflecting on Legal Points." *Japan Labor Bulletin* 41, no. 1. www.jil.go.jp/bulletin/.

Ozaki, Robert S. 1972. *The Control of Imports and Foreign Capital in Japan.* New York: Praeger.

Palich, Leslie E., Laura B. Cardinal, and C. Chet Miller. 2000. "Curvilinearity in the Diversification-Performance Linkage: An Examination of Over Three Decades of Research." *Strategic Management Journal* 21, no. 2: 155–74.

Pascale, Richard, and Thomas P. Rohlen. 1983. "The Mazda Turnaround." *Journal of Japanese Studies* 9, no. 2: 219–63.

Patrick, Hugh T. 1962. *Monetary Policy and Central Banking in Contemporary Japan.* Bombay: University of Bombay Press.

——, ed. 1986. *Japan's High Technology Industries: Lessons and Limitations of Industrial Policy.* Seattle: University of Washington Press.

Patrick, Hugh, and Thomas P. Rohlen. 1987. "Small-Scale Family Enterprises." In *The Political Economy of Japan, Part 1: The Domestic Transformation,* edited by K. Yamamura and Y. Yasuba, 331–84. Stanford: Stanford University Press.

Patrick, Hugh, and Henry Rosovsky, eds. 1976. *Asia's New Giant: How the Japanese Economy Works.* Washington, D.C.: Brookings Institution.

Pempel, T. J. 1998. *Regime Shift: Comparative Dynamics of the Japanese Political Economy.* Ithaca: Cornell University Press.

Penrose, Edith. 1959. *The Theory of the Growth of the Firm.* Oxford: Blackwell.

Pfeffer, Jeffrey. 2006. "Working Alone: What Ever Happened to the Idea of Organizations as Communities?" In *America at Work: Choices and Challenges,* edited by E. E. Lawler III and J. O'Toole, 3–21. New York: Palgrave Macmillan.

Pfeffer, Jeffrey, and James N. Baron. 1988. "Taking the Workers Back Out: Recent Trends in the Structuring of Employment." *Research in Organizational Behavior* 10: 257–303.

Pfeffer, Jeffrey, and Gerald Salancik. 1978. *The External Control of Organizations: A Resource Dependence Perspective.* New York: Harper and Row.

Porter, Michael E. 1980. *Competitive Strategy.* New York: Free Press.

Porter, Michael E. 1985. *Competitive Advantage.* New York: Free Press.

——. 1987. "From Competitive Advantage to Corporate Strategy." *Harvard Business Review* 5, no. 3: 43–59.

——. 1991. "From Competitive Advantage to Corporate Strategy." In *Strategy: Seeking and Securing Competitive Advantage,* edited by C. A. Montgomery and M. E. Porter, 225–55. Boston: Harvard Business School Press.

——. 1992. "Capital Choices: Changing the Way America Invests in Industry." Washington, D.C.: Council on Competitiveness.

Porter, Michael E., Hirotaka Takeuchi, and Mariko Sakakibara. 2000. *Can Japan Compete?* Cambridge: Perseus Publishing.

Prahalad, C. K., and Gary Hamel. 1990. "The Core Competence of the Corporation." *Harvard Business Review* 68, no. 3: 79–91.

Prestowitz, Clyde V., Jr. 1988. *Trading Places: How We Are Giving Our Future to Japan and How to Reclaim It.* New York: Basic Books.

Ravenscraft, D. J., and Frederik M. Scherer. 1987. *Mergers, Sell-Offs, and Economic Efficiency.* Washington, D.C.: Brookings Institution.

Rebick, Marcus. 2005. *The Japanese Employment System: Adapting to a New Economic Environment.* Oxford: Oxford University Press.

Roll, Richard. 1986. "The Hubris Hypothesis of Corporate Takeovers." *Journal of Business* 59, no. 2: 197–216.

Rona-Tas, Akos. 2002. "The Worm and the Caterpillar: The Small Private Sector in the Czech Republic, Hungary, and Slovakia." In *The New Entrepreneurs of Europe and Asia,* edited by V. E. Bonnel and T. B. Gold, 39–65. Armonk, N.Y.: M. E. Sharpe.

Rowley, Ian. 2005. "Japan: Let's Not Make a Deal." *Business Week,* May 30.

Rowley, Ian, and Tashiro, Hiroko. 2004. "So Much for Hollowing Out." *Business Week* online. www.businessweek.com/print/magazine/content04_41/b3903069. htm?chan=mz&.

Rumelt, Richard P. 1974. *Structure, Strategy, and Economic Performance.* Cambridge: Harvard University Press.

Rumelt, Richard P., Dan E. Schendel, and David J. Teece. 1994. *Fundamental Issues in Strategy.* Boston: Harvard Business School Press.

Ryan, P. 2003. "Is China Exporting Deflation Globally, Hollowing Out Japan?" www. marubeni.co.jp/research/eindx/0303. Tokyo: Marubeni Corporation Economic Research Institute.

Saitō, Tarō. 2006. "Hi-seiki koyō no kakudai ga imi suru mono" (Making sense of the expansion in nonregular work). *Nissei kisōken REPORT,* May.

Sakamoto, Hideo. 2004. *Nihon chūshō shōgyō mondai no kaiseki* (An analysis of Japan's problem with small and medium retailers). Tokyo: Dōyūkan.

Samuels, Richard J. 1987. *The Business of the Japanese State: Energy Markets in Comparative and Historical Perspective.* Ithaca: Cornell University Press.

SBJ (Statistics Bureau of Japan). 2007. *Statistical Handbook of Japan 2007* (Chapter 11). www.stat.go.jp/english/data/handbook/pdf/c11cont.pdf. Tokyo.

Schaede, Ulrike. 1989. "Forwards and Futures in Tokugawa-Period Japan: A New Perspective on the Dojima Rice Market." *Journal of Banking and Finance* 13: 487–513.

———. 1990. *Der neue japanische Kapitalmarkt—Finanzfutures in Japan.* Wiesbaden: Gabler.

———. 1994. "Understanding Corporate Governance in Japan: Do Classical Concepts Apply?" *Industrial and Corporate Change* 3, no. 2: 285–323.

———. 1998. "MOF, Money, and the Japanese Banking Crisis of 1995." In *Die Rolle des Geldes in Japans Gesellschaft, Wirtschaft und Politik,* edited by A. Ernst and P. Pörtner, 95–128. Hamburg: Institut für Asienkunde.

———. 2000a. *Cooperative Capitalism: Self-Regulation, Trade Associations, and the Antimonopoly Law in Japan.* Oxford: Oxford University Press.

———. 2000b. *The Japanese Financial System: From Postwar to the New Millennium.* Case No. 9-700-049. Boston: Harvard Business School.

———. 2003. "Industry Rules: From Deregulation to Self-Regulation." In *Japan's Managed Globalization: Adapting to the 21st Century,* edited by U. Schaede and W. W. Grimes, 191–214. Armonk, N.Y.: M. E. Sharpe.

———. 2004. "Cooperating to Compete: Determinants of a Sanctuary Strategy among Japanese Firms." *Asian Business and Management* 3: 435–57.

———. 2005. "The 'Middle-Risk Gap' and Financial System Reform: Small Firm Financing in Japan." *Monetary and Economic Studies* 23, no. 1: 149–76.

———. 2006. "Privatverschuldung und Sozialhilfe in Japan: Kredithaie, das 'Mittelmarkt-Loch' und der japanische Sozialvertrag" (Private debt and social welfare in Japan: Loan sharks, the 'middle-risk gap,' and Japan's social contract). *ZfB (Zeitschrift für Betriebswirtschaftslehre)* 3: 87–108.

———. 2007. "Globalization and the Japanese Subcontractor System." In *Crisis or Recovery in Japan: State and Industrial Economy,* edited by D. Bailey, D. Coffey, and P. Tomlinson, 82–105. London: Edward Elgar.

Schoppa, Leonard J. 2006. *Race for the Exits: The Unraveling of Japan's System of Social Protection.* Ithaca: Cornell University Press.

Schwartzman, David. 1993. *The Japanese Television Cartel: A Study Based on Matsushita v. Zenith.* Ann Arbor: University of Michigan Press.

Segal, Lewis M., and Daniel G. Sullivan. 1997. "The Growth of Temporary Services Work." *Journal of Economic Perspectives* 11: 117–36.

Seth, Anju. 1990. "Value Creation in Acquisitions: A Re-examination of Performance Issues. *Strategic Management Journal* 11: 431–66.

Sheard, Paul. 1989. "The Main Bank System and Corporate Monitoring and Control in Japan." *Journal of Economic Behavior and Organization* 11: 399–422.

———. 1994. "Main Banks and the Governance of Financial Distress." In *The Japanese Main Bank System,* edited by M. Aoki and H. Patrick, 188–230. Oxford: Oxford University Press.

Shimizu, Kaho. 2006. "New Rules to Compel Accurate Accounting by Firms. *Japan Times,* December 29.

Shleifer, Andrei, and Robert W. Vishny. 1990. "The Takeover Wave of the 1980s." *Science* 249: 745–48.

———. 1991. "Takeovers in the '60s and the '80s: Evidence and Implications." *Strategic Management Journal* 12: 51–59.

SMEA (Small and Medium Enterprise Agency). 2003. "Chūshō kigyō hakusho 2003 nenpan: Saisei to "kigyōka shakai" e no michi" (2003 White paper on small and medium enterprises in Japan: The road to regeneration and the creation of an entrepreneurial society). Tokyo.

SMEA (Small and Medium Enterprise Agency). 2004. "Chūshō kigyō hakusho 2004 nenpan" (2004 White paper on small and medium enterprises in Japan: The limitless potential of the diversity of small firms). Tokyo.

———. 2005. "Chūshō kigyō hakusho 2005 nenpan" (2005 White paper on small and medium enterprises in Japan: Structural change in Japanese society and the dynamism of small and medium enterprises). Tokyo.

———. 2006. "Chūshō kigyō hakusho 2006 nenpan" (2006 White paper on small and medium enterprises in Japan). Tokyo.

Smith, Adam. 1937 [1776]. *The Wealth of Nations.* New York: Random House.

Smitka, Michael J. 1991. *Competitive Ties: Subcontracting in the Japanese Automotive Industry.* New York: Columbia University Press.

Softbank. 2007. "Earning Results for the Third Quarter Ended December 31, 2006." http://www.softbank.co.jp/en/irlibrary/presentation/pdf/softbank_presentation_2007_2003.pdf. Tokyo.

SRI (Shoko Research Institute). 2003. "Sangyō kūdōka to chūshō kigyō—kaigai seisan no zōka ga chūshō kigyō ni ataeru eikyō" (Industrial hollowing-out and small firms: How the increase in production abroad has influenced small firms). *Shōkō kinyū* 5: 16–38.

Steiner, George A. 1964. "Why and How to Diversify." *California Management Review* 4: 11–17.

Stiglitz, Joseph E. 1990. "Financial Markets and Development." *Oxford Review of Economic Policy* 5, no. 4: 55–68.

Sugeno, Kazuo. 2006. "Judicial Reform and the Reform of the Labor Dispute Resolution System." *Japan Labor Review* 3, no. 1: 4–12.

Sugino, Isamu, and Masayuki Murayama. 2006. "Employment Practices and Disputing Behavior in Japan." *Japan Labor Review* 3, no. 1: 51–67.

Suwazono, Sadaaki. 2005. "The Features of the Newly Revised Anti-Monopoly Act: Japan's Experience of Making Competition Policy Stronger." www.jftc.go.jp/e-page/policyupdates/speeches/050524suwazono.pdf. Tokyo: Japan Fair Trade Commission.

Suzuki, Ken. 2005. "Kabushiki sogō mochiai no 'kaishō' ni tsuite" (On the "dissolution" of reciprocal shareholdings). *Osaka Keidai Ronshū* 55, no. 5: 7–23.

Suzuki, Yoshio. 1980. *Money and Banking in Contemporary Japan.* New Haven: Yale University Press.

Tago, Hideto. 2003. *Jissen! Rireeshionshippu bankingu* (Relationship banking made real). Tokyo: Kinzai.

Takagi, Shinjirō. 2003. *Kigyō saisei no kisō chishiki* (The basics of corporate rehabilitation). Tokyo: Iwanami Shoten.

Takahashi, Nobuo. 2006. "'Jinkenhi o sagerō' ga seika-shugi no mokuteki datta" ("Let's lower payroll costs" has long been the goal with the meritocracy system). *Ekonomisuto,* April 11: 32.

Takehara, Takenobu, and Takefumi Nihei. 2006. "Corporate Governance Enters a New Era." *International Financial Law Review.* The IFLR Guide to Japan 2006. www.iflr.com.

Takeshima, Kazuhiko. 2006. "Japan's Endeavor for Establishing Rigorous Anti-Cartel Enforcement." www.jftc.go.jp/e-page/policyupdates/speeches/061104IBAspeech.pdf. Tokyo: Japan Fair Trade Commission.

Takeuchi, Koji. 2003. "Japan Has Revamped Its Corporate Insolvency System by Creating New Procedural Rules and Substantive Provisions." Paper presented at the LAWASIA Conference, Tokyo. www.sakaralaw.gr.jp/publication/takeuchi/59.pdf.

Tatsumichi, Shingo, and Motohiro Morishima. 2007. "*Seikashugi* from an Employee Perspective." *Japan Labor Review* 4, no. 2: 79–104.

Taylor, Veronica. 2003. "Re-regulating Japanese Transactions: The Competition Law Dimension." In *Japanese Governance: Beyond Japan Inc.*, edited by J. Amyx and P. Drysdale, 134–55. London: Routledge.

TDB (Teikoku Data Bank). 2006. "Corporate Consolidations in Japan." www.teikoku.com/ArchiveReport. Tokyo.

Teece, David J. 1982. "Toward an Economic Theory of the Multiproduct Firm." *Journal of Economic Behavior and Organization* 3: 39–63.

——. 1988. "Capturing Value from Technological Innovation: Integration, Strategic Partnering, and Licensing Decisions." *Interfaces* 18, no. 3: 46–61.

Teece, David J., Gary Pisano, and Amy Shuen. 1997. "Dynamic Capabilities and Strategic Management." *Strategic Management Journal* 18, no. 7: 509–33.

Teramoto, Yoshio, Yoshimi Yamamoto, and Aya Tomisawa. 2006. "Small Company Portfolio Strategy: January 2006." Tokyo: JP Morgan Asia Pacific Equity Research.

Teranishi, Juro. 2003. *Nihon no Keizai Shisutemu* (Japan's economic system). Tokyo: Iwanami Shoten.

Thomson Financial. 2005. "Introversive M&A Boom." 1Q2005 Japanese M&A League Tables. www.thomsonfinancial.co.jp/pdf/MA1Q2005.pdf. Tokyo.

Tiberghien, Yves. 2007. *Entrepreneurial States: Reforming Corporate Governance in France, Japan, and Korea*. Ithaca: Cornell University Press.

Tilton, Mark. 1995. "Informal Market Governance in Japan's Basic Materials Industries." *International Organization* 48, no. 4: 663–85.

——. 1996. *Restrained Trade: Cartels in Japan's Basic Materials Industries*. Ithaca: Cornell University Press.

TK (Tōyō Keizai). Various issues. *Kigyō Keiretsu Sōran (Data on Keiretsu)*. Tokyo: Tōyō Keizai.

Townsend, Robert M. 1994. "Risk and Insurance in Village India." *Econometrica* 62, no. 3: 539–91.

TSE (Tokyo Stock Exchange). 2006. *Fact Book 2006*. http://www.tse.or.jp/english/data/factbook/fact_book_2006.pdf. Tokyo.

——. 2007. "Heisei 18nendo kabushiki bunpu jōkyō no chōsa kekka ni tsuite" (Results of the 2006 survey on shareholdings). www.tse.or.jp/data/examination/distribute/h18/distribute_h18a.pdf. Tokyo: Tokyo Stock Exchange.

Tsuchiya, Moriaki. 2004. "Sentaku to shūchū: sono rekishiteki kōsatsu" (Choose and focus: A historical perspective). *DIR Keiei senryaku kenkyū* 2: 18–39.

Tsuru, Tsuyoshi. 2004. *Sentaku to shūchū—Nihon no denki, jōhōkanren kigyō ni okeru jittai bunseki* (Selecting and focusing: An empirical analysis of electronics and information technology firms in Japan). Tokyo: Yuhikaku.

Tushman, Michael L., and Philip Anderson. 1986. "Technological Discontinuities and Organizational Environments." *Administrative Science Quarterly* 31: 439–65.

Tushman, Michael L., and Charles A. O'Reilly III. 1996. "Ambidextrous Organizations: Managing Evolutionary and Revolutionary Change." *California Management Review* 38, no. 4: 8–30.

———. 2002. *Winning through Innovation: A Practical Guide to Leading Organizational Change and Renewal.* Boston: Harvard University Press.

Uchida, Takashi. 2002. "Koyō o meguru hō to seisaku" (Employment law and employment policy). *Nihon rōdō kenkyū zasshi* 500: 5–14.

Uesugi, Akinori. 2005a. "Enforcement of Competition Laws in Japan." www.jftc.go.jp/e-page/policyupdates/speeches/050420uesugi.pdf. Tokyo: Japan Fair Trade Commission.

———. 2005b. "Recent Developments in Japanese Competition Policy: Prospect and Reality." www.jftc.go.jp/e-page/policyupdates/speeches/050124uesugi.pdf. Tokyo: Japan Fair Trade Commission.

Upham, Frank. 1993. "Privatizing Regulation: The Implementation of the Large-Scale Retail Law." In *Political Dynamics in Contemporary Japan,* edited by G. D. Allison and Y. Sone, 264–94. Ithaca: Cornell University Press.

———. 1996. "Privatized Regulation: Japanese Regulatory Style in Comparative and International Perspective." *Fordham International Law Journal* 20, no. 2 (December): 396–511.

Ushijima, Tatsuo. 2007. "Evolving Market for Corporate Assets in Japan: Which Firms Enter and How?" Paper presented at the Academy of Management, Philadelphia.

VEC (Venture Enterprise Center). 2006. *Heisei 18nendo benchaa-kyapitaru-tō tōshi kōdō chōsa: Benchaa-kyapitaru fando-tō benchimaruku chōsa* (The 2006 Venture Capital Etc. investment survey: Benchmark survey for VC Funds Etc.). www.vec.or.jp/vc/survey-18j.pdf. Tokyo.

Vogel, Steven K. 2006. *Japan Remodeled: How Government and Industry Are Reforming Japanese Capitalism.* Ithaca: Cornell University Press.

Wada, Ben. 2004. *Jigyō saisei fando: Kigyō-jigyō o baishū shi, saisei suru hitobito* (Corporate reorganization funds: The people that buy and reform companies). Tokyo: Daiyamondo-sha.

Wakasugi, Takaaki. 2006. "Kantoku to keiei no bunri ga sekai no gabanansu no chōryū" (Separation of management and monitoring follows global practices). *Ekonomisuto,* April 11, 28–29.

Wallich, Henry, and Mable Wallich. 1976. "Banking and Finance." In *Asia's New Giant: How the Japanese Economy Works,* edited by H. Patrick and H. Rosovsky. Washington, D.C.: Brookings Institution.

Watts, Jonathan. 2000. "Are Japan's Medical *Sensei* Losing the Public's Respect?" *The Lancet* 355: 995.

Weathers, Charles. 2002. "Women in Japan's Temporary Services Industry." www.jpri.org/publications/workingpapers/wp85.html. San Francisco: Japan Policy Research Institute.

———. 2005. "Equal Opportunity for Japanese Women: What Progress?" *Japanese Economy* 33, no. 4: 16–44.

Wehrfritz, George. 1999. "Japan's Rising Son." *Newsweek International,* December 27.

Weinstein, David E. 1995. "Evaluating Administrative Guidance and Cartels in Japan (1957–1988)." *Journal of the Japanese and International Economies* 9, no. 2: 200–223.

Weinstein, David E., and Yishay Yafeh. 1995. "Japan's Corporate Groups: Collusive or Competitive? An Empirical Investigation of *Keiretsu* Behavior." *Journal of Industrial Economics* 43, no. 4: 359–76.

——. 1998. "On the Costs of a Bank-Centered Financial System: Evidence from the Changing Main Bank Relations in Japan." *Journal of Finance* 53, no. 2: 635–72.

West, Mark D. 2001. "Why Shareholders Sue: The Evidence from Japan." *Journal of Legal Studies* 30, no. 2: 351–82.

Williamson, Oliver E. 1975. *Markets and Hierarchies: Analysis and Antitrust Implications.* New York: Free Press.

——. 1980. "The Organization at Work: A Comparative Institutional Assessment." *Journal of Economic Behavior and Organization* 1: 5–38.

——. 1985. *The Economic Institutions of Capitalism: Firms, Markets, and Relational Contracting.* New York: Free Press.

Witt, Michael A. 2006. *Changing Japanese Capitalism: Social Coordination and Institutional Adjustment.* Cambridge: Cambridge University Press.

Woodall, Brian. 1996. *Japan under Construction: Corruption, Politics, and Public Works.* Berkeley: University of California Press.

Yamada, M. 1999. "Parasaito shinguru no jidai" (The age of the parasite single). www.kyoto-su.ac.jp/-kt1980/book/parasite_single.html.

Yamaguchi, Atsushi. 2003. *Steel Industry: Structural Changes to Lift Earnings* (Part 9). March 11. Tokyo: JP Morgan Asia-Pacific Equity Research.

Yamakawa, Ryūichi, and Takeshi Araki. 2001. "Daiarogu: keiri kaiyō no handan wakugumi: Shingapuuru-Deberoppumento Ginkō jiken" (Dialogue: The case of the Development Bank of Singapore, Osaka branch). *Nihon rōdō kenkyū zasshi* 496: 23–26.

Yamamura, Kozo. 1967. *Economic Policy in Postwar Japan: Growth versus Economic Democracy.* Berkeley: University of California Press.

——. 1982. "Success That Soured: Administrative Guidance and Cartels in Japan." In *Policy and Trade Issues of the Japanese Economy: American and Japanese Perspectives,* edited by K. Yamamura, 77–112. Seattle: University of Washington Press.

Yamamura, Kozo, and Yasuba Yasukichi, eds. 1987. *The Political Economy of Japan,* vol. 1, *The Domestic Transformation.* Stanford: Stanford University Press.

Yoshida, Masayuki. 2003. "The Reluctant Japanese Litigant: A 'New' Assessment." *Electronic Journal of Contemporary Japanese Studies* 5. www.japanesestudies.org.uk/discussionpapers/Yoshida.html.

Yoshihara, Hideki, Akimatsu Sakuma, Hiroyuki Itami, and Tadao Kagono. 1981. *Nihon kigyō no takakuka senryaku—keieishigen aproochi* (Diversification strategies by Japanese firms: A resource-based approach). Tokyo: Nihon Keizai Shinbun-sha.

Yoshino, M. Y. 1968. *Japan's Managerial System.* Cambridge: MIT Press.

Yoshino, M. Y., and Yukihiko Endo. 2005. *Transformation of Matsushita Electric Industrial Co., Ltd. 2005 (A), (B), (C).* Case numbers 9–905–412–414. Boston: Harvard Business School.

Yoshino, M. Y., and Thomas B. Lifson. 1986. *The Invisible Link: Japan's Sogo Shosha and the Organization of Trade.* Cambridge: MIT Press.

Zysman, John. 1983. *Governments, Markets, and Growth: Financial Systems and the Politics of Industrial Change.* Ithaca: Cornell University Press.

INDEX